TRANSPARENCY AND GOVERNANCE IN A GLOBAL WORLD

INTERNATIONAL FINANCE REVIEW

Series Editor: J. Jay Choi

International Finance Review publishes theme-oriented volumes on various issues in international finance, such as international business finance, international investment and capital markets, global risk management, international corporate governance and institution, currency markets, emerging market finance, international economic integration, and related issues in international financial economics.

Volume 3:	Global Risk Management: Financial, Operational, and Insurance Strategies, Edited by J. Jay Choi and Michael R. Powers, 2002, Elsevier Science (ISBN 0-7623-0982-2)
Volume 4:	The Japanese Finance: Corporate Finance and Capital Markets in Changing Japan, Edited by J. Jay Choi and Takato Hiraki, 2003, Elsevier Science (ISBN 0-7623-1068-5)
Volume 5:	Latin American Financial Markets: Developments in Financial Innovations, Edited by Harvey Arbeláez and Reid W. Click, 2004, Elsevier Science (ISBN 0-7623-1163-0)
Volume 6:	Emerging European Financial Markets: Independence and Integration Post-Enlargement, Edited by Jonathan A. Batten and Colm Kearney, 2006, Elsevier Science (ISBN 0-7623-1264-5)
Volume 7:	Value Creation in Multinational Enterprise, Edited by J. Jay Choi and Reid W. Click, 2007, Elsevier Science (ISBN 0-7623-1392-7)
Volume 8:	Asia-Pacific Financial Markets: Integration, Innovation and Challenges, Edited by Suk-Joong Kim and Michael McKenzie, 2008, Elsevier Science (ISBN 978-0-7623-1471-3)
Volume 9:	Institutional Approach to Global Corporate Governance: Business Systems and Beyond, Edited by J. Jay Choi and Sandra Dow, 2008, Emerald Publishing (ISBN 978-1-84855-320-0)
Volume 10:	Credit, Currency, or Derivatives: Instruments of Global Financial Stability or Crisis? Edited by J. Jay Choi and Michael G. Papaioannou, Emerald Publishing, 2009, Emerald Publishing (ISBN 978-1-84950-601-4)
Volume 11:	International Banking in the New Era: Post-Crisis Challenges and Opportunities, Edited by Suk-Joong Kim and Michael D. McKenzie, 2010, Emerald Publishing, 2010 (ISBN: 978-1-84950-912-1)
Volume 12:	Institutional Investors in Global Capital Markets, Edited by Narjess Boubakri and Jean-Claude Cosset, 2011, Emerald Publishing, 2011 (ISBN: 978-1-78052-242-5)

INTERNATIONAL FINANCE REVIEW VOLUME 13

TRANSPARENCY AND GOVERNANCE IN A GLOBAL WORLD

EDITED BY

J. JAY CHOI
Temple University, USA

HEIBATOLLAH SAMI
Lehigh University, USA

United Kingdom – North America – Japan
India – Malaysia – China

Emerald Group Publishing Limited
Howard House, Wagon Lane, Bingley BD16 1WA, UK

First edition 2012

British Library Cataloguing in Publication Data
A catalogue record for this book is available from the British Library

ISBN: 978-1-78052-764-2
ISSN: 1569-3767 (Series)

CONTENTS

LIST OF CONTRIBUTORS

Harvey Arbeláez	Monterey Institute of International Studies, Graduate School of International Policy and Management, Monterey, CA, USA
Josep M. Argilés-Bosch	Department of Accounting, Universitat de Barcelona, Barcelona, Spain
Florian Bitsch	Center for Entrepreneurial and Financial Studies, Technische Universitaet Muenchen, Munich, Germany
Auke de Bos	Erasmus School of Law, Erasmus University Rotterdam, Rotterdam, Netherlands
J. Jay Choi	Department of Finance, Fox School of Business, Temple University, Philadelphia, PA, USA
Fang Fang	College of Business Administration, University of Texas Pan American, Edinburg, TX, USA
Josep García-Blandón	IQS School of Management, Ramon Llull University, Barcelona, Spain
Sid Gray	The University of Sydney Business School, University of Sydney, Sydney, Australia
Moo Sung Kim	Fox School of Business, Temple University, PA, USA
Sung S. Kwon	School of Administrative Studies, York University, Toronto, Ontario, Canada
Andrew Lepone	Faculty of Economics and Business, University of Sydney, NSW, Australia

Mónica Martínez-Blasco	IQS School of Management, Ramon Llull University, Barcelona, Spain
Silvio Hiroshi Nakao	University of Sao Paulo, Ribeirao Preto – Sao Paulo, Brazil
Chinmay Pattnaik	The University of Sydney Business School, University of Sydney, Sydney, Australia
Heibatollah Sami	Lehigh University, College of Business and Economics, Bethlehem, PA, USA
Reuben Segara	Faculty of Economics and Business, University of Sydney, Sydney, Australia
Aloy Soppe	Erasmus School of Law, Erasmus University Rotterdam, Rotterdam, Netherlands
Rie Tanaka	Mizuho Bank, Ltd., Tokyo, Japan
Emna Trabelsi	Institut Superieur de Gestion de Tunis, University of Tunis, Tunisia
Zheng Wang	Department of Accountancy, City University of Hong Kong, Kowloon, Hong Kong
Brad Wong	Booz & Co, New South Wales, Australia
Niels van Zijl	Erasmus School of Law, Erasmus University Rotterdam, Rotterdam, Netherlands
Haiyan Zhou	Faculty of Accounting & Business Law, University of Texas Pan American, Edinburg, TX, USA

PART I
AN OVERVIEW

CORPORATE TRANSPARENCY FROM THE GLOBAL PERSPECTIVE: A CONCEPTUAL OVERVIEW

J. Jay Choi and Heibatollah Sami

ABSTRACT

This is a conceptual overview of transparency from the global and interdisciplinary perspectives. It briefly develops a conceptual framework on transparency as to how it relates to governance and market environments, outlines conditions for transparency, and presents hypotheses concerning the level of transparency in a global world. It then summarizes 12 papers included in the research volume.

Keywords: Transparency; information asymmetry; disclosure; law and finance; global corporate governance

JEL classifications: G30; M40; M16

INTRODUCTION

In some circles, transparency has become a buzzword these days. Firms and organizations are under increasing pressure to be more transparent globally. The pressure for corporate transparency comes from institutional

Transparency and Governance in a Global World
International Finance Review, Volume 13, 3–7

ISSN: 1569-3767/doi:10.1108/S1569-3767(2012)0000013003

shareholders and regulators, as well as from banks and other stakeholders needing to monitor corporate financial conditions and managerial decisions more closely to protect their interests. The call for transparency has also intensified for banks since the recent global financial crises and as a result of a series of egregious financial scandals.

These calls for transparency presume that threat of disclosure could have lessened or deterred some of the financial crises and scandals around the world. Transparency is good because it may offer the promise of accountability and better governance which may lead to efficient allocation of capital and resources. The calls for transparency extend beyond the corporate sector to non-profit entities and public institutions.

From a cultural, institutional or political standpoint, transparency is a country-level issue, depending on the level of democratization of economic, social and political systems, as well as culture that underlies them. If we interpret the work of North (1990), Hofstede (1983) and others in the context of transparency, we can hypothesize that the demand for transparency will increase if the country is more democratic, less authoritative, or more individualistic. From the work of La Porta, de-Silanes, Shleifer and Vishny (1998, 2000) and others, we would expect that transparency should be greater if there is a greater protection of investor rights, if the country has a common law tradition, or if there is a greater regulatory requirement for disclosure and public information.

Within the corporate context, transparency can be understood from the perspective of agency theory (Jensen & Meckling, 1976) or transaction cost theory (Williamson, 1979). A decision to voluntarily disclose firm-specific information is a trade-off between the benefits of disclosure (e.g., visibility or reputation, which may lead to lower cost of capital or more business) and the costs of disclosure (e.g., transaction costs, and potential strategic disadvantage of disclosing proprietary information to one's competitors). In addition, the disclosure may influence agency relationships among stakeholders – whether it is between management and shareholders or between debt and equity holders in a traditional Anglo-Saxon setting (Jensen & Mecking, 1976) or whether it is between controlling insiders such as family, management or banks and a large number of small minority shareholders, which is more likely in the non-Anglo-Saxon world (Shleifer & Vishney, 1986).

What does it take to have transparency in financial reporting to begin with? High level of corporate transparency is contingent upon the existence of certain firm and market characteristics. First, firms should disclose all relevant corporate information (voluntarily or because of regulatory requirements) that has a potential impact on investor values or decisions.

Second, such information should be available to all market participants at the same time without any costs. Third, the market should be functioning efficiently such that the market agents (e.g., analysts or institutions) process and disseminate information and their insights effectively.

Transparency, viewed in this way, is a multi-faceted, interdisciplinary issue with far-reaching implications, and little has been done in academic research to examine the various dimensions of transparency. Bushman, Piotroski and Smith (2004) have surveyed issues pertaining to corporate transparency from an accounting standpoint, but there are many unanswered questions, even at a very basic level.

SOME SPECIFIC QUESTIONS

Here are examples of some non-exhaustive, open questions pertaining to transparency that we used in our call for papers for this volume:

- What is transparency and how is it measured?
- What are the benefits and costs of transparency?
- What mechanisms do firms use to become transparent?
- What are the effects of corporate governance and ownership on transparency?
- Does one view of transparency satisfy the needs of all stakeholders?
- How are the cost of capital and corporate financing related to transparency?
- What is the role of political and social connections in accounting regulation?
- What is the role of auditing or earnings management in shaping transparency?
- What is the role of communication and technology in enhancing transparency?
- Does transparency differ across countries and why?
- How does globalization of financial markets and accounting standards affect transparency?
- What are the effects of culture, law and institutions on transparency?
- What are the effects of economic development and market structure on transparency?
- What is the role of transparency in global financial crisis?

We have collected 12 original research papers dealing with various issues relating to transparency in this volume. These papers may not necessarily answer all these questions directly, but they do address various issues arising from these questions in some specific ways. Some may not concern any of these sample questions but may nevertheless be equally interesting and within the broad spectrum of issues related to transparency in a global context.

Three papers in part two of the volume address issues pertaining to ownership, taxes and transparency. Fang and Zhou show evidence that corporate transparency is positively related to institutional ownership because firms with higher institutional ownership tend to have tighter internal controls as well as more accurate earnings forecast by analysts. Kim conjectures that affiliation with a business group may make the firm more opaque due to the complexity of internal market transactions, but report that Korean chaebol firms improved their transparency after corporate accounting and governance reforms in the aftermath of the Asian financial crisis. Nakao argues that economic and environmental factors such as economic development, financial market structure, ownership concentration and accounting regulations influence tax conformity and hence the informativeness of earnings and transparency.

Part three which is composed of three papers deals with the relationship between governance, operations and transparency. Using firm data for 25 countries, Soppe, Zijl and Bos report that more transparent firms as well as firms with more intense CEO monitoring by the board have better financial performance. Kwon documents the varying sensitivities of executive equity-based compensation to earnings and returns for high-tech versus non-high tech firms. Interestingly, the sensitivity declines for high-tech firms more than for non-high-tech firms when bad earnings news is announced. Pattnaik and Gray examine corporate transparency of multinational corporations (MNC) in India, and show that MNC subsidiaries, as well as domestic firms with high international operations, help improve information environments of Indian market more than domestic firms and facilitate the development of capital market intermediaries such as equity analysts.

Part four contains four papers that examine the relations between investors, analysts and informational transparency. Bitsch documents the presence of a valuation discount for earnings management by listed infrastructure funds, showing that investors punish lack of transparency. The work by Argiles-Bosch, Garcia-Blandon, and Martinez-Blasco documents that Spanish-listed firms change the pattern of earnings management, as well as manipulations of real activities, during the economic downturn. Wang provides evidence on how analysts help improve corporate information environment. In particular, she shows that revisions of analyst recommendations are more valuable for investors when earnings announcements are informationally more complicated. Lepone, Segara and Wong argue that in the presence of significant information asymmetry, broker anonymity can be beneficial because informed traders tend to be less detected.

The last part includes two papers that address transparency in the public sector. Trabelsi theorizes that in a two-player monetary policy game that considers the interaction between the private sector and central bank, an intermediate transparency strategy, rather than a complete transparency, can improve the outcomes of both the private sector and public policy. Envisioning how to deal with corruptions in the context of negotiations for M&As or FDIs, Arbelaez and Tanaka compare the cultural, institutional, political environments of Argentina and Chile, suggesting that governance and opacity are deeply rooted in basic environmental and historical factors.

In sum, these papers analyse the diversity of issues characteristic of the richness of transparency as an essential concept in a global, open economy. Clearly transparency is one of those transcendent topics that span many disciplines – beyond accounting and finance, intersecting economics, law and management, and embracing sociology and political science – offering opportunities for creative interdisciplinary research. We hope this volume is a useful one-stop reference for students and scholars as well as practitioners and policymakers interested in such work.

REFERENCES

Bushman, R. M., Piotroski, J. D., & Smith, A. J. (2004). What determines corporate transparency? *Journal of Accounting Research*, *42*(2), 207–251.

Hofstede, G. (1983). The cultural relativity of organizational practices and theories. *Journal of International Business Studies*, *14*(2), 75–89.

Jensen, M. C., & Meckling, W. H. (1976). Theory of the firm: Managerial behavior, agency costs and ownership structure. *Journal of Financial Economics*, *3*, 305–360.

La Porta, R., Lopez-de-Silanes, F., Shleifer, A., & Vishny, R. (1998). Law and finance. *Journal of Political Economy*, *106*(6), 1113–1155.

La Porta, R., Lopez-de-Silanes, F., Shleifer, A., & Vishny, R. W. (2000). Investor protection and corporate governance. *Journal of Financial Economics*, *58*(1), 3–27.

North, D. C. (1990). *Institutions, institutional change, and economic performance*. New York, NY: Cambridge University Press.

Shleifer, A., & Vishny, R. W. (1986). Large shareholders and corporate control. *Journal of Political Economy*, *94*, 461–488.

Williamson, O. E. (1979). Transaction-cost economics: The governance of contractual relations. *Journal of Law and Economics*, *22*, 233–261.

PART II
OWNERSHIP, TAXES AND TRANSPARENCY

INSTITUTIONAL OWNERSHIP, INTERNAL CONTROL, AND DISCLOSURE TRANSPARENCY

Fang Fang and Haiyan Zhou

ABSTRACT

In this study, we investigate whether higher institutional ownership is related to better internal controls and whether better internal control is associated with a higher quality of transparency.

Keywords: Internal control; institutional ownership; disclosure transparency; earnings management; analyst forecast accuracy; analyst following

JEL classifications: G30; G32; G34; M40

INTRODUCTION

Regulators and policy makers have recognized the need for effective internal controls (ICs) that promote disclosure transparency in the wake of corporate failures and accounting scandals such as Enron, Mahindra Satyam, Parmalat, and Worldcom. Consequently, a variety of acts and regulations

Transparency and Governance in a Global World
International Finance Review, Volume 13, 11–37

ISSN: 1569-3767/doi:10.1108/S1569-3767(2012)0000013004

are implemented to encourage firms to commit to increased disclosure. For instance, in United States, the Sarbanes and Oxley Act Section 404 on the audits of ICs was enacted to increase investor protection, as Gupta, Sami, and Zhou (2011) note that the effectiveness of ICs over the financial reporting process is critical in reasonably assuring the accuracy and reliability of corporate disclosures. In this study, we attempt to document empirical evidence on the relationship among institutional ownership, IC, and disclosure transparency.

A considerable body of empirical research investigates the outcomes of increased disclosures, as well as the association between corporate governance and disclosure transparency (e.g., Gupta et al., 2011; Ogneva, Raghunandan, & Subramanyam, 2006). The effect of increased accounting disclosure and transparency could include reductions in information asymmetry as reflected in bid-ask spreads and bond yield spreads in the securities markets (e.g., Yua, 2005; Zhou, 2007). Transparency may also affect the forecast behavior of financial analysts, that is, analysts mispricing and the accuracy/dispersion of analyst forecasts (Elliott, Krische, & Peecher, 2010; Lang & Lundholm, 1996). These prior observations are consistent with the theory of discretionary disclosure (Verrecchia, 2001), as well as the incomplete accounting information model of Duffie and Lando (2001). Also, Beasley (1996) and Peasnell, Pope, and Young (2000) note that corporate governance mechanisms, such as the independence of board, may deter earnings management behavior and fraudulent financial reporting behaviors of management looking to expropriate stockholder wealth, and hence improve accounting disclosure quality.

The influence of ownership structures in corporate governance and financial disclosure is also examined in the literature. For instance, the role of disclosure transparency lending to a lower cost of capital that is more pronounced with higher level of ownership concentration (Hope, Thomas, & Vyas, 2009). In addition, concentrated ownership is believed to lower the credibility of reported earnings with respect to outside investors. Fang and Wong (2002) note that high ownership concentration may result in agency conflicts between controlling stockholders and outside investors, where controlling stockholders conceal the firms' "rent-seeking" activities from the public. Leuz, Nanda, and Wysocki (2003) report that low levels of disclosure serve as a stanchion for insider control and wealth expropriation, thus shareholders have a financial interest in increasing firm disclosure.

However, little attention has been devoted to the link between IC and transparency until recently (e.g., Felo, 2007; Ogneva et al., 2006). While board involvement in the development, implementation, and maintenance of codes is found to be an important factor in enhancing ethics codes, thus building stronger IC environments and encouraging more information disclosure (Felo, 2000, 2007), there is a disagreement within the literature on the *direct* association between IC weakness and disclosure quality (Ogneva et al., 2006). To address this issue, we investigate the role of IC quality in disclosure transparency drawing from multiple measures within the literature.

The direct link between institutional ownership and ICs has been understudied with an exception of Tang and Xu (2007). Tang and Xu (2007) find that institutional investors with a long investment horizon are less likely to disclose material weakness than those with a short investment horizon. However, they fail to link institutional investor type with firm performance in post-disclosure period. Moreover, the role of institutional owners in corporate disclosures is not addressed within their study.

We address this gap within the literature by testing the unified association between institutional ownership, IC, and disclosure transparency. Specifically, we investigate how institutional ownership relates to ICs and if ICs are associated with higher quality of transparency. Following the literature on disclosure transparency (e.g., Lang & Lundholm, 1996; Roychowdhury, 2006), we use multiple measures of transparency to investigate our hypotheses, including analyst forecast measures (the number of analysts who cover a firm and the accuracy of analyst forecasts) and a variety of earnings management measures.

We find that after controlling for simultaneous effects, firms with higher institutional ownership have significantly higher discretionary accruals, higher abnormal cash flow from operations, higher abnormal production cost, but significantly lower abnormal discretionary expenses, and a lower number of analysts covering the firm. Our findings are different from the conventional notion that increased institutional ownership results in increased disclosure transparency. Instead, our findings indicate that institutional investors may take advantage of their positions to pursue their own interest rather than encourage the firm to commit to better disclosure practice. In addition, employing the IC model we find significant links between institutional ownership and IC quality. It reveals that firms with higher institutional ownership tend to report better IC. Thus, there is a divergence from the theory given the positive link between earnings management and institutional ownership and the positive link between IC quality and institutional ownership. It is possible that institutional investors are more likely to associate with firms of higher yield, smaller size, and less specific firm risks as indicated by the results of the institutional ownership model. These firms tend to report better IC quality, as they are subject to less pressure from their auditors when the auditors are non-Big4. Future research should investigate whether firms with higher institutional investors are more likely to switch their auditors and do opinion shopping. Lastly, we find that firms reporting better IC are associated with fewer analysts following and lower analyst forecast accuracy. This finding is contrary to our expectation that firms with better IC quality are more likely to have greater disclosure transparency, which attracts more analyst followings and subsequently improves analyst's forecasting.

Our study contributes to the extant literature in the following ways. First, our research adds to the current research on transparency by highlighting that IC and institutional ownership are associated with transparency. Our results reveal that the relationship between institutional ownership, IC, and transparency measures may be complicated and demands further research attention.

Second, our results provide more insights regarding previous studies asserting IC is essential to the transparent reporting of financial information. Our results indicate that IC reports and disclosure transparency could be two different concepts. In addition, the quality of IC in perception can be also a different concept from the quality of ICs as reported.

Third, our research uses both accrual-based and real earnings management as proxies for transparency to see whether direct cash flows consequences matter in disclosure transparency. Consistent with Cohen and Zarowin (2010), we find that accrual-based and real earnings management proxies produce various results in terms of the association among institutional ownership, IC, and transparency.

The remainder of the study is organized as follows. The second section introduces the related literature and hypotheses development. The third section describes the sample selection procedures and research design. The fourth section discusses the empirical findings, and the fifth section presents our conclusions.

LITERATURE REVIEW AND HYPOTHESES DEVELOPMENT

The transparency literature has well documented the consequences of increased accounting disclosure and transparency. These consequences include reductions in information asymmetry as reflected in bid-ask spreads and bond yield spreads in the securities markets (e.g., Elliott et al., 2010;

Yua, 2005; Zhou, 2007). For instance, Yua (2005) finds that firms with higher disclosure rankings from Association for Investment Management and Research have lower credit spreads, especially for short-term bonds. Using an environment where ex ante disclosure was relatively low, Zhou (2007) investigates the relationship between new auditing standards, increased accounting disclosure, and information asymmetry – finding that companies experienced significant reduction in the bid-ask spread subsequent to their adoption of new auditing standards in the emerging market of China.

Transparency may also affect financial analysts' forecast accuracy, similarly transparency may influence an analyst's interest in following a firm. Elliott et al. (2010) examine how accounting transparency and investor base jointly affect financial analysts' expectations of mispricing, finding that analysts expect a larger positive deviation when a firm's disclosure is more transparent on earnings management that focus on inflating income and shareholders focus on a shorter-term horizon (low concentration in holdings, high portfolio turnover, and frequent momentum trading). Using data from the Financial Analysts Federation Corporate Information Committee Report (FAF Report), Lang and Lundholm (1996) report that firms who are committed to providing highly informative disclosures have more analyst following, more accurate analyst earnings forecasts, less dispersion among individual analyst forecasts, and less volatility in forecast revisions. Further, Lang, Lins, and Maffett (2011) show, using an international sample, that firms with greater transparency, reflected in accounting standards, auditor choice, earnings management, analyst following and forecast accuracy, experience less liquidity volatility, fewer extreme illiquidity events, and lower correlations between firm-level liquidity as well as market liquidity and market returns.

The corporate governance literature also investigates the link between corporate governance and accounting disclosure quality. Beasley (1996) finds board independence decreases the likelihood of financial fraud. Similarly, Peasnell et al. (2000) examine the deterring role of board monitoring on earnings management by UK firms. They observe that firms with more external board members are less likely to use income-increasing abnormal *accruals* to avoid reporting losses and earnings reductions, though no evidence is found on the direct effect of an audit committee on earnings management by managers to meet or exceed their earnings thresholds. Their findings suggest that boards contribute to the reliability of financial statements, as predicted by agency theory. Similarly, Karamanou and Vafeas (2005) study how corporate boards and audit committees are associated with the voluntary disclosure of management earnings forecasts. They find that managers are more likely to make or update an earnings forecast, their forecasts are more accurate and investor response is greater when firms have effective board and audit committees. Together, the extant empirical evidence is broadly consistent with the notion that effective corporate governance is associated with financial disclosure quality.

However, few studies have specifically investigated the link between IC and transparency (e.g., Felo, 2007; Ogneva et al., 2006). In the wake of Enron, Mahindra Satyam, Parmalat, and Worldcom, regulators and policy makers have recognized the benefits of effective ICs in enhancing disclosure transparency. Consequently, the Sarbanes and Oxley Act Section 404 on the audits of ICs was enacted to increase protection, as Gupta et al. (2011) note that effectiveness of ICs over the financial reporting is critical in reasonably assuring the accuracy and reliability of corporate disclosures. With an implicit assumption that ethics codes will help firms develop more transparent disclosure policies by enhancing their IC environments, Felo (2000) provides evidence that board involvement in the development, implementation, and maintenance of ethics codes is an important factor in whether ethics codes are related to stronger IC environments. In addition, firms having ethics programs overseen by their boards disclose more financial information and board-management information (Felo, 2007). However, there are mixed results in the literature. Ogneva et al. (2006) does not find evidence to support the premise that effective ICs reduce information risk, thereby potentially improving disclosure quality. For firms reporting material weakness of ICs, there is no *direct* association between IC weakness and discretionary accruals, informed trading probability, firm specific risk (Beta), or abnormal price volatility. Although there is a marginally higher cost of equity for firms with material weakness in IC, the differences in cost of equity disappear after controlling for firm characteristics associated with firms disclosing material weaknesses (Ogneva et al., 2006).

The literature also documents the influence of ownership structures in corporate governance and financial disclosure. For instance, ownership concentration is related with disclosure transparency in reducing the cost of capital. Proposing that financial information plays a limited role in decision making process of external investors of private firms, Hope et al. (2009) find that private firms reviewed by an independent external auditor, a proxy for financial transparency, experience significantly less problems and pay less for external financing. They find that such results are more pronounced in the presence of a controlling shareholder, and that this joint effect is more significant in countries with weaker institutional environments. Thus, they provide empirical evidences on the joint role of financial transparency and ownership in a private firm setting.

Using public companies in seven East Asian economies, Fan and Wong (2002) examine the relationships between ownership structure and earnings "informativeness", measured by the earnings and return relation. Postulating that concentrated ownership and the "associated pyramidal and cross-holding" structures create agency conflicts between controlling shareholders and outside investors, they find that controlling shareholders are perceived to report accounting information for private goals, as reflected in lower credibility of the reported earnings from the perspective of outside investors. They also note that concentrated ownership is associated with low earnings disclosure as ownership concentration prevents private information about the firms' "rent-seeking" activities from going to public.

Insiders can use income manipulation to conceal firm performance from outsider shareholders to protect their control benefits, and thus could be associated with low level of disclosures. Leuz et al. (2003), using a global sample, examine the differences in earnings management and find that earnings management decreases with investor protection because a strong protection environment limits an insider's ability to pursuit personal interests. Their results suggest an empirical role of insider owners as a feature of corporate governance affecting reported earnings and accounting disclosure.

However, few studies investigate the direct link between institutional ownership and ICs with an exception of Tang and Xu (2007). Tang and Xu (2007) examine whether a firm's institutional ownership affects its likelihood of disclosing material weaknesses in ICs under SOX 302 and 404. They show that firms with long horizon institutional investors are less likely to disclose material weaknesses than those with short-term horizon, and firms disclosing material weaknesses in IC have worse operating performance and stock returns in the post-disclosure period. However, they find no direct effects of institutional investor type on post-disclosure performance.

In this study, we investigate the comprehensive relation between institutional ownership, IC, and disclosure transparency. We first examine the link between institutional ownership and the quality of IC. As discussed above, ownership concentration results into "pyramidal and cross-holding" structures that create agency conflicts between controlling shareholders and outside investors (Fan & Wong, 2002), and controlling shareholders are perceived to hold private information for their own interests. Hence firms with more ownership concentration have lower disclosure transparency.

Similarly, insiders may use income manipulation to conceal firm performance from outsider shareholders to protect their private control benefits, and thus could be associated with low level of disclosures (Leuz et al., 2003). Different from these types of shareholders, institutional shareholders would have positive impacts on the quality of a firm's governance structure, as institutional investors tend to invest in firms with good governance structure to meet legal and ethical responsibility in addition to saving on monitoring and exit costs (Chung & Zhang, 2011).

First, institutional investors, such as banks, insurance companies, and pension funds, are confronted with greater ethical and legal liabilities than individual shareholders. They tend to focus their portfolios on stocks that are viewed as "prudent" investments (Del Guercio, 1996). For instance, they tend to choose firms with a stable dividends payment history (Grinstein & Michaely, 2005), and firms with first-class governance structures to reduce the risk of wealth expropriation, earn fair rates of return, and preserve the invested capital – thus to meet the prudent-person rule.

In addition, institutional investors have more motivations to monitor firms than individual investors because of their larger stakes in those firms, in particular when trading cost is high. They prefer firms with superior disclosure rankings to reduce monitoring costs (Bushee & Noe, 2000). Given that companies that have better governance structures need less outside monitoring, institutional investors are likely to prefer these firms to those with worse governance structures.

Finally, institutional investors are more likely than individual investors to invest in stocks with high market liquidity because the price changes have more significant impact on institutional investors (Chung & Zhang, 2011). This happens because institutional investors typically trade in larger volumes than individual investors. As better governance structure, in particular, better IC over financial reporting, increases financial transparency thus reducing information asymmetry, firms with better corporate governance show higher market liquidity and lower trading costs (Chung et al., 2010). Therefore, institutional investors are more likely to prefer stocks of a firm with better IC than individual investors.

In sum, institutional shareholders are more likely to encourage firms to develop and implement effective IC governing the financial reporting process, as the latter would help communicate more reliable and transparent information to the public. Therefore, we propose that firms with higher institutional ownership are more likely to have better ICs over financial reporting process and less likely to have IC weakness problems in their disclosures.

H1. Ceteris paribus, firms with more institutional ownership are less likely to have IC weakness.

Second, we investigate the association between IC and disclosure transparency. A common rationale for SOX is that firms with lower transparency are more likely to have IC problems. In contrast, effective ICs can enhance disclosure transparency because effective ICs over financial reporting process would reasonably assure the accuracy and reliability of corporate disclosures (Gupta et al., 2011). For instance, firms having ethics program overseen by their boards, reflecting the tone of top management views on control environment, disclose more overall information, financial information, and board and management information (Felo, 2007). Hence, we propose that firms with better ICs over financial reporting process will be more likely to have greater disclosure transparency.

H2. Ceteris paribus, firms with a better quality of IC are more likely to have greater disclosure transparency.

Third, we investigate whether firms with a higher percentage of institutional ownership are more likely to demonstrate greater disclosure transparency due to increased monitoring effects and takeover threats from concentrated ownership. In line with the argument that institutional investors tend to invest in firms with better corporate governance (Chung & Zhang, 2011), institutional investors prefer firms with forthcoming disclosure practice to fulfill legal and ethical responsibility and reduce monitoring and exit costs. In accord with the prudent-person rule, institutional investors tend to choose firms with better disclosures to reduce the risks of expropriation. Moreover, institutional investors tend to have greater motivation to monitor firms than individual investors due to the size of their holdings, in particular when the trading cost is high, they prefer firms with superior disclosure rankings to reduce monitoring costs (Bushee & Noe, 2000). Subsequently, as institutional investors typically trade in larger quantities, they are more sensitive to stock price changes than individual investors (Chung & Zhang, 2011). As such, institutional investors are more likely to invest in firms that disclosure more information, as these firms exhibit higher market liquidity and lower trading costs (Lang et al., 2011; Leuz & Verrecchia, 2000; Zhou, 2007). Therefore, institutional investors are more likely to prefer firms with superior disclosure transparency, which leads to the following hypothesis.

H3. Ceteris paribus, firms with a greater percentage of institutional ownership are more likely to have greater disclosure transparency.

DATA AND RESEARCH DESIGN

Data

Our sample comes from the COMPUSTAT annual industrial and research files for the period August 2002–December 2009. Additionally, we employ information on analysts following from I/B/E/S. Information on new disclosures of IC is from Audit Analytics' Section 404 Internal Control Data Disclosure that provides detailed information on the effectiveness of a firm's IC. If ineffective IC is found, the underlying reasons for the ineffectiveness are also reported. Lastly, we retrieve institutional ownership data from the CDA/Spectrum database of 113F Institutional Investors for firms. These yield a total of 35,026 firm-year observations. We delete financial firms and utility firms from our sample due to different regulatory environment, delete those firm-year observations with missing data on firm characteristics and winzorize the data on independent variables at 1% and 99%. These processes leave us with a sample of 9,570 observations and the final sample varies with each model after deleting the missing data and winsorizing the data on the dependent variable used in each model (Table 1).

Research Design

Measuring Disclosure Transparency

The accounting and finance literature has documented a variety of transparency measures. In this study, we use two groups of proxies to measure transparency. The first group includes two analyst forecast measures: analyst coverage (NUMEST) and analyst forecast accuracy (ACCURACY). Lang and Lundholm (1996) report that analysts gather and analyze information from both public as well as private sources to derive firm value, and the transmission of private information via analysts forecasts contributes to disclosure transparency. Therefore, an increase in the number of analysts following a firm implies greater disclosure.[1] In addition, analyst forecasts are more likely to be accurate if the firm makes more information available to the analysts and the market. Hence, analyst forecast accuracy can proxy for transparency. These measures are based on prior literature (Brennan & Subrahmanyam, 1995; Lang & Lundholm, 1996; Lang et al., 2011). The second group of measures includes measures of earnings management, to the extent that earning management by managers generates information asymmetry and reduces transparency. Following the literature

Table 1. Sample Selection.

		Sample Construction	Number of Firm-Year Observations
Original sample		All firm-year observations with required data on Compustat, I/B/E/S, Audit Analytics, and CDA/Spectrum database using the sample period August 2002–December 2009	35,026
	Less:	Financial firms and utility firms	27,289
	Less:	Companies with missing data in independent variables	10,465
	Less:	Winsorization of all continuous independent variables at the 1% and 99%	9,570
Final sample			
Measure 1: NA	Less:	Companies with missing data in NA and winsorization of NA at the 1% and 99%	9,158
Measure 2: ACFO	Less:	Companies with missing data in ACFO and winsorization of ACFO at the 1% and 99%	9,294
Measure 3: APRODA	Less:	Companies with missing data in APRODA and winsorization of APRODA at the 1% and 99%	9,376
Measure 4: ADISA	Less:	Companies with missing data in ADISA and winsorization of ADISA at the 1% and 99%	9,377
Measure 5: NUMEST	Less:	Companies with missing data in NUMEST and winsorization of NUMEST at the 1% and 99%	7,931
Measure 6: ACCURACY	Less:	Companies with missing data ACCURACY and winsorization of ACCURACY at the 1% and 99%	7,920

Notes: This table contains sample selection process for the firm-year observations used in the study. Six different proxies for transparency are used as follows: NA, accrual-based earnings management; ACFO, abnormal cash flow from operation; APRODA, abnormal production cost; ADISA, abnormal discretionary expenses; NUMEST, number of analysts following; ACCURACY, estimate of accuracy of analyst forecasts.

(Fan & Wong, 2002; Leuz et al., 2003), we use four measures of earnings management: discretionary accruals, abnormal cash flow from operations, abnormal production costs, and abnormal discretionary expenses.

Analyst coverage is defined as the number of security analysts that provide earnings forecasts or investment recommendations for a stock each month. Data on analyst coverage was obtained from I/B/E/S Summary History-EPS file, which provides information on more than 7,000 analysts affiliated with more than 1,000 institutions. It is important to note that zero analyst coverage does not rule out the possibility that a firm in question receives analyst coverage from institutions not registered with I/B/E/S.

Following Lang and Lundholm (1996), we measure analysts' forecast accuracy (ACCURACY) as minus one times the absolute difference between the I/B/E/S consensus forecast of annual earnings made nine months before the earnings announcement date and the actual annual earnings reported by I/B/E/S, scaled by stock price on the day prior to the measurement of the I/B/E/S consensus forecast. Eq. (1) demonstrates the calculation of ACCURACY. The absolute value of the difference between forecast earnings and actual earnings is normally used as analysts' forecast errors. We multiply it with minus one so that the interpretation of the effect of institutional ownership and ICs on analyst forecast accuracy would be consistent with the sign of the coefficients of the independent variables.

$$\text{ACCURACY} = (-1)\frac{|\text{FCAST} - \text{ACTUAL}|}{\text{PRICE}} \tag{1}$$

where ACTUAL is the actual annual earnings per share reported by I/B/E/S; FCAST is the consensus analyst forecast made nine months prior to the end of the fiscal year; and PRICE is the closing stock price one day before the consensus analyst forecast.

This study considers both real and accrual-based earnings management because firms may use either or both of earnings management. Accruals-based earnings management refers to earnings management activities which have no direct cash flows consequences. In particular, this study uses the modified Jones model (Jones, 1991) to measure discretionary accruals, as described in Dechow, Sloan, and Sweeney (1995). Specifically, we follow the procedure and notations in Cohen, Dey, and Lys (2008), where the modified Jones model is estimated for each industry sector based on the 2-digit SIC code each fiscal year as follows:

$$\frac{\text{TA}_{it}}{Assets_{i,t-1}} = k_{1t}\frac{1}{Assets_{i,t-1}} + k_2\frac{\Delta\text{Rev}_{it}}{Assets_{i,t-1}} + k_3\frac{\Delta\text{PPE}_{it}}{Assets_{i,t-1}} + \varepsilon_{it} \tag{2}$$

where TA, total accruals, is defined as: TA = EBXI − CFO; EBXI represents the earnings before extraordinary items and discontinued operations (annual Compustat data item 123) and CFO is the operating cash flows (annual Compustat data item 308 − annual Compustat data item 124); *Assets* is the total assets (annual Compustat data item 6); ΔREV is the change in revenues (annual Compustat data item 12) from the previous year and PPE is the gross value of property, plant and equipment (annual Compustat data item 7).

Using the coefficient estimates obtained from Eq. (2), we estimate the firm-specific normal accruals (NA) for our sample firms:

$$\mathrm{NA}_{it} = \hat{k}_{1t}\frac{1}{Assets_{i,t-1}} + \hat{k}_2\frac{(\Delta\mathrm{Rev}_{it} - \Delta\mathrm{AR}_{it})}{Assets_{i,t-1}} + \hat{k}_3\frac{\mathrm{PPE}_{it}}{Assets_{i,t-1}} \tag{3}$$

where ΔAR is the change in accounts receivable (annual Compustat data item 2) from the preceding year, and other variables are defined the same as above. Following prior literature, discretionary accruals (DA) are calculated as the difference between total accruals and the fitted normal accruals.

Real earnings management activities impair the transparency of financial reports by adjusting *real* earnings, which can be indistinguishable from optimal business decisions, and thus less likely to draw auditor or regulatory scrutiny. However, real earnings management may imply less commitment of a firm to more disclosure practice when a firm has multiple methods (both real and non-real earnings management) available to manipulate earnings. Meanwhile, real earnings management may imply a firm's commitment to more transparent disclosure practice when a firm has alternative methods (using real earnings management) available to meet target earnings instead of using accruals. As in Roychowdhury (2006), we estimate abnormal cash flows from operations, abnormal production costs, and abnormal discretionary expenses (advertising, R&D, and SG&A) to capture real earnings.

We first estimate the normal levels of cash flows from operations (CFO), production costs, and discretionary expenses. The normal level of CFO is expressed in the following cross-sectional regression for each industry and year combination:

$$\frac{\mathrm{CFO}_{it}}{Assets_{i,t-1}} = k_{1t}\frac{1}{Assets_{i,t-1}} + k_2\frac{Sales_{it}}{Assets_{i,t-1}} + k_3\frac{\Delta Sales_{it}}{Assets_{i,t-1}} + \varepsilon_{it} \tag{4}$$

where CFO is cash flow from operations (Compustat data item 308 − annual Compustat data item 124) and other variables are defined the same as above. The abnormal CFO (*ACFO*) is computed as the difference between the actual values and the normal levels obtained from Eq. (4).

The sum of the cost of goods sold (COGS) is a linear function of contemporaneous *Sales*. Production costs represent the sum of COGS and the change in inventory during a fiscal year.

$$\frac{\text{COGS}_{it}}{Assets_{i,t-1}} = k_{1t}\frac{1}{Assets_{i,t-1}} + k_2\frac{Sales_{it}}{Assets_{i,t-1}} + \varepsilon_{it} \tag{5}$$

where all the variables are defined the same as above. Next, we model inventory growth as a linear function of the contemporaneous and lagged change in sales:

$$\frac{\Delta\text{INV}_{it}}{Assets_{i,t-1}} = k_{1t}\frac{1}{Assets_{i,t-1}} + k_2\frac{\Delta Sales_{it}}{Assets_{i,t-1}} + k_3\frac{\Delta Sales_{i,t-1}}{Assets_{i,t-1}} + \varepsilon_{it} \tag{6}$$

Hence, we estimate the normal level of production costs as:

$$\frac{\text{Pr}od_{it}}{Assets_{i,t-1}} = k_{1t}\frac{1}{Assets_{i,t-1}} + k_2\frac{Sales_{it}}{Assets_{i,t-1}} + k_3\frac{\Delta Sales_{it}}{Assets_{i,t-1}} + k_4\frac{\Delta Sales_{i,t-1}}{Assets_{i,t-1}} + \varepsilon_{it} \tag{7}$$

where Pr*od* represents the production costs in period *t*, the sum of COGS (annual Compustat data item 41) and the change in inventories (annual Compustat data item 3), and all other variables are defined the same as above. Then the abnormal production costs (APRODA) is computed as the difference between the actual values and the normal levels obtained from Eq. (7).

The normal level of discretionary expenses is modeled as a linear function of lagged sales as in Eq. (8). Using lagged sales instead of current sales alleviates the problem that firms managing sales upward in a certain year may result in a significantly lower residual in the regression model.

$$\frac{\text{DiscExp}_{it}}{Assets_{i,t-1}} = k_{1t}\frac{1}{Assets_{i,t-1}} + k_2\frac{Sales_{i,t-1}}{Assets_{i,t-1}} + \varepsilon_{it} \tag{8}$$

where DiscExp represents the discretionary expenditures in period *t*, defined as the sum of advertising expenses (annual Compustat data item 45), R&D expenses (annual Compustat data item 46) and SG&A (annual Compustat data item 189), and all other variables are defined the same as above. Then the abnormal discretionary expenses (ADISA) are computed as the difference between the actual values and the normal levels obtained from Eq. (8).

Measuring Institutional Ownership and IC

Institutional investors are an entity with a large sum of money to invest, such as financial institutions, insurance companies, pension funds, investment trusts, and mutual funds, with equity under management of at least $100 millions. These organizations are required to file Form 13F with the SEC to report their equity holdings. Institutional ownership (INST) in this study is calculated as the total common shares held by institutional investors who meet the above criteria divided by total common shares outstanding.

As firms are mandated to reveal any material weakness in IC under Sections 302 and 404 of Sarbanes–Oxley Act (SOX), Audit Analytics reports on such information. In this study, the IC measure is a binary variable dependent on the presence (1) or absence (0) of effective ICs per the Audit Analytics database.

Control Variables

As in prior research, we include controls for firm characteristics. Prior research indicates that larger firms provide more extensive disclosure than smaller firms (Coulton, James, & Taylor, 2001). Measured as the natural log of a firm's total assets, LTA is expected to be positively associated with the level of transparency.

We employ a binary indicator (Big4) to measure auditor quality. A Big4 auditor is likely to be associated with greater transparency because firms hiring Big4 auditors tend to be profitable and reputable. In addition, a Big4 auditor may have more stringent requirement on corporate transparency; therefore, Big4 is expected to be positively associated with the level of transparency.

We control for inventory and receivables (LINVT and LREC) because Ahmed, Billings, Morton, and Stanford-Harris (2002) argue that sales growth is likely to affect IC because high inventory and receivables will inflate the market's expectations of future cash flows. Consistent with Ahmed et al. (2002), we expect that these variables would be negatively related with the level of transparency. Financial leverage (LEV) is calculated as total long-term debt divided by average total assets. Firms with high levels of leverage tend to have greater agency conflicts, thus a greater transparency is required to reduce agency costs. Therefore, we expect that financial leverage would have a positive impact on the level of transparency. Similarly, return on assets (ROA), earnings before extraordinary item divided by total assets, and BETA, equity beta for the fiscal period, are included in an attempt to control for operating performance and firm's risk, respectively.

Model Specifications for Hypothesis Testing

Transparency (TRANS), institutional ownership and IC can be endogenously affected by some independent variables. If this is the case, then it becomes difficult to derive inferences from regression estimates. To solve this problem, we employ the three-stage least squares analysis using the following equation system.

$$\text{TRANS} = \alpha_0 + \alpha_1\text{INST} + \alpha_2\text{LAT} + \alpha_3\text{ROA} + \alpha_4\text{BETA} + \alpha_5\text{LEV} + \alpha_6\text{LINV} + \alpha_7\text{LREC} + \alpha_8\text{Big4} + \alpha_9\text{IC} \quad (9)$$

$$\text{IC} = \beta_0 + \beta_1\text{INST} + \beta_2\text{LAT} + \beta_3\text{ROA} + \beta_4\text{BETA} + \beta_5\text{LEV} + \beta_6\text{LINV} + \beta_7\text{LREC} + \beta_8\text{EXCHANGE} \quad (10)$$

$$\text{INST} = \gamma_0 + \gamma_1\text{LAT} + \gamma_2\text{ROA} + \gamma_3\text{BETA} + \gamma_4\text{LEV} + \gamma_5\text{LINV} + \gamma_6\text{LREC} + \gamma_7\text{EXCHANGE} \quad (11)$$

where transparency is a general term for the six measures of disclosure transparency discussed earlier, including two analyst forecast measures – the number of analysts who cover a firm (Brennan & Subrahmanyam, 1995) and the accuracy of analyst forecasts (Lang & Lundholm, 1996; Lang, Lins, & Miller, 2004), and four earnings management measures – discretionary accruals, abnormal cash flow from operations, abnormal production cost, and abnormal discretionary expenses (Fan & Wong, 2002; Leuz et al., 2003); INST, the percentage of shares owned by institutional owners of a firm; LAT, the natural log of total assets of a firm (annual Compustat data item 6); ROA, a firm's return on assets, using net income before extraordinary items (annual Compustat data item 18) divided by total assets (annual Compustat data item 6); LEV, the leverage of a firm, calculated as total debt (annual Compustat data item 9 plus annual Compustat data item 34) divided by total assets (annual Compustat data item 6); BETA, a firm's systematic risk measured as beta for the fiscal period; LINV, the natural log of a firm's ending balance of inventory (annual Compustat data item 3); LREC, the natural log of a firm's ending balance of accounts receivable (annual Compustat data item 2); Big4, a dummy variable coded as one if the firm is audited by a Big4 CPA firm, and zero otherwise; IC, a dummy variable coded as one if the firm has effective ICs, and zero otherwise; EXCHANGE, coded as one if the company is exchanged on the NYSE and zero otherwise.

RESULTS

Descriptive Statistics

Table 2 reports descriptive statistics for the full sample of 9,570 observations. On average, the institutional ownership percentage (INST) is 1.82%. The mean of the natural log of total assets of a firm (LAT) is 6.1928. The average ROA is 0.0187. The mean BETA value is 0.9779, indicating the market risk of the sample is slightly below the level of systematic risk observed in the market. The mean leverage (LEV) is 0.1993. The mean of natural log of a firm's ending balance of inventory (LINVT) is 3.8865, and the mean of natural log of a firm's ending balance of accounts receivable (LRECT) is 4.1073. The average discretionary accrual (NA), abnormal cash flow from operations (ACFO), abnormal production cost (APRODA), and abnormal discretionary accruals (ADISA) are 0.0127, 0.0147, − 0.0012, and − 0.1896, respectively. On average, the number of analysts following a firm is 6.8198 and the accuracy of forecast is 0.0351. Out of our final sample firms, 42% observations are from firms audited by one of the Big4 CPA firms and the rest of the observations are from firms audited by other CPA firms. Also 41% observations are from firms listed on New York Stock Exchange. There are 92% observations from firms without IC problems during our sample period and the remaining observations from firms with IC problems.

Main Results

Table 3 reports the Pearson correlation tables for the full sample of 9,570 observations. It shows high correlations (with coefficients higher than 0.4000) between firm size (LAT) and inventory (LINVT), accounts receivables (LREC), number of analyst following (NUMEST), and Big4 auditors (Big4). This indicates that big firms tend to have larger balances of inventory and receivables, more analyst followings and are more likely to hire Big4 auditors.[2] Further calculation of VIF scores in each model suggests that multicollinearity issue is not a serious concern (all VIF scores are less than 6). Table 3 also shows that the abnormal cash flow from operations

Table 2. Descriptive Statistics.

Variable	Mean	Standard Deviation	Min	Max
INST	0.0182	0.0417	0.0000	0.3585
LAT	6.1928	1.8371	2.0166	10.8222
ROA	− 0.0187	0.2032	− 1.2812	0.2865
BETA	0.9779	0.6542	− 0.9958	4.5017
LEV	0.1993	0.1985	0.0000	0.9893
LINVT	3.8865	1.9324	− 1.5945	8.5242
LRECT	4.1073	1.8767	− 0.8771	8.8464
NA	0.0127	0.1440	− 0.9190	0.7986
ACFO	0.0147	0.1765	− 1.0235	0.9708
APRODA	− 0.0012	0.3425	− 1.8604	2.7630
ADISA	− 0.1896	0.8190	− 6.2537	4.7100
NUMEST	6.8198	5.8254	1	28
ACCURACY	0.0351	0.0797	0	0.8421
BIG4	0.4222	0.4939	0	1
EXCHANGE	0.4051	0.4909	0	1
IC	0.9197	0.2716	0	1

Notes: This table contains descriptive statistics for the sample firms used in the study. INST, percentage of institutional ownership of a firm; LAT, first lag of the natural log of total assets of a firm; ROA, a firm's return on assets, using net income before extraordinary items (annual Compustat data item 18) divided by total assets (annual Compustat data item 6); BETA, a firm's systematic risk measured as beta for the fiscal period; LEV, leverage of a firm, calculated as total debt (annual Compustat data item 9 plus annual Compustat data item 34) divided by total assets (annual Compustat data item 6); LINVT, natural log of a firms's ending balance of inventory (annual Compustat data item 3); LREC, natural log of a firm's ending balance of accounts receivable (annual Compustat data item 2); Big4, a dummy variable coded as one if the firm is audited by a Big4 CPA firm, and zero otherwise; EXCHANGE, coded as one if the company is exchanged on New York stock exchange and zero otherwise; IC, a dummy variable coded as one if the firm has effective IC, and zero otherwise. Six different proxies for transparency are used as follows: NA, accrual-based earnings management; ACFO, abnormal cash flow from operation; APRODA, abnormal production cost; ADISA, abnormal discretionary expenses; NUMEST, number of analysts following; ACCURACY, estimate of accuracy of analyst forecasts.

(ACFO) and abnormal production cost is (APRODA) highly correlated at 0.7610. These are alternative measures of independent variable, thus multicollinearity is not a problem here.

Table 3 also presents the correlations between the transparency measures, institutional ownership, and IC. Among these correlations, only analyst following (NUMEST) variable shows a significant and negative correlation with institutional ownership (INST). Since the correlation

Table 3. Pearson Correlation Table.

	INST	LAT	ROA	BETA	LEV	LINVT	LRECT	NA	ACFO	APRODA	ADISA	NUMEST	ACCURACY	BIG4	EXCHANGE	IC
INST	1	−0.2615***	0.0090	−0.1235***	−0.0049	−0.2142**	−0.2449**	0.0112	−0.0050	0.0099	−0.0037	−0.1791**	−0.0032	−0.1101**	−0.0007	−0.0004
LAT		1	−0.0102	0.2786**	0.0238*	0.8487**	0.9259**	−0.0009	0.0281**	−0.0402**	0.0071	0.6588**	0.0019	0.4014**	0.02*	0.0109
ROA			1	0.0495**	0.0101	−0.0226*	−0.0036	0.0021	−0.0050	0.0014	0.0021	0.0341**	−0.1313**	−0.0162	0.2384**	0.0335**
BETA				1	−0.0015	0.1411	0.2063**	−0.0485**	−0.0145	−0.0543**	0.0093	0.1744**	−0.0037	0.2358**	−0.0052	0.0003
LEV					1	0.0026	0.0332**	−0.0062	−0.0008	0.0058	0.0034	0.0211	0.0623**	−0.0606**	0.2980**	0.0089
LINVT						1	0.8654**	0.0163	0.0094	−0.0160	−0.0012	0.4630**	−0.0016	0.3354**	−0.0187	0.0116
LRECT							1	0.0139	0.0250*	−0.0372**	0.0033	0.5579**	−0.0008	0.3554**	0.0163	0.0118
NA								1	−0.1233	−0.1010**	−0.0075	−0.0100	−0.0086	−0.0111	−0.0187	−0.0007
ACFO									1	−0.7610	0.0138	0.0540**	0.0033	−0.0005	0.0088	0.0100
APRODA										1	−0.0147	−0.0665**	−0.0001	0.0061	−0.0014	−0.0002
ADISA											1	0.0094	−0.0016	−0.0044	−0.0080	−0.0023
NUMEST												1	−0.0039	0.2140**	0.0141	−0.0106
ACCURACY													1	−0.0094	−0.0296**	0.0007
BIG4														1	−0.0449	0.0142
EXCHANGE															1	0.0730
IC																1

Notes: The table shows Pearson Pairswise correlation matrix. INST, percentage of institutional ownership of a firm; LAT, first lag of the natural log of total assets of a firm; ROA, a firm's return on assets, using net income before extraordinary items (annual Compustat data item 18) divided by total assets (annual Compustat data item 6); BETA, a firm's systematic risk measured as beta for the fiscal period; LEV, leverage of a firm, calculated as total debt (annual Compustat data item 9 plus annual Compustat data item 34) divided by total assets (annual Compustat data item 6); LINVT, natural log of a firms's ending balance of inventory (annual Compustat data item 3); LREC, natural log of a firm's ending balance of accounts receivable (annual Compustat data item 2); Big4, a dummy variable coded as one if the firm is audited by a Big4 CPA firm, and zero otherwise; EXCHANGE, coded as one if the company is exchanged on New York stock exchange and zero otherwise; IC, a dummy variable coded as one if the firm has effective internal controls, and zero otherwise. Six different proxies for transparency are used as follows: NA, accrual-based earnings management; ACFO, abnormal cash flow from operation; APRODA, abnormal production cost; ADISA, abnormal discretionary expenses; NUMEST, number of analysts following; ACCURACY, estimate of accuracy of analyst forecasts. Significance at the 5% and 1% levels is indicated by *and **, respectively.

coefficients only reflect the univariate analyses but not controlling for the other factors that could also affect these variables yet, any conclusion drawn on the correlation results would be premature without detailed analyses of the multivariate regression models. Hence, we estimate 3SLS models of Eqs. (9–11) and discuss these results as below.

Table 4 reports the 3SLS estimation results of Eqs. (9–11). To simplify the presentation of the table, we report the results in two separate panels. Panel A presents the results regarding discretionary accruals (Measure 1), abnormal cash flow from operations (Measure 2), and abnormal production cost (Measure 3), while Panel B presents the results regarding abnormal discretionary expenses (Measure 4), number of analyst following (Measure 5), and analyst forecast accuracy (Measure 6). The results on transparency models report that after controlling for simultaneous effects, firms with higher institutional ownership have significantly higher discretionary accruals (Measure 1), higher abnormal cash flow from operations (Measure 2), higher abnormal production cost (Measure 3), significantly lower abnormal discretionary expenses (Measure 4), and significantly less number of analyst following (Measure 5). The 3SLS results of the effects of INST on abnormal production cost (Measure 3), and abnormal discretionary expenses (Measure 4) are in the opposite of OLS results (not reported in tables), indicating that the simultaneous effects among these endogenous variables do affect the results under the OLS estimation. These results differ from the notion that firms having a greater percentage of institutional ownership are more likely to have greater disclosure transparency. Instead, it indicates that institutional investors may take advantage of their institutional positions to pursue their own interest rather than to encourage firms to commit to better disclosure practice.

Table 4 reports significant links between institutional ownership and IC quality in the IC model. It shows that firms with higher institutional ownership tend to report better IC (see the results of Measures 3, 5, and 6, and the marginally significant coefficients of INST in the results of Measures 2 and 4). Thus there is a compound relationship between institutional ownership, IC, and transparency given the positive link between earnings management and institutional ownership and the positive link between IC quality and institutional ownership. A possible explanation would be that institutional investors are more likely associated with firms of higher yield, smaller size, and less specific firm risks as indicated by the results of the institutional ownership model. These firms tend to report better IC quality, as they are subject to less pressure from their auditors when the auditors are non-Big4. Future studies are demanded to investigate whether firms with higher institutional investors are more likely to switch their auditors and do opinion shopping.

Again, under the 3SLS approach, firms with better IC tend to have fewer analysts following (Measure 5) and lower analyst forecast accuracy (Measure 6). This is contrary to the expectation that firms having better IC quality are more likely to have greater disclosure transparency, subsequently attracting additional analysts and lowers forecasting error. This finding rules out the simultaneous effects of institutional ownership, ICs, and other factors.

Table 4 further indicates the impact of Big4 auditors on the firm's commitment to transparency after controlling for the simultaneous effects of independent variables. It shows a positive effect of Big4 auditors on deterring accrual management behavior, abnormal production cost manipulation, but a negative effect of these auditors on deterring abnormal accrual expenses. Further, firms with Big4 auditors also tend to have more analyst following and more analyst forecast accuracy.

In sum, different from the notion that disclosure transparency increases with the percentage of institutional ownership, we find in the 3SLS results that institutional investors may take advantage of their institutional positions to pursue their own interest rather than to encourage firms to commit to better disclosure practice. In addition, under the 3SLS approach, we find firms with higher institutional ownership tend to report better IC. Thus, there is a complicated relationship between institutional ownership, IC, and transparency due to the positive link between earnings management and institutional ownership and the positive link between IC quality and institutional ownership. It may suggest that institutional investors are more likely associated with firms of higher yield, smaller size, and less specific firm risks as indicated by the results of the institutional ownership model. These firms tend to receive better IC quality report from their auditors, and these auditors are more likely to be non-Big4 auditors. Finally, contrary to the expectation that firms that have a better IC quality are more likely to have greater disclosure transparency, which attracts more analyst followings with less forecast errors, we find that under the 3SLS approach, firms with better IC tend to have fewer analysts following and lower analyst forecast accuracy.

CONCLUSION

A considerable body of empirical research investigates the consequences of increased disclosures as well as the association between corporate

Table 4. 3SLS Regression Results of the Relationship between Institutional Ownership, Internal Control, and Disclosure Transparency.

Panel A: 3SLS Regression Results Using Discretionary Accruals, Abnormal Cash Flow from Operations, and Abnormal Production Cost as Measures of Disclosure Transparency

	Measure 1			Measure 2			Measure 3		
	NA	IC	INST	ACFO	IC	INST	APRODA	IC	INST
Intercept	0.0211	0.6248**	6.0638***	−0.3117	0.4585	6.0681***	−0.2590	0.3260	6.0909***
	(0.12)	(2.20)	(19.78)	(−1.19)	(1.57)	(19.91)	(−0.66)	(1.17)	(20.12)
INST	0.0163**	0.0470		0.0309***	0.0749		0.0224	0.0956**	
	(2.00)	(1.01)		(2.72)	(1.56)		(1.37)	(2.09)	
LAT	−0.0115	0.0289	−0.6934***	0.0431***	0.0469	−0.6905***	−0.0469***	0.0611*	−0.6801***
	(−1.52)	(0.87)	(−7.04)	(3.99)	(1.38)	(−7.04)	(−3.00)	(1.91)	(−7.00)
ROA	−0.0061	0.0214	0.6024*	−0.0127	0.0064	0.6204*	−0.0369	−0.0037	0.6164*
	(− 0.35)	(0.59)	(1.75)	(−0.48)	(0.17)	(1.81)	(−0.91)	(−0.10)	(1.81)
BETA		0.0198	−0.4583***		0.0358	−0.4663***		0.0488**	−0.5006***
		(0.88)	(−4.30)		(1.51)	(−4.40)		(2.01)	(−4.75)
LEV	0.0041	0.0027	0.1616	−0.0008	0.0032	0.1801	0.0429	0.0071	0.1053
	(0.30)	(0.11)	(0.46)	(−0.04)	(0.12)	(0.51)	(1.39)	(0.26)	(0.30)
LINVT	0.00628*	0.0011	0.1522**	−0.0232***	−0.0029	0.1512**	0.1012***	−0.0035	0.1383*
	(1.80)	(0.13)	(2.02)	(−4.67)	(−0.32)	(2.01)	(13.18)	(−0.41)	(1.85)
LRECT	0.0074*	−0.0010	−0.0246	0.0130**	−0.0005	−0.0271	−0.0360***	−0.0021	−0.0250
	(1.95)	(−0.15)	(−0.24)	(2.42)	(−0.07)	(−0.26)	(−4.28)	(−0.25)	(−0.24)
BIG4	−0.0136***			−0.0015			−0.0484***		
	(−2.63)			(−0.21)			(−3.97)		
EXCHANGE		0.0339***	−0.0918		0.0366***	−0.1077		0.0379***	−0.0940
		(3.23)	(−0.63)		(3.14)	(−0.74)		(3.13)	(−0.65)
IC	−0.0264			0.0615			0.2832		
System adjusted R^2	(−0.15)			(0.23)			(0.71)		
	3.60%			2.32%			5.66%		

Panel B: 3SLS Regression Results Using Abnormal Discretionary Expenses, Number of Analyst Followings, and Analyst Forecast Accuracy as Measures of Disclosure Transparency

	Measure 4			Measure 5			Measure 6		
	ADISA	IC	INST	NUMEST	IC	INST	ACCURACY	IC	INST
Intercept	1.0897	0.5116*	6.0703***	7.0669*	0.4166*	6.2457***	0.5039***	−0.2060	5.6782***
	(1.12)	(1.89)	(20.03)	(1.76)	(1.86)	(18.58)	(2.73)	(−0.59)	(17.46)
INST	−0.1022**	0.0649		−0.6143***	0.0812**		−0.0027	0.1980***	
	(−2.28)	(1.46)		(−3.16)	(2.28)		(−0.38)	(3.24)	
LAT	−0.1575***	0.0416	−0.6758***	0.0906	0.0554*	−0.7734***	−0.0021	0.1191***	−0.6007***
	(−3.78)	(1.35)	(−6.96)	(0.47)	(1.94)	(−8.04)	(−0.35)	(3.08)	(−5.78)
ROA	−0.0118	0.0136	0.6777**	0.7948*	0.0313	0.5143	−0.1336***	−0.1034*	0.6136
	(−0.11)	(0.35)	(1.99)	(1.89)	(0.95)	(1.56)	(−9.00)	(−1.72)	(1.51)
BETA		0.0322	−0.4912***		0.0372**	−0.3760***		0.0980***	−0.4951***
		(1.40)	(−4.66)		(2.35)	(−3.65)		(2.98)	(−4.44)
LEV	−0.1572**	−0.0001	0.0992	0.1751	−0.0335	0.4325	0.0390***	−0.0237	0.2507
	(−2.02)	(−0.01)	(0.29)	(0.68)	(−1.05)	(1.28)	(2.67)	(−0.52)	(0.68)
LINVT	0.0196	−0.0001	0.1363*	0.0381	−0.0100	0.1781***	−0.0009	−0.0241*	0.1381*
	(1.00)	(−0.01)	(1.83)	(0.57)	(−1.15)	(2.49)	(−0.30)	(−1.92)	(1.72)
LRECT	0.0632***	−0.0029	−0.0289	−0.1399**	0.0037	−0.0404	−0.0010	0.0094	−0.0697
	(2.8)	(−0.4)	(−0.28)	(−2.11)	(0.45)	(−0.41)	(−0.28)	(0.71)	(−0.64)
BIG4	0.2657***			0.2033**			0.0080		
	(8.96)			(2.22)			(1.39)		
EXCHANGE		0.0353***	−0.0658		0.0437***	−0.1742		0.0343*	−0.0490
		(3.34)	(−0.45)		(3.35)	(−1.25)		(1.94)	(−0.32)
IC	−0.5873			−5.2354			−0.4900**		
System Adjusted R^2	(−0.58)			(−1.49)			(−2.52)		
	3.61%			13.73%			4.77%		

Notes: This table reports the 3SLS estimates. INST, percentage of institutional ownership of a firm; LAT, first lag of the natural log of total assets of a firm; ROA, a firm's return on assets, using net income before extraordinary items (annual Compustat data item 18) divided by total assets (annual Compustat data item 6); BETA, a firm's systematic risk measured as beta for the fiscal period; LEV, leverage of a firm, calculated as total debt (annual Compustat data item 9 plus annual Compustat data item 34) divided by total assets (annual Compustat data item 6); LINVT, natural log of a firms's ending balance of inventory (annual Compustat data item 3); LREC, natural log of a firm's ending balance of accounts receivable (annual Compustat data item 2); BIG4, a dummy variable coded as one if the firm is audited by a Big4 CPA firm, and zero otherwise; EXCHANGE, coded as one if the company is exchanged on New York stock exchange and zero otherwise; IC, a dummy variable coded as one if the firm has effective internal controls, and zero otherwise. Six different proxies for transparency are used as follows: NA, accrual-based earnings management; ACFO, abnormal cash flow from operation; APRODA, abnormal production cost; ADISA, abnormal discretionary expenses; NUMEST, number of analysts following; ACCURACY, estimate of accuracy of analyst forecasts. *T* statistics are reported in the parenthesis with standard errors clustered by firm. Significance at the 10%, 5%, and 1% levels is indicated by *, **, and ***, respectively (two-tail test).

governance and disclosure transparency (e.g., Gupta et al., 2011; Ogneva et al., 2006). In this study, we bring a new dimension, institutional ownership into the existing research, and attempt to explore the association among institutional ownership, ICs, and disclosure transparency. To fully appreciate the present research on disclosure transparency, we utilize six measures: accrual-based earnings management, abnormal production costs, abnormal cash flow from operation, abnormal discretionary expenses, the number of analysts following, and the accuracy of analyst forecasts.

Using 3SLS approach, we find that after controlling for simultaneous effects, firms with higher institutional ownership have significantly higher discretionary accruals, abnormal cash flow from operations, higher abnormal production cost, but significantly lower abnormal discretionary expenses, and significantly less number of analyst following. In addition, under the 3SLS approach, we find significant links between institutional ownership and IC quality in the IC model. It shows that firms with higher institutional ownership tend to report better IC. Also, firms with better IC tend to have fewer analysts following and lower analyst forecast accuracy.

These results are different from the belief that firms that have a greater percentage of institutional ownership are more likely to have greater disclosure transparency, and the expectation that firms that have a better IC quality are more likely to have greater disclosure transparency, which attracts more analyst followings and less forecast errors. Instead, it indicates that institutional investors may take advantage of their institutional positions to pursue their own interest rather than to encourage firms to commit to better disclosure practice. In addition, we find a positive link between earnings management and institutional ownership, a positive link between IC quality and institutional ownership but a negative link between IC quality and transparency reflected in analyst forecast behaviors. A possible explanation is that institutional investors are more likely associate with firms of higher yield, smaller size, and less specific firm risks as indicated by the results of the institutional ownership model. These firms tend to receive better IC quality report from their auditors, as their auditors are more likely to be non-Big4. Future studies need to investigate whether firms with higher institutional investors are more likely to switch their auditors and do opinion shopping.

Our results would have a few implications for the literature as follows. First, our research contributes to the current literature on transparency by highlighting that IC and institutional ownership are associated with transparency and revealing that the relationship between institutional ownership, IC, and transparency measures may be complicated and demands further research attention. Second, we provide more insights to previous studies asserting IC is essential to the transparent reporting of financial information. Our results suggest that IC reports and disclosure transparency could be two different concepts, as well as the quality of IC in perception and the quality of ICs as reported. Finally, using real earnings management as a proxy for transparency to identify if direct cash flows consequences truly matter in disclosure transparency, our results indicate that real earnings management brings about different schemes from accrual-based earnings management. For instance, we find an inverse effect of institutional ownership on abnormal production cost compared to abnormal discretionary expenses. Further research is needed to investigate how and why real earnings management and accrual based earnings management are employed as alternatives under specific settings.

ACKNOWLEDGMENTS

The authors would like to thank Heibatollah Sami (the guest editor), Williams Pratt, the reviewers, and participants of the first annual Research Day Workshop sponsored by the College of Business Administration at the University of Texas Pan American for their insightful comments and suggestions.

NOTES

1. An alternative explanation could be that increased number of analyst following would increase the disclosure transparency instead of greater disclosures by firms. However, as the literature has documented that transparency may influence an analyst's interest in following a firm (Elliott et al., 2010) and more informative disclosures and greater disclosure transparency are reflected in analyst following (Lang & Lundholm, 1996; Lang et al., 2011), we still keep this measure in our study to provide more information to readers. We owe our thanks to the editor for addressing this alternative possibility.
2. As sensitivity tests, we dropped these variables stepwise and the coefficients remain similar to those reported.

REFERENCES

Ahmed, A. S., Billings, B. K., Morton, R. M., & Stanford-Harris, M. (2002). The role of accounting conservatism in mitigating bondholder-shareholder conflicts over dividend policy and in reducing debt costs. *The Accounting Review*, *77*(4), 867–890.

Beasley, M. (1996). An empirical analysis of the relation between the board of directors composition and financial statement fraud. *The Accounting Review*, *71*(4), 443–465.

Brennan, M., & Subrahmanyam, A. (1995). Investment analysis and price formation in securities markets. *Journal of Financial Economics*, *38*, 361–381.

Bushee, B. J., & Noe, C. F. (2000). Corporate disclosure practices, institutional investors, and stock return volatility. *Journal of Accounting Research*, *38*, 171–202.

Chung, K. H., Elder, J., & Kim, J. (2010). Corporate governance and liquidity. *Journal of Financial and Quantitative Analysis*, *45*, 265–291.

Chung, K. H., & Zhang, H. (2011). Corporate governance and institutional ownership. *Journal of Financial and Quantitative Analysis*, *46*, 247–273.

Cohen, D., Dey, A., & Lys, T. Z. (2008). Real and accrual-based earnings management in the pre- and post-Sarbanes Oxley periods. *The Accounting Review*, *83*(3), 757–787.

Cohen, D., & Zarowin, P. (2010). Accrual-based and real earnings management activities around seasoned equity offerings. *Journal of Accounting and Economics*, *50*(1), 2–19.

Coulton, J., James, C., & Taylor, S., 2001. *The effect of compensation design and corporate governance on the transparency of CEO compensation disclosures*. UTS School of Accounting Working Paper No. 45. Australian School of Business, University of Sydney and University of New South Wales, Australia. Available at SSRN, http://ssrn.com/abstract=273628 or http://dx.doi.org/10.2139/ssrn.273628

Dechow, P., Sloan, R., & Sweeney, A. (1995). Detecting earnings management. *The Accounting Review*, *70*, 193–225.

Del Guercio, D. (1996). The distorting effect of the prudent-man laws on institutional equity investment. *Journal of Financial Economics*, *40*, 31–62.

Duffie, D., & Lando, D. (2001). Term structures of credit spreads with incomplete accounting information. *Econometrica*, *69*(3), 633–664.

Elliott, W. B., Krische, S. D., & Peecher, M. E. (2010). Expected mispricing: The joint influence of accounting transparency and investor base. *Journal of Accounting Research*, *48*(2), 343–381.

Fan, J., & Wong, T. (2002). Corporate ownership structure and the informativeness of accounting earnings in East Asia. *Journal of Accounting and Economics*, *33*, 401–425.

Felo, A. J. (2000). Ethic programs, board oversight, and perceived disclosure credibility: Was the treadway commission correct about ethics and financial reporting? *Research on Accounting Ethics*, *7*, 157–176.

Felo, A. J. (2007). Board oversight of corporate ethics programs and disclosure transparency. *Accounting and the Public Interest*, *7*, 1–25.

Grinstein, Y., & Michaely, R. (2005). Institutional holdings and payout policy. *Journal of Finance*, *60*, 1389–1426.

Gupta, P., Sami, H. & Zhou, H., 2011. Internal control reporting under SOX Sections 302 and 404 and information asymmetry. AAA 2011 Auditing Section Meeting Paper. Lehigh University and University of Texas Pan American, USA.

Hope, O.-K., Thomas, W. B., & Vyas, D., 2009. Financial Credibility, Ownership, and Financing Constraints in Private Firms. AAA 2009 Financial Accounting and Reporting Section (FARS) Paper. Available at SSRN: http://ssrn.com/abstract=1264730 or http://dx.doi.org/10.2139/ssrn.1264730, University of Toronto, Canada and University of Oklahoma, USA.

Karamanou, I., & Vafeas, N. (2005). The association between corporate boards, audit committees, and management earnings forecasts: An empirical analysis. *Journal of Accounting Research, 43*(3), 453–486.

Jones, J. (1991). Earnings management during import relief investigations. *Journal of Accounting Research, 29*, 193–228.

Lang, M., Lins, K., & Miller, D. (2004). Concentrated control, analyst following, and valuation: Do analysts matter most when investors are protected least? *Journal of Accounting Research, 42*, 581–623.

Lang, M., & Lundholm, R. (1996). Corporate disclosure policy and analyst behavior. *The Accounting Review, 71*, 467–493.

Lang, M. H., Lins, K. V., & Maffett, M. G., 2011. *Transparency, liquidity, and valuation: International evidence.* Available at SSRN, http://ssrn.com/abstract=1323514. University of North Carolina, University of Utah and University of Chicago, USA.

Leuz, C., Nanda, D., & Wysocki, P. (2003). Earnings management and investor protection: An international comparison. *Journal of Financial Economics, 69*, 505–527.

Leuz, C., & Verrecchia, R. E. (2000). The Economic consequences of increased disclosure. *Journal of Accounting Research, 38*(Suppl.), 91–124.

Ogneva, M., Raghunandan, K., & Subramanyam, K.R., 2006. *Internal control weakness and cost of equity: Evidence from SOX Section 404 disclosures.* AAA 2006 Financial Accounting and Reporting Section (FARS) Meeting Paper. Available at SSRN: http://ssrn.com/abstract=766104 or http://dx.doi.org/10.2139/ssrn.766104. University of Southern California and Florida International University, USA.

Peasnell, K., Pope, P., & Young, S. (2000). Accrual management to meet earnings targets: UK evidence pre- and post-Cadbury. *British Accounting Review, 32*, 415–445.

Roychowdhury, S. (2006). Earnings management through real activities manipulation. *Journal of Accounting and Economics, 42*, 335–370.

Tang, A. P., & Xu, L., 2007. *Institutional ownership, internal control material weakness and firm performance.* Available at SSRN: http://ssrn.com/abstract=1031270 or http://dx.doi.org/10.2139/ssrn.1031270. Morgan State University and Washington State University, USA.

Verrecchia, R. (2001). Essays on disclosure. *Journal of Accounting and Economics, 32*, 97–180.

Yua, F. (2005). Accounting transparency and the term structure of credit spreads. *Journal of Financial Economics, 75*(1), 53–84.

Zhou, H. (2007). Auditing standards, increased accounting disclosure, and information asymmetry: Evidence from an emerging market. *Journal of Accounting and Public Policy, 26*, 584–620.

CORPORATE TRANSPARENCY OF BUSINESS GROUP FIRMS IN THE ABSENCE OF INTERNAL MARKET BENEFITS

Moo Sung Kim

ABSTRACT

Business group affiliation seems to make a firm more opaque. The benefits of group affiliation (internal market transactions) and the negative aspects of group affiliation (agency problems of group control) both may make group firms more opaque than non-group firms. Using the opacity index developed by Anderson, Duru, and Reeb (2009), this paper reports that Korean group firms are more transparent than non-group firms after the Asian financial crisis (1997–1998) and this leads to better performance of group firms. The improved transparency results from disappeared internal market benefits and diminished agency problems. These results are robust after controlling for the size of internal markets of groups, industry diversification, the existence of group inside financial institutions, and endogeneity.

Transparency and Governance in a Global World
International Finance Review, Volume 13, 39–67

ISSN: 1569-3767/doi:10.1108/S1569-3767(2012)0000013005

Keywords: Corporate transparency; opacity index; business group; Asian financial crisis; agency; performance

JEL classifications: G32; G34; G38; M41; L22

INTRODUCTION

Corporate transparency can enhance performance of firms by reducing agency costs and estimation error, providing lower cost of capital (Diamond and Verrecchia, 1991) and helping corporate insiders make optimal decisions. Despite the obvious benefits from transparency and extensive mandatory disclosure for listed firms, corporate transparency levels of firms vary (Anderson, Duru, & Reeb, 2009) and the agency problem has been considered a principal source of the variation (Healy & Palepu, 2001). Consequently, the research focuses on effective governance mechanisms, such as firm level governance, regulation, information intermediary, and market for control, to enhance the corporate transparency. However, the previous research on corporate transparency has primarily focused on agency problems between managers and owners (Jensen & Meckling, 1976).

After Shleifer and Vishny (1997) introduce the agency problem between controlling owners and outside minority owners, and La Porta, Lopez-de-Silanes, and Shleifer (1999) report the dominance of concentrated ownership around the world, the relationship between concentrated ownership and corporate transparency has been under scrutiny. For example, Anderson et al. (2009) report that U.S. firms with controlling family owners demonstrate lower corporate transparency. Lang, Lins, and Miller (2004), Fan and Wong (2002), and Leuz, Nanda, and Wysocki (2003) also report that concentrated ownership in countries with poor investor protection is related to lower corporate transparency. There is an agreement that agency problems are one of the determinants of corporate transparency, but another aspect must be considered – costs of transparency. For instance, more complex organizational structures cost more to be as transparent as others, and the excess transparency may damage the firm's competitiveness (Hayes & Lundholm, 1996). Corporate transparency is the function of benefits and costs of transparency as well as agency problems. The different organizational structure such as business group structure may provide different set of benefits, costs, and agency problems. However, the impact of business group structure on corporate transparency has not been fully investigated.

Business groups are dominant players not only in emerging markets but also in Europe and Japan. Khanna and Rivkin (2001) define the business group as "a collection of firms which, though legally independent, are bound together by a constellation of formal and informal ties and are accustomed to taking coordinated actions" (Khanna & Rivkin, 2001, p. 47). The benefits of group affiliation are relative benefits from internal markets to external markets (Khanna & Palepu, 2000) and synergy from group network (Nahapiet & Ghoshal, 1998). The internal market transactions among group firms create extra complexity in deciphering group firms' real intentions for outsiders. Business group industrial diversification also increases the complexity of the group firm. Furthermore, closed internal communication channels, group language, and culture provided by group network create an information barrier between group insiders and outsiders. As a result, business group firms have more complex organizational structures and may need additional costs to be as transparent as non-group firms. If the benefits of group affiliation, especially relative benefits of internal markets, are enough to perform well, then business groups do not need to pay extra cost for transparency. Thus, group firms may be more opaque than non-group firms but perform better than non-group firms (*internal market hypothesis*).

The agency problems between group controlling owners and outside minority investors in individual group firms also make group firms more opaque than non-group firms. One form of a group-specific agency problem is the discrepancy of group controlling owners' goals and the goals of investors in each group firms. For example, group controlling owners' goals could be risk-sharing among groups and group level growth, but the goal of investors in individual group firm is profit maximization. A more serious agency problem is tunneling, the expropriation of wealth.[1] If such agency problems exist in group firms, group firms may choose to be more opaque to mask such conflict of goals or expropriation. If the agency problems dominate, group firms may perform worse than non-group firms, because the decision of the group firms cannot be optimal and the market perception of such agency problems invites the discount for group firms' value. Thus, *agency hypothesis* expect lower corporate transparency and worse performance for group firms compared to non-group firms. However, if the external markets, especially the financial market, are well developed (if the relative benefits of internal markets disappear), the business groups should pay additional costs to be transparent to acquire resources from the outside. The external market development also brings more efficient monitoring from outsiders. As a result, group firms may try to be at least as transparent as non-group firms and the agency problems will diminish as the consequence of the transparency or vice versa. If group firms are at least as transparent as or more transparent than non-group firms, they may perform better than non-group firms, because better transparency may give lower costs to external resources and better valuation. Also, benefits from group synergy effects may still help the group firms perform better (*external market hypothesis*).

In this paper, I test the above three hypotheses with Korean business groups, so called chaebols. The business groups are dominant in the Korean economy. The assets of the 30 largest groups are 26.1% larger than the Korean GDP and comprise 95.2% of the Korean GDP in 2011.[2] Also, Korean business groups meet the usual characteristics of business groups except main bank control.[3] I collected data from 2000 to 2007 and the data include financial, accounting, ownership, industry, governance, and opacity-related variables. Korean data provide a unique experimental environment to test the effect of relative benefits of internal markets versus external markets, because, after the Asian financial crisis (1997–1998), the Korean economy improved its business environment (Lee, Park, & Shin, 2009).

I find that group firms are more transparent than non-group firms, using an opacity index measuring relative opacity of firms developed by Anderson et al. (2009). This result supports the external market hypothesis and is robust after controlling for endogeneity issues in constructing control samples. Compared to previous works of Chang, Cho, and Shin (2007), which found that group firms are more opaque using the Korean samples for the data period from 1993 to 2001, the different results through the different time period also support the idea that the change in external markets led to the diminishment of relative benefits of internal markets, and group firms resorted to external markets for the resources and chose to be even more transparent, to compete with non-group firms. Overall, I find that group firms perform better than non-group firms. Along with the results that group firms are more transparent than non-group firms, this result supports the *external market hypothesis*. I examine the impact of characteristics specific to group firms on corporate transparency. Group inside financial institutions and group industry diversification (both group level variables) are positively related to corporate transparency of group firms. This is strong evidence supporting the *external market hypothesis* because group inside financial institutions are believed to facilitate internal capital market transactions, and diversification is related to high benefits from not only internal capital markets, but also from other internal markets to overcome institutional voids from external environment (Khanna & Palepu, 2000). I also examine the impact of corporate transparency among group firms on performance and find that the more transparent group firms perform better than other group firms. This finding also supports the *external market hypothesis*.

I further investigate whether the bigger internal markets provide higher benefits. I assume that the bigger groups have larger internal markets and I divide the business groups by size. I find that the bigger groups are diversified in more industries and have more firms within the group. This could be evidence of larger internal markets following Khanna and Palepu (2001). However, the group firms in bigger groups are more transparent and perform better than smaller group affiliated firms. This also supports the *external market hypothesis*. In relation to agency problems, the ownership disparity between control and cash flow rights is negatively related to corporate transparency among group firms and this supports the idea that high probability of wealth expropriation is related to increased opacity of a firm. Family ownership in group firms also has a negative relation to corporate transparency. This is possible because of the agency problems in concentrated family ownership as reported in Anderson et al. (2009).

This paper contributes to literature in the following ways. First, this paper provides evidence that group firms' corporate transparency improves as the relative benefits of internal markets disappear. Second, I introduce the opacity index in business group opacity literature. Third, by investigating corporate transparency and performance simultaneously, this paper provides the evidence that group firms are robust even if the benefits from internal market disappears. Lastly, I use a propensity score matching method to construct the control samples to better address the endogeneity issue related to group membership.

The remainder of this paper is as follows: the second section develops hypotheses, the third section presents data and explains opacity index, and the fourth section reports main findings. The fifth section tests robustness and the sixth section concludes.

HYPOTHESES DEVELOPMENT

Business group affiliation may affect corporate transparency. The benefits of group affiliation may come from efficient internal markets and the synergy effect from group network. Khanna and Palepu (2000) argue that business group affiliation provides internal capital, labor, and marketing market to overcome the external market failure. The internal capital market attenuates the necessity of external financing. The internal labor and marketing market strengthen the solidarity among group firms and employees. Group solidarity may create a barrier for outside investors in deciphering communication among group firms and being transparent will cost more for group firms than for non-group firms. Similarly, scholars in network perspective argue that the business group structure provides synergy effects to group firms, because the business group structure, as a network, can provide internal channels to share valuable resources such as social connection, technology, know-how, and timely information (Nahapiet & Ghoshal, 1998). Along with resource-sharing, business group headquarters provide similar values, common corporate languages, and various kinds of interactions among group firms to facilitate the intra-group communication. As a result, group firms may have less incentive to be transparent because all benefits are from inside the group. Thus, business group firms may be more opaque than non-group firms, but may perform better than non-group firms (*internal market hypothesis*).

The disadvantage of business group affiliation comes from agency problems between group controlling owners and minority outside investors of individual group firms. The agency problems in group firms are similar to that between majority owners and minority shareholders in non-group firms (Shleifer & Vishny, 1997).[4] However, there is a fundamental difference in agency problems in group firms. A CEO of a non-group firm may create agency conflicts for majority owners of the non-group firms or for herself/himself. However, a CEO of a group firm follows the interest of group controlling owners even though the group controlling owners are not the majority owners of the firm. This is possible because group controlling owners control group firms using the disparity between control and cash flow ownership created by pyramidal ownership structure or cross-holding structure. The group level goals, such as risk-sharing (e.g., Khanna & Yafeh, 2005), group level growth (e.g., Choi & Cowing, 1999), and propping other financially constrained group firms (e.g., Freidman, Johnson & Mitton, 2003), may be deviated from the goals of other shareholders in individual group firms, maximizing the profit of the group firm. Furthermore, if the group controlling owners are expropriating wealth using tunneling ranges from perquisite consumption to asset shifting (e.g., Bae, Kang, & Kim, 2002; Baek, Kang, & Lee, 2006; Bertrand, Mehta, & Mullainathan, 2002; Chang, 2003; Joh, 2003), the agency problem between group controlling owners and minority outside investors would be more severe than any other cases. The agency problems listed above in business groups may hinder the optimal choice for individual group firms to maximize their profits. If this is true, then group controlling owners would entrench their control benefits by affecting corporate transparency. Thus, if agency problems exist in business groups, then I expect that group firms are more opaque than non-group firms and perform worse than non-group firms (*agency hypothesis*).

The benefits of internal markets assume failures in the external markets, such as underdeveloped financial and labor markets, and weak infrastructures and legal protection. However, if the economy develops, and such external market failures diminish, the benefits of internal markets may disappear, the effectiveness of external monitoring may increase, and the importance of corporate transparency may emerge.[5] In this context, to meet the expectations of external markets, group firms may try to be at least as transparent as non-group firms. One way to achieve this could be to decrease the group-specific agency problems mentioned above.

One example is the South Korean economy. In the aftermath of the Asian financial crisis (1997–1998), the Korean economy has experienced fundamental changes. The capital markets have been opened to foreign investors, and accounting and other system have changed to meet the global standard. The volume of capital financing from external markets increased, and the corporate transparency of Korean firms in general have improved (Chang et al., 2007). The agency problems of business groups were blamed to be the main cause of the Asian financial crisis, so the Korean government forbade cross-debt guarantee, and forced improvements in capital structure and accountability. As a result, Lee et al. (2009) find that internal capital market efficiency has disappeared among South Korean business groups after market reforms following the Asian financial crisis and the size of public debt market has increased and is considered a substitute for the internal capital market. Thus, the corporate transparency of group firms may improve as the external business environment develops and such group benefits may disappear. If group firms are at least as transparent as or more transparent than non-group firms, the benefits from the corporate transparency, coupled with benefits of group synergy effect from network perspective, may result in better performance of group firms than non-group firms (*external market hypothesis*).

Both the *internal market hypothesis* and *agency hypothesis* expect that business group firms would be more opaque than non-group firms, while the external market hypothesis expects group firms to be at least as transparent as or more transparent than non-group firms. For performance, the *internal market hypothesis* and *external market hypothesis* expect group firms to better perform than non-group firms, while the *agency hypothesis* expects the opposite. From here four hypotheses are developed.

Hypothesis 1a. (internal market hypothesis and agency hypothesis): The group firms are more opaque than non-group firms, all other things being equal.

Hypothesis 1b. (external market hypothesis): The group firms are at least as transparent as or more transparent than non-group firms, all other things being equal.

Hypothesis 2a. (internal market hypothesis and external market hypothesis): The group firms perform better than non-group firms, all other things being equal.

Hypothesis 2b. (agency hypothesis): The group firms perform worse than non-group firms, all other things being equal.

The next hypotheses are testing the correlation of the difference in group firm corporate transparency and performance. If the *agency hypothesis* holds true, group firms with higher agency problems may have higher opacity than other group firms. Then the higher opacity group firms may have lower performance than group firms with lower opacity. First, the decisions of the more opaque group firms to maximize firm value are inferior to those of less opaque group firms because of the additional agency problems. Second, outside investors notice that opacity of group firms are related to the level of group agency problems and discount the value of the group firms. To test the impact of opacity on performance under dominance of agency problem, I develop Hypothesis 2a.

Hypothesis 3a. If business group firms are more opaque than non-group firm, more opaque group firms perform worse than less opaque group firms, all other things being equal.

Alternatively, if the benefits of group affiliation such as internal markets and group synergy are still dominant to agency problems and the changes in external market, there could be no impact of the different corporate transparency on performance among group firms. However, if the importance of external market is dominant over that of internal market, and if agency problems in group firms are mitigated by such situations, more transparent group firms may perform better than opaque group firms.

Hypothesis 3b. If business group firms are more transparent than non-group firms, more transparent group firms perform better than less transparent group firms, all other things being equal.

OPACITY INDEX AND DATA DESCRIPTION

To test the hypotheses, I use South Korean firms listed in the Korea Stock Exchange (KSE) from 2000 to 2007. I use a total of 3,826 firm observations. I exclude firms in the financial sector. I collect the firm-specific data from the Data Analysis, Retrieval and Transfer System (DART) run by the Korea Financial Supervisory Service (KFTC). DART is an Internet-based public service where Korean firms submit their financial reports and allows outsiders to access such information. Group-related variables are collected from the Online Provision of Enterprises Information System (OPNI) also run by the KFTC. The number of analysts following and analysts forecast error data are collected from FnGuide, which is a Korea-based database that collects financial data from financial institutions in South Korean markets and foreign markets. Bid-ask spread data are collected from Koscom DataMall, which was established by the Korea Ministry of Finance and KSE, and provides information of financial securities traded in South Korean markets. This section presents the methods used to produce opacity index and includes detailed data description.

Opacity Index

I calculate opacity index developed by Anderson et al. (2009) for each firm by the year to proxy corporate transparency. Four variables are used – trading volume, bid-ask spread, analysts following, and forecast error. I follow Anderson et al. as close as possible in the definitions of the four variables. The trading volume is the natural log of annual average of daily trading volume in Korean won (KWR). The bid-ask spread is bid-ask spread over the average of bid and ask price. I use the annual average of bid-ask spread using daily data. The analyst following is the natural log of the number of analysts following a firm. The forecast errors of analysts are the square of difference between analysts' earnings forecast and realized earnings over the stock price. The four variables are divided into ranked deciles. The most opaque deciles for each variable are ranked as 10 and the least opaque deciles as 1. The sum of all four ranking is divided by 40 to obtain an index. The highest opacity index value is 1.0, representing the most opaque firm.

Data Description

I divide the samples into business group firms and non-group firms. Group firms are the firms affiliated with the 30 largest business groups in Korea. The ranking of groups are announced by the KFTC every year by group total assets and this information is available on the OPNI website. The 30 largest groups' concept began because, from 1998 to 2001, the KFTC had monitored the 30 largest groups on their internal transactions to prevent market collapse by unfair trade among group firms. Although the KFTC now monitors business groups by healthiness of group capital structure and not by size, the 30 largest groups' concept is still commonly used in media and other scholars. Unmatched non-group firms are the firms not affiliated with the 30 largest groups' firms. Matched non-group firms are the control samples of the empirical analysis. The matched non-group firms are selected by one-to-one size matching in each industry every year. The industry classification is based on KSIC two-digit codes and the matched sample size is 694 firm observations. The number of group firms, unmatched group firms, and matched group firms by year and by industry is reported in Table 1. The number of group firms has remained almost the same from 2000 to 2002 and gradually increased from 2003. This may be because, during the regime of President Kim Dae-jung (February 1998 to February 2003), the business groups were blamed as the main cause of the Asian financial crisis (1997–1998) and experienced severe restructuring.[6]

The performance measure used in this paper is Tobin's Q industry-adjusted. The individual firm's Tobin's Q is obtained by the sum of the market value of common stock, the book value of preferred stock, and total debts scaled by the book value of total assets. After obtaining the individual Tobin's Q, I subtract the median Tobin's Q of the industry the firm is in from the individual Tobin's Q to produce Tobin's Q industry-adjusted. For control variables, I follow Anderson et al. (2009). Control variables are firm size, risk, lagged ROA, debt ratio, R&D intensity, and firm age. The detailed definitions of each variable are presented in Table 2. All regression models include the same control variables mentioned above and are controlled for year and industry-fixed effects. The statistical significance of the coefficients in all regression models is based on the White heteroscedasticity-consistent standard errors.

Table 1. The Number of Group and Non-group Firms.

	All Firms	Group Firms	Unmatched Non-Group Firms	Matched Non-Group Firms
Panel A: By Year				
2000	337	72	265	72
2001	342	69	273	69
2002	365	71	294	71
2003	525	91	434	91
2004	537	89	448	89
2005	552	98	454	98
2006	565	99	466	99
2007	584	105	479	105
Firm-year observations (*N*)	3,826	694	3,113	694
Panel B: By Industry				
Agriculture	33	0	33	0
Metal mining and metal ores	428	68	360	68
Food, beverage, and tobacco	236	36	200	36
Textiles	227	4	223	4
Wood products	184	4	180	4
Chemicals, petroleum, and coal	804	127	677	127
Primary metal industry	63	15	48	15
Industrial machinery and equipment	164	15	149	15
Electricals and electronics	416	64	352	64
Automobile	265	53	212	53
Communications and utilities	123	45	78	45
Constructions	246	80	166	80
Wholesale and retail services	293	87	206	87
Transportation	129	46	83	46
Other service industries	196	50	146	50
N	3,826	694	3,113	694

Note: This table reports the number of group firms, unmatched non-group firms, and matched non-group firms by year and by industry. All firms are listed in the Korean Stock Exchange from 2000 to 2007. The independent firms affiliated with the 30 largest Korean business groups are the group firms. The independent firms that are not affiliated with the 30 largest business groups are unmatched non-group firms. Matched non-group firms are selected by industry and firm asset size matching for each year. KSIC two-digit codes are used to classify the industry.

Table 3 presents the descriptive statistics (mean, median, and mean and median difference tests) of the variables used in this analysis, comparing group firms and non-group firms. The variable of interest is opacity index. The mean difference between group firms and unmatched non-group firms

Table 2. Descriptions of Empirical Variables.

Group-Related Variables	
Group	A dummy variable to indicate whether a firm belongs to one of the 30 largest business groups in South Korea. The Korea Fair Trade Commission (KFTC) updates the list of the 30 largest business groups annually
Top 5 group	A dummy variable to indicate whether a firm belongs to one of the 5 largest business groups in South Korea
Top 10 group	A dummy variable to indicate whether a firm belongs to one of the 10 largest business groups in South Korea
Group diversification	1 – Herfindahl index of the degree of industrial diversification of the business group with which a firm is affiliated
Ownership disparity	The disparity between control ownership and cash flow ownership of the controlling shareholder in a group firm
Opacity measures	
Trading volume	The natural log of the average daily trade volume of a firm in South Korean won during the fiscal year
Bid-ask spread	The annual average of a firm's bid-ask spread over the average of bid and ask prices
Analyst following	The natural log of the number of analysts following a firm
Forecast error	The square of the difference between analysts' earnings forecast and realized earnings over stock price
Opacity index	An opacity index by Anderson et al. (2009). Details calculating opacity index are presented in the third section
Firm-specific variables	
Family ownership	The percentage of common equity ownership held by the largest shareholder family
Family	A dummy variable to indicate whether the family ownership percentage exceeds 10%
Firm age	The natural log of the number of years since a firm's founding date
Firm size	The natural log of the total assets of a firm in South Korean won
Debt ratio	The ratio of total debts to total assets of a firm
Current ratio	The ratio of current assets to current liabilities of a firm
Export ratio	The ratio of exports to total sales of a firm
R&D intensity	The ratio of the research and development expenditures to total sales of a firm
Dividend yield	The ratio of the annual dividend per share to the price of a share of a firm
Tobin's Q industry-adjusted	A firm's Tobin's Q minus the median Tobin's Q of the industry to which the firm belongs. Tobin's Q is the sum of the market value of common stock, the book value of preferred stock, and total debts, divided by the book value of total assets
ROA_{t-1}	The previous year's ratio of earnings before interest, tax, depreciation, and amortization (EBITDA) to total assets
Turnover	The ratio of trading volume to market capitalization of a firm
Risk	The standard deviation of a firm's stock return for the prior year

Table 3. Difference Tests of Mean and Median for Descriptive Variables.

	Group Firms (1)		Unmatched Non-Group Firms (2)		Matched Non-Group Firms (3)		Difference, (1)–(2)		Difference, (1)–(3)	
	Mean	Median	Mean	Median	Mean	Median	Mean	Median	Mean	Median
Opacity measure										
Opacity index	0.414	0.375	0.514	0.525	0.486	0.475	−0.100***	−0.150***	−0.072***	−0.100***
Trading volume	12.812	10.272	13.532	11.465	13.331	10.743	−0.720***	−1.193***	−0.518***	−0.471**
Bid-ask spread	0.006	0.004	0.009	0.007	0.008	0.006	−0.003***	−0.003***	−0.002***	−0.002***
Analysts following	4.815	5.303	2.813	2.833	3.598	4.007	2.001***	2.470***	1.217***	1.296***
Forecast error	0.401	0.015	0.908	0.021	0.744	0.022	−0.507	−0.006	−0.344	−0.007
Firm Specific variables										
Family ownership	0.121	0.048	0.370	0.364	0.342	0.338	−0.249***	−0.316***	−0.221***	−0.290***
Firm age	3.565	3.555	3.579	3.526	3.654	3.611	−0.014	0.029	−0.089***	−0.056***
Firm size	28.282	28.302	26.286	26.139	27.085	27.000	2.001***	2.162***	1.199***	1.301***
Debt ratio	0.533	0.558	0.435	0.439	0.473	0.483	0.098***	0.119***	0.060***	0.075***
Current ratio	1.113	0.989	1.982	1.460	1.651	1.232	−0.869***	−0.471***	−0.538***	−0.243***
Export ratio	0.344	0.324	0.278	0.128	0.282	0.105	0.066***	0.196***	0.062***	0.219***
R&D intensity	0.008	0.002	0.007	0.001	0.006	0.001	0.001	0.001**	0.002	0.001***
Dividend yield	0.024	0.018	0.027	0.022	0.027	0.022	−0.003*	−0.004***	−0.003*	−0.004***
Tobin's Q	0.096	0.006	−0.070	−0.115	−0.043	−0.100	0.166***	0.121***	0.139***	0.107***
industry-adjusted ROA_{t-1}	28.23	28.27	26.22	26.092	27.016	26.948	2.007***	2.180***	1.217***	1.323***
Turnover	1.427	0.107	3.122	0.374	2.487	0.181	−1.695***	−0.267***	−1.060***	−0.075***
Risk	0.069	0.065	0.070	0.063	0.068	0.064	−0.001	0.001	0.001	0.000
N	582		1,554		569					

Note: This table presents the summary statistics for group firms, unmatched non-group firms, and matched non-group firms. All firms are listed in the Korean Stock Exchange (KSE) and the data period is from 2000 to 2007. This table also provides the mean and median difference tests between group firms and both unmatched and matched non-group firms.

The variables are defined in Table 2.

*, **, and *** denote two-tail significance at 10%, 5%, and 1%, respectively.

is negative and univariate *t*-test result is significant in 1% level. The mean difference between group firms and matched group firms is less than that between group firms and unmatched non-group firms but still negative and significant in 1% level. The negative sign in mean difference means that group firms are less opaque (more transparent) than non-group firms. The cases of median difference are the same. These results preliminarily support Hypothesis 1b that expects group firms to be more transparent than non-group firms. The two individual measures for transparency (bid-ask spread and analysts following) show that group firms are less opaque than non-group firms (both matched and unmatched). Trading volume shows opposite significant results and forecast error shows insignificant results. For other variables, group firms are bigger and younger than non-group firms. Group firms also have lower debt ratio and higher R&D intensity than non-group firms. In performance, group firms perform better than non-group firms in both market-based (Tobin's Q industry-adjusted) and accounting (ROA_{t-1})-based performance measures. The risk level is not significantly different.

The Pearson correlation coefficients are presented in Table 4. Group dummy and opacity index is negatively related, confirming the results from Table 2. Tobin's Q industry-adjusted is also negatively related to opacity index. I can infer that the more transparent firms may perform better in the market. Among individual measures, bid-ask spread and analysts following is highly related to opacity index. Group dummy also has a positive relation with Tobin's Q industry-adjusted. After testing variance inflation factors in every model, results show that the factors are usually lower than 2 for variables of interest and control variables.

MAIN EMPIRICAL RESULTS

In this section, I first examine the impact of group affiliation on corporate transparency and then examine the impacts of group specific characteristics on corporate transparency such as ownership disparity between control rights and cash flow rights, family ownership, group diversification, and group inside financial institutions. Next, I examine the impact of group, opacity, and group × opacity on performance.

Impact of Group Affiliation on Corporate Transparency

I test the impact of group affiliation and other group characteristics on corporate transparency. Column 1 of Table 5 shows that group affiliation

Table 4. Pearson Correlation Coefficients.

	(1)	(2)	(3)	(4)	(5)	(6)	(7)	(8)
(1) Opacity index	1							
(2) Tobin's Q industry-adjusted	−0.2548	1						
(3) Group	−0.2831	0.1701	1					
(4) Family	0.2684	−0.2207	−0.5889	1				
(5) Trading volume	−0.0984	0.0181	−0.1103	−0.049	1			
(6) Bid-ask spread	0.5258	−0.078	−0.1933	0.1612	0.0291	1		
(7) Analysts following	−0.6403	0.2705	0.4114	−0.2655	−0.2715	−0.3441	1	
(8) Forecast error	0.0581	0.025	−0.0233	−0.0619	0.1617	0.1593	−0.0576	1

Note: This table presents the correlation matrix of opacity measures, performance, and group related variables. The variables are defined in Table 2.

has a negative significant impact on firms' opacity index. This result means that group firms are more transparent than non-group firms and supports Hypothesis 1b. This result also indirectly supports the findings of Lee et al. (2009) arguing that the benefits of internal capital markets disappeared in South Korea after the reforms following the Asian financial crisis. This result is contradictory to that of Chang et al. (2007), which finds that the Korean group firms are more opaque than non-group firms after the Asian financial crisis period, using analysts' forecast error and forecast dispersion. This discrepancy may arise from the data period difference. While I am using the data period from 2000 to 2007, the data period of Chang et al. is from 1993 to 2001. One possible explanation can be that the after crisis data period of my research is longer than Chang et al., and thus can examine the long-term effect of market changes. It may also be the case that in 2001, business groups were still undergoing restructuring under President Kim's regime. Their result also supports the *external market hypothesis* because it proves that group firms were initially opaque but became transparent as the market environment changed.

Business groups are not all shaped the same way. Some groups are more diversified. Some have financial institutions within the groups and others do not. Some groups are family controlled and others are not (however, most business groups in South Korea are family controlled groups). Similarly, group firms within the same business groups are not identical. Some group firms have more ownership disparity between control and cash flow ownership, and some groups have less or no disparity. Some group firms have higher group controlling family ownership compared to other group firms in the business group. In this context, I examined the impact of group firm characteristics (ownership disparity between cash flow rights and control rights, and family ownership in a group firms) and group level characteristics (group diversification and inside financial institution) on corporate transparency.

For group firm characteristics, the high ownership disparity means that group controlling owners (mostly family) control the firm in excess of real cash flow ownership of the firm. This ownership disparity is possible because of pyramidal and circular ownership structure. The ownership disparity has been identified as main cause of agency problems between group controlling owners and minority outside investors, because group controlling owners may have incentive to increase their wealth by relocating resources from group firms with lower cash flow ownership to higher cash flow ownership group firms (Johnson et al., 2000). The high ownership disparity helps this expropriation by control of the firm. If this incentive is strong, then group controlling owners may choose the high ownership disparity group firms to be opaque to mask their expropriation from such firms. This expectation is supported by the results in column 2 of Table 5. It shows that ownership disparity between control rights and cash flow rights in group firms has a positive impact on opacity index. The higher the ownership disparity, the more opaque the group firm is.

Compared to the amount of family controlled groups around the world, the role of family ownership in group firms is seldom examined. In non-group settings, Anderson et al. (2009) argue that family owners prefer to make their firms opaque in two competing hypotheses. First, in the entrenchment hypothesis, family owners want to entrench their expropriation of firm wealth, thus wanting their firm to be opaque. Second, in the monitoring hypothesis, the family owners are diligent inside monitors and firms with such family owners do not need to be transparent because the costs to be transparent may exceed the benefits of being transparent. Thus, family firms are less transparent than other firms. Column 3 of Table 5 also shows positive significant impact of group × family on opacity index, which means group firms with higher family ownership are more opaque than other group firms. However, the question of whether the entrenchment hypothesis or monitoring hypothesis holds true is not the scope of this paper and can be discussed in future research.

For group level characteristics, I first examine the effect of group diversification. One of the business characteristics is the industry diversification. Group diversification usually becomes subject to more complex organization and thus increases information asymmetry problems between insiders and outsiders. In the U.S. diversified conglomerate research, scholars found that the diversification has a relation with lower information asymmetry, and argue that diversification of conglomerate diversify away the volatility of stock return. However, this portfolio theory cannot be used in business group studies because each group firms are separately traded in the markets. The real effect of diversification on corporate transparency can be found in business group studies because of the absence of the portfolio effect. If business group is diversified in many industries, outside investors of a group firm should hardly expect the impact of events such as financial problems or litigation issues of other group firms in remote industries. However, if the internal capital market benefits disappear and the more diversified group firms are perceived as more opaque than less diversified group firms, the group firms in diversified groups may try to

Table 5. Impact of Business Group Affiliations and Group Characteristics on Corporate Transparency.

This table presents panel regression results of opacity index on business group affiliation and group characteristics (the detailed calculation of opacity index is presented in the third section). The regression models are the following:

Model 1: *Opacity index* = $\beta_0 + \beta_1 \times$ *group* + *control variables* + *industry and year dummies*
Model 2: *Opacity index* = $\beta_0 + \beta_1 \times$ *group* + $\beta_2 \times$ *group* × *ownership disparity* + *control variables* + *industry and year dummies*
Model 3: *Opacity index* = $\beta_0 + \beta_1 \times$ *group* + $\beta_2 \times$ *group* × *family* + $\beta_3 \times$ *family* + *control variables* + *industry and year dummies*
Model 4: *Opacity index* = $\beta_0 + \beta_1 \times$ *group* + $\beta_2 \times$ *group* × *financial institution* + *control variables* + *industry and year dummies*
Model 5: *Opacity index* = $\beta_0 + \beta_1 \times$ *group* + $\beta_2 \times$ *group diversification* + *control variables* + *industry and year dummies*

where control variables are firm size, risk, ROA_{t-1}, debt ratio, R&D intensity, and firm age. All independent variables are defined in Table 2. The sample period is from 2000 to 2007. The t-statistics are shown in parentheses. *, **, and *** imply two-tail significance at 10%, 5%, and 1%, respectively. F-values are given for the overall group impact from the null: group × (1 + ownership disparity + family + financial institution) = 0; similarly for the overall family impact: family × (1 + group) = 0.

Dependent Variable: Opacity Index	(1)	(2)	(3)	(4)	(5)
Group	− 0.020**	− 0.053***	− 0.042*	− 0.012	− 0.003
	(−2.20)	(−4.64)	(−1.76)	(−1.27)	(−0.28)
Group × ownership disparity		0.124***			
		(4.86)			
Group × family			0.047*		
			(1.77)		
Group × financial institution				− 0.020*	
				(−1.92)	
Group diversification					− 0.039*
					(−1.95)
Family			− 0.006		
			(−0.25)		
Firm size	− 0.019	− 0.016	− 0.021	− 0.020	− 0.020
	(−1.39)	(−1.19)	(−1.53)	(−1.47)	(−1.49)
Risk	− 0.062	− 0.095	− 0.055	− 0.069	− 0.060
	(−0.31)	(−0.49)	(−0.28)	(−0.35)	(−0.31)
ROA_{t-1}	− 0.030**	− 0.030**	− 0.028**	− 0.029**	− 0.030**
	(−2.24)	(−2.25)	(−2.08)	(−2.18)	(−2.23)
Debt ratio	0.175***	0.171***	0.169***	0.177***	0.179***
	(6.63)	(6.51)	(6.42)	(6.75)	(6.81)

Table 5. (*Continued*)

Dependent Variable: Opacity Index	(1)	(2)	(3)	(4)	(5)
R&D intensity	−0.737***	−0.707***	−0.716***	−0.730***	−0.715***
	(−3.66)	(−3.46)	(−3.71)	(−3.61)	(−3.58)
Firm age	0.020***	0.020***	0.017**	0.020***	0.019***
	(2.85)	(2.99)	(2.46)	(2.95)	(2.83)
Industry dummies	Yes	Yes	Yes	Yes	Yes
Year dummies	Yes	Yes	Yes	Yes	Yes
Intercept	Yes	Yes	Yes	Yes	Yes
F-value for overall group impact		12.23	0.18	8.90	
F-value for overall family impact			15.25		
N	1,151	1,151	1,151	1,151	1,151
Adjusted R^2	0.329	0.340	0.336	0.331	0.331

achieve higher transparency to attract outside investors. The results show a negative significant impact of group diversification on opacity index. Group firms in more diversified groups are more transparent and this supports the latter proposition above. The group inside a financial institution also has a negative significant impact on opacity index. The explanation for this result may be similar to that of group diversification. The existence of the group inside financial institution may signal the possible opacity of group firms in the group to external financial markets and such group firms may pay more attention to offset such signals. The two results from group diversification and inside financial institution also support *external market hypothesis.*

Impacts of Group Affiliation and Corporate Transparency on Firm Performance

To confirm whether group firms choose to be transparent because the benefits of internal markets are relatively lower than external markets, I test the impact of group dummy, opacity index, and group × opacity index on firm performance measured by Tobin's Q industry-adjusted. The results are presented in Table 6. Group has a positive impact on performance. Using Korean data from 1990 to 1995, Ferris, Kim and Kitsabunnarat (2003) find the business group discount on group firms and argue that group level agency problems, such as risk-sharing, over-investment, and

Table 6. Group Affiliation, Corporate Transparency, and Performance.

This table presents panel regression results of Tobin's Q industry-adjusted on group, opacity index, and group × opacity index (the detailed calculation of opacity index is presented in the third section). The regression models are the following:

Model 1: $Tobin's\ Q\ industry-adjusted = \beta_0 + \beta_1 \times group + control\ variables + industry\ and\ year\ dummies$

Model 2: $Tobin's\ Q\ industry-adjusted = \beta_0 + \beta_1 \times group + \beta_2 \times group \times opacity\ index + control\ variables + industry\ and\ year\ dummies$

Model 3: $Tobin's\ Q\ industry-adjusted = \beta_0 + \beta_1 \times group + \beta_2 \times group \times opacity\ index + \beta_3 \times opacity\ index + control\ variables + industry\ and\ year\ dummies$

where control variables are firm size, risk, ROA_{t-1}, debt ratio, R&D intensity, and firm age. All independent variables are defined in Table 2. The sample period is from 2000 to 2007. The t-statistics are shown in parentheses. *, **, and *** imply two-tail significance at 10%, 5%, and 1%, respectively. F-values are presented for the overall group impact from the null: group × (1 + opacity index) = 0; in the same way the overall opacity impact from the null: opacity × (1 + group) = 0.

Dependent Variable: Tobin's Q Industry-Adjusted	(1)	(2)	(3)
Group	0.064**	0.306***	0.010
	(2.06)	(4.43)	(0.12)
Group × opacity index		−0.527***	0.086
		(−4.30)	(0.56)
Opacity index			−0.702***
			(−6.37)
Control variables	Yes	Yes	Yes
Industry dummies	Yes	Yes	Yes
Year dummies	Yes	Yes	Yes
Intercept	Yes	Yes	Yes
F-value for overall group impact		10.77	1.50
F-value for overall opacity impact			25.43
N	1,151	1,151	1,151
Adjusted R^2	0.190	0.201	0.226

propping, may be the main causes of the discount. Improved transparency of group firms after the Asian crisis and improved performance of group firms confirm that group firms are trying to be transparent to match the market trend and have succeeded in doing so. Thus, the *external market hypothesis* is supported.

I expect that if the *external market hypothesis* holds, then the more transparent group firms will perform better than other group firms. The results show that group × opacity index has a negative significant effect.

This means that the more transparent group firms perform better in the markets. This result supports Hypothesis 3b (see column 2 of Table 6). However, in column 3 of Table 6, the significance of group × opacity index disappears when the model has opacity index together. This may be because the impact of corporate transparency is so dominant on performance compared to group impact. Thus, the market perceives corporate transparency to be a priority to other concerns. This also helps to support the external market hypothesis.

ROBUSTNESS

In this section, the two robustness checks are performed. First, the impacts of business group rankings on corporate transparency and performance are checked and second, endogenous group affiliation issues are checked.

Internal Market Size

The larger groups engage in more industry diversification and have more group firms (See panel A of Table 7). These facts are related to more complexity of group level decisions and make it harder for outsiders to monitor the larger groups' internal transactions. Furthermore, the larger groups may still have benefits from internal capital markets because of their scale and may not need to use external capital markets as smaller groups do. Thus, the larger groups can be more opaque than smaller groups. To check the difference in transparency, I divided group firms in three sub-groups: the 5 largest group firms; the 10 largest group firms; and the 30 largest group firms (the same as the group variable definition). The results show a positive relationship between opacity index and group ranking. The five largest group firms show the strongest negative coefficient and the most significant results. The 10 largest group firms show the next strongest negative coefficient and the 30 largest group firms show the highest coefficient and the least significant level (which is 5% significant level). Thus, business group firms are more transparent than non-group firms and the group firms affiliated with larger groups tend to have higher corporate transparency level. I also checked the difference in performance and find that group firms affiliated with larger groups tend to have higher performance. These results mean that even larger group-affiliated firms, which could have more benefits from the bigger internal markets, are more transparent

Table 7. Impact of Internal Market Size: Group Ranking, Corporate Transparency, and Performance.

Panel A: Group level summary statistics.

Groups are divided by ranking into the five largest groups (top 5 groups), groups ranked between 6th and 10th, and groups ranked between 11th and 30th places in the Korea Fair Trade Commission ranking system of 2007.

	Mean	Median	Minimum	Maximum
Top 5 groups				
Total group assets (billion Korean won)	69,651	60,376	40,208	129,078
Number of industry	26	26	20	32
Number of group firms	45.4	44	31	59
Ownership disparity (%)	32.31	32.50	24.80	37.91
Top 6–10 groups				
Total group assets (billion Korean won)	26,085	25,136	22,224	32,661
Number of industry	19	17	14	25
Number of group firms	31	25	19	48
Ownership disparity (%)	19.47	21.84	0.69	37.51
Top 11–30 groups				
Total group assets (billion Korean won)	8,609	6,826	4,764	20,573
Number of industry	14	14	4	33
Number of group firms	17.8	14.5	5	64
Ownership disparity (%)	30.89	29.45	0.03	57.72

Panel B: Impact of group ranking on corporate transparency and performance.

This panel presents panel regression results of opacity index and Tobin's Q industry-adjusted on group ranking (the detailed calculation of opacity index is presented in the third section). The regression models are the following:

Model 1: $\textit{Opacity index} = \beta_0 + \beta_1 \times \textit{top 5 group} + \textit{control variables} + \textit{industry and year dummies}$

Model 2: $\textit{Opacity index} = \beta_0 + \beta_1 \times \textit{top 10 group} + \textit{control variables} + \textit{industry and year dummies}$

Model 3: $\textit{Opacity index} = \beta_0 + \beta_1 \times \textit{group} + \textit{control variables} + \textit{industry and year dummies}$

Model 4: $\textit{Tobin's Q industry} - \textit{adjusted} = \beta_0 + \beta_1 \times \textit{top 5 group} + \textit{control variables} + \textit{industry and year dummies}$

Model 5: $\textit{Tobin's Q industry} - \textit{adjusted} = \beta_0 + \beta_1 \times \textit{top 10 group} + \textit{control variables} + \textit{industry and year dummies}$

Model 6: $\textit{Tobin's Q industry} - \textit{adjusted} = \beta_0 + \beta_1 \times \textit{group} + \textit{control variables} + \textit{industry and year dummies}$

where control variables are firm size, risk, ROA_{t-1}, debt ratio, R&D intensity, and firm age. Business groups are divided into the five largest groups (top 5 group), 10 largest groups (top 10 group), and 30 largest groups (group). All independent variables are defined in Table 2. The sample period is from 2000 to 2007. The *t*-statistics are shown in parentheses. *, **, and *** imply two-tail significance at 10%, 5%, and 1%, respectively.

Table 7. (*Continued*)

	Opacity Index			Tobin's Q Industry-Adjusted		
	(1)	(2)	(3)	(4)	(5)	(6)
Top 5 group	− 0.068***			0.159***		
	(− 6.02)			(3.22)		
Top 10 group		− 0.058***			0.116***	
		(− 5.60)			(2.87)	
Group			− 0.020**			0.064**
			(− 2.20)			(2.06)
Control variables	Yes	Yes	Yes	Yes	Yes	Yes
Industry dummies	Yes	Yes	Yes	Yes	Yes	Yes
Year dummies	Yes	Yes	Yes	Yes	Yes	Yes
Intercept	Yes	Yes	Yes	Yes	Yes	Yes
N	815	901	1,151	815	901	1,151
Adjusted R^2	0.363	0.354	0.329	0.194	0.184	0.190

and thus perform better than other group firms and support the *external market hypothesis*.

Endogeneity

One of the edogeneity problems comes from a sample selection bias. I use yearly industry and size one to one matching to select the control sample. To do this, I sort all firms by year and industry and match one group firm by one non-group firm without replacement. The selected non-group firm is nearest in size to a group firm. This matching process minimizes the size difference between group firms and matched sample within year and industry. However, it may be not enough to use two-dimensional matching because there would be more ex ante firm characteristics from non-group firms to be considered. Thus, I want to check whether the results from industry and size matched control samples are still valid after taking care of possible sample selection bias.

I use a propensity score matching method to handle this issue. The propensity score is the probability of being business group firms conditional on x:

$$P(x) = pr(D = 1|x)$$

Table 8. Endogeneity: Estimating Propensity to be a Group Firm and Re-estimating Relations Among Group, Corporate Transparency, and Performance.

This table presents logistic regression estimates to determine the propensity for business group membership in Panel A. Panel B and panel C estimate the impacts of predicted group affiliation on corporate transparency and performance, respectively. *, **, and *** denote two-tail significance at 10%, 5%, and 1%, respectively.

Panel A: Propensity to be a group firm.

This panel reports logistic estimates from a model of a firm's propensity to be a group firm. The dependent variable is one for group firms and zero for non-group firms. All regressions include intercept and are controlled for year and industry fixed effects.

	Coefficient	*z*-Statistics
Firm size	1.313***	17.61
Debt ratio	−0.074	−0.13
Current ratio	−0.458***	−3.92
Export ratio	−0.314	−1.08
R&D intensity	0.050	0.01
Dividend yield	−0.218	−0.08
Tobin's Q industry-adjusted	0.344**	1.96
ROA	−1.685	−1.44
Firm age	−0.036***	−6.57
Turnover	−0.063***	−2.84
Industry dummies	Yes	
Year dummies	Yes	
Intercept	Yes	
N	3,696	

Panel B: Group affiliation and corporate transparency.

Table 5 is re-estimated using predicted group propensity estimates. The dependent variable is opacity index. The regression models are the following:

Model 1 : $\textit{Opacity index} = \beta_0 + \beta_1 \times \textit{group} + \textit{control variables} + \textit{industry and year dummies}$

Model 2 : $\textit{Opacity index} = \beta_0 + \beta_1 \times \textit{group} + \beta_2 \times \textit{group} \times \textit{ownership disparity} + \textit{control variables} + \textit{industry and year dummies}$

Model 3 : $\textit{Opacity index} = \beta_0 + \beta_1 \times \textit{group} + \beta_2 \times \textit{group} \times \textit{family} + \beta_3 \times \textit{family} + \textit{control variables} + \textit{industry and year dummies}$

Model 4 : $\textit{Opacity index} = \beta_0 + \beta_1 \times \textit{group} + \beta_2 \times \textit{group} \times \textit{financial institution} + \textit{control variables} + \textit{industry and year dummies}$

Model 5 : $\textit{Opacity index} = \beta_0 + \beta_1 \times \textit{group} + \beta_2 \times \textit{group diversification} + \textit{control variables} + \textit{industry and year dummies}$

where control variables are firm size, risk, ROA_{t-1}, debt ratio, R&D intensity, and firm age.

Table 8. *(Continued)*

	(1)	(2)	(3)	(4)	(5)
Group	− 0.026***	− 0.052***	− 0.043**	− 0.019**	− 0.010
	(− 3.10)	(− 4.85)	(− 2.35)	(− 2.08)	(− 0.86)
Group × ownership disparity		0.098***			
		(3.84)			
Group × family			0.042**		
			(2.02)		
Group × financial institution				− 0.019*	
				(− 1.85)	
Group diversification					− 0.038*
					(− 1.89)
Family			0.002		
			(0.12)		
Control variables	Yes	Yes	Yes	Yes	Yes
Industry dummies	Yes	Yes	Yes	Yes	Yes
Year dummies	Yes	Yes	Yes	Yes	Yes
Intercept	Yes	Yes	Yes	Yes	Yes
F-value for overall group impact		5.03	0.00	13.18	
F-value for overall family impact			18.38		
N	1,164	1,164	1,164	1,164	1,164
Adjusted R^2	0.376	0.383	0.385	0.377	0.378

Panel C: Group affiliation, corporate transparency, and performance

Table 6 is re-estimated using predicted group propensity estimates. The dependent variable is Tobin's Q industry-adjusted. The regression models are the following:

Model 1 : $\textit{Tobin's Q industry} - \textit{adjusted} = \beta_0 + \beta_1 \times \textit{group} + \textit{control variables} + \textit{industry and year dummies}$

Model 2 : $\textit{Tobin's Q industry} - \textit{adjusted} = \beta_0 + \beta_1 \times \textit{group} + \beta_2 \times \textit{group} \times \textit{opacity index} + \textit{control variables} + \textit{industry and year dummies}$

Model 3 : $\textit{Tobin's Q industry} - \textit{adjusted} = \beta_0 + \beta_1 \times \textit{group} + \beta_2 \times \textit{group} \times \textit{opacity index} + \beta_3 \times \textit{opacity index} + \textit{control variables} + \textit{industry and year dummies}$

where control variables are firm size, risk, ROA_{t-1}, debt ratio, R&D intensity, and firm age.

	(1)	(2)	(3)
Group	0.061**	0.288***	− 0.035
	(2.02)	(4.16)	(− 0.40)
Group × opacity index		− 0.493***	0.164
		(− 4.00)	(1.07)
Opacity index			− 0.782***
			(− 7.17)

Table 8. (*Continued*)

	(1)	(2)	(3)
Control variables	Yes	Yes	Yes
Industry dummies	Yes	Yes	Yes
Year dummies	Yes	Yes	Yes
Intercept	Yes	Yes	Yes
F-value for overall group impact		9.30	2.79
F-value for overall opacity impact			25.79
N	1,164	1,164	1,164
Adjusted R^2	0.181	0.191	0.221

where D is a dummy variable to indicate 1 for group firms and 0 for non-group firms. The conditional probability is computed using a logistic model. Conditioning variables used to estimate the propensity score are firm size, debt ratio, current ratio, export ratio, dividend yield, Tobin's Q industry-adjusted, ROA, firm age, and turnover (the detailed definition of variables are presented in Table 2). The logistic regression estimation results are presented in panel A of Table 8.

Panel B and panel C re-estimate Table 5 and Table 6 with propensity matched control samples. In panel B, the results of group affiliation on opacity index are in support of Hypothesis 1b that group firms are more transparent than non-group firms as in Table 5. Other group firms and group level characteristics have the same direction and significance. Panel C presents the regression result of group, opacity index, and group × opacity index on Tobin's Q industry-adjusted. The results are almost identical to those in Table 6. Thus, after controlling the endogeneity issue, the results of this paper are strong in support of the external market hypothesis.

CONCLUSION

The complex organizational structure, well-documented agency problems such as propping and tunneling, and the existence of internal markets make us assume that business groups are opaque by itself. Some scandals of business group controlling owners almost confirm the opaqueness of group firms as fact. The previous research on corporate transparency of group firms also confirms these beliefs (Chang et al., 2007). However, I find the business group firms in Korea are more transparent than non-group firms and perform better than non-group firms. I argue that business groups need to be more transparent because the benefits of internal markets disappeared as a result of the Korean economy's external market development. The increase in corporate transparency may be related to better performance of group firms because of low cost of capital, better valuation from market, and reduced agency problem. The positive relation between group diversification and corporate transparency support the main results. Other tests related to the impact of internal markets such as internal market size and group inside financial institutions also support the main results. From the results, I can infer that business groups may be more flexible in transforming their group firms to adjust to the changes of the business environment than commonly thought.

Further research should identify the component of the corporate transparency of group firms and test whether the transparency is driven by business group's decisions or by external forces such as regulation or market enforcement. Along with these, to be more generalized, business groups of other countries should be added to future research.

NOTES

1. The pyramidal or circular ownership structure of business group yields ownership disparity between control and cash flow rights of group controlling owners. This disparity may provide incentives for group controlling owners to shift resources from the low cash flow right group firms to high cash flow right group firms to increase their own wealth in the sacrifices of minority outside investors in resource shifting group firms (Johnson, La Porta, Lopez-de-Silanes, & Shleifer, 2000).
2. http://news.mk.co.kr/newsRead.php?year = 2012&no = 86524 (accessed August 3, 2012).
3. The main bank control is observed in Japanese business groups, *keiretsu*. In Chinese groups, the government control is found but family controlled groups are common around world.
4. If a group firm's majority owner is the group controlling owner and the controlling owner's goal is to maximize the group firm's profit itself, then the agency problem of the group firm is identical to the non-group firm's agency problem between majority shareholder and minority shareholders.
5. Khanna and Palepu (2000) expect that as an economy, where business groups reside, develops and institutional voids disappear, the business group affiliation will lose its benefits over non-group firms.
6. President Kim Dae-jungs regime (1998–2003) put restrictions on group firms such as government driven restructuring, lowering the limit of total internal investments and reinforcing scrutiny on group internal transactions. However, President

Noh Moo-hyun's regime eased the previous restrictions on business groups as they appeared strengthened after a series of restructuring.

REFERENCES

Anderson, R., Duru, A., & Reeb, D. (2009). Founders, heirs, and corporate opacity in the United States. *Journal of Financial Economics*, *92*, 2005–2222.

Bae, K., Kang, J., & Kim, J. (2002). Tunneling or value added? Evidence from mergers by Korean business groups. *Journal of Finance*, *57*, 2695–2740.

Baek, J., Kang, J., & Lee, I. (2006). Business groups and tunneling: Evidence from private securities offerings by Korean chaebols. *Journal of Finance*, *56*, 2415–2449.

Bertrand, M., Mehta, P., & Mullainathan, S. (2002). Fretting out tunneling: An application to Indian business groups. *Quarterly Journal of Economics*, *117*, 121–148.

Chang, J., Cho, Y., & Shin, H. (2007). The change in corporate transparency of Korean firms after the Asian financial crisis: An analysis using analysts' forecast data. *Corporate Governance*, *15*, 1144–1167.

Chang, S. (2003). Ownership structure, expropriation and performance of group affiliated companies in Korea. *Academy of Management Journal*, *46*, 238–254.

Choi, J., & Cowing, T. (1999). Firm behavior and group affiliation: The strategic role of corporate grouping for Korean firms. *Journal of Asian Economics*, *10*, 195–209.

Diamond, D., & Verrecchia, R. (1991). Disclosure, liquidity and the cost of equity capital. *Journal of Finance*, *46*, 1325–1360.

Fan, P., & Wong, T. (2002). Corporate ownership structure and the informativeness of accounting earnings in East Asia. *Journal of Accounting and Economics*, *33*, 401–426.

Ferris, S., Kim, K., & Kitsabunnarat, P. (2003). The costs (and benefits?) of diversified business groups; the case of Korean chaebols. *Journal of Banking and Finance*, *27*, 251–273.

Freidman, E., Johnson, S., & Mitton, T. (2003). Propping and tunneling. *Journal of Comparative Economics*, *31*, 732–750.

Hayes, R., & Lundholm, R. (1996). Segment reporting to the capital market in the presence of a competitor. *Journal of Accounting Research*, *34*, 261–279.

Healy, P., & Palepu, K. (2001). Information asymmetry, corporate disclosure, and the capital markets: A review of the empirical disclosure literature. *Journal of Accounting and Economics*, *31*, 405–440.

Jensen, M., & Meckling, W. (1976). Theory of the firm: Managerial behavior, agency costs and ownership structure. *Journal of Financial Economics*, *3*, 305–360.

Joh, S. (2003). Corporate governance and firm profitability: Evidence from Korea before the economic crisis. *Journal of Financial Economics*, *58*, 141–186.

Johnson, S., La Porta, R., Lopez-de-Silanes, F., & Shleifer, A. (2000). Tunneling. *American Economic Review Papers and Proceedings*, *90*, 22–27.

Khanna, T., & Palepu, K. (2000). Is group affiliation profitable? An analysis of Indian business groups. *Journal of Finance*, *55*, 867–891.

Khanna, T., & Rivkin, J. (2001). Estimating the performance effects of business groups in emerging markets. *Strategic Management Journal*, *22*, 45–74.

Khanna, T., & Yafeh, Y. (2005). Business groups and risk sharing around the world. *Journal of Business*, *78*, 301–340.

Lang, M., Lins, K., & Miller, D. (2004). Concentrate control, analyst following, and valuation: Do analysts matter most when investors are protected least? *Journal of Accounting Research*, *42*, 589–623.

La Porta, R., Lopez-de-Silanes, F., & Shleifer, A. (1999). Corporate ownership around the world. *Journal of Finance*, *54*, 471–517.

Lee, S., Park, K., & Shin, H. (2009). Disappearing internal capital markets: Evidence from diversified business group in Korea. *Journal of Banking and Finance*, *33*, 326–334.

Leuz, C., Nanda, D., & Wysocki, P. (2003). Earnings management and investor protection: An international comparison. *Journal of Financial Economics*, *69*, 505–527.

Nahapiet, J., & Ghoshal, S. (1998). Social capital, intellectual capital and the organizational advantage. *Academy of Management Review*, *23*, 242–266.

Shleifer, A., & Vishny, R. (1997). A survey of corporate governance. *Journal of Finance*, *52*, 737–783.

INFLUENCE OF TAX ACCOUNTING ON TRANSPARENCY

Silvio Hiroshi Nakao

ABSTRACT

The purpose of this chapter is to discuss the relation between tax reporting and financial reporting, their influence on transparency, and empirical implications.

Keywords: Tax accounting; transparency; book-tax conformity; book-tax differences; tax planning; earnings management

JEL classifications: M41; D82

INTRODUCTION

This chapter provides a conceptual approach of economic incentives, factors, and mechanisms that surround the relation between tax and financial accounting and their influence on the transparency of financial reporting information, as well as related empirical implications.

Income tax represents an important concern of managers and stakeholders due to several reasons. First of all, income tax may represent a significant portion of income, what attracts attention by itself. Moreover, taxable

Transparency and Governance in a Global World
International Finance Review, Volume 13, 69–96

ISSN: 1569-3767/doi:10.1108/S1569-3767(2012)0000013006

income may be calculated in a different way of income for financial reporting and it may have an important influence on transparency. Managers have to report accounting information to tax authorities as well as to investors and creditors, but many times with different regulations. However, a link between accounting for tax and for reporting purposes may exist. It can explain why accounting scandals are frequently accompanied by tax frauds.

Since the regulations are different and tax expense reduces net income for financial reporting purposes, there are different economic incentives related to both reports. To report a higher income to investors and creditors, a manager would attempt to reduce taxable income with tax planning strategies or even managing earnings.

There is a long discussion about increasing book-tax conformity (BTC). Increasing required BTC would limit opportunistic behavior of managers, improving the transparency of financial reporting information. According to opponents, if required BTC is increased, tax policymakers will interfere in the standard-setting process, what would reduce the quality of reported information.

Therefore, there is a clear influence of tax accounting on transparency of financial reporting. Tax accounting involves economic incentives and mechanisms of protection against opportunistic behavior that may improve or reduce transparency of financial reporting.

The next sections deal with the concept of transparency related to tax reporting, the influence of choices of managers for tax and financial reporting accounting purposes on transparency, and the mechanisms of protection of investors and tax authorities against opportunism. In sequence, the chapter has a discussion about the factors that influence book-tax differences (BTDs) and similarities and their influence on transparency. Finally, the chapter discusses empirical implications covering research and practical aspects.

TRANSPARENCY IN FINANCIAL REPORTING AND TAX REPORTING

Publicly held companies have to provide their information to at least two main audiences. Each of whom has a stake in assessing how much income is being generated. The first audience is constituted by investors and creditors, among others. The second is consisting of tax authorities, such as the United States' Internal Revenue Service (IRS) (Shackelford, Slemrod, & Sallee, 2011).

Both have interests in companies, but the mechanisms to protect their interests may be sometimes divergent, other times convergent. In all cases, the information for both audiences needs to be transparent. Transparency is usually associated with information to investors and creditors, but the tax authorities require transparency as well.

Bushman, Piotroski, and Smith (2004) conceptualize corporate transparency within a country as the joint output of a multifaceted system whose components collectively produce, gather, validate, and disseminate information to market participants outside the firm.

Financial reporting works like a "glass window" that permits investors and creditors to see through it the company's performance. Distortions on "glass window" reduce their ability to have the perception of the real situation of the company. Investors would see a bigger or distorted image that does not match with the real figure.

As investors and creditors want to make decisions about the company, they would like to see the ability that the company has today to have a good (or bad) future. They have to decide whether to invest and funding the company or not and it will depend on a company's ability of generating cash flows in the future. Financial information is transparent as it allows investors and creditors to see the company from this perspective without distortions on the "glass window."

Transparency to the tax authority has the same meaning but what it needs to "see" is a different thing. It needs to "see" the ability of the company to pay taxes. It wants to "see" if the company has earned money to pay taxes. If the company earned some money yesterday, it has money to pay taxes today. Tax authority doesn't want to decide about the future, about the things that will happen, the value of the company: it wants to "see" just if the company had income to pay taxes in the last period. The company just has to "twist" in front of the "window" in a way that would allow the tax authority to see it from this perspective.

Tax authorities can see the public financial statements, which helps them to detect any understatement of taxable income. Although investors cannot see the tax return, investors receive some information about taxes in the financial statements, what may be informative to both tax authorities and investors (Shackelford et al., 2011).

Thus, to be transparent, companies have to allow investors, creditors, and tax authorities to "see through the window" from different perspectives. It implies that transparency of financial and tax reporting should be defined as the quality of allowing observation of economic phenomenon of an entity from relevant perspectives for investors, creditors, and tax authorities. This definition covers financial and tax reporting because there are many situations that the information for an audience cannot be unlinked of the other.

Transparency is resulting from the quality of information produced by managers for both audiences following (or not) accounting tax rules and financial accounting standards. Hereafter, the chapter refers to transparency as the quality of financial reporting information.

ACCOUNTING CHOICES OF MANAGERS FOR FINANCIAL REPORTING PURPOSES

The manager has full access to information about the company and is responsible for producing information to report to investors and creditors. However, the process of producing information is not "automatic" and requires from manager to make choices about how information should be reported.

Managers have to make decisions about how long a financial asset will be held, how long a machine will be used, or criteria to estimate the amount of receivables that are likely to be collected, for example. Aside of impact on operations of the company, these choices have an impact on accounting information to investors and creditors.

Fields, Lys, and Vincent (2001, p. 256) define that an accounting choice is "any decision whose primary purpose is to influence (either in form or substance) the output of the accounting system in a particular way, including not only financial statements published in accordance with GAAP, but also tax returns and regulatory filings."

Manager's accounting choices can provide a high-quality information since the manager has full access to information about the company and makes operational decisions and estimates that may influence financial information. Thus, the manager is able to provide a faithful representation of the economic situation of the company since the accounting choices can represent his operational decisions and projections.

However, the manager, as an agent of the shareholders (or the controlling shareholder himself), has economic interests that cannot be aligned with shareholders' interests. Economic interests of managers may include bias in information and that should not faithfully represent the performance of the company. For example, managers can make choices that result in anticipating revenues and postponing expenses in self-interested attempts to produce a higher income and increase his participation in profit or increase the stock price prior to the expiration of stock options they hold.

Thus, there are accounting choices made by managers that should represent manipulation of information to achieve a goal, a practice known as earnings management.

Healy and Wahlen (1999, p. 368) state that "earnings management occurs when managers use judgment in financial reporting and in structuring transactions to alter financial reports to either mislead some stakeholders about the underlying economic performance of the company or to influence contractual outcomes that depend on reported accounting numbers."

According to Fields et al. (2001, p. 260), "although not all accounting choices involve earnings management, and the term earnings management extends beyond accounting choice, the implications of accounting choice to achieve a goal are consistent with the idea of earnings management."

The earnings management procedure depends on the objective that should promote the achievement of their economic interests. It should occur by income smoothness, for example.

Accounting information can have so high-level incentives to convey self-serving information that managers may present an aggressive financial reporting, making choices that are not allowed by generally accepted accounting principles (GAAP). Frank, Lynch, and Rego (2009, p. 468) define aggressive financial reporting as "upward earnings management that may or may not be within the confines of generally accepted accounting principles (GAAP)." This definition includes fraudulent reporting. Some managers can be so aggressive in financial reporting that they are willing to pay more taxes just to not attract attention to BTD.

Therefore, accounting choices of managers can improve or reduce transparency to the extent that the accounting choices of managers can or cannot lead to a faithful representation of the real economic situation of the company.

ACCOUNTING CHOICES OF MANAGERS FOR TAX PURPOSES

Managers can make choices for tax purposes as well as they make choices for financial reporting. However, the economic interests may be different, since the taxable income results in a tax expense that reduces the net income of the company. In general, there is an economic incentive to reduce taxable income. The reduction of taxable income through accounting choices is generally included in most of the tax planning definitions.

Tax planning is an action that aims to minimize tax payments and maximize income. Hanlon and Heitzman (2010) define tax avoidance broadly as "the reduction of explicit taxes," not distinguishing between real activities that are tax-favored, avoidance activities specifically undertaken to reduce taxes, and target tax benefits from lobbying activities.

According to Scholes, Wolfson, Erickson, Maydew, and Shevlin (2002), tax planning can be accomplished in three ways:

1. Shifting the result of one type to another, which can happen, e.g., by shifting the nature of revenues and expenses, the method of distribution of income, or the method of calculation of taxable income;
2. Shifting the result from one "pocket" to another. The shifting of "pocket" can occur by shifting the responsibility for tax payments, by creation of new entities, or by changing taxing jurisdiction. For example, a company can save taxes by shifting the location of its subsidiaries to other countries;
3. Shifting the result of one period to another. The shifting of results from one period to other deals with the concept of time value of money. The economy may happen with the postponement of taxable income, with the anticipation of deductible expenses or with the change of the taxation system (accrual to cash basis). For example, managers can invest in a tax favored activity to accelerate depreciation for tax purposes.

Tax planning strategies can be implemented by modifying operations, what can or cannot produce differences between book and tax income. For example, if a company decides to shift the location of its subsidiary to another jurisdiction to reduce tax, book and tax income of the subsidiary may be accounted in the same way and no difference will arise. However, it is also possible to use tax planning strategies involving temporary or permanent BTD. For example, if a company invests in an incentivized activity and there is a full depreciation for tax purposes on acquisition of equipment, a temporary BTD will arise as a result of postponing tax payments. For the same activity, legislation would provide a tax incentive that allows a double deduction of an expense, e.g., resulting in a permanent BTD. Sometimes tax planning may imply on an increasing taxable income in some periods to deduct tax losses.

Managers can have an aggressive behavior in their reporting to tax audience. Frank et al. (2009) define aggressive tax reporting as "downward manipulation of taxable income through tax planning that may or may not be considered fraudulent tax evasion." They use a measure of aggressive tax reporting based on permanent differences between book and tax income. The main reason is that relying on permanent difference is more consistent with anecdotal evidence regarding the nature of tax shelter activity. A temporary difference should represent a simple postponement of taxable income that would result merely in a time value of money saving.

Another possibility that cannot be discharged is a fraudulent reporting for tax purposes.

MECHANISMS OF PROTECTION OF INVESTORS AND CREDITORS

The audience constituted by investors and creditors needs financial reporting to make economic decisions. Investors need information to make valuation of companies and decide to invest or disinvest. Creditors need information whether to provide or not capital to companies, what includes a bankrupt and credit risk evaluation.

All of these things are related to future, because investors want a return on investment in future and creditors want to get the loans back and earn interest. Valuation of a firm requires future cash flow projections.

Investors and creditors are interested in financial reporting to minimize their information risks about the economic situation of companies. As it is related to future cash flows, investors and creditors need information about the tendency of earnings in the future.

However, projections depend on premises used by investors and on reported information that is taken as a basis for projecting. If information is biased by manager's self-interested attempts to produce higher income, e.g., the information would take investors for making wrong decisions.

Earnings have higher ability of prediction of future cash flows. Dechow, Kothari, and Watts (1998, p. 133–134) consider that one explanation for the prominence of accounting earnings and the reasons for its usage is that earnings reflect cash flow forecasts and have a higher correlation with value than does current cash flow. Earnings' inclusion of those forecasts causes earnings to be a better forecast of (and so a better proxy for) future cash flows than current cash flows. This can help explain why earnings are often used instead of operating cash flows in valuation models and performance measures.

A role of financial accounting standard setters is to avoid misleading information by setting principles that aim to constrain most possibilities of bias that should result from conflicts of economic interests of investors and creditors and managers that provide information.

Regulators must, therefore, understand the advantages and disadvantages of allowing choice and determine the "optimal" level of discretion (Fields et al., 2001).

However, the earnings have subjectivity on their measurement. There is uncertainty involved in realization of earnings in cash. The future cash flow method of measuring assets increases relevance but decreases reliance. This method would be able to provide representation of the real value of assets and results in a timely earnings recognition, but carries subjective of premises used by the manager to measure the asset.

A way that financial accounting standard setters have to set more reliable information is setting alternative measures of assets instead of using future cash flows. Fair value is one of the alternatives. Historical cost is another alternative method. Using the historical cost method increases reliance but decreases the relevance of information.

Accounting standard setters choose alternative measures for assets depending on the magnitude of uncertainty that is related to the realization of cash benefits in future. Any alternative measurement method has a downward degree of ability to represent the real economic value, but it can bring reliability to the measurement of asset. The income of the period is affected by the selected method of measurement of assets and liabilities.

Selection of the method by accounting standard setters can make earnings include more (or less) information about future cash flows. For example, if a biological asset is measured by its market value instead of historical cost, increases or decreases in its market value will be recognized in income of the period, while no result would be recognized in historical cost measurement up to its selling. As the benefits of the biological asset will be realized in cash in the future, the recognition of these results increases prediction of current income related to future cash flows.

Accounting standard setters can also use the conservatism mechanism. Losses are timely recognized but gains are postponed and recognized when realized. It is a mechanism that avoids opportunism of managers related to theirs "optimism" on estimates of changes of future cash flows of the assets. LaFond and Watts (2008) argue that conservative financial reporting is a governance mechanism that reduces the managers' ability to manipulate and overstate financial performance and increases the firm's cash flows and value. The manager's asymmetric loss function gives him incentives to use his private information to attempt to transfer wealth from investors to himself by overstating financial performance and consequently stock prices during his tenure at the firm.

LaFond and Watts (2008) consider that by their nature, growth options (future positive net present value projects) are unverifiable so that, it is expected, the larger the information asymmetry between managers and outside investors, the greater is the growth options. If conservatism reduces the information asymmetry generated by growth options proportionately, then they expect conservatism to vary positively with observed information asymmetry. Using cross-sectional regressions, they find that the larger the measure of conservatism, the larger the information asymmetry measure.

Bushman and Piotroski (2006, p. 108) find that investor protection embodied in corporate law and the efficiency and impartiality of the judicial system play a significant role in creating incentives for timely loss recognition (TLR). Firms in countries with strong investor protections and high-quality judicial systems reflect bad news in reported earnings numbers in a more timely fashion than firms in countries characterized by weak investor protections and low-quality judicial systems.

Standard setters can improve transparency as the information may reveal the current economic situation in their relevant aspects with a reliable estimate of future cash flows of companies.

MECHANISMS OF PROTECTION OF TAX AUTHORITIES

The government collects income tax from companies, but it depends on companies' reporting to collect. However, as there is information asymmetry in this relation, tax authority attempts to set rules to obtain transparent information from taxpayers.

Information to tax authorities can be transparent when it contains a reliable representation of the ability of companies to pay taxes. Reliability is the main quality of information to tax authorities because the objective is to collect taxes and not make decisions.

Making economic decisions about a company is not important to tax authorities. Relevance based on timely information and predictive and feedback values is not important since the information about taxable income is not useful to make decisions. Thus, estimates about the amounts and timing of benefits of assets and liabilities that would impact earnings and permit better cash flow projection are not important.

As due tax payments are usually based on past income, tax authorities should be concerned about taxable income measurement instead of asset and liability measurements. Taxable income is the earned amount that represents the ability of entity to pay income tax during a period. Objectively, the ability to pay taxes is defined by the measurement of income stated by tax accounting rule setters.

The historical cost may be the predominant method of measuring earnings as it represents a reliable basis due to its verifiability with documentation of realized transactions. Historical cost is also more directly related to cash basis and requires fewer estimates than other methods of measuring assets and liabilities. Fair value measurements of assets, e.g., are not important for tax purposes because its ability to predict future cash flows is not relevant to collect taxes.

Tax accounting rule setters should be concerned about avoiding misleading information about the companies' ability to pay taxes. They should set rules to protect the interests of government since the information asymmetry can represent an incentive to self-interest attempt of manager.

A set of mechanisms to avoid misleading information is related to accounting estimates. Estimation criteria about cost allocation on the timeline like depreciation cost can be defined by tax authorities instead of allowing managers to make the choice, since the decisions and estimates of managers about future benefits or return on investments may not be relevant to define past taxable income. Tax authorities can use their own estimate criteria as a mechanism to avoid misleading information from managers, which would estimate a short useful life of depreciable assets to reduce taxable income of the first years and postponing tax payments, for example.

When there is high uncertainty on recognition of expenses, the government uses to postpone recognition up to the cash payment moment. For example, if there is uncertainty on timing or amount of payments of a provision, the tax authority may require recognition of deductible expense on cash basis.

Tax authorities also adopt certain mechanisms in order to avoid or to incentive manager's actions. For example, they can prohibit the deduction of a penalty, accelerate the deduction of depreciation expense of a favored activity, or deduct a non-recognized expense.

Tax accounting is a minded system that is rule based and rigid and has very small space for judgment. As pointed by Fields et al. (2001), an obvious problem with a rigid accounting system is providing rules for all facts and circumstances. New situations arise regularly (e.g., debt/equity hybrids, securitizations) requiring that new accounting rules be devised.

Thus, to protect its interests, government attempts to set rules to avoid managers anticipating expenses and postponing incomes. It is nearly the opposite mechanism of conservatism used by financial accounting standard setters.

As there are mechanisms of protection of government interests that are different from the mechanisms used by financial accounting standard setters, the tax accounting information may have characteristics that should not be useful and transparent for investors and creditors.

BOOK-TAX DIFFERENCES

Accounting choices of financial accounting standard setters, government, and managers can make the reported income different from taxable income. The periodical difference of financial and tax income is called BTD. BTD contains a reconciliation of both income measures.

BTD can be temporary, e.g., a provision that is recognized for financial accounting purposes but it shouldn't be recognized at this moment for tax purposes, postponing its recognition. When this expense is paid, the expense can be recognized for tax purpose. A BTD may arise in the first moment and this difference is reverted in the second moment. Other differences are permanent, like a bad penalty that is definitely not deductible.

Different criteria can lead to a BTD. For example, a sale for future delivery can be recognized as revenue for tax purposes but may be recognized for financial reporting purposes only at the moment of delivery. Depreciation criteria can be defined by tax authorities, but financial accounting standards can require an estimate from the manager about the useful life of assets. Provisions can be deducted from taxable income on a cash basis but the expense must be recognized timely for financial reporting purposes.

There is also a BTD when a tax rule permits deduction of an expense that is not recognized for financial accounting reporting. For example, Brazil has a deduction that is calculated by the interest on ownership capital. So it is possible to deduct this interest for tax purposes, but it is a kind of distribution of dividends for financial accounting purposes.

Shackelford et al. (2011, p. 463) argue that the income reported in financial reports may differ from taxable income for at least three reasons:

1. There are explicit differences in the intent of the two reports. The objective of financial statements is to reduce information asymmetries through reliable and relevant disclosures. The objective of tax returns is to reduce asymmetries through information that reflects the economic and political objectives of revenue collection;

2. Financial accounting strives to record underlying economics of a transaction, while the tax system is designed to induce or reward particular behavior;
3. There are incentives to mislead both the audiences about ongoing operations.

The rules can differ from each other because the objectives are different. The objective of financial accounting is to provide information to investors and creditors to make decisions related to their capacity in providing capital to companies. They have to decide about investing or disinvesting. They have to decide whether to lend money to companies or not and that depends on whether the companies have a healthy financial situation or not. The appraisal of financial situation depends on the valuation of companies, that is based on making projections of cash flows. However, the objective of tax reporting is to provide information to collect taxes.

The concerns of financial accounting standard setters are different from that of tax rule setters because the problems are different. The problems of financial accounting standard setters are related to earnings management risks related to information asymmetry between investors and creditors and the manager. There is also an information asymmetry between minority shareholders and controlling shareholders. The tax authorities have another kind of problem, because they have to deal with problems related to asymmetry in information that should be caused by minimization of taxes.

In a review of tax research, Hanlon and Heitzman (2010, p. 128) point out that the evidence to date suggests that BTD provide information about current and future earnings (e.g., earnings persistence and future earnings growth) and potentially indicate pre-tax earnings management.

BOOK-TAX SIMILARITIES

Despite the reasons for the pointed differences, there are many reasons to have earnings being recognized as the same way to both audiences. There are several transactions, e.g., wages, where earnings have to be recognized in the same way to both sets of accounting rules.

The similarities between book and tax accounting also may be related to the degree of connection between tax rules and accounting practice.

Lamb, Nobes, and Roberts (1998) construct a method for assessing the degree of connection between tax rules and practices and financial reporting rules and practices in a country with five types of connection improved by Nobes and Schwencke (2006) with the inclusion of one more type of connection. Table 1 contains a description of the types of connection:

Lamb et al. (1998) and Nobes and Schwencke (2006) provide a cross-country approach that considers the differences and similarities between book and tax rules and following a financial reporting rule for tax purposes and vice-versa. It implies that practicing may lead to accounting choices that would improve the similarities between book and tax income.

Depending on its bargaining power, taxation rule setters can use financial accounting information for the interest of government. Financial accounting earnings recognition and measurement criteria can be convenient to taxation objective of reducing risk of opportunism. By imposing BTC, the economic interest of managers to report good performance can be useful for taxation rule setters because it works as a mechanism to avoid tax planning by shifting of periods.

Table 1. Cases of Linkage Between Tax and Financial Reporting.

Disconnection (Case I)	The different tax and financial reporting rules (or different options) are followed for different purposes[a]
Identify (Case II)	Identity between specific (or singular) tax and financial reporting rules
Accounting leads (Case III)	A financial reporting rule is followed for financial reporting purpose, and also for tax purpose. This is possible because of the absence of a sufficiently specific (or singular) tax rule
Accounting leads (but with reverse effect) (Case III†)	Financial reporting rules contain options or allow interpretations, some of which lead to lower or to the later profit than others do. This is a motivation for choosing these options so that they will then also be used for tax purpose, in the absence of a specific or singular tax rule
Tax leads (Case IV)	A tax rule or option is followed for tax purposes, and also for financial reporting purposes. This is possible because of the absence of a sufficiently specific (or singular) financial reporting rule
Tax dominates (Case V)	A tax rule or option is followed for tax and financial reporting purposes instead of a conflicting financial reporting principle

[a]Such disconnection will be recognized when distinct, independent, and detailed tax and financial reporting operational rules exist. Even if measurement outcomes are essentially the same, the particular arena may still be characterized as Case I; the independence and completeness of the sets of rules "disconnect" tax and accounting in an operational sense.
Source: Nobes and Schwencke (2006).

Income taxation would be on cash basis, but the recognition of revenues in accrual basis used in financial accounting can be interesting for tax purposes since it should avoid some kind of manipulation of operations that would have a cash impact but not accrual impact. For example, if a company negotiates with its client to postpone receipt of some revenues to avoid payment of taxes on a cash basis, it should not have an effect on accrual basis. At the same time, recognition of expenses in accrual basis should avoid undue deduction of assets not consumed. Expenses can be postponed in relation to cash method when there is, e.g., an expense paid in anticipation. There is a cash payment at first time and the expense being recognized later.

Financial accounting standard setters would use tax accounting criteria to protect the interests of investors and creditors (increasing BTC) because it works as a mechanism of conservatism, avoiding earnings management. By the point of view of financial accounting there are incentives related to tax minimization that can reduce earnings management practices because the incentive is related to reduction of taxable income. A postponement of revenue avoids earnings management related to increasing income reported to investors and creditors. It should be an interesting mechanism when there is a large risk of information manipulation.

If managers use depreciation rates for tax purposes, e.g., it can be used by financial accounting standard setters to reduce earnings management risk because there is a unique criterion to recognize a depreciation expense in a period.

In countries with higher BTC, if managers use depreciation rates for tax purposes, e.g., it would also be used in financial reporting. The result is that the freedom to manipulate earnings is reduced.

Hanlon, Laplante, and Shevlin (2005) consider that several recent events have led to the suggestion that the calculation of taxable income be conformed to or more closely tied to financial accounting income. The recent accounting scandals, such as those involving Enron, WorldCom, Adelphia, and Qwest, in which firms overstated corporate income, also attracted attention to the large gap between book income and taxable income.

Economic incentives related to tax minimization can reduce the risk of earnings management practice. Tax minimization can occur in several ways, including the manipulation of accounting values. A reduction of tax payments can increase net income and improve cash flows. If a manager has economic interests on tax minimization, he would manage accounting earnings not just for tax purposes. If there is imposed BTC, the manager would manage financial accounting earnings to report a lower BTD to not attract attention to tax minimization actions. An extended discussion about mandatory BTC is provided in the next section.

Frank et al. (2009) document a strong and positive relationship between financial and tax reporting aggressiveness with a sample of firms that engaged in tax shelter activity. These results suggest that financial accounting standards and tax law allow firms to manage book income upward and taxable income downward in the same reporting period because there are insufficient costs to offset financial and tax reporting incentives. These results represent evidence that firms do not always trade-off financial and tax reporting but do report higher book income to investors and lower taxable income to the tax authorities at the same time.

A BTC may imply in a reduction in the level of earnings management and hence an increasing transparency in financial reporting. However, due to the economic incentives related to tax minimization, BTC can produce less transparent information on financial reporting.

FACTORS THAT INFLUENCE THE RELATIONSHIP BETWEEN TAX AND FINANCIAL ACCOUNTING INFORMATION

Interests of managers, government, and investors and creditors can explain the existence of differences and similarities between tax and financial accounting information. To this effect, some factors help to explain the differences of economic interests that affect the book-tax relation. Governance, capital structure, economic development, International Financial Reporting Standards (IFRS) adoption, and mandatory BTC are some of these factors.

Governance problems of companies with lower ownership concentration are related to the conflicting relation of shareholders and managers. Since capital market pressures managers for economic performance as higher as the volume of shares traded, ownership concentration is a factor that influences the relationship between financial and tax reporting.

Managers of companies with a lower ownership concentration attempt to manage earnings to report income as a proxy of companies' performance. Companies with lower ownership concentration are frequently oriented to minority investor, which is frequently interested in dividend distribution and market value of shares.

Companies with higher ownership concentration have different incentives related to accounting choices by managers. They have a controlling shareholder or a little group of shareholders that control the company, and different problems of governance arise. Managers can be an agent of the shareholders or the controlling shareholder themselves. They are likely to persecute the interests of controlling shareholders instead of minority investors' interests. For that reason, financial accounting standard setters use to be concerned about protection of interests of minority investors against the opportunism of controlling shareholders.

As the ownership concentration is higher, the controlling shareholder can use their bargaining power to expropriate minority shareholders. It means that financial accounting information that is the basis for dividend distribution can be manipulated to favor controlling shareholders.

Scholes et al. (2005) suggest that large shareholders who closely held firms have an incentive to monitor managers' tax-saving activities. These firms are more likely to choose tax-saving opportunities involving permanent BTD even if these opportunities reduce accounting income.

Usually, managers of higher ownership concentration companies are more concerned about companies' value than payment of dividends in the short term. As taxable income is usually based on adjusted recognized earnings, managers of higher ownership concentration companies can make choices conforming earnings to tax legislation and reduce tax payments.

Klassen (1997) arguments that financial reporting is an important non-tax consideration since many managers may wish the company to appear very profitable to reflect appropriately firm value or managerial performance, or to facilitate the issuance of new debt or equity securities. But at the same time, these managers may not wish the company to appear as profitable when preparing tax returns. The tension between financial and tax reporting is pervasive because many actions that increase income for one reporting purpose will increase income for the other as well and managers should have to trade-off between financial and tax reporting.

Zeng (2011) examines how ownership concentration affects firms' effective tax rates in China and finds that firms' effective tax rate is negatively associated with the concentration of share ownership. This result suggests that firms with higher ownership concentration are more concerned with tax reporting.

The presence of high ownership concentration in financial markets is frequently associated with weak investor protection. If economic system and financial markets do not provide mechanisms to protect the economic interests of minority investors, financial accounting information can be influenced by controlling shareholders' interests.

Van Tendeloo and Vanstraelen (2005) examine if voluntary adoption of IFRS is associated with lower earnings management in Germany, and the results suggest that IFRS adopters do not present different earnings management behavior compared to companies under German GAAP. These results suggest that high quality standards may not be sufficient in countries with weak investor protection rights and weak corporate governance system.

Companies with higher ownership concentration tend to have a more tax planning aggressiveness because minimization of tax payments by reduction of reported income avoids dividend distribution to minority shareholders and increases future income and future value of companies.

Klassen (1997) uses inside ownership concentration as a proxy of reduced capital market pressure. He finds that firms with larger inside ownership concentration were found, on average, to take larger losses or smaller gains when they were highly taxable. The results imply that ownership structure produces greater differences in the incentive to increase financial reporting income when there is a tax cost to income acceleration. In the absence of the tax cost, the inside ownership concentration of the firm is less influential on the behavior of managers.

Capital structure can influence financial and tax accounting relationship since the proportion of debt-financed influences tax incentives on financial accounting information. Banks have more access to managerial information than a minority investor since they usually can have more information provided directly by managers. Thus, managers can be more concerned about management of earnings for tax purposes even with no BTC.

If the financial market is sufficiently developed in a country, a company will have higher market pressure to produce relevant information to investors. Some countries have special listings on their stock exchange, e.g., Germany and Brazil. Companies within the listing have an additional attraction because of imposing governance mechanisms. If financial market is not sufficiently developed, managers have lower market pressure and can turn their choices to tax minimization, which can improve the value of the company since expenses and payments of tax are reduced.

Clements, Neill, and Stovall (2010) examine the influence of cultural diversity and country size on the IFRS adoption decision of 61 countries. They are unable to document any cultural influences on the decision, but IFRS adoption decision is significantly related to the size of the country. This result is consistent with the notion that larger countries have a well-established set of financial accounting and reporting standards already in place, and therefore would be reluctant to incur the costs of changing to an international set of standards.

Financial markets, legislation, and external monitoring are improved in developed countries. In consequence, more transparency is required and provided by companies as well. Tax incentives may not be prevalent over financial market incentives, so earnings should be more informative. The country can reduce the risk of evasion because the monitoring of large companies is more efficient.

Guenther and Young (2000) find that because of differences in legal systems and the demand for accounting information, differences in the legal protection for external shareholders, and differences in the degree of tax conformity, the United Kingdom and the United States are more closely related to underlying economic activity than are accounting earnings in France and Germany. Gaio (2010) tests an aggregate earnings quality measure based on seven earnings attributes (accruals quality, persistence, predictability, smoothness, value relevance, timeliness, and conservatism). The results indicate that firm and industry characteristics today explain much more of the variation in earnings quality rankings than country characteristics.

In many countries, IFRS adoption is a factor that improves transparency since standards are investor-oriented and its implantation requires the break of the BTC. The influence of taxation on earnings is lower.

Soderstrom and Sun (2007) review the literature about IFRS adoption and accounting quality and conclude that cross-country differences in accounting quality are likely to remain following IFRS adoption because accounting quality is a function of the overall institutional setting of firms, including the legal and political system of the country in which the firms reside.

Liu, Yao, Hu, and Liu (2011) examine the impact of IFRS on accounting quality in China. They find that accounting quality improved with decreased earnings management and increased value relevance since 2007. It is evident that IFRS can be relevant to markets that are still disciplined mainly by regulators rather than by market mechanisms.

Tan, Wang, and Welker (2011) find that mandatory IFRS adoption improves foreign analysts' forecast accuracy and the change increases with the distance between local GAAP and IFRS.

Landsman, Maydew, and Thornock (2012) examine whether the information content of earnings announcements increases in countries following mandatory IFRS adoption. They find that there are three mechanisms through which IFRS adoption increases information content: reducing reporting lag, increasing analyst following, and increasing foreign investment. It means that the monitoring activity is relevant to increasing transparency.

IFRS is usually adopted by countries at the same time of breaking of mandatory BTC, when it is the case. However, the influence of tax accounting on financial reporting is not over with IFRS adoption since interests related to tax minimization still remain. Taxation can have influence on financial accounting information even with no mandatory BTC.

If financial market pressure is lower, there is a larger space for enforcement power of tax authorities to determine rules for financial accounting reporting purposes, since it should represent a mechanism to prevent risk of evasion.

On mandatory BTC, investors can be aware about tax legislation and make decisions with financial accounting information driven by tax rules and search other sources of information.

With BTC, financial accounting reporting follows tax accounting rules. It is a particular situation because taxation rules are used for financial accounting purposes, which induces managers to produce financial accounting reporting following tax incentives or trade-off to financial market incentives and pay higher taxes. As a result, financial accounting information can be more affected by tax incentives.

This means that some revenues can be postponed and some expenses can be anticipated. Expenses that are not deductible temporarily may not be recognized and some revenues that are not taxable temporarily may not be recognized at the first moment.

As the managers have to follow financial accounting information to calculate income tax, managers can be oriented to recognize their earnings for financial purposes to conform with tax rules and save money for tax purposes. So, it avoids the manager's tendency to anticipate revenues and postpone expenses.

In countries with BTC, managers know that investors and creditors are aware about legislation that imposes BTC and search information with other sources and understand information with the tax bias. In certain circumstances, financial accounting standard setters can make use of this mechanism to reduce earnings management ability. There is a long discussion about financial accounting standards to have more BTC to avoid earnings management, because it goes by the opposite way of economic incentives.

Hanlon and Maydew (2009) present the argument of proponents of BTC that because managers attempt to maximize financial accounting income and minimize taxable income and are "unconstrained" by the rules in the other system (i.e., the tax and book rules are not conformed), they can act opportunistically, thereby reporting lower income to the tax authorities and also misleading shareholders. By requiring book-tax conformity, they contend that firms will be forced to trade off reporting high earnings numbers to shareholders and reporting low earnings to the taxing authority, resulting in improved financial reporting and less tax avoidance. Reduced compliance costs and easier auditing have also been cited as potential benefits of BTC.

Atwood, Drake, and Myers (2010) present the arguments of proponents and opponents of increasing BTC. According to proponents, increasing required BTC will limit opportunistic management behaviors, allowing tax authorities to act as additional monitors of reported profits, and allow shareholders to observe taxes paid, making the overall economic performance of firms more transparent. According to opponents, if required BTC is increased, tax policymakers will interfere in the standard-setting process, eroding the quality of earnings reported to investors.

Hanlon et al. (2005) argue that a way to reduce accounting scandals and aggressive tax shelters is to reduce the gap between the calculation of book and taxable income. When a wide divergence between a high financial accounting income and a low taxable income exist, suspicions often arise that one or possibly both of the measures have been reported in an opportunistic way. However, they find results that suggest that if the book income measure is conformed to taxable income and based on tax rules, there is an information loss of financial reporting.

Hanlon, Maydew, and Shevlin (2008) find that increasing BTC results in earnings that are less informative, examining firms forced to change from the cash method to accrual method for tax purposes.

Calegari (2000) finds that firms adjust debt ratios and discretionary accruals with relatively high BTC to achieve tax planning goals and use discretionary accruals with relatively low BTC to accomplish financial reporting objectives. Even countries with no imposed BTC can present some degree of BTC.

Guenther, Maydew, and Nutter (1997) find that firms forced to switch from cash to accrual method have a little trade-off between tax planning and reporting goal before. However, after the switch, the recognition criteria of book and tax accounting became more alike.

However, Atwood et al. (2010) examine the level of required BTC affects earnings persistence and the association between earnings and future cash flows. They find that earnings have lower persistence and a lower association with future cash flows when conformity is higher. Evidence suggests that BTC is an important determinant of the properties of accounting earnings, and that BTC should be considered in.the design of cross-country studies.

By documenting the information content of each income measure, Hanlon et al. (2005) quantify the loss in information to investors if the two income measures are constrained to be the same. The tests indicate significantly greater explanatory power for book income. An incremental information content test indicates that both income measures have significant incremental explanatory power. They conclude that conforming the two measures at a minimum results in the loss of incremental explanatory power, and if book income is conformed to the tax rules, a 50 percent loss in the explanatory power of earnings (estimated as the reduction in R^2 value of a regression of stock returns on earnings).

BTC AND QUALITY OF INFORMATION

Since tax accounting influences financial reporting, the quality of financial information could be related to the level of BTC as a level indicator of this influence.

The literature uses some proxies for earnings quality instead of defining "quality" because it is contingent on the decision content. Researchers have used various measures as indications of "earnings quality" including persistence, accruals, smoothness, timeliness, loss avoidance, and investor responsiveness (Dechow, Ge, & Schrand 2010).

Dechow et al. (2010) identify two broad streams of research on persistence. The first stream is motivated by an assumption that more persistent earnings will yield better inputs to equity valuation models, and hence a more persistent earnings number is of higher quality than a less persistent earnings number. A second stream of research attempts to address the broader issue of whether earnings decision is useful in that it improves equity valuation outcomes. An important issue in this literature is the benchmark used to evaluate the equity market outcomes.

Financial reporting of companies with higher BTC is likely to have lower persistence since tax planning incentives prevail. Investors and creditors are aware about BTC and expect from managers' tax planning actions. Atwood et al. (2010) find that earnings have lower persistence and a lower association with future cash flows when BTC is higher.

Companies with lower BTC are likely to have higher persistence. The distribution of accruals over the time is better with the prevalence of investor-oriented financial accounting standards.

Hung and Subramanyam (2007) examine IFRS adoption by Germany and find that the variability of book value and income are significantly higher under IAS than under the local German GAAP. The information is more value relevant and persistent under International Accounting Standards (IAS). It means that the quality of information is higher with a financial accounting standards oriented to provide information to investors and creditors. German GAAP emphasizes a "prudent" approach to asset valuation and liability recognition to facilitate contracting among stakeholders and is driven by tax-book conformity considerations.

Earnings management is frequently measured with regressions of accruals. According to Dechow et al. (2010), commonly used models to estimate normal levels of accruals are Jones (1991) model, modified Jones model (Dechow, Sloan, & Sweeney 1995), performance matched (Dechow & Dichev, 2002; Kothari, Leone, & Wasley, 2005), approach and discretionary estimation errors (Francis, LaFond, Olsson, & Schipper, 2005). Residuals from accrual models represent management discretion or estimation errors, both of which reduce decision usefulness (Dechow et al., 2010).

Companies with higher BTC are likely to have lower levels of discretionary accruals because managers have restrictions to manage earnings for reporting purposes as it would affect taxable income. Companies with lower BTC are likely to have higher levels of discretionary accruals. Since the requirements of tax authorities have lower impact on financial reporting, managers have more discretionary power to manage earnings for financial reporting purposes.

Dechow et al. (2010) remind that a basic tenet of an accrual-based earnings system is that earnings smooth cash payments and receipts, making earnings more informative about performance than cash flows. Hence, smoothing cash flows can improve earnings informativeness. However, managers attempting to smooth permanent changes in cash flows will lead to a less timely and less informative earnings number.

Companies with higher BTC are likely to have lower levels of smoothness because financial accounting earnings are influenced by tax planning incentives. Earnings management with the goals of reducing taxable income can reduce the level of smoothness. Companies with lower BTC are likely to have higher levels of smoothness because investor-oriented financial reporting standards improve allocation of earnings at the time.

TLR is demanded to combat management's natural optimism. TLR represents high-quality earnings (Dechow et al., 2010). TLR is frequently referred to as a proxy of conservatism. The most frequently used measure of TLR has been the regression from Basu (1997). Companies with higher BTC are likely to have lower TLR because tax planning strategies attempt to postpone the recognition of expenses. Companies with lower BTC are likely to have higher TLR because financial accounting standards have several mechanisms, e.g., impairment of assets, to avoid postponing expenses.

Dechow et al. (2010) retrieve studies that examine an earnings response coefficient (ERC) as a measure of investor responsiveness to earnings. The studies explicitly state (or at least strongly imply) that investor responsiveness to earnings is a direct proxy for earnings quality (or for earnings informativeness). Companies with higher BTC are likely to have a lower ERC because earnings are oriented to tax conformity that are not necessarily oriented to reflect economic movements that affect economic performance of companies. Companies with lower BTC are likely to have a higher ERC because financial accounting standards are more oriented to reflect economic movements.

Barth, Landsman, and Lang (2008) examine whether application of IAS is associated with higher accounting quality. They find evidence that the use of IAS by firms from 21 countries is associated with less earnings management, more TLR, and greater value relevance.

EMPIRICAL IMPLICATIONS

This chapter discusses the influence of tax accounting on transparency and some points should be highlighted by the point of view of empirical implications. There are empirical research and practical implications.

Despite several papers concerned with transparency of financial reporting do not consider the tax dimension, tax accounting considerations should have an impact on transparency research. Researchers would consider tax implications in designing quantitative researches involving transparency, even as a control variable. Qualitative research on transparency also would have to be concerned about tax accounting considerations.

As discussed before, as managers can be aggressive of tax planning and aggressive of earnings management at the same time, there may not exist a trade-off between book and tax reporting, producing lower levels of BTD. However, a trade-off can exist with higher levels of BTC. Thus, quantitative studies involving persistence, discretionary accruals, ERC, TLR, and other measures of informativeness should consider variables related to BTC. If the managers can trade-off to tax interests in producing information to investors and creditors, the quality of information is likely to decrease. Thus, it is relevant that the research involving accounting choices and earnings management be concerned about the presence of a trade-off for tax interests that would influence their results.

BTC results from a set of factors and may influence in some extent the quality of financial information. Empirical research involving information quality has to deal with the influence of BTC even if it is not mandatory.

As discussed previously, many factors that may be present in economic environment can drive the existence of a BTC. Culture, politics, economic development, financial market strength, ownership concentration, and other factors influence the level of BTC, whether mandatory or not.

Companies can present some level of BTC even in a country with no mandatory BTC, given all these factors and the interaction with the economic interest of managers, controlling shareholders, minority investors, creditors, and tax authorities. If some level of BTC can exist, taxation can influence on financial reporting information quality because the interests involving tax planning can interfere the earnings and related information to some extent.

A measure of BTC can be used or developed in quantitative studies involving informativeness measurement. Atwood et al. (2010) developed cross-country measures of BTC.

Research involving IFRS adoption has to consider the effects of a break of the BTC. Countries that have adopted IFRS have to break mandatory BTC. It does not mean that BTC is extinguished because there are factors that lead companies to keep some level of BTC.

The research about BTD would deal with differences that would exist with no BTC but are hidden in financial reporting income due to tax planning strategies. Since managers can modify earnings not to attract attention to the BTD, the financial accounting information can be distorted by tax planning incentives. Thus, BTD can contain not all differences resulting from tax planning strategies.

The concepts and arguments presented in this chapter have practical implications as well. The first practical implication is that standard setters have to be concerned about the influence of BTC on the quality of financial reporting information. Accounting for income tax cannot be able to deal with BTC since the influence of taxation on financial information does not involve only BTD. Managers can use tax accounting rules as financial accounting practice, and it does not result in a BTD and it is not captured by accounting for income tax, since there is no permanent or temporary difference. The difference will be detected only in accruals of financial accounting information. As a result, financial accounting standard setters have to deal with the influence of tax considerations on subjects that may deteriorate information quality.

The second implication is that investors and creditors have to consider a number of factors and the level of BTC to make decisions using financial accounting information. If there is a higher level of BTC, investors and creditors must be aware of the influence of taxation on information quality. Recognition of provisions and impairments are examples of issues that investors and creditors must be aware of because the related results are usually not deductible before cash payments and cannot be recognized for financial reporting purposes as well.

Choices resulting from measurement processes can be even more difficult to identify because in most cases it is difficult to adjust the value of assets and liabilities with external information. Assets and liabilities that would be measured with fair value measurements can be biased by managers for tax purposes in a BTC environment. Earnings that are allocated along the time can be modified by managers to conform to tax and produce an information that does not match to the economic reality. Thus, there would be infinite examples that would be given that investors and creditors would be aware of the information that they receive that would be biased by an interest of tax planning purposes.

Investors and creditors have to be aware of IFRS adoption followed by breaking of mandatory BTC because managers can keep making accounting choices for tax purposes on financial reporting depending on the found factors in a country. Thus, the information quality cannot be significantly improved with the IFRS adoption for companies with high ownership concentration, for example.

On the other side, BTC can reduce informational risk by reducing the natural "optimism" of managers that would imply on earnings management, improving financial information quality.

CONCLUDING REMARKS

The chapter deals with the relation between transparency and tax reporting. This relation is determined by the choices of managers for tax and financial reporting accounting purposes and the mechanisms of protection of investors and tax authorities against opportunism. In turn, the level of BTC that may be contained in financial reporting is influenced by a wide range of factors. BTC has a direct influence on transparency since the information may contain some level of manipulation for tax planning purposes.

Tax accounting may reduce transparency because economic incentives related to tax minimization can reduce earnings informativeness. It can be mostly observed in countries with mandatory BTC, because it imposes on the manager a trade-off between financial market incentives or pays higher taxes. If there is a prevalence of economic incentives related to tax minimization, BTC may affect the financial reporting accounting and therefore the informativeness of earnings.

Tax accounting may reduce transparency even with no mandatory BTC because managers may have interests on tax minimization and make choices on financial accounting earnings to not attract attention to the size of the BTD.

On the other side, economic incentives related to tax minimization can improve transparency as it should reduce earnings management practice.

These theoretical propositions have research implications. Research involving information quality would have to deal with the influence of BTC and BTD that would exist with no BTC, but are hidden in financial reporting income due to tax planning strategies.

The propositions lead to practical implications as well. Financial accounting standard setters have to be concerned about the influence of BTC on the quality of financial reporting information, and investors and creditors have to consider a number of factors and the level of BTC to make decisions using financial accounting information.

ACKNOWLEDGMENTS

The author gratefully acknowledges the comments of the editors J. Jay Choi and Heibatollah Sami and the support of Fundação de Amparo à Pesquisa do Estado de São Paulo (Fapesp), University of São Paulo, and University of Sydney.

REFERENCES

Atwood, T. J., Drake, M. S., & Myers, L. (2010). Book-tax conformity, earnings persistence and the association between earnings and future cash flows. *Journal of Accounting and Economics*, *50*, 111–125.

Barth, M. E., Landsman, W. R., & Lang, M. H. (2008). International Accounting Standards and accounting quality. *Journal of Accounting Research*, *46*(3), 467–498.

Basu, S. (1997). The conservatism principle and the asymmetric timeliness of earnings. *Journal of Accounting and Economics*, *24*, 3–37.

Bushman, R. M., & Piotroski, J. D. (2006). Financial reporting incentives for conservative accounting: The influence of legal and political institutions. *Journal of Accounting and Economics*, *42*, 107–148.

Bushman, R. M., Piotroski, J. D., & Smith, A. J. (2004). What determines corporate transparency? *Journal of Accounting Research*, *42*(2).

Calegari, M. J. (2000). The effect of tax accounting rules on capital structure and discretionary accruals. *Journal of Accounting and Economics*, *30*, 1–31.

Clements, C. E., Neill, J. D., & Stovall, O. S. (2010). Cultural diversity, country size, and the IFRS adoption decision. *Journal of Applied Business Research*, *26*(2), 115.

Dechow, P., Ge, W., & Schrand, C. (2010). Understanding earnings quality: A review of the proxies, their determinants and their consequences. *Journal of Accounting and Economics*, *50*, 344–401.

Dechow, P. M., & Dichev, I. (2002). The quality of accruals and earnings: The role of accrual estimation errors. *The Accounting Review*, *77*(Suppl), 35–59.

Dechow, P. M., Kothari, S. P., & Watts, R. L. (1998). The relation between earnings and cash flows. *Journal of Accounting and Economics*, *25*, 133–168.

Dechow, P., Sloan, R., & Sweeney, A. (1995). Detecting earnings management. *The Accounting Review*, *70*, 193–225.

Fields, T. D., Lys, T. Z., & Vincent, L. (2001). Empirical research on accounting. *Journal of Accounting and Economics*, *31*, 255–307.

Francis, J., LaFond, R., Olsson, P., & Schipper, K. (2005). The market pricing of accruals quality. *Journal of Accounting and Economics*, *39*, 295–327.

Frank, M. M., Lynch, L. J., & Rego, S. O. (2009). Tax reporting aggressiveness and its relation to aggressive financial reporting. *The Accounting Review*, *84*(2), 467–496.

Gaio, C. (2010). The relative importance of firm and country characteristics for earnings quality around the world. *European Accounting Review*, *19*(4), 693–738.

Guenther, D. A., Maydew, E. L., & Nutter, S. E. (1997). Financial reporting, tax costs, and BTC. *Journal of Accounting and Economics*, *23*, 225–248.

Guenther, D. A., & Young, D. (2000). The association between financial accounting measures and real economic activity: A multinational study. *Journal of Accounting and Economics*, *29*, 53–72.

Hanlon, M., & Heitzman, S. (2010). A review of tax research. *Journal of Accounting and Economics*, *50*, 127–178.

Hanlon, M., Laplante, S. K., & Shevlin, T. (2005). Evidence for the possible information loss of conforming book income and taxable income. *Journal of Law and Economics*, *XLVIII*, 407–442.

Hanlon, M., & Maydew, E. L. (2009). BTC: Implications for multinational firms. *National Tax Journal*, *LXII*(1), 127–153.

Hanlon, M., Maydew, E. L., & Shevlin, T. (2008). An unintended consequence of book-tax-conformity: A loss of earnings informativeness. *Journal of Accounting and Economics*, *46*, 294–311.

Healy, P. M., & Wahlen, J. M. (1999). A review of the earnings management literature and its implications for standard setting. *Accounting Horizons*, *13*(4), 365–383.

Hung, M., & Subramanyam, K. R. (2007). Financial statement effects of adopting International Accounting Standards: The case of Germany. *Review of Accounting Studies*, *12*, 623–657.

Jones, J. J. (1991). Earnings management during import relief investigations. *Journal of Accounting Research*, *29*(2), 193–228.

Klassen, K. J. (1997). The impact of inside ownership concentration on the trade-off between financial and tax reporting. *The Accounting Review*, *72*(3), 455–474.

Kothari, S. P., Leone, A. J., & Wasley, C. E. (2005). Performance matched discretionary accrual measures. *Journal of Accounting & Economics*, *39*(1), 163–197.

LaFond, R., & Watts, R. L. (2008). The information role of conservatism. *The Accounting Review*, *83*(2), 447–478.

Lamb, M., Nobes, C., & Roberts, A. (1998). International variations in the connections between tax and financial report. *Accounting and Business Research*, *28*(3), 173–188.

Landsman, W. R., Maydew, E. L., & Thornock, J. R. (2012). The information content of annual earnings announcements and mandatory adoption of IFRS. *Journal of Accounting and Economics*, *53*, 34–54.

Liu, C., Yao, L. J., Hu, N., & Liu, L. (2011). The impact of IFRS on accounting quality in a regulated market: An empirical study of China. *Journal of Accounting, Auditing and Finance*, *26*(4), 659–676.

Nobes, C., & Schwencke, H. R. (2006). Modelling the links between tax and financial reporting: A longitudinal examination of Norway over 30 years up to IFRS adoption. *European Accounting Review*, *15*(1), 63–87.

Scholes, M. S., Wolfson, M. A., Erickson, M., Maydew, E. L., & Shevlin, T. (2002). *Taxes and business strategy: A planning approach* (2nd ed.). Upper Saddle River, NJ: Prentice Hall.

Shackelford, D., Slemrod, J., & Sallee, J. (2011). Financial reporting, tax, and real decisions: Toward a unifying framework. *International Tax and Public Finance*, *18*(4), 461–494.

Soderstrom, N. S., & Sun, K. J. (2007). IFRS adoption and accounting quality: A review. *European Accounting Review*, *16*(4), 675–702.

Tan, H., Wang, S., & Welker, M. (2011). Analyst following and forecast accuracy after mandated IFRS adoptions. *Journal of Accounting Research*, *49*(5), 1307–1357.

Van Tendeloo, B., & Vanstraelen, A. (2005). Earnings management under German GAAP versus IFRS. *European Accounting Review*, *14*(1), 155–180.

Zeng, T. (2011). Ownership concentration, state ownership, and effective tax rates: Evidence from China's listed firms. *Accounting Perspectives*, *9*(4), 271–289.

PART III
GOVERNANCE, OPERATIONS AND TRANSPARENCY

BOARD TRANSPARENCY, CEO MONITORING AND FIRMS' FINANCIAL PERFORMANCE

Aloy Soppe, Niels van Zijl and Auke de Bos

ABSTRACT

This international empirical study analyses the relation between board transparency, CEO monitoring policy and financial performance.

Keywords: Corporate governance; board transparency; CEO monitoring; stock ownership; firms' financial performance

JEL classification: G32

INTRODUCTION

The urgent need for transparent accounting information and 'good' corporate governance has become painfully apparent following the major financial scandals at the beginning of the twenty-first century.[1] There is a general 'textbook' agreement that information asymmetry is the driving theoretical factor behind the demand for disclosure of information in the modern capital market economy. In that line of thinking, the inherent agency costs of

Transparency and Governance in a Global World
International Finance Review, Volume 13, 99–125

ISSN: 1569-3767/doi:10.1108/S1569-3767(2012)0000013007

insufficiently disclosed markets are the main cause of an increase in capital costs, hence decreasing financial performance. More generally speaking, information asymmetry and moral hazard are endangering the informational efficiency of the capital markets. The problem with this line of argument is that it invokes just as many new questions as it answers. The broad research field on disclosure is categorized into four major topics by Healy and Palepu (2001). First, there are the questions concerning the regulations of disclosure. Why is there a need for regulation of disclosure and which types of disclosures should be regulated? Second, there are the questions on the effectiveness of auditors and intermediaries. Do they enhance the credibility of financial statements? The third group of questions deals with the disclosure decisions of managers. What factors affect management disclosure choices? Lastly, Healy and Palepu (2001) distinguish the capital market consequences of disclosure. How do investors respond? In this chapter, we only deal with this last question by relating the level of board transparency and the level of CEO monitoring to financial performance. By implementing a capital market approach, we strive to answer the question of whether a 'good' corporate governance policy is recognized by the market and rewarded with higher financial performance.

This chapter focuses on one aspect of corporate transparency called *board transparency*. At company, country and sector level, the chapter analyses whether the general Anglo-Saxon governance model, with its highly competitive and high transparency board standards, actually increases a firm's value. 'Good governance' is interpreted as a company with highly transparent (board and stock) ownership information, together with a clear and published set of corporate governance principles and policies. In this research, CEO monitoring signifies extensive public board information with independent audit and remuneration procedures. Theoretically, it is expected that companies with strongly monitored CEOs have lower agency costs and hence lower costs of capital and better financial performance. In order to conclude on the financial performance of these types of basic corporate governance attributes, we apply the Fama and French (1993) and Carhart (1997) capital market model. This model is used as a robust and well-tested financial benchmark with which to conclude on the performance of governance attributes.

The next section deals first with the theoretical background of corporate transparency and disclosure of governance information in relation to financial firm performance. Concepts such as information asymmetry, 'good governance', and their theoretical implications will be discussed. Then, the dataset is described extensively and several descriptive statistics of the data are provided. This section also explains the choice of the four-factor model as the framework for measuring financial performance. Thereafter, we present the empirical results and all their interpretations. The last section summarizes and concludes.

THE THEORETICAL BACKGROUND OF CORPORATE GOVERNANCE TRANSPARENCY, MONITORING POWER AND FIRM PERFORMANCE

Corporate transparency, as a concept, is described extensively in Bushman, Piotroski, and Smith (2004). They define it generally as 'the availability of firm specific information to those outside publicly traded firms'. Then, a specific distinction is made between three components of corporate transparency. The first component is called *corporate reporting* and includes disclosure intensity, financial disclosures, governance disclosures, accounting principles, timelines of disclosures, and the credibility of disclosures. The second component is called *private information acquisition and communication*, and concerns the communication with external financial analysts and institutional investors. The third component distinguished is *information dissemination*, representing media penetration of the company in general. Bushman et al.'s research implemented this entire corporate transparency concept empirically and it was concluded that the governance transparency factor is primarily dependent on a country's legal/judicial regime, whereas financial transparency is primarily related to political economy.

Corporate ownership is very much dispersed in the 27 wealthiest economies in the world. La Porta et al. (1999) found that except in economies with very good shareholder protection, relatively few of these firms are widely owned, in contrast with the well-known Berle and Means (1932) image of ownership. Based on data collected between 1993 and 1997, they found that large- and medium-sized firms are controlled either by families or the state. The transparency of the governance systems also varies widely and can be classified into two types of disclosure: mandatory and voluntary. The mandatory type of disclosure depends first on the country in which a firm is located.

Easterbrook and Fischel (1991) extensively discussed the need for and importance of the legal structure of the business environment. The 'lemon problem'[2] in particular, as argued by the seminal paper of Akerlof (1970), is the crux of the economic argument. This Akerlof paper states that a market needs strong legal protection against low quality products ('lemons') because of moral hazard and adverse selection. The problem in a non-protected market economy is that suppliers tend to offer 'lemons' at regular (higher) market prices, undermining the informational efficiency of the market. Voluntary disclosure goes beyond the minimal legal requirements. Companies choose to disclose additional information in order to be more transparent to outsiders and this is usually part of a good investor relations policy by the company.

Our study does not distinguish between mandatory (legal) and voluntary transparency, but does differentiate between countries based on common law and on civil law. The focus, however, is on the examination of a firm's simultaneous choice of disclosure quality and corporate governance structure in relation to financial performance. The sustainability data, as applied in this chapter, measures the level of governance disclosure in 25 different countries and hence in many different legal and political regimes. In order to contribute to the general economic question of the capital market performance of governance transparency, and rather than looking at the reasons behind disclosure, we focus primarily on sectoral and regional distribution, sign and the magnitude of the relationship along with the robustness of the model.

TRANSPARENCY AND FINANCIAL PERFORMANCE

From a theoretical perspective, it was Diamond and Verrecchia (1991) that first argued convincingly that revealing public information to reduce information asymmetry can reduce a firm's cost of capital, the major reason being that disclosure of information reduces information asymmetries and therefore attracts increased demand from large investors. This line of argument is what Healy and Palepu (2001) called 'increased information intermediation'. Bhushan (1989a, 1989b) and Lang and Lundholm (1996) argued that voluntary disclosure lowers the cost of information acquisition for analysts and hence increases their supply of information. Expanded disclosure enables financial analysts to create valuable new information such as superior forecasts, thereby increasing demand for their services.

There are more economic reasons to hypothesize the value-increasing influence of financial disclosure through a lower capital cost. For example, increased disclosure reduces the estimation risk regarding the distributions of returns (e.g. Clarkson et al., 1996). Vander Bauwhede and Willekens

(2008) found for European Union countries that the level of disclosure is lower for companies with a higher ownership concentration and higher for companies in common law countries. Core (2001) presented a review of the empirical disclosure literature and discussed the relation between disclosure quality, disclosure credibility and management incentives. Yet another similar empirical result is that the level of corporate transparency is highly dependent on the legal regime of the home country (Healy & Palepu, 2001).

An alternative explanation for firms disclosing information is that it is the 'socially responsible thing to do' (Gelb & Strawser, 2001). Based on a rating of the Council of Economic Priorities as proxies for the degree of social responsibility, they found a positive relationship between the level of disclosure and corporate social responsive activities. Once again, we are not pursuing the 'why' of the disclosure, but merely looking at the influence of either mandatory or voluntary corporate governance disclosure on the financial performance of the company itself. It is essential to know that there are good a priori theoretical reasons for assuming a positive relation between corporate transparency and financial performance. This chapter therefore tests the following hypothesis.

> **H1**. Companies with highly transparent governance structures show better financial performance than companies with poor transparency on governance.

CEO MONITORING AND FINANCIAL PERFORMANCE

Another issue addressed in this chapter is the influence of CEO monitoring on firm performance. International empirical studies show that better legal protection for investors is associated with a higher stock market valuation (e.g. La Porta et al., 2002). Based on a dataset of 494 companies from 24 countries, scored in the year 2000, Durnev and Kim (2005) found that (i) firms with better investment opportunities, higher concentration of ownership and greater needs for external financing practice better governance, (ii) firms that practice better governance are valued higher, and (iii) that these relations are stronger in weaker regimes. They argued that ownership concentration matters because 'one does not steal from oneself' (p. 1462). In other words, firms with a high ownership concentration exert strong monitoring power and do not allow incompetent managers to be their agents. In their view, the quality of corporate governance is dependent on the proportion of firm value diverted for private gains. Private gains include a wide range of value-decreasing activities from what Jensen and Meckling (1976) define as 'excessive shirking and corporate perks to outright stealing of tangible or intangible corporate resources'. This definition of the quality of governance captures various governance and managerial practices that may or may not be legally binding. Examples of diverting values by CEOs are the costs of reputation loss, costs of fines and costs of fraud. By using this broad definition of governance quality, both mandatory and voluntary disclosure of governance information is needed in order to reduce the shirking behaviour of some CEOs.

A strict quantitative approach towards corporate governance and performance was applied by Bhagat and Bolton (2008). Based on the GIM index, they found, among other things, a positive correlation between 'better' governance and contemporaneous and subsequent operating performance.[3] Gompers, Ishii, and Metrick (2003) constructed a 'Governance Index' based on 24 governance rules and tested whether strong shareholder rights also implied better financial performance in the 1990s. They found that firms with better shareholder rights had a higher firm value, higher profits, higher sales growth, lower capital expenditures and made fewer corporate acquisitions.

A more qualitative approach towards evaluating the quality of the board of directors was presented by Van den Berghe and Levrau (2004). In addition to the quantitative and structural elements as often discussed in literature (board size, board composition, and board leadership construction), they introduced 'soft' factors into the analysis. The construction of that particular tool was deduced from an international comparison of corporate governance codes, former research and practitioners' views. Based on 60 in-depth interviews with directors of Belgian listed companies on Euronext and on Nasdaq Europe, they developed an evaluation tool of performance criteria with which to measure superior corporate governance and value creation. The authors ultimately identified three areas of improvement or challenge for the board. First, a formal board and director evaluation system is needed, both for the directors as a group but also for individual directors. A professionalization of the selection process of new outside directors is also needed in order to reduce the influence of the 'old boys network'. Finally, they stressed the importance of improving the disadvantageous position of external directors with regard to information gathering.[4] This chapter therefore tests the following hypothesis.

H2. Companies with high levels of CEO monitoring show better financial performance than companies with low levels of CEO monitoring.

Stock exchanges all over the world require a specific level of disclosure of information from the listed companies simply because financial markets need that information for a proper pricing process. However, the disclosure on corporate governance is relatively poor. Based on a Danish dataset, Parum (2005), for example, concluded that the quality of information on the independence and qualification of the leading shareholder coalition, the management processes and strategic and financial goals have, at the least, 'room for improvement' (p.707). An interesting aspect of the underlying study is that this kind of 'soft' information is specifically acquired by the sustainability rating agencies used for our quantitative analysis. The following section will elaborate on the distinguished variables.

DATASET AND METHODOLOGY

The implemented dataset consists of two types of variables. First, there are the scores from the rating agencies on transparency and the monitoring power of a company. Second, a description is presented of the quantitative economic variables on the company's performance as retrieved from Thomson International. The employed methodology is then discussed, and finally, the section concludes with some descriptive statistics.

THE DATA ON TRANSPARENCY, CEO MONITORING AND 'CG PERFORMANCE'

The dataset consists of qualitative scores on the corporate governance performance of 2008 major companies quoted on stock exchanges in 25 different countries all over the world in the year 2007 (see Appendix A for more details). The scores of these companies are based on questionnaires produced by the SiRi research agencies[5] and covering the years 2003–2007. Sustainalytics, formerly part of Triodos Bank in the Netherlands and a former member of the SiRi group, put the dataset at our disposal. In this chapter, transparency (TRANSP) is measured by the scores resulting from questions regarding the availability of public reports on directors' biographies, directors' remuneration, CEO's remuneration, the number and nature of board committees, primary stock ownership and voting rights, and the availability of a set of published corporate governance principles as based on the GRI guidelines (see Appendix B for the entire list of questions (questions C.1 and C.2)). The question scores are recalculated to a percentage between 0 and 100, according to strict criteria based on the level of disclosure for a specific question. For example, the question on directors' biographies results in a '100' if the company annually discloses biographies of all members of its board (including the supervisory board in a two-tier system) containing the member's name, age, position in the company, other positions held in listed companies or major institutions, and a broad outline of their past career. A score of '40' is provided if the company publishes biographies of only some but not all directors , or does not include all the information included in the SiRi guidelines. A score of '0' results if the company does not provide any information whatsoever on its directors in its public report. Although they are based on years of experience and development, it is important to realize that the resulting corporate governance scores are relative numbers, representing a systematic but qualitative perception of transparency.

The CEO monitoring (CEO-MON) variable represents the questions appearing under the heading 'management systems' in Appendix B. Transparency aims exclusively to provide information to all relevant stakeholders; CEO monitoring, on the other hand, focuses on the management systems in place. CEO monitoring represents the policy applied to reduce agency costs and to create a competitive and monitored environment for the board. This variable concerns information on the existence of a performance evaluation system, board effectiveness and the number of non-executive directors (NEDs) on the board, the position of the chairman of the board, and the existence and composition of an audit and/or nomination committee. The existence of independent remuneration and compensation committees are also considered. The criteria for a company's scores are structured in such a way that the higher the level of monitoring and competition among board members, the higher the score on CEO monitoring. This variable can also result in scores between 0% and 100% and represents the percentage of 'good' governance in terms of the reduction of agency costs. The number of questions was changed in 2005 in order to improve the efficiency, relevancy and variability of the variables. However, the structure of the questions remained unchanged and aims to provide similar governance information.

The third variable in our research is called the 'GOV-total', and aims to measure the total 'good governance' practices of a company and is the average score of both Transparency and CEO monitoring. The first variable (TRANSP) is based on information as provided by the company itself (e.g. annual reports). By adding the reported management systems and the realizations of the policy through controversies and realizations that can be measured externally, we gain a more complete score of the companies' total quality of governance. We hypothesize that 'good' governance results in higher financial performance.

The fourth distinguished governance variable is called 'the free float number of shares': NOSHFF. The data was retrieved from Thomson International and the variable calculated as the percentage of total shares in issue available to ordinary investors, also defined as the total number of shares less the strategic holdings.[6] This governance indicator proxies the power (including monitoring power) of shareholders in the sense that theoretically the higher the free float of shares, the lower the strategic holdings of shares and therefore the lower the monitoring power. A high free float indicates that there is a highly dispersed shareholdership for which it is difficult to raise a majority during the annual shareholder meeting of the company. Or, vice versa, the lower the free float of shares, the higher the strategic shareholdings, which makes it easier for the more major shareholders to create a coalition with other shareholders and thus monitor the board more closely.

DATA ON FIRMS' FINANCIAL PERFORMANCE

In addition to the corporate governance data as gathered by the SiRi research group, the financial data of the companies involved was retrieved from Thomson International. All relevant financial information of the analysed companies was gathered, ranging from annual balance sheet data to monthly stock prices. The research period covers 2003_01 to 2007_12, and in that period 60 monthly logarithmic total stock returns per company were calculated based on closing prices (including reinvestment gains such as dividend and bonus shares).

R_m and R_f represent the market return in the country of the company and the risk-free rate, respectively. For the risk-free rate, the 1-month US treasury bills were selected for all countries because similar short-term treasury rates were not available for all the 25 countries involved. Griffin (2002) shows that ignoring country specific differences in risk-free rates yields similar outcomes. Panel A in Table 1 shows the descriptive statistics and the two-sided Pearson's correlation coefficients of the main variables in this research. The research period represented in the table shows an upward international market with an average annual return of 20.2%.

Table 1. Descriptive Statistics.

Panel A shows the descriptive statistics and the two-sided Pearson correlation coefficients of the main variables in this research. TRANSP represents the quality of the internal written and published communication of the companies' corporate governance indicators. The variable CEO-MON indicates the level of monitoring power as derived from the applied management system concerning the corporate governance issues of the company. The scores of these two variables range from 0 to 100. The higher the score, the better the company fulfils the requirements of the SiRi research group. FFNOSH is the free float number of shares as a percentage of the total number of issued shares. All the other variables represent economic indicators. R_i is the total return of company *i* in the years 2003–2007. Also the market value (MV) and the price to book value (PtBV) are based on the years 2003–2007.

Panel B shows the descriptives and correlations of the monthly returns of the selected (hedge) portfolios in the research period. A hedge portfolio is calculated as the difference in total returns between the top 20% companies of the entire sample minus the bottom 20%, as selected for a specific variable. Further is R_i, the return of company *i*, R_f the risk-free rate, R_m the return on the local market portfolio. SMB represents the small minus big portfolio, measured by market value; HML represents the high book to market stocks minus the low book to market stocks and MOM the momentum variable, being the 6 month top performing stocks minus the 6 month worst performing stocks.

Panel A	*N*	Min	Max	Mean	Std. Dev.	TRANSP	CEO-MON	FFNOSH	R_i	MV	PtBV
TRANSPARENCY	6058	0	100	61.3	23.8	1					
CEO-MONITORING	6058	19.2	100	66.7	13.4	0.516**	1				
FFNOSH (in %)	10,178	0	100	71.1	22.9	0.056**	0.096	1			
R_i	10,229	−3.22	2.78	0.202	0.303	0.020**	−0.011	−0.1021	1		
Market value[a]	10,289	1.94	470,434	12,413	25,490	0.224	0.025	0.120	−0.71	1	
PtBV	10,273	−2940	622	2.70	32.2	0.027**	0.013	0.008	0.013*	0.011	1

Panel B	*N*	Min[b]	Max[b]	Mean[b]	Std. Dev.	$R_m - R_f$	SMB	HML	MOM
$R_m - R_f$	60	−4.8	7.7	0.92	2.7	1			
SMB	60	−2.8	4.4	0.70	1.6	0.222	1		
HML	60	−3.2	4.4	0.77	1.8	0.264	0.677	1	
MOM	60	−8.6	10.5	0.69	3.1	0.264	0.202	−0.45	1

*Correlation is significant at the 0.05 level (two-tailed).
**Correlation is significant at the 0.01 level (two-tailed).
[a]In millions of euros.
[b]In percentages per month.

There are over 6000 governance observations available in this research as a result of the 1211 (average) companies measured for 5 years. The positive correlations between the corporate governance variable TRANSP with all other variables are particularly interesting. Transparency shows a positive relation to all the other variables but in particular to CEO monitoring and the market value of the firm. This indicates that better transparency of the companies' board is coupled with increased CEO monitoring and larger company size, without drawing any conclusions about causality. A higher free float of shares (FFNOSH) reduces the CEO monitoring power and shows a negative relation to the total returns of companies.

THE METHODOLOGY APPLIED

To measure the financial performance of 'good governance' variables, we chose to apply the three-factor Fama and French (1993) and the 4-factor Carhart (1997) models in order to measure the influence of governance variables on financial performance. Although there is an ongoing debate as to whether these factors represent the correct proxies for risk, we accept the framework as a robust methodology for both financial and non-financial firms (see also Barber & Lyon, 1997). By using capital asset pricing models, it is implicitly assumed that it is the financial market (i.e. the stockholder and the debt holder) that ultimately disciplines the management and determines equity prices. This framework is therefore considered optimal for benchmarking the exact measurement of the influence of 'good governance' on financial performance. On the other hand, the problem with this methodology is that we need to assume informationally efficient markets and, more importantly, the main value drivers of the return-generating process have to be specifically identified. Ultimately, we calculate and apply the constant factor α in the regression as used before in Gompers et al. (2003). The applied model is

$$R_{it} - R_{ft} = \alpha_i + b_i(R_{mt} - R_{ft}) + c_i\mathrm{SMB}_t + d_i\mathrm{HML}_t + e_i\mathrm{MOM}_t + \varepsilon_{it} \qquad (1)$$

where

R_{it} = the return on portfolio i in month t of companies representing a specific selection of governance aspects

R_{mt} = return on market in month t

R_{ft} = risk-free interest rate in month t

SMB_t = value weighted Small Minus Big zero investment hedge portfolio of companies in month t
HML_t = value weighted zero investment hedge portfolio of value (high B/M) stocks and growth stocks (low B/M) in month t
MOM_t = momentum portfolio, which is the return difference between a portfolio of the last 12-month winners and a portfolio of past 12-month losers in month t.

The estimated 'α' can be interpreted as the abnormal return in excess of what could be achieved by passive investing in the applied factors. A hedge portfolio implies that an investor buys a portfolio of companies that belong to the top of a specific criterion (a long position), e.g. transparent companies, and finances that transaction with the sale of the bottom portfolio (a short position) of that variable in such a proportion that a zero investment remains. All portfolios are reset annually in June. The return earned with that arbitrage portfolio is supposed to be generated by the isolated selection criterion. It must finally be noted that the methodology produces robust results, but is still a joint test of the validity of the general capital market model and the identity of the tested variable in question.

RESULTS

Panel B in Table 1 shows, in accordance with theory, that the financial hedge portfolios (Small Minus Big, Price to Book Value and Momentum) all showed positive mean returns of respectively 8.4%, 9.3% and 8.3% per year. With regard to the correlation matrix, it is important to note the high correlation between the size and the value of a hedge portfolio. This may create a bias in the independence of the explaining variables in the applied asset pricing models.

Following the methodology of Gompers et al. (2003), explained in the previous section, the annualized idiosyncratic returns of the selected portfolios are analysed for, respectively, the entire dataset (2008 companies in 25 countries) and the data broken down into region and sector. Additionally, we have also performed an analysis using various legal jurisdictions as proposed by La Porta et al. (1998).

Table 2 shows that in our dataset, after correction for market risk, size, value and momentum, the hedge portfolio of the top 20% companies with highly transparent governance structures outperforms the bottom quintile portfolio by 65.2 basis points per month. On a yearly basis, this comes down to a return of 7.8% per annum. Similar results are calculated for companies with good CEO monitoring structure and, as we take both governance elements transparency and CEO monitoring together, an international portfolio of 'good governance' companies. The CEO monitor hedge portfolio earns a 3.8% and the total good governance hedge position yields 7.3% per annum. It is concluded that despite the wide-ranging legal structures used around the world, transparency in governance systems and a good CEO monitoring structure have a positive influence on a company's financial performance. This conclusion is supported by the results of the variable FFNOSH, the percentage free float of shares. Table 2 shows the portfolios of companies with the highest free float compared to the bottom quintile portfolio, which has a negative return of 46.6 basis points, or −5.6% per annum. Once again, it must be concluded that – in accordance with agency theory – company boards that are insufficiently disciplined by block holdings of shares show lower financial performance.

REGIONAL AND LEGAL ANALYSIS OF COUNTRIES AROUND THE WORLD

After the general conclusion as derived from the widely dispersed general dataset, let us first take a more in-depth look at the details of the results distributed per geographic region or type of legal jurisdiction. The results are presented in Table 3.

The first interesting observation is that Northern Europe (Scandinavia) has a statistically significant negative return on governance transparency, whereas Asia and countries with the English legal origin show clear positive results. Two different types of explanations for these dispersed returns were explored; first, the statistically different levels of 'good governance' between countries and regions, and second, the differences in legal and organizational cultures between the distinguished geographic regions.

La Porta et al. (1998) argue that commercial laws are not written from scratch, but originate from two broad traditions: common law and civil law. In contrast to common law tradition with its lay judges, broad legal principals and oral arguments, civil law tradition is characterized by professional judges, legal codes and written arguments (see also Glaeser & Shleifer, 2002). While common law is English in origin, the roots of civil law go as far back as the Roman Empire. Within the civil law tradition, a division can be made into the French, German and Scandinavian legal

Table 2. Performance–Attribution Regressions for Top and Bottom 20% Portfolios Ranked by Governance Scores for All Companies (2025) in the Research Period 2003_1 to 2007_12.

We estimate four factor regressions (Eq. (1) from the text) of value weighed monthly returns for 20% top and bottom portfolios of all companies (2063) ranked by a specific governance attribute. $R_{mt}-R_{ft}$ represents the returns of the market proxy in excess of the risk-free rate. SMB denotes the difference in return between a small cap portfolio and a large cap portfolio. HML denotes the return spread between a value portfolio and a growth portfolio. SMB and HML are discussed in Fama and French (1993). The sample period is January 2003 until December 2007 (60 months). All portfolios are reset five times (in June of every year). Per attribute we subtract the constant return of the top and bottom portfolio in order to estimate the monthly return difference for a zero-investment portfolio in basis points (top minus bottom). Diff BP is the monthly difference in basis points between the top and the bottom portfolio as measured by the α of the estimated equations. See Gompers (2003, p. 123). For example, the first row shows an idiosyncratic return of 28.1 basis points if we buy the top 20% of companies ranked transparency scores. Corrected for factor risks, we see that the bottom portfolio costs 37.2 basis points. The difference between the two portfolios is 65.2 basis point per month, equalling 7.8% per year. It can be concluded that investing in a portfolio with high transparency scores and financing that by a short position in low transparent companies is a successful strategy. t-values are between brackets.

$$R_{it} - R_{ft} = \alpha_i + b_i(R_{mt} - R_{ft}) + c_i\text{SMB}_t + d_i\text{HML}_t + e_i\text{MOM}_t + \varepsilon_{it}$$

Governance Characteristic Hedge	α	R_m-R_f	SMB	HML	MOM	Adj. R^2	Diff BP
Transparency							
Top	28.1	1.04	−0.25	−0.055	−0.024	90.4	
		(23.1)***	(−2.4)**	(−0.59)	(−0.061)		
Bottom	−37.2	0.81	0.41	0.55	−0.097	78.5	65.2
		(10.3)***	(2.7)***	(3.4)***	(−1.41)		
CEO-monitoring							
Top	27.6	1.03	0.07	−0.24	0.02	87.9	
		(20.4)***	(0.58)	(−2.34)**	(0.45)		
Bottom	−4.1	0.96	0.06	0.13	−0.004	87.3	31.7
		(18.5)***	(0.47)	(1.26)	(−0.08)		

Governance							
Top	22.4	0.98	−0.14	−0.10	0.004	93.5	
		(28.7)***	(−1.76)*	(−1.37)	(0.13)		
Bottom	−38.6	0.89	0.33	0.54	−0.13	78.0	61.0
		(10.5)***	(1.79)*	(3.27)***	(−1.85)*		
FFNOSH							
Top	8.7	0.91	0.08	0.23	−0.055	88.4	
		(18.7)***	(0.11)	(2.29)**	(−1.28)		
Bottom	55.3	0.98	0.12	−0.02	0.028	86.3	−46.6
		(18.3)***	(0.95)	(−0.22)	(0.60)		

T-statistics are reported in parentheses and statistical significance at the 10%, 5% and 1% levels are indicated by *, ** and ***, respectively.

Table 3. Expected Abnormal Return in Per cent Per Year of Quintile Portfolios of Governance Transparency and Monitoring Strategies Per Geographical Distribution.

This table reports the risk-adjusted yearly abnormal return (bold numbers) as estimated by the constant α in the multifactor regressions described in Eq. (1) for various regional breakdowns. The independent variable is a value weighed factor mimicking zero-investment strategy based on governance scores provided by the SiRi rating agencies. TRANSP, for example, represents the return difference between respectively the top 20% of stocks, ranked by transparency scores, and the bottom 20% of companies in the very same countries. Similarly, the so-called zero investment hedge portfolios are also calculated for governance scores on CEO-monitoring, total governance (GOV), and the free float of shares FFNOSH. *t*-values are between brackets and the sample period is 2003_01 to 2007_12. Number of companies included in the total sample: 2008.

	Transparency		CEO-monitoring		Governance		FFNOSH	
	α	Diff BP[a]	α	Diff BP[a]	α	Diff BP[a]	α	Diff BP[a]
All Countries		7.8		3.8		7.3		−5.6
Japan	−0.003	−3.3	−0.003	−3.4	0.002	2.6	−0.003	−3.0
($n=405$)	(−0.44)		(−0.54)		(0.35)		(−0.59)	
United Kingdom	0.003	4.0	−0.005	−5.6	0.003	3.1	0.001	1.3
($n=136$)	(0.85)		(−0.88)		(0.53)		(0.31)	
United States	0.001	0.7	−0.001	−0.7	0.002	2.7	−0.002	−2.5
($n=627$)	(0.23)		(−0.157)		(0.63)		(−0.56)	
Asia	0.010	11.4	0.002	1.9	0.007	8.3	−0.008	−9.5
($n=86$)	(1.71)		(0.18)		(1.01)		(−1.49)	
Europe North	−0.012	−14.6	0.004	4.9	−0.002	−2.6	−0.032	−38.7
($n=103$)	(−1.81)*		(0.45)		(−0.29)		(−2.99)***	
Europe Central	0.000	0.3	−0.011	−12.8	−0.000	−0.4	−0.006	−7.6
($n=344$)	(0.07)		(−2.98)***		(−0.07)		(−1.35)	
Europe South	−0.003	−4.1	−0.008	−10.1	−0.002	−1.8	0.003	3.7
($n=105$)	(−0.77)		(−2.10)**		(−0.30)		(0.77)	
English Legal Origin ($n=1059$)	0.001	1.0	0.000	0.4	0.004	4.3	−0.004	−5.2
	(0.27)		(0.08)		(0.78)		(−1.25)	
French Legal Origin ($n=225$)	−0.003	−4.0	−0.007	−7.9	−0.008	−10.0	−0.007	−8.4
	(−0.89)		(−1.90)*		(−1.72)*		(−1.44)	
German Legal Origin ($n=615$)	0.011	13.2	0.010	11.4	0.013	15.7	−0.003	−3.9
	(2.76)***		(2.09)**		(2.77)***		(−1.00)	

T-statistics are reported in parentheses and statistical significance at the 10%, 5% and 1% levels are indicated by *, ** and ***, respectively.
[a]On a yearly basis.

families. Together with French and German legal families, common law has been spread around the world by conquest and imperialism.

There are two main legal channels through which legal traditions impact contemporaneous finance: the political channel and the adaptability channel (see Beck et al., 2003). The political channel argues that legal traditions differ in the way they prioritize individual property rights versus the rights of the state. French and German legal families are established in order to protect the rights of the state, and the common law family attaches greater priority to individual property rights. The political channel conjectures that civil law countries give preference to state power at the cost of financial development. The adaptability channel conjectures that the legal traditions differ to the extent that they are able to adapt to a changing environment. As a result, the law in common law countries can change more efficiently in alignment with the needs of the economy. The discretion of judges enables them to challenge inefficient laws and replace them with more efficient ones that are better suited to the current situation. Laws in civil law countries seem to evolve less efficiently, which results in negative implications for finance.

Returning to the statistically significant results of Table 3, it is shown that the German civil law legal tradition (Germany, Austria, Switzerland, Japan and Korea) scores a positive return of 13.2 % on transparency, 11.4% on CEO monitoring leading to a 15.7 % in total on Governance. Our first conclusion is that 'good' corporate governance – transparent and high CEO monitoring – is a prized factor in countries with German civil law traditions. Financial markets obviously appreciate transparent companies with strict CEO monitoring policies. The German civil law tradition using the political channel to monitor the economy obviously blurs clear company statements. This interpretation is confirmed by the relatively low levels of transparency and, to a lesser extent, the CEO monitoring power, as compared to other regions and countries.[7]

With a negative return of −4% and −14.6% respectively for transparency, French and Scandinavian legal origins both represent the other extreme of the civil law-based countries. It is important to note that the general level of transparency for these companies is higher than average. This indicates that Scandinavian and French legal origins encourage higher transparency than the German legal origin. The top transparent countries (the United States and the United Kingdom) show slightly positive results but which are not significantly different from zero statistically. A final significant result is that for the Scandinavian countries, a high free float of stocks shows a very negative financial performance (−38% per annum). In other words, blocks of stocks are needed to monitor the management of the company.

RESULTS PER SECTOR

Two striking observations can be made if we analyse the results per sector. While most coefficients do not differ statistically from zero, the *industrials* sector exhibits a clear positive result for transparent companies (+14.7% return per annum), whereas *consumer discretionary* obviously needs shareholder blocks in order to discipline management (−9.3% annual return for a portfolio with a high free float of stocks).

Despite the correction for size, value and momentum, there remains a strong positive return for industrial companies. We conclude therefore that industrial companies with highly transparent board structures perform better than similar companies that have boards with low transparency.

Most important, however, is the general conclusion resulting from Table 4 in which all governance coefficients are positive. This implies that from a strict international sector economic perspective – eliminating the legal, cultural and regional differences through diversification –'good' governance does pay off. This is supported by the fact that all returns for the higher free float portfolios are negative, with the exception of the sector *consumer staples*. Once again, in the international financial markets, block holdings of shares, higher transparency and strict CEO monitoring help to improve financial performance. Agency theory still holds strong in the international stock markets.

SUMMARY AND CONCLUSIONS

This substantial international empirical study analyses the relation between board transparency, CEO monitoring policy and financial performance. The study basically analyses corporate governance and agency relations between the boards of major international companies and their residual claimants: the shareholders. 'Good governance' is interpreted as a company with highly transparent board and stock ownership information, together with a clear and published set of corporate governance principles and policies. In this research, CEO monitoring signifies extensive public board information and management systems with independent audit and remuneration procedures. Agency theory argues that companies with strongly monitored CEOs have lower agency costs and hence lower costs of capital. Based on Fama and French (1996) and Carhart (1997), the Gompers et al. (2003) methodology is a robust and well-tested capital

Table 4. Expected Abnormal Return in Per cent Per Year of Quintile Portfolios of Various Governance Variables Distributed Per Sector.

This table reports the risk-adjusted yearly abnormal return (bold numbers) as estimated by the constant α in the multifactor regressions described in Eq. (1) for various breakdowns per sector. The independent variable is a value weighed factor mimicking zero-investment strategy based on governance scores provided by the SiRi rating agencies. TRANSP, for example, represents the return difference between respectively the top 20% of stocks, ranked by transparency scores, and the bottom 20% of companies in the very same countries. Similarly, the so-called zero investment hedge portfolios are also calculated for governance scores on CEO-monitoring, total governance (GOV), and the free float of shares FFNOSH. T-values are between brackets and the sample period is 2003_01 to 2007_2012. Number of companies included in the total sample: 2008.

	Transparency		CEO-monitoring		Governance		FFNOSH	
	α	Diff BP	α	Diff BP	α	Diff BP	α	Diff BP
All Countries		7.8		3.8		7.3		−5.6
10 Energy (n = 112)	0.006	7.5	0.002	1.9	0.006	6.6	−0.004	−5.0
	(1.12)		(0.23)		(0.85)		(−0.80)	
15 Materials (n = 173)	0.003	3.0	0.004	4.5	0.005	5.4	−0.004	−4.5
	(0.43)		(0.50)		(0.50)		(−0.83)	
20 Industrials (n = 325)	0.012	14.7	0.008	9.5	0.007	8.4	−0.005	−6.1
	(2.56)**		(1.34)		(1.03)		(−0.88)	
25 Consumer Dis-cretionary (n = 352)	0.003	4.1	0.004	5.0	0.004	5.1	−0.008	−9.3
	(0.60)		(0.67)		(0.81)		(−2.10)**	
30 Consumer Staples (n = 142)	0.003	4.0	0.003	3.7	0.007	7.9	0.003	4.2
	(0.80)		(0.57)		(1.26)		(0.92)	
35 Health Care (n = 137)	0.005	5.6	0.001	1.5	0.006	7.6	−0.009	−10.7
	(0.75)		(0.20)		(0.99)		(−1.31)	
40 Financials (n = 417)	0.006	6.7	0.003	4.0	0.005	5.6	−0.003	−3.6
	(0.97)		(0.73)		(0.80)		(−1.09)	
45 Information Technology (n = 212)	0.010	11.6	0.007	8.1	0.005	6.3	−0.003	−3.4
	(1.31)		(0.90)		(0.66)		(−0.40)	
50 Telecommunication Services (n = 46)	0.008	9.8	0.002	2.4	0.006	7.1	0.003	3.9
	(1.05)		(0.24)		(0.65)		(0.60)	
55 Utilities (n = 87)	0.006	7.2	0.006	7.4	0.003	4.0	−0.003	−3.4
	(1.25)		(1.38)		(0.60)		(−0.54)	

T-statistics are reported in parentheses and statistical significance at the 10%, 5% and 1% levels are indicated by *, ** and ***, respectively.

market model with which to measure the financial performance of international companies in the finance literature. Controlling for size, risk, book-to-market value and a momentum factor, it is concluded that the quintile zero hedge portfolios in the overall international sample showed a statistically significant annual return of 7.8% in the research period of 2003–2007. In other words, it is concluded that firms which provide transparent board information are better rewarded by the investor. This result is in line with theoretical literature as presented extensively in the second section (e.g. Diamond & Verecchia, 1991; Healy & Palepu, 2001). The different results between the Scandinavian civil law system and that of German civil law are attributed to the low average level of transparency in German civil law countries, which provides investors with the opportunity to reveal the better-functioning governance structures.

A second conclusion is that there is evidence that a more intense CEO monitoring policy by a company's board does lead to a statistically higher financial performance in countries with the German legal origin but a negative return in those with the French legal origin. On average, we found a positive return for the CEO monitoring policies in the entire sample. Taking transparency and CEO monitoring together – and calling it 'good governance' – we found that good governance paid off (7.3% per year) in the international capital markets during the 2003–2007 sample period. Moreover, the results of the variable free float of shares underpin the general conclusion that better-monitored management of companies by – in this case – shareholders and blocks of shareholders show better financial performance. Despite the increasing influence of stewardship theory, these results indicate that the opposing agency theory still dominates the international capital markets.

NOTES

1. Ahold, WorldCom and Parmalat are well-known examples in the real economy, and Bernard L. Madoff and the banking crisis of 2008 emphasize the importance of transparency in the financial sector.

2. The "lemons problem" is based on Akerlof (1970) and basically argues that due to asymmetrical information, general market prices are always overvalued because low-quality suppliers get the same market price as good quality suppliers. This encourages suppliers with low morality to enlarge the business at the expense of high moral suppliers.

3. See page 261 of Bhagat and Bolton (2008) for a description of all relevant variables.

4. These qualitative results are part of our quantitative input as can be read in Appendix B, questions 6–11.

5. SiRi was a cooperation of 10 social research companies (in 2008) that developed a research questionnaire for analysing companies from different countries according to an identical international structure. The sources of information for the analyst are: 1) company documents that are publicly released; 2) national and international press articles 3) associations, non-profit and non-governmental organisations, and 4) contacts between SiRi group members and the company. The SiRi organisation went out of business in 2009.

6. *Source*: Thomson Financial Limited, Infostream, October 2002, p. 16.

7. The average level of 45% and 63% respectively for *transparency* and *CEO-monitoring* in the group German Legal Origin is clearly lower than the world averages of 61% and 66%. See Appendix C for an overview of the average levels of governance variables per region.

REFERENCES

Akerlof, G. A. (1970). The market for 'Lemons': Qualitative uncertainty and the market mechanism. *Quarterly Journal of Economics*, *84*(3), 488–500.

Barber, B. M., & Lyon, J. D. (1997). Firm size, book-to-market ratio and security returns: A holdout sample of financial firms. *Journal of Finance*, *52*(2), 875–883.

Beck, T., Demirgüç-Kunt, A., & Levine, R. (2003). Law and finance: Why does legal origin matter? *Journal of Comparative Economics*, *31*(4), 653–675.

Berle, A. A., & Means, G. C. (1932). *The modern corporation and private property*. New York, NJ: Commerce Clearing House.

Bhagat, S., & Bolton, B. (2008). Corporate governance and firm performance. *Journal of Corporate Finance*, *14*(3), 257–273.

Bhushan, R. (1989a). Collection of information about publicly traded firms: Theory and evidence. *Journal of Accounting and Economics*, *11*(2–3), 183–206.

Bhushan, R. (1989b). Firm Characteristics and Analysts Following. *Journal of Accounting and Economics*, *11*(2–3), 255–275.

Bushman, R. M., Piotroski, J. D., & Smith, A. J. (2004). What determines corporate transparency. *Journal of Accounting Research*, *42*(2), 207–252.

Carhart, M. M. (1997). On persistence in mutual fund performance. *Journal of Corporate Finance*, *52*(1), 57–82.

Clarkson, P., Guedes, J., & Thompson, R. (1996). On the diversification, observability, and measurement of estimation risk. *Journal of Financial and Quantitative Analysis*, *31*(1), 69–84.

Core, J. E. (2001). A review of the empirical disclosure literature: Discussion. *Journal of Accounting and Economics*, *31*(1-3), 441–456.

Diamond, D. W., & Verrecchia, R. E. (1991). Disclosure, liquidity, and the cost of capital. *Journal of Finance*, *46*(4), 1325–1359.

Durnev, A., & Kim, E. H. (2005). To steal or not to steal: Firm attributes, legal environment, and valuation. *Journal of Finance*, *60*(3), 1461–1493.

Easterbrook, F. H., & Fischel, D. R. (1991). *The economic structure of corporate law*. Cambridge: Harvard University Press.

Fama, E. F., & French, K. R. (1993). Common risk factors in the returns on stocks and bonds. *Journal of Financial Economics*, *33*(1), 3–56.

Fama, E. F., & French, K. R. (1996). Multifactor explanations of asset pricing anomalies. *Journal of Finance*, *51*(1), 55–84.

Gelb, D. S., & Strawser, J. A. (2001). Corporate social responsibility and financial disclosures: An alternative explanation for increased disclosure. *Journal of Business Ethics*, *33*(1), 1–13.

Glaeser, E. L., & Shleifer, A. (2002). Legal origins. *The Quarterly Journal of Economics*, *117*(4), 1193–1229.

Gompers, P., Ishii, J., & Metrick, A. (2003). Corporate governance and equity prices. *The Quarterly Journal of Economics*, *118*(1), 107–155.

Griffin, J. M. (2002). Are the fama and french factors global or country specific? *The Review of Financial Studies*, *15*(3), 783–803.

Healy, P. M., & Palepu, K. G. (2001). Information asymmetry, corporate disclosure and the capital markets: A review of the empirical disclosure literature. *Journal of Accounting and Economics*, *31*(1–3), 405–440.

Jensen, M. C., & Meckling, W. H. (1976). Theory of the firm: Managerial behavior, agency costs and ownership structure. *Journal of Financial Economics Volume*, *3*(4), 305–360.

La Porta, R., Lopez-de-Silanes, F., & Shleifer, A. (1999). Corporate ownership around the world. *Journal of Finance*, *54*(2), 471–517.

La Porta, R., Lopez-de-Silanes, F., Shleifer, A., & Vishny, R. W. (1998). Law and finance. *The Journal of Political Economy Volume*, *106*(6), 1113–1155.

La Porta, R., Lopez-de-Silanes, F., Shleifer, A., & Vishny, R. W. (2002). Investor protection and corporate valuation. *Journal of Finance*, *57*(3), 1147–1170.

Lang, M. H., & Lundholm, R. J. (1996). Corporate disclosure policy and analyst behavior. *The Accounting Review*, *71*(4), 467–492.

Parum, E. (2005). Does disclosure on corporate governance lead to openness and transparency in how companies are managed? *Corporate Governance: An International Review*, *13*(5), 702–709.

Van den Berghe, L. A. A., & Levrau, A. (2004). Evaluating boards of directors: What constitutes a good corporate board? *Corporate Governance: An International Review*, *12*(4), 461–478.

Vander Bauwhede, H., & Willekens, M. (2008). Disclosure on corporate governance in the European union. *Corporate Governance: An International Review*, *16*(2), 101–115.

APPENDIX A: NUMBER OF COMPANIES PER REGION AND SECTOR IN 2007

GICS Sector	
10 Energy	112
15 Materials	173
20 Industrials	325
25 Consumer Discretionary	352
30 Consumer Staples	142
35 Health Care	137
40 Financials	417
45 Information Technology	212
50 Telecommunication services	46
55 Utilities	87
Other (non-listed companies)	5
Major countries outside Europe	**1168**
Japan	405
United Kingdom	136
United States	627
Asia	**86**
Hong Kong (China)	48
South Korea	1
Singapore	37
Europe North	**103**
Denmark	19
Finland	21
Norway	19
Sweden	44
Europe Central	**344**
Austria	15
Belgium	21
France	69
Germany	65
Ireland	15
Netherlands	30
Switzerland	129

English Legal Origin	*1059*
Australia	81
Canada	102
Hong Kong (China)	48
Ireland	15
New Zealand	13
Singapore	37
United Kingdom	136
United States	627
French Legal Origin	*225*
Belgium	21
France	69
Greece	21
Italy	38
Netherlands	30
Portugal	9
Spain	37
German Legal Origin	*615*
Austria	15
Germany	65
Japan	405
South Korea	1
Switzerland	129
Scandinavian Legal	*103*
Denmark	19
Finland	21
Norway	19
Sweden	44
Total	
Other	*6*
China	1
International	5
Total	***2008***

Appendix A. (*Continued*)

Europe South	**105**
Greece	21
Italy	38
Portugal	9
Spain	37

APPENDIX B: SHORT DESCRIPTION OF THE CORPORATE GOVERNANCE DATA QUESTION LIST

Transparency 2003–2004		**Transparency 2005–2007**	
C.1.a Directors' biographies		C.1.a Directors' biographies	
C.1.b Directors' remuneration/compensation		C.1.b Directors' and/or CEOs' remuneration/compensation	
C.1.c CEOs' remuneration/compensation		C.1.c Public reporting based on GRI guidelines	
C.1.d Number and nature of board committees			
C.1.e Primary stock ownership and voting rights	5		3
C.2.a The company has a set of corporate governance principles	1	C.2.a Formal policy statement on remuneration	1
CEO Monitoring 2003–2004		**CEO Monitoring 2005–2007**	
C.3.a Directors' term of office		C.3.a Separate position for chairman of board and CEO	
C.3.b Board performance evaluation		C.3.b Number of independent NEDs in the Board (and %)	
C.3.c Board effectiveness		C.3.c Audit committee composition	
C.3.e Number of NEDs in the Board		C.3.d Remuneration/compensation committee composition	
C.3.f Number of independent NEDs in the Board		C.3.e Variable remuneration linked to sustainability performance	
C.3.g Separate position for chairman of board and CEO			
C.3.h Existence of audit committee			
C.3.h.1 Audit committee composition			

Appendix B. (*Continued*)

CEO Monitoring 2003–2004		**CEO Monitoring 2005–2007**	
C.3.i Existence of remuneration/compensation committee			
C.3.i.1 Remuneration/ Compensation committee composition			
C.3.j Existence of nomination committee			
C.3.j.1 Nomination committee composition	12		5
C.4.a The company adheres to the 'one share, one vote' principle		C.4.a The company adheres to the one share, one vote principle	
C.4.b.3 % non-audit fees of audit fees		C.4.b % non-audit fees of audit fees	
C.4.f Absence of anti-takeover devices		C.4.c Controversies over remuneration	
C.4.g Remuneration		C.4.d Controversies over shareholders' rights	
C.4.h Shareholders' rights		C.4.e Controversies over governance structures	
C.4.i Governance structures or practices	6		5

APPENDIX C: AVERAGE LEVELS OF TRANSPARENCY PER REGION AND JURISDICTION

	Transparency	CEO-Monitoring	Governance	FFNOSH
United Kingdom	79.3	73.1	76.2	69.9
United States	71.6	67.9	69.7	69.5
Asia	47.6	67.8	57.7	55.6
Europe Central	64.3	65.3	64.8	67.4
Europe North	54.2	64.4	59.3	70.6
Europe South	55.1	59.9	57.5	56.4
English Legal Origin	71.3	70.7	71.0	69.4
French Legal Origin	63.2	61.2	62.2	62.5
German Legal Origin	44.8	62.9	53.9	77.5
Scandinavian Legal Origin	54.2	64.4	59.3	70.6
Total	61.3	65.9	63.6	66.5

SYMMETRY IN THE SENSITIVITY OF EXECUTIVE BONUS COMPENSATION TO EARNINGS AND RETURNS IN HIGH-TECHNOLOGY FIRMS

Sung S. Kwon

ABSTRACT

This chapter examines the sensitivity of executive incentive compensation to market-adjusted returns and changes in earnings for high-tech (HT) firms vis-à-vis firms (NHT) in other industries. Consistent with the hypotheses, this chapter uncovers the following evidence: First, the sensitivity of executive bonus compensation to market-adjusted returns is weaker and more symmetric for HT firms than for NHT firms (a control group), which implies that the problem of ex post settling up, documented in Leone et al. (2006), may be far less serious in HT firms than in NHT firms. Second, the sensitivity of executive incentive compensation to earnings changes is generally more symmetric for HT firms than for NHT firms, which is consistent with the view that HT firms engage in more conservative financial reporting than NHT firms. Third, the sensitivity of executive equity-based compensation to market-adjusted returns is

Transparency and Governance in a Global World
International Finance Review, Volume 13, 127–172

ISSN: 1569-3767/doi:10.1108/S1569-3767(2012)0000013008

significantly negative for HT firms compared to NHT firms when bad earnings news is announced. The results imply that HT firms, with a strong motive to attract and retain their highly talented executives, judiciously use both short-term and long-term incentive compensation schemes by compensating for a reduction of short-term incentive pay with an increase in long-term incentive pay. The issue of executive compensation has been a longstanding one in the United States and Canada, and the issue of executive compensation-performance sensitivity for HT firms is also relevant in this era of the information technology (IT) revolution, especially when prior research has shown that HT firms differ from NHT firms in their market-valuation process.

Keywords: Bonus compensation; equity-based compensation; high-tech firms; compensation-performance sensitivity; conservatism

JEL classifications: J33; L2; M41

INTRODUCTION

Prior research has shown that the market valuation for high-tech stocks differs from that for traditional stocks.[1] Amir and Lev (1996) provide empirical evidence that financial data pertaining to high-tech firms (e.g., cellular companies) are less value-relevant than data for less technology-dependent firms. In addition, Trueman, Wong, and Zhang (2000) fail to find a significant positive correlation between net income and market prices for Internet stocks in their sample. In an attempt to explain such a weak association, Hand (2000) claims that the conventional assumption that accounting information maps into equity market value in a linear and stationary fashion is not relevant to technology-intensive firms.

It is also widely accepted that reported earnings play an informational role both in the determination of firm value and the compensation of top corporate executives. Bushman et al. (2000) develop an agency-based model that provides a direct theoretical connection between compensation-earnings sensitivities and value-earnings sensitivities. The authors assert that this relationship between valuation and managerial stewardship derives from the fact that the capitalization rate of earnings into value also influences the marginal product of current period managerial actions that impact current earnings. The authors' empirical tests of the model provide evidence of a positive link between compensation-earnings sensitivities and value-earnings sensitivities.

The question then arises as to whether high-tech firms (HT firms hereafter) and firms that do not belong to high-tech industries (NHT firms hereafter) differ in the degree of sensitivity of executive incentive compensation to both stock and accounting performance in the setting of efficient compensation contracts.[2] The purpose of this chapter is to examine this question and provide empirical evidence on the differences, if any, between HT and NHT firms with respect to the sensitivity of executive incentive compensation to both stock and accounting performance.[3]

According to Leone et al. (2006), the problem of ex post settling up under conservative accounting is mitigated when executives' compensation contracts are based directly on earnings because unrealized gains are excluded and unrealized losses are timely recognized.[4] The authors further note that the degree of symmetry in the sensitivity of cash compensation to accounting earnings would increase as the level of accounting conservatism ratchets up. A firm's conservative accounting is a function of litigation, taxes, other accounting-based contracts (e.g., debt covenants), and accounting regulation.

Whether or not HT firms' earnings are more conservative in comparison to NHT firms' earnings, however, has not yet been conclusively documented in prior research.[5] On one hand, recent cases involving accounting fraud and manipulations by HT firms such as Adelphia, Tyco International, and WorldCom suggest that some HT firms aggressively report their earnings (aggressive accounting). It is conceivable that many young, fast-growing HT firms are under great pressure to generate favorable accounting numbers to attract external capital.

On the other hand, HT firms have more incentives to engage in conservative accounting reporting than NHT firms. Current generally accepted accounting principles (GAAP) require HT firms to be more conservative in accounting reporting than NHT firms. For example, HT firms are affected to a greater degree by accounting standards such as SFAS 121 on asset impairments, SFAS 5 on contingencies, and SFAS 2, which requires immediate expensing of most R&D costs. HT firms are also more affected by industry-specific accounting standards such as SFAS 86 on software development costs and AICPA SOP 97-2 that requires deferral of certain software revenue.

Greater growth opportunities and heightened risk due to volatile stock prices render HT firms more vulnerable to shareholder litigation (Francis, Philbrick, & Schipper, 1994; Jones & Weingram, 1996; Johnson,

Kasznik, & Nelson, 2001). About one-third of federal securities law class actions involve tech firms (Grundfest & Perino, 1997). Investors in HT firms are more likely to resort to class suits than investors in NHT firms because investors in HT firms have a greater stake in high-tech stocks, and the higher volatility of high-tech stocks is likely to cause investors to experience a large decline in wealth at some time. The threat of shareholder litigation increases high-tech managers' incentives to practice conservative accounting. HT firms are also more politically sensitive when investors lose money from alleged overstated income, and net assets and conservative accounting can result in lower political costs.

Because of technological innovations, HT firms are more likely to fund operating activities by raising capital from external investors (Trueman et al., 2000). HT firms that publicly commit to conservative accounting choices convey credible and favorable private information about future cash flow by signaling that they have the ability to meet investors' expectations about future growth. As a result, HT firms have an incentive to engage in conservative reporting.

Furthermore, HT firms attract more attention from financial analysts and the investment community than NHT firms because of HT firms' enormous opportunities for growth and favored status in the technology-based New Economy. As a result, HT firms undergo closer scrutiny by financial analysts as objects of investment recommendations to their customers and are likely to be more prudent in their financial reporting.[6]

Davis and Edge (2004) identify key compensation issues and total compensation perspective for high-growth entities as follows: (1) they must attract employees and maintain long-term incentive opportunities, and (2) they must be competitive to ensure the ability to attract and retain employees. HT firms are generally considered high-growth firms. All four components of the investment opportunity set (IOS) for HT firms are significantly higher than those in low-tech firms, according to a recent study by Kwon and Yin (2006).[7] Due to the nature of their businesses, HT firms invest more in intangible assets, such as R&D, human resources, customer acquisition, brand development, and other information technology (IT).[8] HT firms also incur more unusual or nonrecurring expenses, such as inventory write-downs, restructuring/reorganization expenses, and write-downs or write-offs of receivables and intangibles in order to survive in today's fast-changing, fiercely competitive market.[9] Since investment projects are typically more difficult to observe and monitor than assets-in-place (Smith & Watts, 1992; Krishnan & Kumar, 2001), greater information asymmetry exists between the principal (shareholders) and the agent (managers) in HT firms, creating a need for costly monitoring through incentive compensation contracts (Fama & Jensen, 1983; Jensen & Meckling, 1976).

On one hand, CEOs of HT firms are expected to be compensated more because of the increased risk exposure related to investment opportunities and for informational advantages on investment projects. On the other hand, HT firms are more likely to rely on compensation incentives to reduce agency costs arising from informational asymmetry, i.e., to tie CEO compensation closely to managerial efforts to accomplish investment goals in the best interest of shareholders.[10] Furthermore, since large expenses incurred to generate and exploit investment opportunities may lower accounting earnings, managers may be myopic and forgo projects with positive net present value if a large portion of compensation is tied to accounting earnings. To alleviate this managerial decision horizon problem and to avoid penalizing managers for engaging in activities that reduce current income, yet improve the long-term prospects of the company, HT firms are likely to increase proportions of long-term incentives such as stock options grants and tie compensation to stock returns since a firm's stock price captures intangible growth.[11]

Since the turnover of CEOs in HT firms is high (Reingold, 2000), long-term compensation contracts can be used to induce managers with valuable private information to stay with the firm (Clinch, 1991). Because of the vesting provisions of stock options and the likelihood of options increasing in value with tenure, it is common for HT companies to use stock options as a vehicle to attract and retain talented executives. In order to retain those highly talented executives, HT firms are likely to adopt a policy that compensates reduced short-term incentive pay (e.g., bonus) with increased long-term incentive pay (e.g., equity-based compensation) when bad earnings news is announced.

Using HT and NHT samples based on prior research, this chapter documents the following empirical results. First, the sensitivity of executive bonus compensation to HT firms is more symmetric to both stock and accounting performance than NHT firms. This finding is consistent with the conjecture that the compensation committees of HT firms, compared to NHT firms, do not actively seek to mitigate the ex post settling up problem partly due to their fear of losing their stellar CEOs. Second, HT firms, relative to NHT firms, show a higher level of accounting conservatism when three different proxies of conservatism are used. Finally, HT firms' compensation committees do compensate reduced bonus compensation with equity-based compensation in the event of negative earnings changes (bad news) whereas NHT firms' compensation committees do not adopt such a policy. This finding is also consistent with the view that HT firms are more concerned about losing important managerial talent.

This chapter's contribution to the extant literature is in the following five areas. First, Ely (1991) documents that the relationship between compensation and firm performance measures depends on the firm's production environment. The author defines environment as technology, product markets, and the operating and financing risk faced by firms. I am able to provide evidence that industry participation, i.e., HT versus NHT, has differential effects on the sensitivity of executive incentive compensation to both accounting and market performance measures (e.g., earnings and market returns).

Second, the issue of executive compensation has been a longstanding one in the United States and Canada because many feel that executives are overpaid. In addition, the issue of the executive compensation-performance sensitivity for HT firms is also relevant for accounting and finance researchers to pursue in this era of the IT revolution, especially when prior research has shown that HT firms differ from NHT firms in their market-valuation process. Therefore, this chapter is expected to contribute to the literature directly related to executive compensation, high-tech industries, and accounting conservatism.

Third, this chapter's evidence of more symmetric sensitivity of executive bonus compensation to changes in earnings and market-adjusted returns, and the use of executive equity-based pay to compensate executives for a loss in bonus pay when bad earnings news is announced in HT firms, is likely to become useful information for managers, politicians, investors, regulators, and academics in their assessment of the equitable relationship between executive efforts and executive compensation for technology-intensive (HT) firms.

Fourth, comparing the executive compensation of HT firms with that of NHT firms is important because empirical evidence has shown that the total sensitivity of executive wealth to changes in shareholder wealth has become dominated by executives' stock and stock option portfolios, as opposed to cash compensation or other components of executive pay packages (Bushman & Smith, 2001, p. 242). This chapter's results suggest that one explanation may be the increasing number of HT firms and their changing compensation strategies as the business environment becomes more uncertain.

Fifth, this chapter has relevance to the literature of corporate governance and transparency in financial reporting. According to Wikipedia, the free encyclopedia, corporate governance is defined as "The system by which companies are directed and controlled. It involves a set of relationships between a company's management, its board, its shareholders and other stakeholders; it deals with prevention or mitigation of the conflict of interests of stakeholders. Ways of mitigating or preventing these conflicts of interests include the processes, customs, policies, laws, and institutions which have impact on the way a company is controlled. An important theme of corporate governance is the nature and extent of accountability of people in the business, and mechanisms that try to decrease the principal–agent problem."[12]

Therefore, this chapter's major research issue that deals with the sensitivity of executive bonus compensation to earnings and returns is consistent with the corporate governance issue that deals with prevention or mitigation of the conflicts of stakeholders including executives and executive compensation committees that promote the well-being of firms or their shareholders. In addition, since financial reporting has an important role in motivating executive performance and controlling manager power, transparency, accountability, and conservatism in financial reporting are expected to influence prevention or mitigation of conflicts of interests between executives and shareholders.

In addition, Garcia Lara et al. (2009) recently document that firms with stronger corporate governance is associate with a higher degree of accounting conservatism. Therefore, this chapter's finding that HT firms have an incentive to engage in more conservative reporting than NHT firms because HT firms, through conservative financial reporting, can convey credible and favorable private information about future cash flows and growth is clearly linked with a corporate governance issue.

The remainder of this chapter is organized as follows. The second section develops the hypotheses by exploring and discussing previous relevant research. The third section describes sample selection procedures and the measurement of variables. The fourth section presents the results of empirical tests involving the comparison of the sensitivity of executive compensation to earnings changes and returns and the level of conservatism between HT and NHT firms. The fifth section provides discussion on sensitivity analyses. Concluding comments are offered in the sixth section.

HYPOTHESES DEVELOPMENT

Leone et al. (2006) claim that managers, like shareholders, have limited tenure and limited liability, which creates costly ex post settling up when managers are paid for unrealized gains that evaporate. Recovery of excess compensation payments and reparation for excess investments is difficult when the manager leaves the firm before the cash flows materialize (Watts, 2003).[13] In contrast to unrealized gains, cash compensation reflects unrealized losses to prevent managers from evading the cash compensation consequences of these losses (Leone et al., 2006). This differential treatment of unrealized gains and unrealized losses has led the authors to find that CEO cash compensation is twice as sensitive to negative stock returns as it is to positive stock returns.[14]

The ex post settling up problem may not be serious for HT firms vis-à-vis NHT firms for the following reasons: First, many HT firms attract and retain talent by offering stock options (long-term incentive pay) with generous payoff possibilities and rely on equity as a major component of compensation packages (Lublin & Scism, 1999; Unifi Network, 2000). That is, short-term incentive pay such as a bonus has a lesser weight in total executive compensation for HT firms than for NHT firms. This, in turn, would reduce the sensitivity of executive bonus compensation to both positive and negative stock returns for HT firms. Most of the largest U.S. manufacturing corporations, including HT firms, use a bonus plan based on accounting earnings to remunerate managers (Fox, 1980; Healy, 1985). In light of these facts, I conjecture that HT firms are less likely to tie short-term incentive compensation (e.g., bonus) to stock returns than NHT firms.

Second, HT firms are more likely to adopt conservative financial reporting policies than their NHT counterparts for reasons indicated in the introduction section (i.e., vulnerability to shareholder litigation, subjection to stricter accounting standards which conveys credible and favorable private information to investors, and widespread analyst attention due to favored status in the technology-based New Economy. Watts (2003) points out that "conservatism constrains managerial opportunistic behavior and offsets managerial biases with its asymmetrical verifiability requirement... In addition to conservatism offsetting managerial bias in financial reporting, noncontracting parties in society also value conservatism's *constraint* on opportunistic payments to managers (emphasis added) and other contracting parties." Therefore, the ex post settling up problem for HT firms can be significantly reduced if they adopt more conservative reporting policies.

Third, according to the study by Davis and Edge (2004), the key compensation issues and total compensation perspective/for high-growth entities (e.g., HT firms) are to attract employees and maintain long-term incentive opportunities, and to be competitive to ensure the ability to attract and retain employees. Therefore, compensation committees of HT firms, relative to compensation committees of NHT firms, have a stronger incentive to treat both unrealized gains and unrealized losses equally, which will increase the symmetry in the sensitivity of executive bonus compensation to stock returns for HT firms. Asymmetric treatment of unrealized gains and losses can take place in HT firms only when the benefit of adopting such a policy exceeds the cost to be incurred resulting from the loss of a high-quality executive who is difficult to replace in a tight managerial labor market for high-technology industries. Gibbons and Murphy (1990) and Sloan (1993) find that, consistent with the theory of relative performance evaluation, executive compensation is more sensitive to firm-specific changes in value than to market-wide changes in firm value. Therefore, I adopt market-adjusted returns to measure stock performance. This chapter's first hypothesis, in its alternate form, is constructed as follows:

H1. Ceteris paribus, the sensitivity of executive bonus compensation to market-adjusted returns is weaker and more symmetric for HT firms than for NHT firms.

Leone et al. (2006) indicate that an important feature of conservative accounting is that it generally excludes unrealized gains from earnings and recognizes unrealized losses in a timely fashion. Accounting earnings fully reflect unrealized losses and partially reflect unrealized gains. For example, a loss contingency from pending or threatened litigation is recognized in the accounts when the chance of the litigation loss is high, and the amount of loss can be reasonably estimated. However, a gain contingency such as possible refunds from the government in tax disputes is at best footnoted, but not recognized in the accounts. In contrast to contingencies, unrealized holding gains and losses on trading securities and derivatives are fully reflected in accounting earnings.[15] Leone et al. (2006) further note that if the accounting system were designed solely for use in compensation contracts (unrealized gains are excluded from income and unrealized losses are recognized as incurred), there would be no asymmetry in the relationship between cash compensation and accounting earnings.[16]

Since HT firms are more likely to be in favor of conservative accounting policies, the above discussion can lead us to propose this chapter's second hypothesis in its alternate form as follows:

H2. Ceteris paribus, the sensitivity of executive incentive compensation to earnings changes is more symmetric for HT firms than for NHT firms.

Selecting investment projects requires higher managerial skills than supervising existing assets-in-place, and therefore the larger the proportion of firm value represented by growth options, the greater the executive's pay package (Gaver & Gaver, 1995; Smith & Watts, 1992). Moreover, HT firms are likely to be riskier than their counterparts and, as a result, are likely to offer higher compensation packages to CEOs for taking on increased risk and uncertainties related to growth opportunities. Also, the use of incentive-based compensation to encourage CEOs to take on investment projects imposes additional managerial risk, and HT firms are likely to pay a higher risk premium in the total compensation package. In addition, the turnover of CEOs in HT firms has been reported to be high (Reingold, 2000). To mitigate the effects of high CEO turnover and the potential cash shortage problem resulting from paying a higher risk premium discussed in the above, HT firms have a strong incentive to resort to more equity-based compensation contracts to induce managers with valuable private information to stay with the firm (Clinch, 1991). Because of the vesting provisions of stock options and the likelihood of these options increasing in value with tenure, it is common for HT companies to use stock options as a vehicle to attract and retain talented executives. In a similar vein, to attract and retain highly talented executives, HT firms are also likely to adopt a policy that compensates for reduced short-term incentive pay (e.g., bonus) with increased long-term incentive pay (e.g., equity-based compensation) when bad earnings news is announced. The third hypothesis in its alternate form is the following:

H3. Ceteris paribus, the sensitivity of executive equity-based compensation to market-adjusted returns is significantly negative for HT firms compared to NHT firms when bad earnings news is announced.

SAMPLE SELECTION AND METHODOLOGY

Sample Selection and Descriptive Statistics

Table 1 summarizes the sample selection procedures of this chapter. Financial data are obtained from COMPUSTAT, stock return data from CRSP, and executive compensation data from ExecuComp. The sample period begins in 1992 because that is the first year for which detailed compensation information is available from ExecuComp. The sample begins with 25,653 firm-year observations and ends with 5,653 firm-year observations from

Table 1. Sample Selection.

Panel A: Sample selection process		
Firm-year observations with CEO compensation data in ExecuComp from 1992 to 2005 (both bonus and equity compensation)		25,653
Less		
Observations with insufficient data to compute the change form of compensation and missing non-compensation data (ExecuComp)		8,314
Observations with insufficient CRSP data		2,995
Observations with insufficient COMPUSTAT and institutional investors' ownership data		5,373
Observations from financial institutions and utilities		3,318
Total usable firm-year observations (1993–2005) for highest-paid executives		5,653
Panel B: Total usable firm-year observations for the sample period (1993–2005)		
HT (high-tech firms)	Highest-paid executives	1,438
	Highest-paid CEOs	1,038
NHT (non-HT firms)	Highest-paid executives	4,215
	Highest-paid CEOs	2,983
Panel C: Yearly usable observations for highest-paid executives		
HT		
1993(60), 1994(90), 1995(108), 1996(103), 1997(108), 1998(102), 1999(126), 2000(136), 2001 (112), 2002(106), 2003(116), 2004(129), 2005(142)		
NHT		
1993(209), 1994(276), 1995(292), 1996(305), 1997(318), 1998(311), 1999(348), 2000(361), 2001(324), 2002(328), 2003(356), 2004(393), 2005(394)		
No. of firms that have appeared at least once out of 13 years (1993–2005)		
Final samples	HT: 194 firms and NHT: 487 firms	

1993 to 2005 after eliminating missing observations and computing the change form of compensation. The total usable firm-year observations are dichotomized into both HT and NHT samples. As in the work of Francis and Schipper (1999), I define HT firms as those in the computer, electronics, pharmaceutical, and telecommunications industries. NHT firms are all other firms except financial institutions (SICs between 6,000 and 6,999) and utilities (SICs between 4,400 and 5,000).[17] This sample selection procedure results in 194 HT firms (1,438 firm-year observations) and 487 NHT firms (4,215 firm-year observations). I limit the executive compensation observations to the highest-paid executives; I assume they are the ultimate decision-makers at the firms. Later, I replicate the tests using highest-paid

CEOs as in several other prior studies and find qualitatively similar results. In this replication, firm-year observations with the change of CEOs are deleted to mitigate potential biases from partial-year compensation. For this analysis, I use 1,038 HT and 2,983 NHT firm-year observations.

Table 2 presents the distribution of this chapter's samples in HT (NHT) industries as measured by three (two)-digit SIC codes. Slightly more than half of the HT firms fall in the electronic components and accessories, computer and data processing services, drugs, and computer and office equipment industries. The five most common industries in the NHT sample include industrial machinery and equipment, chemicals and allied products, food and kindred products, transportation equipment, and oil and gas extraction.

Table 3 shows the means, medians, and standard deviations of compensation variables, performance measurement variables, other financial variables, and time-series variables, and the results from both parametric (two-sample Student's *t*) and nonparametric (Wilcoxon rank-sum *Z*) tests of differences in these variables between HT and NHT firms. These financial and time-series variables are assumed to influence the sensitivity of executive incentive compensation to earnings and stock prices as documented in prior research. HT firms pay greater amounts of short-term (i.e., bonuses) and long-term (e.g., stock options and restrictive stock grants) incentive-based compensation than NHT firms. The differences are statistically very significant (far less than 1%). Smith and Watts (1992) indicate that selecting investment projects requires greater managerial skill than supervising existing assets-in-place. Therefore, executive compensation increases as growth options represent a larger proportion of a firm's value (Gaver & Gaver, 1995). HT firms generally carry higher risk and uncertainty related to growth opportunities than their NHT counterparts. Thus, HT firms are likely to use more incentive-based compensation to encourage their executives to take on new investment projects that are risky but have profitable long-term prospects.

HT firms show greater negative changes in equity-based compensation than NHT firms during the sample period spanning 1993–2005. HT firms fared considerably better than NHT firms in the performances of return on assets (ROA), return on equity (ROE), annual stock returns (ANNMRR), and annual market-adjusted stock returns (ANNMAR). The differences are statistically significant at 5% or lower in two-tailed tests. When a firm's performance is measured by earnings per share (EPS) deflated by stock price at the beginning of the fiscal year, however, HT firms did more poorly than NHT firms.[18] The changes in ROA and ROE are similar between HT and NHT firms during the sample period whereas

Table 2. Three-Digit (Two-Digit) SIC Codes of High-Tech (Non-HT) Sample.

Panel A: High-Tech (HT) Firms

3-Digit SIC Code	Industry	Number of Firms (Percent)
272	Periodicals	1(0.52)
283	Drugs	24(12.37)
355	Special industry machinery	4(2.06)
357	Computer and office equipment	19(9.79)
361	Electric distribution equipment	2(1.03)
362	Electrical industrial apparatus	6(3.09)
363	Household appliances	3(1.55)
364	Electric lighting and wiring equipment	3(1.55)
366	Communications equipment	14(7.22)
367	Electronic components and accessories	34(17.53)
369	Misc. electrical equipment & supplies	2(1.03)
381	Search and navigation equipment	4(2.06)
382	Measuring and controlling devices	16(8.25)
386	Photographic equipment and supplies	3(1.55)
481	Telephone communications	6(3.09)
573	Radio, TV, and electronic stores	3(1.55)
621	Security brokers and dealers	8(4.12)
679	Miscellaneous investing	2(1.03)
733	Mailing, reproduction, stenographic	1(0.52)
737	Computer and data processing services	33(17.01)
738	Miscellaneous business services	2(1.03)
873	Research and testing services	4(2.06)
Total		194(100.00)

Panel B: Non-High-Tech (NHT) Firms

2-Digit SIC Code (Percent)	Industry	Number of firms (Percent)
10	Metal mining	6(1.23)
12	Coal mining	1(0.21)
13	Oil and gas extraction	27(5.54)
14	Nonmetallic minerals, except fuels	2(0.41)
15	General building contractors	10(2.05)
16	Heavy construction	2(0.41)
17	Special trade contractors	2(0.41)
20	Food and kindred products	28(5.75)
21	Tobacco products	2(0.41)
22	Textile mill products	5(1.03)
23	Apparel and other textile products	9(1.85)

Table 2. (*Continued*)

Panel B: Non-High-Tech (NHT) Firms

2-Digit SIC Code (Percent)	Industry	Number of firms (Percent)
24	Lumber and wood products	7(1.44)
25	Furniture and fixtures	5(1.03)
26	Paper and allied products	16(3.29)
27	Printing and publishing	23(4.72)
28	Chemicals and allied products	29(5.95)
29	Petroleum and coal products	15(3.08)
30	Rubber and misc. plastics products	9(1.85)
31	Leather and leather products	5(1.03)
32	Stone, clay, and glass products	7(1.44)
33	Primary metal industries	23(4.72)
34	Fabricated metal products	17(3.49)
35	Industrial machinery and equipment	40(8.21)
37	Transportation equipment	28(5.75)
38	Instruments and related products	21(4.31)
39	Miscellaneous manufacturing industries	9(1.85)
40	Railroad transportation	3(0.62)
42	Trucking and warehousing	6(1.23)
50	Wholesale trade__durable goods	22(4.52)
51	Wholesale trade__nondurable goods	13(2.67)
52	Building materials and garden supplies	3(0.62)
53	General merchandise stores	10(2.05)
54	Food stores	4(0.82)
55	Automotive dealers and service stations	2(0.41)
56	Apparel and accessory stores	12(2.46)
57	Furniture and homefurnishings stores	4(0.82)
58	Eating and drinking places	12(2.46)
59	Miscellaneous retail	9(1.85)
70	Hotels and other lodging places	4(0.82)
72	Personal services	5(1.03)
73	Business services	13(2.67)
75	Auto repair services, and parking	1(0.21)
79	Amusement and recreation services	2(0.41)
80	Health services	5(1.03)
82	Educational services	2(0.41)
87	Engineering and management services	7(1.44)
Total		487(100.00)

the changes in EPS with or without extraordinary items and discontinued operations are positive but smaller in HT firms than in NHT firms.

Consistent with the contracting hypotheses set forth in Myers (1977) and Smith and Watts (1992), HT firms are less leveraged (measured by debt-to-asset ratio) than NHT firms.[19]

HT firms are larger than NHT firms when the firm size is measured by the logarithm of the market value of equity. HT firms show higher market-to-book ratios (MTB) than NHT firms. Kole (1997) claims that high market-to-book value firms are research-intensive firms (HT firms), use more equity-based compensation plans (HT firms), and have longer vesting periods in their stock option plans. In addition, Smith and Watts (1992) document that firms with more growth options (higher MTB) employ more stock-option-based compensation.

As expected, HT firms turn out to be younger and fewer are owned by institutions when compared to NHT firms.[20] The CEOs of HT firms also are younger than their NHT counterparts during the sample period from 1993 through 2005. Baber et al. (1998) indicate that the sensitivity of executive compensation to earnings is greater for cases where executives are approaching retirement. HT firms' executives have a higher degree of equity interest measured by the total of restricted stock grants and option grants, deflated by total compensation including option grants whereas HT firms' equity-based incentives, measured by the total of restricted stock holdings, exercisable options, unexercisable options, and shares owned by the CEOs deflated by shares outstanding, are smaller than NHT firms only in parametric tests.[21]

The effects of the noise components in stock returns and accounting earnings on the sensitivity of executive compensation have been well documented in prior studies, including Lambert and Larcker (1987), Banker and Datar (1989), and Sloan (1993) among others.[22] The results of the comparison between HT and NHT firms in Table 3 show that the variability (i.e., the noise component) of basic and diluted EPSs is smaller in HT firms than in NHT firms.[23] The variability of EPSs is measured by standard deviation of annual EPSs over the past 7 years. The smaller variability of accounting earnings for HT firms may reflect a higher level of accounting conservatism in HT firms vis-à-vis NHT firms. The variability (the noise component) of annual stock returns, measured by the standard deviation of monthly returns over the prior 60 months, is higher for HT firms and than for NHT firms.[24] These variability measures are similar to those adopted in Leone et al. (2006).

A recent study by Baber et al. (1998) demonstrates that the sensitivity of executive cash compensation to earnings varies directly with earnings

Table 3. Descriptive Statistics 1993–2005.

Variable[a]	HT Mean	HT Median	HT SD	NHT Mean	NHT Median	NHT SD	Student t^b	Wilcoxon Z^b
Compensation variables								
Bonus compensation (BON)	1.830	0.868	5.324	1.134	0.780	1.963	7.17***	3.75***
Equity-based compensation (STOCK)	5.248	1.664	13.713	2.541	1.016	7.358	9.44***	8.96***
Change in bonus (CBON)	0.049	0.013	3.866	0.059	0.000	1.888	−0.13	0.99
Change in equity-based compensation (CSTOCK)	−5.237	−1.648	13.704	−2.580	−1.007	7.616	−9.12***	−8.81***
Change in cash salary and bonus (CSALBON)	0.335	0.140	4.835	0.271	0.103	1.985	0.70	2.25**
Change in total compensation (CTCOG)	0.741	0.230	26.399	0.598	0.199	9.526	0.30	0.70
Performance measurement variables								
Return on assets (ROA)	0.089	0.078	0.063	0.073	0.066	0.050	10.06***	7.84***
Return on equity (ROE)	0.196	0.165	0.281	0.190	0.153	0.312	0.71	3.69***
EPS including extraordinary items and discontinued operations (EPSEIP)	0.049	0.044	0.043	0.063	0.057	0.051	−8.57***	−13.29***
EPS excluding extraordinary items and discontinued operations (EPSP)	0.050	0.045	0.038	0.064	0.057	0.043	−10.76***	−14.06***
Change in ROA (CROA)	0.001	0.002	0.050	0.001	0.002	0.031	−0.26	0.75
Change in ROE (CROE)	0.001	0.003	0.239	0.006	0.002	0.309	−0.59	−0.12
Change in EPS including extraordinary items and discontinued operations (CEPSEIP)	0.004	0.003	0.061	0.006	0.005	0.070	−0.83	−2.45**
Change in EPS excluding extraordinary items and discontinued operations (CEPSP)	0.003	0.003	0.049	0.005	0.005	0.038	−1.88*	−2.34**
Annual stock returns (ANNMRR)	0.231	0.158	0.545	0.169	0.127	0.383	4.72***	2.10**

Table 3. (*Continued*)

	HT			NHT			Student	Wilcoxon
Variable[a]	Mean	Median	SD	Mean	Median	SD	t^b	Z^b
Annual abnormal return (ANNMAR)	0.120	0.037	0.488	0.068	0.010	0.375	4.21***	2.26**
Other financial variables								
Total assets (ASSET)	16,517	1,446	71,497	5,750	1,533	19,648	8.85***	− 1.05
Sale	5,814	1,193	13,605	6,379	1,854	19,001	− 1.04	− 7.85***
Log of market value of equity (LMVE)	7.992	7.798	1.769	7.556	7.438	5.483	9.05***	7.26***
Long-term debt divided by total assets (LEVERAGE)	0.158	0.119	0.167	0.228	0.227	0.147	− 15.01***	− 17.11***
Market-to-book value of equity (MTB)	4.560	3.279	8.094	3,498	2.407	14.559	2.63***	14.51***
Institutional ownership percent (Pct_Inst)	62.63	65.56	22.14	63.87	65.63	19.48	− 2.01**	− 0.19
Firm age (FAGE)	27.35	23.00	16.51	32.45	28.00	18.90	− 9.12***	− 9.75***
Executive's age (CEOAGE)	72	74	9.73	73	75	11.08	− 3.17***	− 5.08***
Equity incentive (EQUITYINC)	0.039	0.017	0.058	0.044	0.015	0.074	− 2.56**	− 0.23
Equity interest (EQUITYINT)	0.389	0.400	0.299	0.307	0.290	0.257	9.94***	8.85***
Stock price at the beginning of the current fiscal year (PFYM1)	37.62	33.38	22.16	35.98	30.07	37.65	1.98**	4.40***
Negative net income–dummy variable (1 if NI is negative) (LOSSDUM)	0.722	1.000	0.448	0.708	1.000	0.455	1.02	1.02
Taxrate (Taxrate)	0.328	0.340	0.092	0.358	0.368	0.081	− 11.53***	− 14.30***
Litigation (Litig)	0.004	0.000	0.024	0.017	0.000	0.123	− 3.73***	− 7.97***

Table 3. *(Continued)*

Variable[a]	HT Mean	HT Median	HT SD	NHT Mean	NHT Median	NHT SD	Student t^b	Wilcoxon Z^b
Time-series variables								
Variability of basic EPS (EPSBSTD)	0.852	0.617	0.807	0.977	0.637	1.292	-3.47^{***}	-2.14^{**}
Variability of diluted EPS (EPSDSTD)	0.838	0.602	0.794	0.954	0.624	1.178	-3.49^{***}	-2.07^{**}
Variability of returns (RETSTD)	0.118	0.113	0.046	0.098	0.095	0.032	17.73^{***}	15.64^{***}
Persistence measure–integrated moving average (IMA)	0.914	0.947	0.324	0.941	0.952	0.339	-2.69^{***}	-2.56^{**}
Persistence measure–integrated autoregressive (ARI)	0.421	0.468	0.283	0.450	0.494	0.269	-3.45^{***}	-3.22^{***}

[a]BON = $BONUS_t/SALARY_{t-1}$; STOCK = (Restricted stock $grants_t$ + Black–Scholes option $awards_t$)/$SALARY_{t-1}$; CBON = $BON_t - BON_{t-1}$; CSTOCK = $STOCK_t - STOCK_{t-1}$; CSALBON = $SALBON_t - SALBON_{t-1}$, where SALBON = SALARY + BON and SALARY = $SALARY_t/SALARY_{t-1}$; CTCOG = $TCOG_t - TCOG_{t-1}$, where TCOG = total compensation including option grants deflated by $SALARY_{t-1}$; ROA = net income before extraordinary items and discontinued operations/total assets; ROE = net income before extraordinary items and discontinued operations/average common equity; EPSEIP = (EPS including extraordinary items and discontinued $operations)_t$/(stock $price)_{t-1}$; EPSP = EPS excluding extraordinary items and discontinued $operations)_t$/(stock $price)_{t-1}$; CROA = $ROA_t - ROA_{t-1}$; CROE = $ROE_t - ROE_{t-1}$; CEPSEIP = $EPSEIP_t - EPSEIP_{t-1}$; CEPSP = $EPSP_t - EPSP_{t-1}$; ANNMRR = cumulative monthly raw returns for fiscal year t from CRSP; ANNMAR = cumulative monthly market-adjusted returns for fiscal year t from CRSP where market-adjusted returns = raw returns – value-weighted market returns; ASSET = total assets (compustat #6); Sale = net sales (compustat #12); LMVE = log(market value of equity from ExecuComp); LEVERAGE = long-term debt plus the current portion of long-term debt (compustat #9 + compustat #34)/total assets (compustat #6); MTB = market value of equity/book value of common equity from ExecuComp; Pct_Inst = institutional ownership in % from the TFSD ownership database; FAGE = fiscal year t of the observation minus the year the firm first appeared on CRSP; CEOAGE = the age of the highest-paid executive in year t; EQUITYINC = (RSHN + OPTIONN + EOPN + UEOPN + SHOWN)/(SHOUT × 1,000), where RSHN = restricted stock holdings (in thousand shares), OPTIONN = options granted (in thousand shares), EOPN = exercisable options (in thousand shares), UEOPN = unexercisable options (in thousand shares), SHOWN = shares owned with options excluded (in thousand shares), and SHOUT = common shares outstanding (in million shares); EQUITYINT = (RSG + OPTION)/TCOG, where RSG = restricted stock grants ($), OPTION = option grants ($), and TCOG = total compensation ($); taxrate = total income taxes for $t-1$ fiscal year(compustat #16)/pretax income for $t-1$ fiscal year (compustat #170); Litig = total contingent liabilities (compustat #327) for past three fiscal years at the beginning of the current fiscal year/total Assets (compustat #6) at the beginning of the current fiscal year; EPSBSTD = earnings volatility measured by standard deviation of annual basic earnings per share over the past 7 years; EPSDSTD = earnings volatility measured by standard deviation of annual diluted earnings per share over the past 7 years; RETSTD = stock return volatility measured by standard deviation of monthly returns over the prior 60 months; and IMA = persistence measure based on the integrated moving average model; ari = persistence measure based on the integrated autoregressive model.

[b]*, **, and** *** indicate statistical significance levels of 10%, 5%, and 1%, respectively, in two-tailed tests.

persistence. Earnings persistence is defined as the degree to which future earnings are induced by a \$1.00 innovation in current earnings. Valuation theory suggests that analysts and investors should place greater emphasis on forecasting high-persistence earnings than low-persistence earnings, because a given amount of the former has a greater valuation impact than the same amount of the latter. This time series properties of earnings (earnings persistence) are positively related to ERC, the magnitude of the relation between earnings and returns (Collins & Kothari, 1989; Easton & Zmijewski, 1989; Kormendi & Lipe, 1987).

The role of persistence can be explained by comparing the values of an unexpected dollar of permanent earnings and transitory earnings. Prior empirical studies predict that transitory earnings surprises have an empirical ERC of one, while the ERC of permanent earnings is one plus the inverse of discount rate such that analysts and investors are relatively uninterested in transitory earnings because the trading profits that could be earned from private foreknowledge of a dollar of transitory earnings are smaller than the profits from private foreknowledge of a dollar of permanent earnings (Freeman & Tse, 1992).

Since earnings follow a nonstationary process, the persistence can be better measured with a first differenced time-series model. In order to estimate firm-specific persistence levels, we adopt an ARIMA (1,1,0) or ARI (1,1,0) (Easton & Zmijewski, 1989; Kormendi & Lipe, 1987) and an IMAMA (0,1,1) or IMA (0,1,1) (Ali & Zarowin, 1992b; Baber et al., 1998; Beaver, 1970; Beaver et al., 1980; Collins & Kothari, 1989) time-series characterization of quarterly earnings, each of which considers seasonality of quarterly earnings and facilitates parsimonious empirical specifications of both earnings innovations and earnings persistence.

The ARI (1,1,0) model or the first differenced AR (1) model with seasonality can be expressed as follows:

$$(1\phi B)(1B^4)X_t = a_t$$

X is quarterly actual earnings, ϕ is persistence parameter, B is backshift operator, and a_t is white noise. This can be also represented as

$$X_t = X_{t4} + \phi(X_{t1}X_{t5}) + a_t$$

$$\Delta X_t \phi \Delta X_{t1} = a_t$$

ϕ is a firm-specific persistence level estimate similar to the autocorrelation of seasonally differenced earnings over the 32 quarters that end in each year of the sample period 1993–2005.

We can easily find that if ϕ is low, then current-earnings innovation would be more transitory. On the other hand if ϕ is high, then current-earnings innovation would be more permanent. Thus parameter ϕ measures the extent to which earnings innovations are permanent as opposed to transitory and quantifies the notion of earnings persistence.

The IMA (0,1,1) model with seasonality can also be expressed as follows:

$$(1B^4)Xt = (1\theta B^4)a_t$$

where (1θ) is persistence parameter.

$$X_t = X_{t4}\theta a_{t4} + a_t$$

If $\theta = 1$, then earnings follow a mean reverting process, and all earnings innovations are expected to be transitory. In contrast, when $\theta = 0$, earnings follow a random walk process, and all earnings innovations are expected to be permanent. Thus parameter (1θ) measures the extent of persistence level.[25]

As demonstrated in the time-series variables section of Table 2, HT firms' earnings are less persistent than NHT firms' earnings when the persistence is measured in either the IMA (0,1,1) model or the ARI (1,1,0) model.[26] The *t*-statistic (Wilcoxon *Z*), which measures the difference in persistence levels between HT and NHT firms, is 2.69 (2.56) under the IMA (0,1,1) model and 3.45 (3.22) under the ARI (1,1,0) model. They are all statistically significant at the 5% level or higher in two-tailed tests.

METHODOLOGY

CEO Performance Measures

I adopt four different versions of accounting earnings performance metrics normally found in prior research as follows[27]:

Change in Earnings per Share excluding EI and DO (CEPSP)[28]

$$\text{CEPSP}_t = \frac{\Delta\ (\text{Earnings per share excluding EI and DO})_t}{(\text{Stock Price})_{t1}}$$

Change in Earnings per Share including EI and DO (CEPSEIP)

$$\text{CEPSEIP}_t = \frac{\Delta\ \text{(Earnings per share including EI and DO)}_t}{\text{(Stock Price)}_{t1}}$$

Change in Return on Assets (CROA)

$$\text{CROA}_t = \text{ROA}_t\text{ROA}_{t1}$$

Where: ROA = Net Income before EI and DO/Total Assets;

Change in Return on Equity (CROE)

$$\text{CROE}_t = \text{ROE}_t\text{ROE}_{t1}$$

Where: ROE = Net Income before EI and DO/Average Common Equity

Annual Market-Adjusted Return (ANNMAR)

Annual Market-Adjusted Returns (ANNMAR) are cumulative monthly returns for the fiscal year where a return is computed by subtracting a value-weighted market index from a monthly return obtained from the CRSP monthly returns file.

$$\text{ANNMAR}_t = \prod_{\tau=1}^{12} (\text{RET}\tau + 1) - 1$$

where RET = Monthly Raw ReturnValue-Weighted Market Index.

Annual Raw Return (ANNMRR)

Annual Raw Returns (ANNMRR) are cumulative monthly returns for the fiscal year obtained from the CRSP monthly returns file.

$$ANNMRR_t = \prod_{\tau=1}^{12} (RET\tau + 1) - 1$$

where RET = Monthly Raw Return

Regression Models

Pooled Regression Model

$$\begin{aligned}\text{CBON}_{i,t} = {} & \beta_0 + \beta_1\text{D}_{i,t} + \beta_2\text{ANNMAR}_{i,t} + \beta_3 D_{i,t} \times \text{ANNMAR}_{i,t} \\ & + \beta_4\Delta\text{EPS}_{i,t} + \beta_5 D_{i,t} \times \Delta\text{EPS}_{i,t} + \beta_6\text{SALE}_{i,t} + \beta_7\text{SALE}^2{}_{i,t} \\ & + \beta_8\text{FAGE}_{i,t} + \beta_9\text{PERS}_{i,t} + \beta_{10}\text{LOSSDUM} \\ & + \beta_{11}\text{EQUITYINC}_{i,t} + \beta_{12}\text{LMVE}_{i,t} + \beta_{13}\text{MTB}_{i,t}\end{aligned}$$

$$+ \beta_{14}\text{EPSSTD}_{i,t} + \beta_{15}\text{RETSTD}_{i,t} + \beta_{16}\text{INST}_{i,t} + \beta_{17}\text{CEOAGE}_{i,t} + \beta_{18}\text{LEVERAGE}_{i,t} + \Sigma\gamma_j\text{YEAR}_j + \varepsilon_{i,t} \quad (1)$$

$$\text{CSTOCK}_{i,t} = \beta_0 + \beta_1 D_{i,t} + \beta_2\text{ANNMAR}_{i,t} + \beta_3 D_{i,t} \times \text{ANNMAR}_{i,t} + \beta_4\Delta\text{EPS}_{i,t} + \beta_5 D_{i,t} \times \Delta\text{EPS}_{i,t} + \beta_6\text{SALE}_{i,t} + \beta_7\text{SALE}^2{}_{i,t} + \beta_8\text{FAGE}_{i,t} + \beta_9\text{PERS}_{i,t} + \beta_{10}\text{EQUITYINC}_{i,t} + \beta_{11}\text{LMVE}_{i,t} + \beta_{12}\text{MTB}_{i,t} + \beta_{13}\text{EPSSTD}_{i,t} + \beta_{14}\text{RETSTD}_{i,t} + \beta_{15}\text{INST}_{i,t} + \beta_{16}\text{CEOAGE}_{i,t} + \beta_{17}\text{LEVERAGE}_{i,t} + \Sigma\gamma_j\text{YEAR}_j + \varepsilon_{i,t} \quad (2)$$

where for firm i in year t,
CBON = $\text{BON}_t\text{BON}_{t1}$;
BON = $\text{BONUS}_t/\text{SALARY}_{t1}$;
CSTOCK = $\text{STOCK}_t\text{STOCK}_{t1}$;
STOCK = (restricted stock grants$_t$ + BlackScholes option awards$_t$)/SALARY$_{t1}$;
D = 1 if the annual market-adjusted return (ANNMAR) is negative, and 0 otherwise;
ANNMAR = cumulative monthly marketadjusted returns for fiscal year t from CRSP
where market-adjusted returns = raw returnsvalue-weighted market returns;
CEPSEIP = $\text{EPSEIP}_t\text{EPSEIP}_{t1}$;
EPSEIP = (EPS including EI and DO)$_t$/(stock price)$_{t1}$;
CEPSP = $\text{EPSP}_t\text{EPSP}_{t1}$;
EPSP = (EPS excluding EI and DO)$_t$/(stock price)$_{t1}$;
CROA = $\text{ROA}_t\text{ROA}_{t1}$;
ROA = net income before EI and DO$_t$/total assets$_t$;
CROE = $\text{ROE}_t\text{ROE}_{t1}$;
ROE = net income before EI and DO$_t$/average common equity for t and t 1;
ASSET = total assets$_t$ (compustat #6);
SALE = net sales$_t$ (compustat #12);
FAGE = fiscal year t of the observation minus the year the firm first appeared on CRSP;
PERS = persistence measure$_t$ based on the integrated moving average model;
LOSSDUM = 1 if net income including EI and DO$_t$ < 0 and 0 otherwise;
EQUITYINC = ($\text{RSHN}_t + \text{OPTIONN}_t + \text{EOPN}_t + \text{UEOPN}_t + \text{SHOWN}_t$)/($\text{SHOUT}_t \times 1{,}000$)

where RSHN = restricted stock holdings (in thousand shares), OPTIONN = options granted (in thousand shares), EOPN = exercisable options (in thousand shares), UEOPN = unexercisable options (in thousand shares), SHOWN = shares owned with options excluded (in thousand shares), and SHOUT = common shares outstanding (in million shares);
LMVE = log(market value of equity$_t$ from ExecuComp);
MTB = market value of equity$_t$/book value of common equity$_t$ from ExecuComp;
EPSSTD = earnings volatility$_t$ measured by standard deviation of annual basic earnings per share over the past 7 years;
RETSTD = stock return volatility$_t$ measured by standard deviation of monthly returns over the prior 60 months;
INST = institutional ownership$_t$ in % from the TFSD ownership database/100;
CEOAGE = the age of the highest-paid executive in fiscal year *t*;
LEVERAGE = long-term debt$_t$ plus the current portion of long-term debt$_t$ (compustat #9 + compustat #34)/total assets$_t$ (compustat #6);
YEAR$_t$ = 1 if the firm is in year *t* and 0 otherwise.

I deflate year *t* change in executive compensation by the prior year's (*t* 1) base salary to control for size-related factors that vary cross-sectionally and to minimize the effect of year *t*1 performance on compensation metrics. The compensation metric is also used in the work of Baber et al. (1996). The market-adjusted stock returns, instead of raw stock returns, are used because Sloan (1993) indicates that firm-specific movements in stock returns should be viewed as a more concentrated measure of CEO performance than raw stock returns.[29] The log of the market value of equity (LMVE) is included to control for firm size effect (Dikolli et al., 2005; Garvey & Milbourn, 2006).

Francis and Schipper (1999, p. 342) indicate that market-to-book ratios have been used in prior research as a proxy for unrecognized intangible assets. Givoly and Hayn (2000) and others demonstrate that to the extent that equity valuation by investors is based on the present value of future cash flows, the market-to-book ratio as well as earnings multiples would tend to be higher when the accounting measurement is more conservative.[30] This suggests that the market-to-book ratio, measured by the value of the equity divided by the book value of the equity (MTB), can also be used as a proxy for accounting conservatism, which may affect the sensitivity of CEO compensation to market and accounting performance.

Prior research such as work by Banker and Datar (1989), Lambert and Larcker (1987), Sloan (1993), and Leone et al. (2006) demonstrates that earnings volatility and stock return volatility may influence the sensitivity of CEO cash compensation to market and accounting performance. I measure earnings volatility as the standard deviation of annual basic earnings per share over the last 7 years and stock return volatility as the standard deviation of monthly returns over the prior 60 months, which are similar to the measures used by Dikolli et al. (2005).

Other control variables that are expected to influence the sensitivity of CEO compensation to CEO performance measures include institutional ownership (INST) (Dikolli et al., 2005, 2006), the age of CEO (CEOAGE) (Dikolli et al., 2006; Garvey & Milbourn, 2006), firm age, sales (SALE) and sales^2 (Leone et al., 2006), and leverage (LEVERAGE) measured by total debt divided by total assets (Leone et al., 2006). Baber et al. (1998) demonstrate that the sensitivity of compensation to earnings varies directly with earnings persistence, measured by MA1 based on an IMA (1,1) time-series characterization of earnings.

According to Cheng and Warfield (2005), managers with high equity incentives are more likely to sell shares in the future, and this motivates these managers to engage in earnings management to increase the value of the shares to be sold. The managers' earning management can affect the level of earnings persistence and quality, which in turn can affect the sensitivity of compensation to earnings. I include, in the regression model, an independent variable, EQUITYINC, as a proxy for earnings management. The LOSSDUM variable, which takes a value of 1 if net income with EI and DO is less than 0.0 and 0 otherwise, is included as an independent variable to control for earnings persistence when earnings are negative. Finally, year dummies (YEAR) are included to capture time-specific factors. I run the two models separately on HT and NHT firms.

Fama–MacBeth Regression Model

I also estimate regression Eqs. (1) and (2) using the Fama–MacBeth (1973) procedure, which has the advantage of controlling for cross-sectional correlation in the residuals by assuming independence through time.[31] The presence of a positive cross-sectional correlation in the residuals in the pooled regression would understate standard errors and overstate the *t*-statistics. Reported coefficients, adjusted R^2s, and number of observations will be the means of 13 annual regressions from 1993 to 2005. In addition, the standard errors will be the time-series standard deviations of the coefficients divided by the square root of 13. *t*-statistics will be accordingly computed as follows:

$$t(Y_j) = \frac{Y_j}{s(Y_j)/\sqrt{n}}$$

where Y_j = the mean coefficient of 13 annual cross-sectional regressions from 1993 through 2005 for variable j;
$s(Y_j)$ = the time-series standard deviations of the 13 coefficients divided by the square root of 13; and
n = the number of years tested.

Modified Jones Model and Performance-Matched Discretionary Accruals

I compute discretionary accruals using the cross-sectional modified Jones model estimated by industry and year. The cross-sectional approach has the advantage of controlling for the effects of industry-wide economic changes on total accruals and allowing the coefficients to change across years due to possible structural changes.[32]

$$\mathrm{TACCR}_{i,t}/\mathrm{A}_{i,t1} = \mathrm{a}_t(1/A_{i,t1}) + \mathrm{b}_{1t}(\Delta\mathrm{REV}_{i,t}\Delta\mathrm{REC}_{i,t})/\mathrm{A}_{i,t1} + \mathrm{b}_{2t}(\mathrm{PPE}_{i,t}/A_{i,t1}) + \varepsilon_{i,t} \quad (3)$$

where for firm i at time t,
$\mathrm{TACCR}_{i,t}$ = total accruals[33];
$\mathrm{A}_{i,t1}$ = lagged total assets (item #6);
$\Delta\mathrm{REV}_{i,t}$ = change in sales (item #12);
$\Delta\mathrm{REC}_{i,t}$ = change in accounts receivable (item #2);
$\mathrm{PPE}_{i,t}$ = gross property, plant, and equipment (item #7); and
$\varepsilon_{i,t}$ = error term.

Discretionary accruals are estimated as the difference between reported total accruals and fitted values of total accruals (nondiscretionary accruals) using coefficient estimates from Eq. (3) for the period spanning 1993–2005:

$$\mathrm{DA}_{i,t} = \mathrm{TACCR}_{i,t}/\mathrm{A}_{i,t1}[\mathrm{a}_t\,(1/A_{i,t1}) + \mathrm{b}_{1t}(\Delta\mathrm{REV}_{i,t}\Delta\mathrm{REC}_{i,t})/A_{i,t1} + \mathrm{b}_{2t}(\mathrm{PPE}_{i,t}/\,\mathrm{A}_{i,t1})] \quad (4)$$

where $\mathrm{DA}_{i,t}$ is discretionary accruals and $\Delta\mathrm{REC}_{i,t}$ is the change in accounts receivable (item #2). I adjust discretionary accruals for performance and industry effects as suggested by Kothari, Leone, and Wasley (2005) because potential measurement errors in discretionary accruals may correlate with industry membership, growth, or performance. I calculate performance-matched discretionary accruals for firm i as discretionary

Table 4. Spearman Correlation Coefficients[a].

Panel A: HT firms (N=1,438)

	CBON	CSTOCK	ANNMAR	ANNMRR	CEPSEIP	CEPSP	CROA	CROE
CBON	1.00	−0.07**	0.21***	0.24***	0.25***	0.30***	0.31***	0.37***
CSTOCK		1.00	−0.02	0.04	0.05*	0.03	0.01	0.02
ANNMAR			1.00	0.88***	0.13***	0.15***	0.17***	0.20***
ANNMRR				1.00	0.17***	0.17***	0.19***	0.22***
CEPSEIP					1.00	0.86***	0.61***	0.60***
CEPSP						1.00	0.71***	0.70***
CROA							1.00	0.87***
CROE								1.00

Panel B: NHT firms (N=4,215)

	CBON	CSTOCK	ANNMAR	ANNMRR	CEPSEIP	CEPSP	CROA	CROE
CBON	1.00	−0.09**	0.18***	0.17***	0.29***	0.32***	0.33***	0.35***
CSTOCK		1.00	−0.05***	−0.01	−0.02	−0.01	−0.02	−0.02
ANNMAR			1.00	0.82***	0.13***	0.14***	0.17***	0.14***
ANNMRR				1.00	0.17***	0.14***	0.17***	0.15***
CEPSEIP					1.00	0.87***	0.65***	0.65***
CEPSP						1.00	0.76***	0.75***
CROA							1.00	0.86***
CROE								1.00

[a]The variables are defined in Table 2. The symbols *, **, and *** indicate statistical significance levels of 10%, 5%, and 1%, respectively, in two-tailed tests.

accruals of firm *i* minus discretionary accruals of firm *j* that exhibits the closest ROA in the same industry.

EMPIRICAL RESULTS

Panel A(B) of Table 4 shows Spearman correlation coefficients among key compensation and performance measurement variables used in the regressions for HT (NHT) firms.[34] As expected, most of the correlations are statistically significant at the level of 5% or higher in two-tailed tests except for generally insignificant correlations between equity-based compensation (CSTOCK) and performance measures based on accounting earnings and stock returns. It is also interesting to note that two incentive compensation variables – bonus (short-term) and stock (long-term) – are negatively correlated in both HT and NHT firms. These variables are statistically significant at the 5% level. The negative association between changes in bonus pay and changes in equity-based compensation suggests that both HT and NHT firms compensate for a reduction in one type of incentive compensation with an increase in the other type of incentive compensation, keeping the total change in incentive compensation constant. However, it should be noted that correlation tests are limited in that they cannot control for contemporaneous changes in other variables that might affect the correlation between a change in compensation and a change in executive performance.

Since Fama–MacBeth regressions have the advantage of controlling cross-sectional correlation in the residuals over the pooled regressions, and they are the procedure used by prior research (Leone et al., 2006), I also adopt the Fama–MacBeth procedure in this study for the purpose of comparison.

The empirical evidence in Panel A of Table 5 is consistent with the claim that positive (negative) firm-specific returns generally do not significantly increase (decrease) executive bonus pay in HT firms. For *t*-statistics for coefficients of ANNMAR are 1.10, 1.17, 0.03, 0.03, and 0.21 when the measures of ΔEPS are CEPSEIP, CEPSP, CROA, and CROE, respectively. The *t*-statistics for coefficients of ANNMAR in the case of bad news (negative firm-specific returns) are 0.28, 0.38, 0.70, and 0.08 when the measures of ΔEPS are CEPSEIP, CEPSP, CROA, and CROE, respectively. There are no significant differences between positive and negative firm-specific returns in their impact on executive bonus pay in HT firms. In other words, HT firms demonstrate more symmetry in the sensitivity of

Table 5. The Relationship between Changes in Bonus Compensation and Independent Variables, including Changes in EPS, Annual Abnormal Return, and Other Control Variables Fama–MacBeth Regressions from 1993 through 2005 (t-Statistics in Parentheses)[a].

Panel A: HT firms

Model: $\text{CBON}_{i,t} = \beta_0 + \beta_1 D_{i,t} + \beta_2\text{ANNMAR}_{i,t} + \beta_3 D_{i,t}\times\text{ANNMAR}_{i,t} + \beta_4\Delta\text{EPS}_{i,t} + \beta_5 D_{i,t}\times\Delta\text{EPS}_{i,t} + \beta_6\text{SALE}_{i,t} + \beta_7\text{SALE}^2_{i,t} + \beta_8\text{FAGE}_{i,t} + \beta_9\text{PERS}_{i,t} + \beta_{10}\text{LOSSDUM} + \beta_{11}\text{EQUITYINC}_{i,t} + \beta_{12}\text{LMVE}_{i,t} + \beta_{13}\text{MTB}_{i,t} + \beta_{14}\text{EPSSTD}_{i,t} + \beta_{15}\text{RETSTD}_{i,t} + \beta_{16}\text{INST}_{i,t} + \beta_{17}\text{CEOAGE}_{i,t} + \beta_{18}\text{LEVERAGE}_{i,t} + \Sigma\gamma_j\text{YEAR}_j + \varepsilon_{i,t}$ (1)

ΔEPS	CEPSEIP	CEPSP	CROA	CROE
β_0 (intercept)	−0.011(−0.32)	−0.023(−0.59)	−0.020(−0.55)	−0.027(−0.65)
β_1 (D)	−0.054(−1.87)*	−0.070(−2.37)**	−0.044(−1.57)	−0.054(−1.89)*
β_2 (ANNMAR)	0.030(1.10)	0.032(1.17)	0.001(0.03)	−0.010(−0.21)
β_3 (D*ANNMAR)	0.008(0.28)	−0.013(−0.38)	0.022(0.70)	0.003(0.08)
β_4 (ΔEPS)	0.047(1.12)	0.061(1.94)*	0.158(2.36)**	0.221(2.94)***
β_5 (D*ΔEPS)	0.075(1.31)	0.173(1.44)	−0.030(−0.41)	0.022(0.39)
β_6 (SALE)	−0.079(−0.41)	−0.073(−0.39)	−0.031(−0.14)	−0.009(−0.04)
β_7 (SALE^2)	0.139(0.39)	0.143(0.41)	0.088(0.20)	−0.041(−0.10)
β_8 (FAGE)	0.006(0.14)	0.017(0.38)	0.003(0.08)	−0.005(−0.12)
β_9 (PERS)	−0.015(−0.75)	−0.016(−0.87)	−0.022(−0.96)	−0.020(−0.99)
β_{10} (−OSSDUM)	−0.038(−2.03)**	−0.045(−2.65)**	−0.045(−2.29)**	−0.040(−2.00)**
β_{11} (EQUITYINC)	0.011(0.39)	0.006(0.23)	0.006(0.23)	0.010(0.42)
β_{12} (LMVE)	0.042(0.73)	0.039(0.75)	0.042(0.71)	0.054(1.05)
β_{13} (MTB)	−0.020(−0.75)	−0.025(−0.88)	−0.024(−0.76)	−0.005(−0.09)
β_{14} (EPSSTD)	0.013(0.45)	0.008(0.24)	−0.009(−0.32)	−0.004(−0.13)
β_{15} (RETSTD)	−0.026(−1.63)	−0.027(−1.56)	−0.027(−1.56)	−0.024(−1.57)
β_{16} (INST)	0.019(0.88)	0.018(0.81)	0.015(0.68)	0.013(0.63)
β_{17} (CEOAGE)	0.018(1.04)	0.020(1.04)	0.025(1.19)	0.027(1.23)
β_{18} (LEVERAGE)	0.005(0.15)	−0.001(−0.04)	−0.004(−0.10)**	−0.007(−0.21)
Adj. R^2	0.103	0.121	0.127	0.142
No. of observations	1,438	1,438	1,438	1,438

Panel B: NHT firms

Model: $\text{CBON}_{i,t} = \beta_0 + \beta_1 D_{i,t} + \beta_2\text{ANNMAR}_{i,t} + \beta_3 D_{i,t} \times \text{ANNMAR}_{i,t} + \beta_4\Delta\text{EPS}_{i,t} + \beta_5 D_{i,t} \times \Delta\text{EPS}_{i,t} + \beta_6\text{SALE}_{i,t} + \beta_7\text{SALE}^2_{i,t} + \beta_8\text{FAGE}_{i,t} + \beta_9\text{PERS}_{i,t} + \beta_{10}\text{LOSSDUM} + \beta_{11}\text{EQUITYINC}_{i,t} + \beta_{12}\text{LMVE}_{i,t} + \beta_{13}\text{MTB}_{i,t} + \beta_{14}\text{EPSSTD}_{i,t} + \beta_{15}\text{RETSTD}_{i,t} + \beta_{16}\text{INST}_{i,t} + \beta_{17}\text{CEOAGE}_{i,t} + \beta_{18}\text{LEVERAGE}_{i,t} + \Sigma\gamma_j\text{YEAR}_j + \varepsilon_{i,t}$ (1)

ΔEPS	CEPSEIP	CEPSP	CROA	CROE
β_0 (intercept)	−0.012(−0.43)	−0.009(−0.35)	−0.009(−0.32)	−0.012(−0.37)
β_1 (*D*)	0.027(1.83)*	0.029(2.01)**	0.032(2.08)**	0.027(1.70)*
β_2 (ANNMAR)	0.113(4.01)***	0.107(4.18)***	0.100(3.54)***	0.100(3.53)***
β_3 (*D**ANNMAR)	0.039 (1.84)*	0.039(1.85)*	0.040(2.45)**	0.044(2.30)**
β_4 (ΔEPS)	0.120 (4.18)***	0.131 (4.91)***	0.128(3.86)***	0.276(3.35)***
β_5 (*D**ΔEPS)	0.070(5.60)***	0.057(5.32)***	0.017(0.72)	0.053(1.17)
β_6 (SALE)	0.023(0.24)	0.013(0.13)	−0.011(−0.11)	−0.001(−0.01)
β_7 (SALE^2)	−0.295 (−0.84)	−0.256(−0.71)	−0.178(−0.46)	−0.222(−0.59)
β_8 (FAGE)	−0.008(−0.59)	−0.005(−0.38)	0.001(0.06)	−0.009(−0.65)
β_9 (PERS)	−0.011(−0.79)	−0.009(−0.75)	−0.010(−0.76)	−0.010(−0.66)
β_{10} (LOSSDUM)	−0.080(−4.93)***	−0.080(−4.72)***	−0.070(−4.12)***	−0.075(−4.73)***
β_{11} (EQUITYINC)	0.033(1.73)*	0.025(1.31)	0.034(1.70)*	0.031(1.57)
β_{12} (LMVE)	0.026(1.06)	0.025(0.92)	0.023(0.90)	0.030(1.10)
β_{13} (MTB)	0.046(1.37)	0.039(1.11)	0.031(0.95)	0.017(0.71)
β_{14} (EPSSTD)	0.003(0.53)	0.001(0.05)	−0.001(−0.09)	0.004(0.38)
β_{15} (RETSTD)	−0.003(−0.25)	−0.004(−0.32)	−0.002(−0.15)	0.005(0.36)
β_{16} (INST)	0.015(1.19)	0.017(1.34)	0.019 (1.42)	0.017(1.17)
β_{17} (CEOAGE)	−0.008(-0.71)	−0.007(−0.62)	−0.008(−0.77)	−0.009(−0.85)
β_{18} (LEVERAGE)	0.014(1.46)	0.015(1.59)	0.023(2.70)***	0.015(1.78)*
Adj. R^2	0.096	0.106	0.100	0.097
No. of observations	4,215	4,215	4,215	4,215

[a]The variables are defined in Table 2. The symbols *, **, and *** indicate statistical significance levels of 10%, 5%, and 1%, respectively, in two-tailed tests. The "LOSSDUM" variable is omitted in the Fama–MacBeth regression tests because these tests are based on much smaller number of yearly observations that are often all zeros for HT firms, which led to the problem of linear dependence among independent variables. To match the tests with HT firms, I also omit the LOSSDUM variable in the tests for NHT firms.

executive bonus compensation to market-adjusted returns than NHT firms.

In contrast to the results of HT firms in Panel A, the empirical evidence of Panel B of Table 5 for NHT firms is consistent with the claim that positive firm-specific returns (ANNMAR) significantly increase executive bonus pay, and negative firm-specific returns decrease executive bonus pay on even a greater scale. The *t*-statistics for coefficients of ANNMAR are 4.01^{***}, 4.18^{***}, 3.54^{***}, 3.53^{***} when the measures of ΔEPS are CEPSEIP, CEPSP, CROA, and CROE, respectively. The *t*-statistics for coefficients of ANNMAR in the case of bad news (negative firm-specific returns) are 1.84^{*}, 1.85^{*}, 2.45^{**}, and 2.30^{**} when the measures of ΔEPS are CEPSEIP, CEPSP, CROA, and CROE, respectively.

The empirical evidence in Panel B of Table 5 supports the claim of Leone et al. (2006) that CEO cash compensation is more sensitive to negative stock returns than it is to positive stock returns.[35] Therefore, this chapter's first hypothesis that ceteris paribus, the sensitivity of executive bonus compensation to market-adjusted returns is weaker and more symmetric for HT firms than for NHT firms has been supported.

In the case of the sensitivity of executive bonus pay to changes in earnings (ΔEPS), the empirical evidence in Panel A of Table 5 is consistent with the claim that positive changes in earnings generally significantly increase executive bonus pay, and negative changes in earnings decrease executive bonus pay in a similar scale for HT firms. For *t*-statistics for coefficients of ΔEPS are 1.12, 1.94^{*}, 2.36^{**}, and 2.94^{***} when the measures of ΔEPS are CEPSEIP, CEPSP, CROA, and CROE, respectively. The *t*-statistics for coefficients of ΔEPS in the case of bad news (negative firm-specific returns) are 1.31, 1.44, 0.41, and 0.39 when the measures of ΔEPS are CEPSEIP, CEPSP, CROA, and CROE, respectively. There are no significant differences between good and bad news cases in the sensitivity of executive bonus pay to changes in earnings in HT firms. In other words, HT firms demonstrate more symmetry in the sensitivity of executive bonus compensation to changes in earnings than NHT firms.

In contrast to the earnings results of HT firms in Panel A, the empirical evidence of Panel B of Table 5 for NHT firms is consistent with the claim that when positive changes in earnings significantly increase executive bonus pay, but negative changes in earnings decrease executive bonus pay on even a greater scale for NHT firms. The *t*-statistics for coefficients of ΔEPS are 4.18^{***}, 4.91^{***}, 3.86^{***}, and 3.35^{***} when the measures of ΔEPS are CEPSEIP, CEPSP, CROA, and CROE, respectively. However, the *t*-statistics for coefficients of ΔEPS in the case of bad news (negative firm-specific returns) are 5.60***, 5.32***, 0.72, and 1.17 when the measures of ΔEPS are CEPSEIP, CEPSP, CROA, and CROE, respectively.

The sensitivity of executive bonus pay to negative changes in earnings for NHT firms is also negative (i.e., positive coefficients) and statistically significant in at least two out of four different measures of ΔEPS. This shows that there are some significant differences between good and bad news cases in the sensitivity of executive bonus pay to changes in earnings in NHT firms. In other words, HT firms demonstrate more symmetry in the sensitivity of executive bonus compensation to changes in earnings than NHT firms. The above finding is consistent with this chapter's second hypothesis that ceteris paribus, the sensitivity of executive incentive compensation to earnings changes is more symmetric for HT firms than for NHT firms.

The results of Table 6 are also based on Fama–MacBeth regressions and deal with the sensitivity of equity-based executive compensation to market-adjusted returns and changes in earnings for HT (Panel A) and NHT firms (Panel B). The empirical evidence in Panel A of Table 6 is consistent with the claim that both positive and negative firm-specific returns do significantly increase executive equity-based compensation in HT firms. For *t*-statistics the coefficients of ANNMAR are 3.64***, 3.66***, 3.75***, and 3.12*** when the measures of ΔEPS are CEPSEIP, CEPSP, CROA, and CROE, respectively. The *t*-statistics for coefficients of ANNMAR in the case of bad news (negative firm-specific returns) are 2.52**, 2.57**, 2.48**, and 2.57** when the measures of ΔEPS are CEPSEIP, CEPSP, CROA, and CROE, respectively. HT firms indeed adopt a policy that compensates for reduced short-term incentive pay (e.g., bonus) with increased long-term incentive pay (e.g., equity-based compensation) when bad earnings news is announced.

In contrast to the results of HT firms in Panel A of Table 6, the empirical evidence of Panel B for NHT firms does not demonstrate any significant sensitivity of equity-based executive compensation to changes in earnings or market-adjusted returns, consistent with the results of Leone et al. (2006, Table 4). The *t*-statistics for coefficients of ANNMAR in the case of good (bad) news are 0.23 (1.26), 0.26 (1.34), 0.33 (0.88), and 0.37 (1.22) when the measures of ΔEPS are CEPSEIP, CEPSP, CROA, and CROE, respectively. Similarly, the *t*-statistics for coefficients of ΔEPS in the case of good (bad) news are 1.14 (0.72), 0.08 (0.21), 0.79 (0.52), and 1.13 (1.11) when the measures of ΔEPS are CEPSEIP, CEPSP, CROA, and CROE, respectively.

Table 6. The Relationship between Changes in Equity-based Compensation and Independent Variables Including Changes in EPS, Annual Abnormal Return, and Other Control Variables** Fama–MacBeth Regressions from 1993 through 2005 (t-statistics in parentheses)[a].

Panel A: HT firms

Model: $\text{CSTOCK}_{i,t} = \beta_0 + \beta_1 D_{i,t} + \beta_2\text{ANNMAR}_{i,t} + \beta_3 D_{i,t}\times\text{ANNMAR}_{i,t} + \beta_4\Delta\text{EPS}_{i,t} + \beta_5 D_{i,t}\times\Delta\text{EPS}_{i,t} + \beta_6\text{SALE}_{i,t} + \beta_7\text{SALE}^2_{i,t} + \beta_8\text{FAGE}_{i,t} + \beta_9\text{PERS}_{i,t} + \beta_{10}\text{EQUITYINC}_{i,t} + \beta_{11}\text{LMVE}_{i,t} + \beta_{12}\text{MTB}_{i,t} + \beta_{13}\text{EPSSTD}_{i,t} + \beta_{14}\text{RETSTD}_{i,t} + \beta_{15}\text{INST}_{i,t} + \beta_{16}\text{CEOAGE}_{i,t} + \beta_{17}\text{LEVERAGE}_{i,t} + \Sigma\gamma_j\text{YEAR}_j + \varepsilon_{i,t}$ (2)

ΔEPS	CEPSEIP	CEPSP	CROA	CROE
β_0 (intercept)	0.094(4.29)***	0.092(4.37)***	0.089(4.24)***	0.097(4.79)***
β_1 (D)	−0.008(−0.28)	−0.004(−0.14)	−0.012(−0.43)	−0.003(−0.11)
β_2 (ANNMAR)	0.082(3.64)***	0.080(3.66)***	0.071(3.75)***	0.076(3.12)***
β_3 (D*ANNMAR)	−0.080(−2.57)**	−0.076(−2.57)**	−0.066(−2.48)**	−0.064(−2.57)**
β_4 (ΔEPS)	0.065(1.72)*	0.047(1.42)	0.048(1.89)*	0.080(1.73)*
β_5 (D*ΔEPS)	0.003(0.11)	−0.011(−0.38)	−0.030(−1.47)	−0.021(−1.00)
β_6 (SALE)	−0.077(−0.57)	−0.075(−0.57)	−0.098(−0.76)	−0.094(−0.68)
β_7 (SALE^2)	0.045(0.19)	0.057(0.26)	0.067(0.31)	0.050(0.22)
β_8 (FAGE)	0.124(4.81)***	0.128(4.87)**	0.130(4.94)*	0.132(4.88)***
β_9 (PERS)	−0.058(−2.67)**	−0.063(−2.84)***	−0.062(−3.17)*	−0.057(−2.79)***
β_{10} (EQUITYINC)	0.045(2.16)**	0.045(2.05)**	0.038(1.87)*	0.038(1.87)*
β_{11} (LMVE)	−0.129(−3.42)***	−0.132(−3.27)	−0.124(−3.33)***	−0.123(−2.84)***
β_{12} (MTB)	−0.096(−2.98)***	−0.096(−3.05) **	−0.107(−3.28)***	−0.072(−1.09)
β_{13} (EPSSTD)	−0.039(−1.55)	−0.040(−1.49)	−0.045(−1.82)*	−0.040(−1.59)
β_{14} (RETSTD)	−0.059(−2.55)**	−0.054(−2.36)**	−0.046(−2.16)**	−0.054(−2.51)**
β_{15} (INST)	−0.074(−4.32)***	−0.069(−4.32)*	−0.068(−4.43)***	−0.073(−4.54)***
β_{16} (CEOAGE)	0.003(0.28)	0.008(0.60)	−0.003(−0.22)	−0.004(−0.34)
β_{17} (LEVERAGE)	−0.088(−4.18)***	−0.086(−4.31)***	−0.083(−4.15)***	−0.089(−4.28)***
Adj. R^2	0.129	0.130	0.127	0.137
No. of observations	1,438	1,438	1,438	1,438

Panel B: NHT firms

Model: $CSTOCK_{i,t} = \beta_0 + \beta_1 D_{i,t} + \beta_2 ANNMAR_{i,t} + \beta_3 D_{i,t} \times ANNMAR_{i,t} + \beta_4 \Delta EPS_{i,t} + \beta_5 D_{i,t} \times \Delta EPS_{i,t} + \beta_6 SALE_{i,t} + \beta_7 SALE^2_{i,t} + \beta_8 FAGE_{i,t} + \beta_9 PERS_{i,t} + \beta_{10} EQUITYINC_{i,t} + \beta_{11} LMVE_{i,t} + \beta_{12} MTB_{i,t} + \beta_{13} EPSSTD_{i,t} + \beta_{14} RETSTD_{i,t} + \beta_{15} INST_{i,t} + \beta_{16} CEOAGE_{i,t} + \beta_{17} LEVERAGE_{i,t} + \Sigma\gamma_j YEAR_j + \varepsilon_{i,t}$ (2)

ΔEPS	CEPSEIP	CEPSP	CROA	CROE
β_0 (intercept)	0.083(3.40)***	0.083(3.35)***	0.089(3.77)***	0.082(3.14)***
β_1 (*D*)	0.018(1.41)	0.015(1.22)	0.004(0.38)	0.011(0.89)
β_2 (ANNMAR)	−0.006(−0.23)	−0.007(−0.26)	−0.009(−0.33)	−0.009(−0.37)
β_3 (*D**ANNMAR)	0.032(1.26)	0.037(1.34)	0.023(0.88)	0.031(1.22)
β_4 (ΔEPS)	0.022(1.14)	0.001(0.08)	0.021(0.79)	0.078(1.13)
β_5 (*D**ΔEPS)	−0.017(−0.72)	0.006(0.21)	−0.014(−0.52)	−0.127(−1.11)
β_6 (SALE)	−0.139(−1.66)*	−0.148(−1.75)*	−0.163(−1.93)*	−0.161(−1.90)*
β_7 ($SALE^2$)	0.543(1.72)*	0.566(1.78)*	0.619(1.95)*	0.591(1.87)*
β_8 (FAGE)	0.037(4.13)***	0.038(4.10)***	0.037(4.17)***	0.037(4.06)***
β_9 (PERS)	−0.001(−0.14)	−0.001(−0.12)	−0.003(−0.32)	−0.001(−0.12)
β_{10} (EQUITYINC)	−0.008(−0.96)	−0.007(−0.79)	−0.007(−0.78)	−0.007(−0.79)
β_{11} (LMVE)	−0.197(−7.22)***	−0.195(−7.52)***	−0.190(−7.43)**	−0.186(−7.81)***
β_{12} (MTB)	−0.067(−1.64)	−0.071(−1.65)*	−0.076(−1.87)*	−0.072(−2.34)**
β_{13} (EPSSTD)	−0.040(−1.70)*	−0.041(−1.73)*	−0.034(−1.59)	−0.038(−1.60)
β_{14} (RETSTD)	−0.058(−5.40)***	−0.056(−5.18)***	−0.056(−4.80)**	−0.055(−4.75)***
β_{15} (INST)	−0.037(−3.92)***	−0.036(−3.82)***	−0.038(−4.33)*	−0.037(−3.80)***
β_{16} (CEOAGE)	0.015(2.64)***	0.013(2.17)**	0.013(2.45)**	0.013(2.29)**
β_{17} (LEVERAGE)	−0.023(−1.80)*	−0.022(−1.66)*	−0.024(−2.08)**	−0.024(−1.85)*
Adj. R^2	0.148	0.149	0.158	0.153
No. of observations	4,215	4,215	4,215	4,215

[a]The variables are defined in Table 2. The symbols *, **, and *** indicate statistical significance levels of 10%, 5%, and 1%, respectively, in two-tailed tests. The "LOSSDUM" variable is omitted in the Fama–MacBeth regression tests because these tests are based on much smaller number of yearly observations that are often all zeros for HT firms, which led to the problem of linear dependence among independent variables. To match the tests with HT firms, I also omit the LOSSDUM variable in the tests for NHT firms.

Therefore, based on the empirical evidence of Panel A (HT firms) and Panel B (NHT firms), this chapter's third hypothesis is supported, that ceteris paribus, the sensitivity of executive equity-based compensation to market-adjusted returns is significantly negative for HT firms compared to NHT firms when bad earnings news is announced. The evidence of negative sensitivity to market-adjusted returns for HT firms in the case of bad news is consistent with the view that for the purpose of attracting and retaining highly talented executives, HT firms are likely to adopt a policy that makes up for reduced short-term bonus pay with increased long-term equity-based compensation when bad earnings news is announced. When good earnings news is announced, HT firms' compensation committees have also significantly increased both short-term bonus pay and long-term equity-based pay in order to retain and motivate their highly valued executives.

SENSITIVITY TESTS AND ALTERNATIVE SPECIFICATIONS

Extreme Values and Alternative Specifications of Proxies

For all regression analyses in this study, I use several methods of truncation: deletions of observations outside mean ± 3 SD, mean ± 4 SD, and mean ± 5 SD; deletion of extreme 1% of variable distributions; and deletion of extreme 2% of variable distributions. The results presented in Tables 5and 6 are robust to such alternative treatments.[36]

As in the work of Cheng and Warfield (2005), I replicate the regressions in Tables 5 and 6 by replacing the equity incentive variable (EQUITYINC) with the equity interest variable (EQUITYINT). The results are qualitatively the same as before. In addition, I replace the persistence measure, MA1, with AR and obtain results similar to those in Tables 5 and 6.

Highest-Paid Executives versus Highest-Paid CEOs

I replicate the regression tests for highest-paid executive compensation with the data based on highest-paid CEO compensation because many prior studies use CEO compensation data, rather than compensation data of the highest-paid executives. The regression tests (not tabulated) reveal that empirical results of both HT (NHT) firms about the sensitivity of both short-term and long-term executive incentive compensation to market-adjusted returns do not materially differ between highest-paid executives and highest-paid CEOs. For example, the *t*-statistics for coefficients of ANNMAR for the regressions involving changes in bonuses as the dependent variable in the case of bad news for HT (NHT) firms are 0.23 (3.62***), 0.25 (4.56***), 0.27 (3.94***), and 0.06 (3.21***) when the measures of ΔEPS are CEPSEIP, CEPSP, CROA, and CROE, respectively. The *t*-statistics for coefficients of ANNMAR for the regressions involving changes in equity-based compensation as the dependent variable in the case of bad news for HT (NHT) firms are 1.94* (1.14), 2.04** (0.23), 2.04** (0.23), and 1.84* (0.13) when the measures of ΔEPS are CEPSEIP, CEPSP, CROA, and CROE, respectively. However, the sensitivity of CEO bonus compensation to earnings is indistinguishable between HT and NHT firms. Therefore, it can be concluded that inferences about market-adjusted returns made in previous tables are robust to this alternative specification of executive compensation.

Conservatism Measures

The results of Table 7 show a higher level of accounting conservatism for HT firms than for NHT firms when three different measures of accounting conservatism, including the market-to-book value of equity (Panel A), Performance-matched Discretionary Accruals (Panel B), and Basu's (1997) earnings-return association, are used (Givoly & Hayn, 2000). The market-to-book value of equity (MTB) variable for HT firms during the sample period spanning 1993–2005 is significantly higher in magnitude than that for NHT firms. Student's *t*-test (Wilcoxon rank-sum *Z*) is 2.63 (14.51), which is significant at the 1% level or higher.

The theory of conservatism predicts that earnings are more correlated with stock movements in periods characterized by bad earnings news than in periods characterized by good earnings news. If HT firms are more conservative in financial reporting than NHT firms, the association between stock price movements and earnings in periods of bad earnings news, compared with that in periods of good earnings news, would be stronger for HT firms than for NHT firms.

Panel C of Table 7 shows the earnings-return association based on pooled cross-sectional results. In the model, the coefficient on RDR, β_1, which measures the incremental response to bad earnings news relative to good earnings news, is positive and significant for HT firms (1.112, $t=3.33$). β_1 is insignificant and negative for NHT firms (0.032, $t=1.59$).

Table 7. Conservatism Measures 1993–2005[a].

HT			NHT			Student's	Wilcoxon
Mean	Median	SD	Mean	Median	SD	t	Z
Panel A: Market-to-book value of equity (MTB)							
4.560	3.279	8.094	3,498	2.407	14.559	2.63***	14.51***
Panel B: Performance-matched discretionary accruals (PMDA)							
1. PMDA							
1.182	− 0.002	22.387	0.305	0.025	12.076	1.23	− 1.33
2. |PMDA|							
6.320	1.275	21.507	4.367	0.591	11.263	2.88***	5.44***

Panel C: Earnings-return association (1993–2005)

$EPSP_{it} = \alpha_0 + \alpha_1 DR_{it} + \beta_0 ANNMRR_{it} + \beta_1 ANNMRR_{it} \times DR_{it} + \varepsilon_{it}$[b]

	α_0[c]	α_1	β_0	β_1	F-Value	Adj. R^2
HT	− 0.043(−2.15)*	− 0.045(−1.45)	0.067(1.76)*	1.112 (3.33)***	29.52(0.00)***	0.057
NHT	− 0.050(−4.16)***	− 0.014(−0.73)	0.215(7.73)***	− 0.032 (−1.59)	71.68(0.00)***	0.049

[a]The symbols *, **, and *** indicate statistical significance levels of 10%, 5%, and 1%, respectively, in two-tailed tests. Whenever a violation occurs with respect to the assumptions of homoskedastic errors, independence between the errors and regressors, or the linear specification of the model, White's (1980) heteroscedasticity-consistent t-statistics are reported. t-values are reported in parentheses. The top and bottom 1% of EPS and R are deleted. Also, the top and bottom 2% of the PMDA are deleted to mitigate the effects of extreme values.

[b]For firm i in year t, $EPSP_{it} = EPS_{it} / P_{it-1}$ where EPS_{it} = earnings per share; P_{it-1} = price per share at the beginning of the year; $ANNMRR_{it}$ = Annual Stock Returns; $DR_{it} = 1$ if $ANNMRR_{it} < 0$ and 0 otherwise; and ε_{it} = error term.

[c]Results are based on pooled cross-sectional time-series data.

This indicates that in HT firms the association between earnings and return in the periods of bad earnings news is stronger than that for NHT firms, consistent with the view that supports this chapter's second hypothesis that ceteris paribus, the sensitivity of executive incentive compensation to earnings changes is more symmetric for HT firms than for NHT firms. This is because HT firms engage in more conservative financial reporting (Leone et al., 2006).

CONCLUDING REMARKS

This chapter examines the sensitivity of executive incentive compensation to market-adjusted returns and changes in earnings for HT firms vis-à-vis NHT firms. Leone et al. (2006) recently found that CEO cash compensation is twice as sensitive to negative stock returns as it is to positive stock returns. They attribute this difference in sensitivity to boards of directors structuring cash compensation to mitigate the ex post settling up problem so that CEOs are rewarded less for unrealized gains than they are penalized for unrealized losses.[37]

This ex post settling up problem may not be serious for HT firms vis-à-vis NHT firms for the following reasons: First, many HT firms attract and retain high-quality executives by offering stock options (long-term incentive pay) with generous payoff possibilities and rely on equity as a major component of compensation packages. This focus on stock options in HT firms would reduce the sensitivity of executive bonus compensation to both positive and negative stock returns for HT firms (H1).

Second, HT firms are more likely to adopt conservative financial reporting policies than their NHT counterparts for reasons illustrated in the introduction section (i.e., vulnerability to shareholder litigation, subjection to stricter accounting standards which conveys credible and favorable private information to investors, and widespread analyst attention due to favored status in the technology-based New Economy. Accounting conservatism reduces both managerial bias in financial reporting and opportunistic payments to managers and other contracting parties (Watts, 2003). Therefore, the ex post settling up problem for HT firms can be significantly mitigated if they adopt more conservative reporting policies.

Third, in order to attract and retain highly talented executives, compensation committees of HT firms, relative to compensation committees of

NHT firms, have a stronger incentive to treat both unrealized gains and unrealized losses equally, which will increase the symmetry in the sensitivity of executive bonus compensation to stock returns for HT firms. Asymmetric treatment of unrealized gains and losses can take place in HT firms only when the benefit of adopting such a policy exceeds the cost to be incurred resulting from the loss of a high-quality executive who is difficult to replace in a tight managerial labor-market for high technology industries.

Prior studies also document that financial data pertaining to HT firms are less value-relevant than data belonging to NHT firms and also suggest the existence of a positive link between compensation-earnings sensitivities and value-earnings sensitivities. Leone et al. (2006) claim that the symmetry in the sensitivity of CEO cash compensation to earnings is an increasing function of the level of accounting conservatism because conservative accounting generally excludes unrealized gains from earnings and recognizes unrealized losses. Since HT firms are more likely to advocate conservative accounting policies, I hypothesize that the sensitivity of executive incentive compensation to earnings changes is more symmetric for HT firms than for NHT firms.

I also hypothesize that the sensitivity of executive equity-based compensation to market-adjusted returns is significantly negative for HT firms compared to NHT firms for the following reasons: The turnover rate for CEOs in HT firms was reported high in prior studies. In order to retain high-quality executives, HT firms are likely to adopt a policy that compensates reduced short-term pay (e.g., bonus) with increased long-term incentive pay (e.g., equity-based compensation) when bad earnings news is announced.

I find empirical evidence consistent with the above hypotheses. First, the sensitivity of executive bonus compensation to market-adjusted returns is weaker and more symmetric for HT firms than for NHT firms (a control group). Second, the sensitivity of executive incentive compensation to earnings changes is generally more symmetric for HT firms than for NHT firms. Third, the sensitivity of executive equity-based compensation to market-adjusted returns is significantly negative for HT firms compared to NHT firms when bad earnings news is announced. The results imply that HT firms, with a strong motive to attract and retain highly talented executives, judiciously use both short-term and long-term incentive compensation schemes by compensating for a reduction in short-term incentive pay with an increase in long-term incentive pay. Finally, consistent with prior research, HT firms show a higher level of accounting conservatism than NHT firms when three different proxies (market-to-book value of equity, performance-matched discretionary accruals, and earnings-return association) for accounting conservatism are adopted.

Our main results are robust to the use of highest-paid CEOs instead of highest-paid executives at least in the case of the sensitivity of executive compensation to market-adjusted returns, to the use of five different extreme value treatments, and to the use of alternative proxies of factors that are known to affect executive sensitivity to earnings and returns.

The issue of executive compensation has been a longstanding one in the United States and Canada because many feel that executives are overpaid. In addition, the issue of executive compensation-performance sensitivity for HT firms is also relevant for accounting/finance researchers to pursue in this era of the IT revolution, especially when prior research has shown that HT firms differ from NHT firms in their market-valuation process.

This chapter's evidence of greater symmetry in the sensitivity of executive bonus compensation to changes in earnings and market-adjusted returns, and the use of executive equity-based pay to compensate executives for a loss in bonus pay when bad earnings news is announced in HT firms is likely to become useful information to managers, politicians, investors, regulators, and academics in their assessment of the equitable relationship between executive efforts and executive compensation for technology-intensive (HT) firms. Therefore, this chapter is expected to contribute to the literature related to executive compensation, high-tech industries, and accounting conservatism.

ACKNOWLEDGMENTS

Comments from Kathryn Bewley, Brian Gaber, Patrice Gelinas, Michel L. Magnan, Peggy Ng, Flora Niu, Inho Suk, Jennifer Yin, and seminar participants at the CAAA annual conference in Montreal, Canada are greatly appreciated. The author acknowledges financial support from Research Grant programs at York University. Data used in this study are available from public sources identified in the chapter.

NOTES

1. A *BusinessWeek* article (Becker 2003) provides a good incentive to compare high-tech firms with less technology-dependent firms. The author argues: "I continue to believe that even after the burst of the bubbles in ***high-tech stocks***, the U.S. economy is in the relatively early stages of a major technological revolution (IT

revolution). The previous tech advance started at the end of the 19th century and was due mainly to the development of both the electric motor and the internal-combustion engine. The large spurt in technological progress during the past eight years is mainly due to a series of developments: rapid progress in computer capabilities, the explosive growth of the Internet, advances in cellular and other wireless technologies, the growth of fiber optics, advances in biotech, greater world competition for U.S. companies, which induced improvements in business efficiency, and myriad other smaller improvements in technology." The author, Professor Gary Becker, was the 1992 Nobel Laureate in Economics at the University of Chicago.

2. Many executive compensation plans are based on two performance measures – net income and share price.

Sloan (1993) indicates that empirically firms use both stock-price-based incentives and accounting-earnings-based incentives. The theoretical analyses demonstrated in the studies of Holmstrom (1979) and Feltham and Xie (1994) support that multiple performance measures increase contracting efficiency.

3. As Smith and Watts (1992) did, this study specifies bonus plans (short-term) and stock-option plans (long-term) as two incentive compensation plans. Also, Healy (1985) notes that although both bonus schemes and performance plans explicitly depend on accounting numbers, bonus contracts specify annual earnings goals, and performance plans specify long-term (three or five years) earnings goals. Moreover, Sloan (1993, p. 56) observes that top executive compensation is explicitly linked to earnings through annual bonus plans and long-term performance plans.

4. Leone et al. (2006) recently document that CEO cash compensation is twice as sensitive to negative stock returns as it is to positive stock returns. They attribute this difference in sensitivity to boards of directors structuring cash compensation to mitigate the ex post settling up problem so that CEOs are rewarded less for unrealized gains than they are penalized for unrealized losses.

5. Kwon et al. (2006) show that the level of accounting conservatism is higher in HT firms than in low-tech (LT) firms using several proxies of conservatism.

6. The results of Kwon (2002) support this explanation. Kwon (2002) finds that the absolute forecast errors and forecast dispersion are *negatively* related to the number of analysts and market-to-book value of assets.

7. Those four IOS components are investment intensity, geometric mean annual growth rate of market value of total assets, market-to-book value of total assets, and research and development expenditure to total assets.

8. Prior research has used market-to-book value of asset (MTBA) as a proxy for a firm's growth opportunities (Smith & Watts, 1992) and R&D spending as a percentage of total assets (RNDA) as a proxy for a firm's investment in unrecorded intangible assets (Francis & Schipper, 1999). Kwon and Yin (2006) report that the average MTBA and RNDA for high-tech (low-tech) firms are 3.2113 (1.9069) and 0.1037 (0.0208), respectively. The differences in these ratios between the two groups are significant at the .001 level.

9. Kwon (2002) reports that expenditures on special items in HT firms are anywhere between 3 and 28 times greater than those in low-tech firms during the period of 1990–1997.

10. Agency costs are defined as the sum of (i) the monitoring expenditures by the principal, (ii) the bonding expenditures by the agent, and (iii) the residual loss. For more details, see Jensen and Meckling (1976, pp. 81–83).

11. Lublin and Scism (1999), in a Wall Street Journal article, report that many HT firms attract and retain talent by offering stock options with generous payoff possibilities. In addition, a recent compensation study by PricewaterhouseCoopers on 123 public Internet companies indicates that these companies rely on equity as a major component of compensation packages (PricewaterhouseCoopers, 2000).

12. http://en.wikipedia.org/wiki/Corporate_governance (accessed August 6, 2012).

13. Leone et al. (2006) also indicate that if the firm pays the executive a cash bonus for an unrealized gain, but that gain does not later materialize, the executive can quit the firm and the shareholders will have difficulty recovering the cash paid for that unrealized gain.

14. Very recently, however, Shaw and Zhang (2010) demonstrate using a three-way performance partition that an ex post settling up in CEO cash compensation based on poor firms performance does not systematically occur. This is in stark contrast to the empirical evidence documented in Leone et al. (2006). Dechow (2006) also suggests that what appears to be ex post settling up enforced by compensation committees upon poorly performing executives could in fact reflect the result of compensation committees mechanically applying bonus contract formulas to earnings.

15. See Statement of Financial Accounting Standards No. 115 Accounting for Certain Investments in Debt and Equity Securities issued by FASB in May 1993 and Statement of Financial Accounting Standards No. 133 Accounting for Derivative Instruments and Hedging Activities issued by FASB in June 1998. This study uses the term "partially recognized" when it comes to unrealized gains because in some cases they are fully recognized (e.g., trading securities and derivatives), and are not recognized at all in some other cases (e.g., contingencies).

16. The studies by Watts (2003) and Leone et al. (2006) also imply that additional factors such as other accounting-based contracts (e.g., debt covenants), litigation, taxes, and regulation can cause the firm to deviate from the optimal level of accounting conservatism chosen solely for compensation contracts, potentially creating asymmetry in the relation between cash compensation and earnings.

17. These firms are excluded because Cheng and Warfield (2005) and Burgstahler and Eames (2003) point out that managers in these regulated industries might have different motivations to manage earnings.

18. HT firms' lower levels of EPS may indicate that HT firms engage in more conservative financial reporting, whether it is a mandatory requirement or voluntary choice, than NHT firms.

19. Under the contracting argument, firms with more growth options tend to use less debt to avoid severe incentive problems associated with debt (Myers, 1977; Smith & Watts, 1992, p. 278).

20. Leone et al. (2006) include firm age (FAGE) as a control variable in testing asymmetry in CEO compensation relative to stock returns. Khan et al. (2005) examine how institutional ownership concentration and dispersion affect levels of CEO compensation, pay mix, and stock option pay sensitivity.

21. These equity incentives and equity interest metrics are the same as those used in Cheng and Warfield (2005).

22. Specifically, Lambert and Larker find that CEO compensation is relatively less sensitive to earnings performance and more sensitive to stock-price performance when the time-series variance of earnings is high relative to the time-series variance of stock-price performance.

23. The fact that the variability of EPSs is lower in firms than in NHT firms may also imply a higher level of accounting conservatism in financial reporting for HT firms vis-à-vis NHT firms.

24. In light of the fact that the 1990s are characterized by the irrational exuberance in the U.S. stock market and the formation of record budget surpluses from government tax revenues. During this period HT firms with high growth potential were more susceptible to economic volatility. In addition, the burst of bubbles in high-tech stocks in 2001 also contributes to higher variability for HT firms.

25. In this paper, $(1-\Theta)=0.914$ (0.941) for HT (NHT) firms during the sample period 1993–2005, which implies that $\Theta=0.086$ (0.059). Similarly, Baber et al. (1998, p. 176) find, using 1974–1993 earnings per share data, that the mean value of the IMA parameter $(1-\Theta)=0.857$ and hence $\Theta=0.143$. The differences, which seem to be inconsiderable, possibly reflect differences in the sample period, sample size, and data availability requirement. This study also reports the results based on an alternative time-series model, Integrated Autoregressive Process [ARI (1,1,0)]. AR is the proxy for earnings persistence in this model.

26. Amir and Lev (1996) examine independent cellular companies and conclude that nonfinancial variables, such as total population in the licensed area and market penetration, account for stock prices better than financial indicators, such as earnings and cash flow from operations. This suggests that the financial information of HT firms is less market-value-relevant compared to that of NHT firms.

27. Many different versions of accounting performance measures appear in the following studies: Sloan (1993), Baber, Janakiraman, and Kang (1996), Gaver and Gaver (1998), Baber, Kang, and Kumar (1998), Baber, Kang, and Kumar (1999), Leone, Wu, and Zimmerman (2006), etc.

28. EI = Extraordinary items; DO = Discontinued operations.

29. Sloan (1993) further notes that even market-adjusted returns still contain other sources of noise that are beyond the CEO's control, such as exchange rate fluctuations and unexpected changes in input and output prices. The failure to incorporate these other sources of noise will reduce the power of the empirical tests and will create biases against finding the hypothesized relations. In this respect, the market-adjusted returns are not considered as a pure signal of CEO actions.

30. Also, see Feltham and Ohlson (1995) and Ohlson and Zhang (1998).

31. Leone et al. (2006) and Herrmann et al. (2001) among others used the Fama–MacBeth procedure in their empirical analyses. Theil (1971, p. 160) discusses a theoretical aspect of correlated residuals (disturbances) in a panel data regression.

32. Guay, Kothari, and Watts (1996) investigate the relative merit of various discretionary accrual models and conclude that the cross-sectional Jones and cross-sectional modified Jones models are most the effective in identifying discretionary accruals. DeFond and Jiambalvo (1994), Subramanyam (1996), Bartov, Gul, and

Tsui (2001), and Gul, Leung, and Srinidhi (2000) further support the adoption of the cross-sectional modified Jones model.

33. $TACCR_{i,t} = \Delta CA_{i,t} - \Delta CL_{i,t} - \Delta Cash_{i,t} + \Delta STD_{i,t} - Dep_{i,t}$, where, for firm i at time t, $\Delta CA_{i,t}$ = change in current assets (item #4); $\Delta CL_{i,t}$ = change in current liabilities (item #5); $\Delta Cash_{i,t}$ = change in cash and cash equivalents (item #1); $\Delta STD_{i,t}$ = change in debt included in current liabilities (item #34); and $Dep_{i,t}$ = depreciation and amortization expense (item #14).

34. Unlike Pearson's product moment correlation method, Spearman's rank correlation method does not require the association between two variables to be linear and thus is more suitable for measuring certain relationships that are not linear.

35. The only difference between my study and Leone et al. (2006) is the use of cash bonus in my study, instead of salary and bonus in Leone et al. (2006).

36. Murphy (1999) reports that earnings-based bonus contracts usually contain bogeys and caps, and most bonus plans use accounting earnings in a piece-wise linear fashion. In order to preclude the chance that extreme values of earnings per share may reduce the sensitivity of CEO compensation, I use five different deletion rules such as delete any independent or dependent variable whose observation exceeds the mean of the variable ± 3 standard deviations, ± 4 standard deviations, or ± 5 standard deviations. Also, following the deletion rule of Baber et al. (1996), independent or dependent variables in the top or the bottom 0.5% (2%) of their respective distributions are omitted from the regression.

37. Leone et al. (2006) further note that the ex post settling up problem also exists in other types of CEO compensation although it is likely more severe when payments are made in cash. This is because the unrealized gain may evaporate before equity claims vest when payments are made in stock options.

REFERENCES

Ali, A., & Zarowin, P. (1992). The role of earnings levels in annual earnings-return studies. *Journal of Accounting Research, 30*(2), 286–296.

Amir, E., & Lev, B. (1996). Value-relevance of non-financial information: The wireless communications industry. *Journal of Accounting and Economics, 22*, 3–30.

Baber, W., Janakiraman, S., & Kang, S. (1996). Investment opportunities and the structure of executive compensation. *Journal of Accounting and Economics, 21*(3), 297–318.

Baber, W. R., Kang, S. H., & Kumar, K. R. (1998). Accounting earnings and executive compensation: The role of earnings persistence. *Journal of Accounting and Economics, 25*, 169–193.

Baber, W. R., Kang, S. H., & Kumar, K. R. (1999). The explanatory power of earnings levels vs. earnings changes in the context of executive compensation. *The Accounting Review, October*, 459–472.

Banker, R. D., & Datar, S. M. (1989). Sensitivity, precision, and linear aggregation of signals for performance evaluation. *Journal of Accounting Research, 27*(1), 21–39.

Bartov, E., Gul, F. A., & Tsui, J. S. J. (2001). Discretionary-accruals models and audit qualifications. *Journal of Accounting and Economics, 30*(3), 421–452.

Basu, S. (1997). The conservatism principle and the asymmetric timeliness of earnings. *Journal of Accounting and Economics, 24*, 3–37.

Beaver, W. (1970). The time series behavior of earnings variables, empirical research in accounting: Selected studies. *Supplement to Journal of Accounting Research*, 62–99.

Beaver, W., Lambert, R., & Morse, D. (1980). The information content of security prices. *Journal of Accounting and Economics, 2*, 3–28.

Becker, G. (2003). The productivity boom is just warming up. *BusinessWeek, 20*, 29.

Burgstahler, D. C., & Eames, M. J. (2003). Earnings management to avoid losses and earnings decreases: Are analysts fooled? *Contemporary Accounting Research, 20*(2), 253–294.

Bushman, R., Engel, E., Milliron, J., & Smith, A. (2000). *An analysis of the relation between the stewardship and valuation roles of earnings*. Working Paper, University of Chicago.

Bushman, R., & Smith, A. (2001, December). Financial accounting information and corporate governance. *Journal of Accounting and Economics, 32*, 237–333.

Cheng, Q., & Warfield, T. D. (2005). Equity incentives and earnings management. *The Accounting Review, 80*(2), 441–476.

Clinch, G. (1991). Employee compensation and firms' research and development activity. *Journal of Accounting Research, 29*(1), 59–78.

Collins, D. W., & Kothari, S. P. (1989). An analysis of the intertemporal and cross-sectional determinants of earnings response coefficients. *Journal of Accounting and Economics, 11*, 143–181.

Davis, M. L., and Edge, J. T. (2004). Executive compensation? The professional's guide to current issues & practices, Windsor Professional Information, LLC.

Dechow, P. (2006). Asymmetric sensitivity of CEO cash compensation to stock returns: A discussion. *Journal of Accounting and Economics, 42*, 193–202.

DeFond, M. L., & Jiambalvo, J. (1994). Debt covenant violation and manipulation of accruals. *Journal of Accounting and Economics, 17*, 145–176.

Dikolli, S. S., Kulp, S. L., & Sedatole, K. L. (2005). *Transient institutional ownership and the contracting use of returns and earnings*. Working Paper, University of Texas at Austin.

Dikolli, S. S., Kulp, S. L., & Sedatole, K. L. (2006). *Transient institutional ownership and CEO contracting*. Working Paper, Duke University.

Easton, P. D., & Zmijewski, M. E. (1989). Cross-sectional variation in the stock-market response to accounting earnings announcements. *Journal of Accounting and Economics, 11*, 117–141.

Ely, K. (1991). Interindustry differences in the relation between compensation and firm performance variables. *Journal of Accounting Research, 29*(1), 37–58.

Fama, E., & Jensen, M. C. (1983). Separation of ownership and control. *Journal of Law and Economics, 26*, 301–325.

Feltham, G. A., & Ohlson, J. A. (1995). Valuation and clean surplus accounting for operating and financial activities. *Contemporary Accounting Research, 11*(2), 689–731.

Feltham, G. A., & Xie, J. (1994). Performance measure congruity and diversity in multi-task principal/agent relations. *The Accounting Review, 69*(3), 429–453.

Fox, H. (1980). *Top executive compensation*. New York, NY: The Conference Board.

Francis, J., Philbrick, D., & Schipper, K. (1994). Shareholder litigation and corporate disclosures. *Journal of Accounting Research, 32*, 137–164.

Francis, J., & Schipper, K. (1999). Have financial statements lost their relevance? *Journal of Accounting Research, 37*(2), 319–352.

Freeman, R. N., & Tse, S. (1992). A nonlinear model of security price responses to unexpected earnings. *Journal of Accounting Research*, *30*, 185–209.

Garcia Lara, J. M., Garcia Osma, B., & Penalva, F. (2009). Accounting conservatism and corporate governance. *Review of Accounting Studies*, *14*, 161–201.

Garvey, G. T., & Milbourn, T. T. (2006). Asymmetric benchmarking in compensation: Executives are rewarded for good luck but not penalized for bad. *Journal of Financial Economics*, *82*, 197–225.

Gaver, J. J., & Gaver, K. M. (1995). Compensation policy and the investment opportunity set. *Financial Management*, *24*(1), 19–32.

Gaver, J. J., & Gaver, K. M. (1998). The relation between nonrecurring accounting transactions and CEO compensation. *The Accounting Review*, *73*, 235–253.

Gibbons, R., & Murphy, K. (1990). Relative performance evaluation for chief executive officers. *Industrial and Labor Relations Review*, *43*, 30S–51S.

Givoly, D., & Hayn, C. (2000). The changing time-series properties of earnings, cash flows and accruals: Has financial reporting become more conservative? *Journal of Accounting and Economics*, *29*, 287–320.

Grundfest, J., and Perino, M. (1997). *Ten things we know and ten things we don't know about the Private Securities Litigation Reform Act of 1995*. Joint Written Testimony to the U.S. Congress, July 24. Retrieved from http://securities.stanford.edu/research/articles/19970723sen1.html. Accessed on August 9, 2012.

Guay, W. R., Kothari, S. P., & Watts, R. L. (1996). A market-based evaluation of discretionary accrual models. *Journal of Accounting Research*, *34*, 83–105.

Gul, F.A., Leung, S., & Srinidhi, B. (2000). *The effect of investment opportunity set and debt level on earnings-returns relationship and the pricing of discretionary accruals*. Working Paper, City University of Hong Kong.

Hand, X. (2000). *Profit, losses and the non-linear pricing of internet stocks*. Working Paper, University of North Carolina.

Healy, P. M. (1985). The effect of bonus schemes on accounting decisions. *Journal of Accounting and Economics*, *7*(1–3), 85–107.

Herrmann, D., Inoue, T., & Thomas, W. B. (2001). The relation between incremental subsidiary earnings and future stock returns in Japan. *Journal of Business Finance & Accounting*, *28*(9/10), 1115–1139.

Holmstrom, B. (1979). Moral hazard and observability. *Bell Journal of Economics*, *10*, 74–91.

Jensen, M., & Meckling, W. (1976). Theory of the firm: Managerial behavior, agency costs and ownership structure. *Journal of Financial Economics*, *3*(4), 305–360.

Johnson, M., Kasznik, R., & Nelson, K. (2001). The impact of securities litigation reform on the disclosure of forward-looking information by high-technology firms. *Journal of Accounting Research*, *39*, 297–327.

Jones, C., & Weingram, S. (1996). *The determinants of 10b-5 litigation risk*. Working Paper, Stanford University.

Khan, R., Dharwadkar, R., & Brandes, P. (2005). Institutional ownership and CEO compensation: A longitudinal examination. *Journal of Business Research*, *58*(8), 1078–1088.

Kole, S. (1997). The complexity of compensation contracts. *Journal of Financial Economics*, *43*, 79–104.

Kormendi, R. C., & Lipe, R. (1987). Earnings innovations, earnings persistence, and stock returns. *Journal of Business*, *60*(3), 323–346.

Kothari, S. P., Leone, A. J., & Wasley, C. E. (2005). Performance matched discretionary accrual measures. *Journal of Accounting and Economic, 39*(February), 163–197.

Krishnan, G. V., & Kumar, K.R. (2001). *Investment opportunities and the informativeness of cash flows*. Working Paper, George Washington University.

Kwon, S. S. (2002). Financial analysts' forecast accuracy and dispersion: High-tech versus low-tech stocks. *Review of Quantitative Finance and Accounting, 19*(1), 65–91.

Kwon, S. S., & Yin, J. (2006). Executive compensation, investment opportunities, and earnings management: High-tech versus low-tech firms. *Journal of Accounting, Auditing and Finance, Spring*, 1–36.

Kwon, S. S., Yin, Q. J., & Han, J. (2006). The effects of differential accounting conservatism on the 'over-valuation' of high-tech firms relative to low-tech firms. *Review of Quantitative Finance and Accounting, 27*, 143–173.

Lambert, R., & Larcker, D. (1987). An analysis of the use of accounting and market measures of performance in executive compensation contracts. *Journal of Accounting Research, 25*(3), 85–125.

Leone, A. J., Wu, J. S., & Zimmerman, J. L. (2006). Asymmetric sensitivity of CEO compensation to stock returns. *Journal of Accounting and Economics, 42*, 167–192.

Lublin, J. S., & Scism, L. (1999). Stock options at firms irk come investors. *The Wall Street Journal*, C1–C4, January 12.

Myers, S. (1977). Determinants of corporate borrowing. *Journal of Financial Economics, 5*(2), 147–175.

Ohlson, J. A., & Zhang, X. J. (1998). Accrual accounting and equity valuation. *Journal of Accounting Research, 36*, 85–111.

PricewaterhouseCoopers (2000). An analysis of public documents for 123 public internet companies?

Reingold, J. (2000, April 17). Executive pay: It continues to explode – And options alone are creating paper billionaires. *BusinessWeek*, 100–102.

Shaw, K. W., & Zhang, M. H. (2010). Is CEO cash compensation punished for poor firm performance? *The Accounting Review, 85*(3), 1065–1093.

Sloan, R. G. (1993). Accounting earnings and top executive compensation. *Journal of Accounting and Economics, 16*, 55–100.

Smith, C. W., & Watts, R. L. (1992). The investment opportunity set and corporate financing, dividend, and compensation policies. *Journal of Financial Economics, 32*, 263–292.

Subramanyam, K. R. (1996). The pricing of discretionary accruals. *Journal of Accounting and Economics, 22*(1-3), 249–281.

Theil, H. (1971). *Principles of econometrics*. Wiley.

Trueman, B., Wong, F., & Zhang, X. (2000). The eyeballs have it: Searching for the value in internet stocks. *Journal of Accounting Research, 38*, 137–162.

Unifi Network. (2000). *An analysis of public documents for 123 public internet companies*. Retrieved from http://www.pwcunifionline.com

Watts, R. (2003). Conservatism in accounting part I: Explanations and implications. *Accounting Horizons, 17*, 207–221.

White, H. (1980). Heteroskedasticity consistent covariance matrix estimator and a direct test of heteroskedasticity. *Econometrica, 48*, 817–838.

DIFFERENCES IN CORPORATE TRANSPARENCY BETWEEN MNC SUBSIDIARIES AND DOMESTIC CORPORATIONS: EMPIRICAL EVIDENCE FROM INDIA

Chinmay Pattnaik and Sid Gray

ABSTRACT

This study examines the differences in corporate transparency between subsidiaries of multinational corporations (MNCs), and domestic corporations (DCs) in India.

Keywords: Corporate transparency; corporate governance; market intermediaries; equity analysts; India; emerging market economies

JEL classifications: G34; G14; G17; L22

Transparency and Governance in a Global World
International Finance Review, Volume 13, 173–196

ISSN: 1569-3767/doi:10.1108/S1569-3767(2012)0000013009

INTRODUCTION

Corporate transparency refers to the disclosure of firm-specific information to outside constituents of the firm, and is an integral part of corporate governance practice. Corporate transparency plays an important role in reducing the information asymmetry between firms and their stakeholders, and contributes to the efficient functioning of financial, product, and labor markets in a country (Durnev, Errunza, & Molchanov, 2009; Rajan & Zingales, 1995). It also allows investors and stakeholders to monitor performance and contractual commitments of firms (Bushman & Smith, 2001). Therefore, market regulators enact numerous rules and regulations to ensure timely and accurate disclosure of information by public firms.

The existing literature on corporate transparency provides several useful insights on the determinants of corporate disclosure and transparency (Healy & Palepu, 2001). However, despite the recent interest among scholars in the corporate governance practices of multinational corporations or MNCs (Kriger, 1988; Luo, 2005; Strange & Jackson, 2008), comparisons between multinational and domestic firms on corporate governance practices in general and on corporate transparency in particular have received very little attention. While MNCs share many common features of corporate governance with domestic corporations (DCs), they also face additional complexities and challenges due to the diversity of corporate governance rules, regulations, and stakeholder expectations in the various host countries in which they operate (Luo, 2005). While some studies have examined the differences in corporate disclosure between MNC corporate headquarters and domestic firms (Alpay, Bodur, Ener, & Talug, 2005; Kiel, Hendry, & Nicholson, 2006; Krigger, 1988; Leksel & Lindgren, 1982), very few studies have examined the differences between MNC subsidiaries and DCs in their corporate governance, and in particular, their corporate disclosure practices in a host country (Cahan, Rahman, & Perera, 2005; Duru & Reeb, 2002).

MNCs generally have two related tiers of corporate governance structures – at headquarters and at subsidiary levels. In the case of MNCs with subsidiaries listed on local stock exchanges in different countries, those subsidiaries need to simultaneously conform to the host country's legal requirements as well as to governance practices of the MNC (Luo, 2005; Kiel et al., 2006). Therefore, MNC subsidiaries face dual pressures, from the demands of the host country environment and also from corporate headquarters (Kostova & Zaheer, 1999; Rosenzweig & Singh, 1991). On the other hand, DCs need to conform only to the demands of their domestic rules, regulations, and stakeholder expectations (Alpay et al., 2005).

In this study, we seek to examine how MNC subsidiaries and domestic firms differ in corporate transparency. We argue that subsidiaries of MNCs disclose more information than DCs. Considering the fact that MNCs conduct business in multiple institutional environments that require different disclosure rules, they maintain higher disclosure standards than DCs. Secondly, we separate DCs on the basis of their level of internationalization, and argue that DCs with high levels of internationalization disclose more information than those with purely local operations. Highly internationalized domestic firms need to conform to rules and regulations across different host countries. Moreover, internationalization increases the information asymmetry between the firm and its investors, as investors may find it difficult to gather information on the firm's foreign operations. As a result, firms with high levels of internationalization have a greater mandate to disclose more and reduce this information asymmetry. Finally, we differentiate domestic firms based on whether or not they are affiliated to business groups. The Indian corporate landscape is dominated by business groups. These are groups of legally independent firms operating in a wide variety of industries under common ownership and control (Ghemawat & Khanna, 1998; Khanna & Palepu, 2000). Firms affiliated with business groups trade capital, products, and managerial resources among themselves (Khanna & Palepu, 1997). The reliance on group-specific internal capital, product, and managerial/labor markets provides little motivation or incentives for affiliated firms to disclose information to stakeholders outside the groups. This in turn exacerbates the problem of information asymmetry between group-affiliated firms and the market (Douthett, Jung, & Kwak, 2004). Hence, we argue, business group affiliated firms are less transparent compared to unaffiliated domestic firms and subsidiaries of MNCs.

Our measure of corporate transparency is based on the characteristics of equity analysts' forecast behavior. Equity analysts serve as intermediaries between firms and the financial market. They collect information about a firm, evaluate its current performance, and make future forecasts about the firm. The accuracy and dispersion of analysts' forecasts depend on, and reflect the extent to which firms disclose information in the markets (Healy & Palepu, 2001; Lang & Lundholm, 1996). Previous studies have demonstrated that corporate disclosure is positively linked to analysts' forecast accuracy, and negatively to the dispersion among analysts covering a given firm in their forecasts (Bhat, Hope, & Kang, 2006; Hope, 2003; Irani & Karamanou, 2003; Lang & Ludholm, 1996).

The rest of the chapter is organized as follows: The following section presents our hypotheses on differences in corporate transparency between MNC subsidiaries and DCs, and between DCs differentiated in terms of their degree of internationalization and affiliation with business groups. The next section describes our data and the measurement of variables. The results of the empirical analysis are presented in the next section, and we discuss the implications of these in the final section.

DIFFERENCES IN CORPORATE TRANSPARENCY BETWEEN MNC SUBSIDIARIES AND DCs

Subsidiaries of MNCs face two conflicting pressures in global market. In order to survive and prosper, subsidiaries of MNCs need to conform to the laws, values, and norms of the host country in which they operate. This pressure to adapt to the local environment arises from host country legal and regulatory requirements. On the other hand, they also face pressures for consistency within the MNCs. Due to the ambiguity and uncertainty of international operations, MNCs strive to be internally consistent in their strategy through centralizing control and coordination of foreign operations, and by establishing similar organizational structure and processes in multiple host countries (Rosenzweig & Singh, 1991). Kostova and Zaheer (1999) argue that one of the critical issues faced by MNCs is acquiring legitimacy in their multiple host country environments. Survival of each subsidiary is contingent both on support from the parent company (internal legitimacy), and from the host country (external legitimacy). Subsidiaries of MNCs thus face two institutional environments, viz., the external environment of host country, and the internal environment of the MNCs.

Existing research has found substantial cross-country differences in practices related to corporate governance (La Porta, Lopez-de-Silanes, & Shleifer, 1999) and disclosure (Bushman, Piotroski, & Smith, 2003). In a study investigating corporate transparency across 45 countries worldwide, for example, Bushman et al. (2003) found substantial differences in corporate disclosure practices that arose from a country's legal/judicial regime and political economy.

To deal with the diversity of corporate governance norms they face in different countries, MNCs develop standardized financial reporting, accounting, and related practices to implement in their overseas subsidiaries. Such standardized corporate governance practices tend to be stronger than those of host country firms, especially in countries where corporate governance rules and regulations are weak. DCs, on the other hand, typically adopt the corporate governance practices of their home country. In instances of host countries where corporate governance rules are weak, DCs do not have any incentive to disclose a lot of information. Existing evidence suggests that the lack of corporate transparency is particularly prevalent in emerging market economies like India where corporate governance rules and enforcement are ineffective (Bushman et al., 2003; Oman, Fries, & Buiter, 2003).

Based on the above arguments, we posit that, compared to DCs in India, subsidiaries of MNCs have stronger disclosure practices.

> **H1**. The corporate transparency of MNC subsidiaries is higher than that of DCs.

DIFFERENCES IN CORPORATE TRANSPARENCY AMONG DCs

Firms in a country differ along several dimensions including their ownership, strategy, and organizational structure (Peng, 2006). In this study, we consider two such dimensions and their impact on corporate transparency. Firstly, we consider the impact of a firm's degree of internationalization. As argued in the previous section, firms that are geographically diversified need to conform to the rules and regulations of multiple host countries. This requires maintenance of higher disclosure levels than domestic firms. Secondly, we consider the impact of the structure of the corporation on corporate transparency. The Indian corporate sector is dominated by business groups. Firms affiliated with business groups trade capital, products, and managerial resources among group associates (Khanna & Palepu, 1997). This reliance on group-specific internal capital, product, and managerial/labor markets provide little motivation or incentive to disclose information to stakeholders outside the groups, exacerbating the problem of information asymmetry in the market (Douthett et al., 2004). Consequently, we argue that firms affiliated with business groups are less transparent than unaffiliated firms.

FIRM INTERNATIONALIZATION AND CORPORATE TRANSPARENCY

MNCs, compared with domestic firms, operate in a more complex business, financial reporting, and information environment. The degree of complexity increases as MNCs diversify their operations into different geographical markets and are exposed to diverse sets of rules and regulations (Hope, 2003). This complexity of operations increases the information asymmetry between the MNC managers and investors. Firstly, geographical diversification increases volatility of earnings due to subsidiaries' exposure to political or economic risk, and to regulatory intervention. Secondly, investors have more information about their home countries than on the foreign operations of a MNC (Duru & Reeb, 2002). Finally, compared to managers in the home country, subsidiary managers in the host country have more specific knowledge about the future cash flows (Cahan et al., 2005). All these factors exacerbate information asymmetry between firms with significant foreign operations and its investors. As a result, MNCs have incentives to reduce information asymmetry by disclosing information to reduce the cost of external financing (Lee et al., 2008). Existing empirical evidence also suggests a positive association between geographical diversification and higher corporate disclosure (Behn, Nichols, & Street. 2002; Cahan et al., 2005; Khanna, Palepu, & Srinivasan, 2004). For example, Cahan et al. (2005) found that managers disclose more information to reduce the information asymmetry and agency costs associated with geographical diversification. Also, Khanna et al. (2004) found that non-US firms interacting with the US product, capital, and labor markets are more likely to use disclosure practices similar to the those in the United States.

After the liberalization of Indian economy in 1991, Indian firms have substantially expanded their operation abroad. Also, due to the relaxation of foreign ownership rules, international investors have increased their ownership in Indian firms. As a result, Indian firms are exposed to international product and capital markets. We argue that Indian firms with higher levels of interaction with foreign markets, that is, with higher levels of internationalization, disclose more information relative to firms that operate only in the domestic market.

H2. The corporate transparency of DCs increases with their level of internationalization.

BUSINESS GROUP AFFILIATION AND CORPORATE TRANSPARENCY

Emerging markets are quite distinct from their developed country counterparts in terms of their institutional context and transaction costs that firms face in the market (Khanna & Palepu, 1997; North, 1990; Williamson, 1985).

External markets in emerging economies are often underdeveloped, or lack effective regulations for trade, contract enforcement, and communication. Weak information disclosure and the absence of information intermediaries, especially in capital, labor, and product markets, create "institutional voids," which in turn lead to high transaction costs (Khanna & Palepu, 1997; Khanna & Rivkin, 2001). In such circumstances, business groups turn to and draw from their internal capital, labor, and product markets, and allocate scarce resources among their affiliated firms. Business groups also resort to internal markets to reduce transaction costs that arise from information asymmetry between investors and the firm.

As a result, group-affiliated firms, by virtue of their access to internal capital markets, lack incentives and motivation to improve their transparency by disclosing information, say for the purpose of mitigating information asymmetry and reducing financing costs (Krishnaswami, Spindt, & Subramaniam, 1998; Rajan & Zingales, 1995). Furthermore, business groups in India have access to various privileges from governmental policies. For example, groups receive capital on preferential lending terms. This reduces their reliance on external equity markets and limits their incentives to build credibility through improved transparency in external capital markets (Khanna & Yafeh, 2007).

Based on arguments espoused in the above literature, we propose that business group-affiliated firms are less transparent than nonbusiness group firms.

H3. The corporate transparency of corporations affiliated with business groups is lower than that of unaffiliated corporations.

DATA AND METHODOLOGY

Data and Sample

We use analyst forecast error and forecast dispersion as proxies for corporate transparency, our dependent variable. We obtained analyst forecast data from the Institutional Brokers Estimate System (I/B/E/S) Summary History Tape. The I/B/E/S has collected data on Indian firms since 1993, but we only used data from 1995 to 2003 as some data points for the period 1993–1994 were missing. We also restricted our data to firms listed on the Bombay Stock Exchange (BSE). In order to ensure that regulatory changes during the study period for corporate governance, especially for corporate disclosure, did not impact our results, we referred to the corporate disclosure regulations as set out by the Securities and Exchange Board of India

(SEBI). SEBI is the statutory body responsible for listed firms' compliance with corporate governance and disclosure practices. Strict disclosure practices were not mandatory for listed firms until the mid-1990s. In order to improve corporate governance practices, SEBI set up the Kumar Mangalam Committee in 1999. But recommendations for mandatory and stricter disclosure practices were introduced in Clause 49 of the SEBI Act only in 2002. Since our study period ends in 2003, after which the strict enforcement of these laws occurred, we assume that changes in regulatory policies on disclosure practices do not affect our results.

We used the PROWESS database, compiled by the Center for Monitoring Indian Economy (CMIE), for financial data, and for data on MNC subsidiary and business group affiliations. PROWESS is the most reliable Indian corporate database, covers about 4,500 of the approximately 6,000 firms listed on the BSE, and has been extensively used in previous empirical studies (Bertrand, Mehta, & Mullainathan, 2002; Khanna & Palepu, 2000). The BSE classifies shares into three major groups: specified shares, that is, A group, and non-specified, that is, B1 and B2 group shares. However, only specified A-group shares are actively traded in the secondary market. Specified shares typically have a large capital base with a widespread shareholding, good growth record, a steady dividend, and high trading volume in the secondary market. Fairly liquid securities are included in the B1 category, and all newly listed securities are placed in the B2 group. The BSE periodically moves companies across categories, but classifies fewer than 200 shares as A group at any one time. In terms of the volume specified, A group accounts for more than 90% of total annual turnover. We include only specified A-group shares in our study in the expectation that, due to their large trading volume, disclosure standards will be higher in these firms. We exclude firms with missing values for forecast error and forecast dispersion, along with financial institutions and regulated utilities under government supervision. Using these criteria, we ended up with 911 firm-year observations in our final sample. This includes 206 MNC subsidiaries, 705 domestic firms, and 548 affiliates of business groups.

MEASUREMENT OF VARIABLES

Dependent Variable

We use two dependent variables for corporate transparency or disclosure: analysts' forecast error and dispersion. Firms make information available to the market through periodic disclosures (annual reports), occasional disclosures, and investor-relations activities. Together with direct information, equity analysts access and interpret information from other sources as well (McNichols & Trueman, 1994). Lang and Lundholm (1996) find that analyst forecasts are more accurate and less dispersed for firms with more open disclosure policies. Therefore, in this study, as in prior studies, we examine the changes in corporate transparency of Indian firms by tracking error and dispersion in analysts' forecasts.

Forecast error, which captures analysts' forecast accuracy, is the absolute value of the difference between actual earnings per share (EPS) and the median analyst forecast of EPS. We deflate this difference by stock price to facilitate comparisons across firms. The median analyst forecast we use is the final one calculated before the actual EPS figure is released.[1] In this study, we use a logarithmic transformation of forecast error to account for its highly skewed distribution.[2] The way we compute Log(Forecast Error) is:

$$\text{Log(Forecast Error)} = \text{Log}(|(\text{actual EPS} - \text{median analyst forecast of EPS})/\text{stock price}|)$$

Forecast dispersion among analysts is the standard deviation of analysts' forecasts of EPS. Again, we deflate the standard deviation by stock price to facilitate across firm comparisons. The standard deviation we use here is the final one calculated before the actual EPS figure is released. As in the case of forecast error, we use a logarithmic transformation.[3] The equation for computing Log(Forecast Dispersion) is as follows:

$$\text{Log(Forecast Dispersion)} = \text{Log}(|\text{standard deviation of analyst forecastsof EPS}/\text{stock price}|)$$

Independent Variables

We use a dummy variable, *MNC Subsidiary Dummy* that takes the value of 1 if the firm belongs to a MNC and 0 otherwise. We measure internationalization of Indian firms in two ways. The first variable relates to product market internationalization, measured as ratio of *Foreign Sales to Total Sales*. This measure captures the extent of exposure to foreign product markets. Several scholars have used ratio of foreign to total sales to measure international operations (e.g., Capar & Kotabe, 2003; Geringer,

Tallman, & Olsen, 2000; Tallman & Li, 1996). Our second measure of domestic firms' internationalization is their *Ratio of Foreign Ownership*. We consider a high degree of foreign ownership in domestic firms to indicate its closeness to international capital markets (Rubach & Sebora, 1998). Finally, our *Business Group Dummy* takes the value of 1 for firms that belong to any business group at the fiscal year-end, and 0 otherwise. We stick to the PROWESS classification of business-group affiliation. There is no legal definition for identifying business groups in India, but PROWESS provides a comprehensive classification of business group affiliation, which takes into account historical family ties, and is based on information from government and company sources. This classification is not only comprehensive and up-to-date, but also has been used in previous studies (Bertrand et al., 2002; Khanna & Palepu, 2000).

Control Variables

Based on prior studies, we included five control variables that influence analyst forecast error and dispersion. We proxy firm size with *Log(Market Value)*, the market value of the firm's equity. We defined this as the closing price of the firms' common stock at the fiscal year-end, multiplied by the number of outstanding common shares. Previous studies have found positive correlations between forecast accuracy and market value, between firm size and less dispersed forecasts (Lang & Lundholm, 1996), and between firm size and lower forecast error (Brown, Richardson, & Schwager, 1987; Eddy & Seifert, 1992). We also control for *Standard Deviation of Stock Returns*, the historical standard deviation of daily stock returns computed for one year. This measure reflects the internal uncertainty of a firm, which naturally affects analysts' forecasts. As this variable reflects the reliability of information contained in a stock price, forecasts for firms with higher standard deviation of stock returns becomes more difficult, and less accurate (Chang, Cho, & Shin, 2007). *Number of Analysts* is the number of analysts following a firm in a given year. We expect the number of analysts to have a negative impact on forecast error and dispersion, as they represent the quantity and quality of information about the firm being disseminated into the market (Alford & Berger, 1999; Lang & Lundholm, 1996). *Leverage* is the firm's debt-to-asset ratio; we expect a positive relationship between leverage and analyst forecast error and dispersion. Finally, variability in earnings increases the difficulty in predicting earnings, especially for firms that show losses. So variability leads to greater forecast error and dispersion

(Hope, 2003). Our *Earnings Dummy* takes a value of 1 if earning is negative and 0 otherwise (Chang et al., 2007). We expect a positive relationship between the negative earnings dummy and forecast error and dispersion.

In each regression, we include nine *Industry Dummies* to control for industry effects, and eight *Year Dummies* to control for any year-specific effects.

EMPIRICAL RESULTS

Descriptive Statistics

We report descriptive statistics for our variables in Table 1. The mean and median of forecast error are 5% and 1%, respectively, of the actual stock price. The mean and median of forecast dispersion are 2% and 1% of the actual stock price. The mean and median values of Log(Forecast Error) are −4.45 and −4.46, and those of Log(Forecast Dispersion), −4.46 and −4.47. The distribution of Log(Forecast Error) and Log(Forecast Dispersion) are thus less skewed and closer to normality.

Panel B compares the descriptive statistics of MNC subsidiaries and domestic firms. Our sample includes 206 MNC subsidiaries and 705 domestic firms. Both the mean and median of forecast error and forecast dispersion are higher for domestic firms. Both Log(Forecast Error) and Log(Forecast Dispersion) show the same pattern. The differences in the mean of the log variables are significant at the 1% level, indicating that transparency of MNC subsidiaries is higher than that for domestic firms.

Panel C compares the descriptive statistics of business-group and non-group firms. Our sample includes 548 business group-affiliated firms and 363 nonaffiliated (independent) firms. Both the mean and median of forecast error and forecast dispersion are higher for group-affiliated firms than for nongroup firms. Log(Forecast Error) and Log(Forecast Dispersion) show the same pattern. The differences in mean and median of the log variables are significant at the 1% level, indicating that transparency for business group-affiliated firms is lower than that for nonaffiliated firms.

Table 2 shows the Pearson correlations between variables used in this study. Log(Forecast Error) has a significant positive correlation with Log (Forecast Dispersion). Both Log(Forecast Error) and Log(Forecast Dispersion) have a negative and significant correlation with the MNC subsidiary dummy, firm internationalization variables (i.e., foreign sales to total sales and ratio of foreign ownership), and a positive and significant

Table 1. Descriptive Statistics for Variables.

Panel A: Pooled Sample (1995–2003)

Variables	Mean	Median	Standard Deviation	Minimum	Maximum
Forecast Error	0.05	0.01	0.16	0.00	2.38
Log(Forecast Error)	−4.45	−4.46	1.77	−11.54	0.86
Forecast Dispersion	0.02	0.01	0.06	0.00	1.01
Log(Forecast Dispersion)	−4.46	−4.47	1.30	−8.4	1.01
MNC Subsidiary Dummy	0.22	0.00	0.41	0	1
Foreign sales to total sales	0.10	0.03	0.16	0	0.89
Ratio of foreign ownership	6.60	4.13	7.43	0	44.97
Business group dummy	0.60	1.00	0.48	0	1
Number of analysts	1.69	1.79	0.69	0	2.94
Leverage	0.67	0.71	0.31	0	1.77
Earnings dummy	0.15	0.00	0.36	0	1
Log(Market Value)	6.33	6.25	1.80	−0.96	11.64
Standard deviation of stock returns	11.70	7.54	17.85	0	185.18

Panel B: Comparison between MNC Subsidiaries and DCs

	MNC Subsidiaries			Domestic Firms			Difference
	N	Mean	Median	N	Mean	Median	Mean
Forecast Error	206	0.03	0.00	705	0.05	0.01	0.02^{*}
Log(Forecast Error)	206	−5.19	−5.33	705	−4.32	−4.16	0.95^{***}
Forecast Dispersion	206	0.01	0.00	705	0.03	0.01	0.02^{**}
Log(Forecast Dispersion)	206	−5.18	−5.37	705	−4.25	−4.26	0.93^{***}
MNC Subsidiary Dummy	206	1	1	705	0	0	-1^{***}
Foreign sales to total sales	206	0.11	0.07	705	0.10	0.03	−0.01

Ratio of foreign ownership	206	3.90	1.81	705	4.49	0.10	0.58
Business group dummy	206	0	0	705	0.77	1.00	0.77***
Number of analysts	206	1.60	1.60	705	1.72	1.79	0.11**
Leverage	206	0.54	0.54	705	0.71	0.75	0.16***
Earnings dummy	206	0.08	0	705	0.17	0.00	0.09***
Log(Market Value)	206	6.56	6.53	705	6.27	6.20	−0.29***
Standard deviation of stock returns	206	10.12	7.78	705	21.74	10.47	0.67**

Panel C: Comparison between Business Group-Affiliated and Unaffiliated Corporations

	Business Group Firms			Nonbusiness Group Firms			Difference
	N	Mean	Median	*N*	Mean	Median	Mean
Forecast Error	548	0.05	0.01	363	0.04	0.00	−0.01
Log(Forecast Error)	548	−4.29	−4.20	363	−4.70	−4.89	−0.41***
Forecast Dispersion	548	0.03	0.01	363	0.02	0.00	−0.00**
Log(Forecast Dispersion)	548	−4.29	−4.29	363	−4.71	−4.87	−0.42***
MNC Subsidiary Dummy	548	0.00	0.00	363	0.56	1.00	0.56***
Foreign sales to total sales	548	0.11	0.04	363	0.08	0.02	−0.02**
Ratio of foreign ownership	548	4.66	0.34	363	3.91	0.69	−0.74
Business group dummy	548	1	1	363	0.00	0.00	−1***
Number of analysts	548	1.71	1.79	363	1.67	1.60	−0.03
Leverage	548	0.75	0.77	363	0.55	0.59	−0.20***
Earnings dummy	548	0.18	0	363	0.11	0.00	−0.06**
Log(Market Value)	548	6.20	6.09	363	6.54	6.58	0.33**
Standard deviation of stock returns	548	19.43	10.36	363	18.64	8.93	−0.79

Table 2. Correlation Coefficients.

Variables	1	2	3	4	5	6	7	8	9	10	11
1. Log(Forecast Error)	1										
2. Log(Forecast Dispersion)	0.66***	1									
3. MNC Subsidiary Dummy	−0.22***	−0.29***	1								
4. Foreign sales to total sales	−0.13***	−0.12***	0.02	1							
5. Ratio of foreign ownership	−0.17***	−0.11***	−0.14***	0.16***	1						
6. Business Group Dummy	0.11***	0.15***	−0.66***	0.07*	0.16***	1					
7. Number of analysts	−0.26***	−0.15***	−0.07*	0.06	0.26***	0.02	1				
8. Leverage	0.02	0.03	−0.23***	0.10***	0.09*	0.32***	0.01	1			
9. Earnings dummy	0.16***	0.15***	−0.11***	−0.21***	−0.14***	0.09**	−0.03	−0.22***	1		
10. Log(Market Value)	−0.32***	−0.28***	0.06*	0.06	0.18***	−0.09***	0.52***	0.05	−0.11***	1	
11. Standard deviation of stock returns	0.05	0.01	−0.08***	0.05	−0.02	0.00	−0.10**	0.10**	0.00	−0.23***	1

correlation with the business group dummy. The MNC subsidiary dummy has a negative and significant correlation with business group dummy. The group dummy has a significant and positive correlation with leverage, indicating that listed firms often invest and lend or borrow from other group firms (Khanna & Palepu, 1999; Lensink, Van der Molen, & Gangopadhyay, 2003). Both Log(Forecast Error) and Log(Forecast Dispersion) have a negative and significant correlation with Log(Market Value) and number of analysts, and a positive and significant correlation with the negative earnings dummy.

REGRESSIONS OF LOG(FORECAST ERROR) AND LOG(FORECAST DISPERSION)

Table 3 provides results for our hypotheses. We used multiple regression to test our hypotheses. The regression model is divided into two different panels. Each Panel (A and B) measures the independent impact of our independent variables on forecast error and forecast dispersion. Panels A and B are constructed as follows:

$$\begin{aligned}\text{Panel A : Log (Forecast Error)} &= \text{a} + \text{b}_1\text{MNC Subsidiary Dummy}\\ &+ \text{b}_2\text{Foreign to Total Sales} + \text{b}_3\text{Ratio of Foreign Ownership}\\ &+ \text{b}_4\text{BusinessGroup Dummy} + \text{b}_5\text{Number of Analysts} + \text{b}_6\text{Leverage}\\ &+ \text{b}_7\text{Earnings Dummy} + \text{b8Log (Market Value)}\\ &+ \text{b9Standard Deviation of Stock Returns}\\ &+ \text{Industry Dummy} + \text{Year Dummy} + e\end{aligned}$$

$$\begin{aligned}\text{Panel B : Log (Forecast Dispersion)} &= \text{a} + \text{b}_1\text{MNC Subsidiary Dummy}\\ &+ \text{b}_2\text{Foreign Sales to Total Sales} + \text{b}_3\text{Ratio of Foreign Ownership}\\ &+ \text{Ownership} + \text{b}_4\text{Business Group Dummy} + \text{b}_5\text{Number of Analysts}\\ &+ \text{b}_6\text{Leverage} + \text{b7Earnings Dummy} + \text{b8Log (Market Value)}\\ &+ \text{b9Standard Deviation of Stock Returns} + \text{Industry Dummy}\\ &+ \text{Year Dummy} + e\end{aligned}$$

Panel A shows the regression results for Log(Forecast Error). We used 788 firm-year observations between 1995 and 2003. We report the standard error-adjusted (White's adjusted) results for our independent and control variables. Model I shows the result for the impact of the MNC subsidiary

Table 3. Regression Results of Log(Forecast Error) and Log(Forecast Dispersion).

Panel A: Log(Forecast Error)	MODEL I	MODEL II	MODEL III	MODEL IV
MNC Subsidiary Dummy	−0.22***			
Foreign sales to total sales		−0.13***		
Ratio of foreign ownership			−0.14***	
Business group dummy				0.11***
Number of analysts	−0.21***	−0.16***	−0.17***	−0.18***
Leverage	0.07*	0.14***	0.11***	0.09**
Earnings dummy	0.27***	0.27***	0.27***	0.28***
Log(Market Value)	−0.20***	−0.23***	−0.22***	−0.21***
Standard deviation of stock returns	0.00	0.03	0.01	0.02
Industry dummy	Yes	Yes	Yes	Yes
Year dummy	Yes	Yes	Yes	Yes
Adjusted R^2	0.29	0.24	0.25	0.24
N	788	788	788	788

Panel B: Log(Forecast Dispersion)	MODEL I	MODEL II	MODEL III	MODEL IV
MNC Subsidiary Dummy	−0.28***			
Foreign sales to total sales		−0.11***		
Ratio of foreign ownership			−0.19***	
Business group dummy				0.15***
Number of analysts	−0.09**	−0.03	−0.05	−0.06*
Leverage	−0.07*	0.16***	0.13***	0.10***
Earnings dummy	0.21***	0.22***	0.21***	0.22***
Log(Market Value)	−0.21***	−0.27***	−0.26***	−0.24***
Standard deviation of stock returns	−0.02	0.01	0.01	0.00
Industry dummy	Yes	Yes	Yes	Yes
Year dummy	Yes	Yes	Yes	Yes
Adjusted R^2	0.26	0.20	0.23	0.21
N	788	788	788	788

dummy on forecast error. The MNC subsidiary dummy has a negative association with forecast error after controlling for the number of analysts, leverage, earnings dummy, market value, and standard deviation of stock returns. The estimated coefficient of the MNC subsidiary dummy suggests that analyst forecast error is 20% lower for MNC subsidiaries than for domestic firms.[4] This result supports H1, and indicates that MNC subsidiaries have higher transparency than domestic firms in India. Model

II and III show the impact of internationalization of domestic firms on forecast error. In line with H2, we expect higher levels of transparency for firms with high levels of internationalization. The regression results show that both foreign to total sales and ratio of foreign ownership in a domestic firm have significant negative associations with forecast error. In other words, greater level of internationalization by domestic firms leads to lower forecast error. Model IV shows the impact of a domestic firm's affiliation with business group and its impact on forecast error. We hypothesized that business group firms have little incentive and motivation to disclose information to the market. Consistent with this (H3), Model IV shows that our business group dummy variable has positive and significant association with forecast error. Among the control variables, number of analysts and Log(Market Value) have a significant negative association, and leverage and negative earnings dummy have positive and significant association with Log(Forecast Error). This suggests that larger firms with positive earnings and a large analyst following disclose comparatively more information (Brown et al., 1987; Eddy & Seifert, 1992).

Panel B shows the regression results for Log(Forecast Dispersion). In H1, we predicted MNC subsidiaries would have lower forecast dispersion than domestic firms. Model I shows that the MNC subsidiary dummy has a negative and significant association with Log(Forecast Dispersion). The estimated coefficient signifies that analysts' forecasts are 25% less dispersed for MNC subsidiaries than for domestic firms.[5] Consistent with H1, this result indicates that MNC subsidiaries in India have higher corporate transparency than domestic firms. Model II shows the impact of internationalization of domestic firms on Log(Forecast Dispersion). In H2, we expected higher corporate transparency for domestic firms with higher levels of internationalization. Consistent with our hypothesis, the regression results show that domestic firms' foreign to total sales and ratio of foreign ownership have significant and negative associations with forecast dispersion. The group dummy maintains its positive significance with forecast dispersion in model IV, consistent with H3. Log(Market Value) has a negative association and earnings dummy, a positive association with Log (Forecast Dispersion), suggesting that larger firms with positive earnings disclose more information than smaller firms.

Table 4 reports the combined impact of our independent variables on Log(Forecast Error) and Log(Forecast Dispersion). In the regression we included our independent variables incrementally to measure the combined impact. Panel A shows the regression results of the independent variables on Log(Forecast Error). The MNC subsidiary dummy and degree of

Table 4. Regression Results of Log(Forecast Error) and Log(Forecast Dispersion).

Panel A: Log(Forecast Error)

	MODEL I	MODEL II	MODEL III	MODEL IV	MODEL V
MNC Subsidiary Dummy	− 0.22***	− 0.22***	− 0.20***		− 0.23***
Foreign sales to total sales		− 0.12***	− 0.12***	− 0.13***	− 0.11***
Ratio of foreign ownership			− 0.03**	− 0.06**	− 0.07**
Business group dummy				0.13***	− 0.01
Number of analysts	− 0.21***	− 0.20***	− 0.20***	− 0.17***	− 0.19***
Leverage	0.07*	0.08**	0.08**	0.10***	0.09***
Earnings dummy	0.27***	0.26***	0.26***	0.26***	0.25***
Log(Market Value)	− 0.20***	− 0.20***	− 0.20***	0.20***	− 0.20***
Standard deviation of stock returns	0.00	0.01	0.01	0.03	0.00
Industry dummy	Yes	Yes	Yes	Yes	Yes
Year dummy	Yes	Yes	Yes	Yes	Yes
Adjusted R^2	0.29	0.29	0.32	0.26	0.32
N	788	788	788	788	788

Panel B: Log(Forecast Dispersion)

	MODEL I	MODEL II	MODEL III	MODEL IV	MODEL V
MNC Subsidiary Dummy	− 0.28***	− 0.28***	− 0.25***		− 0.30***
Foreign sales to total sales		− 0.10***	− 0.10***	− 0.12***	− 0.09*
Ratio of foreign ownership			− 0.06**	− 0.07**	− 0.07**
Business group dummy				0.17***	− 0.02
Number of analysts	− 0.09	− 0.08**	− 0.08**	− 0.05	− 0.07*
Leverage	− 0.07*	0.08**	0.08***	0.11***	0.09**
Earnings dummy	0.21***	0.20***	0.20***	0.21***	0.19***
Log (Market Value)	− 0.21***	− 0.24***	− 0.23***	− 0.23***	− 0.24***
Standard deviation of stock returns	− 0.02	− 0.01	− 0.01	0.01	0.01
Industry dummy	Yes	Yes	Yes	Yes	Yes
Year dummy	Yes	Yes	Yes	Yes	Yes
Adjusted R^2	0.26	0.27	0.31	0.23	0.31
N	788	788	788	788	788

Significance level: *5–10%; **1–5%; ***less than 1%.

internationalization of domestic firms (i.e., foreign to total sales and ratio of foreign ownership) have a negative and significant impact on the Log (Forecast Error) in model I, II, and III, respectively. The results are consistent with our H1 and H2. Model IV shows the impact of business group dummy variable on Log(Forecast Error). Considering the high and significant correlation between MNC subsidiary dummy and business group dummy, we excluded the MNC subsidiary dummy in the regression. The results show positive and significant impact of business group dummy on forecast error. This result is consistent with H3. We also ran additional regression including the MNC dummy in the regression as reported in model V. The business group dummy is not significant, and we suspect this is due to high correlation between the MNC subsidiary dummy and business group dummy. Panel B shows the impact of independent variables on Log(Forecast Dispersion). Consistent with H1 and H2, results show that MNC subsidiary dummy and domestic firm internationalization variables (i.e., ratio of foreign to total sales and ratio of foreign ownership) have negative and significant association with Log(Forecast Dispersion). These can be seen in models I, II, and III respectively. Model IV shows the regression results of business group dummy on Log(Forecast Dispersion). Similar to the results in Panel A, we excluded the MNC subsidiary dummy considering the high and significant correlation. Results show that business group dummy has positive and significant association with Log(Forecast Dispersion) consistent with H3. We also ran an additional regression with the MNC subsidiary dummy as reported in model V. The business group dummy lost its significance in the model, again, due to the high correlation between our business group and MNC subsidiary dummies.

The results in Panels A and B in Tables 3 and 4 support our three hypotheses that MNC subsidiaries and Indian firms with greater level of internationalization have higher corporate transparency. Business group-affiliated firms, however, in comparison to unaffiliated firms, have lower corporate transparency.

CONCLUSION AND IMPLICATIONS

In this study, we measured the corporate transparency of subsidiaries of MNCs, internationalized domestic firms, and firms affiliated with business groups in India. Our empirical findings suggest that subsidiaries of MNCs are more transparent than domestic Indian firms. But domestic firms with higher levels of internationalization are more transparent compared to firms which operate only in the Indian market. Furthermore, firms affiliated with business groups are less transparent compared to unaffiliated or independent firms.

Our findings have several implications for the corporate governance practices of MNCs and their impact on host country environments where corporate disclosure rules are weak in comparison to developed economies. Our findings on the greater transparency of subsidiaries of MNCs are consistent with the few prior studies on the effectiveness of corporate board structure, and performance of MNC subsidiaries and DCs (Alpay et al., 2005). Our results reveal that subsidiaries of MNCs adopt the standard disclosure rules of their corporate headquarters, which is usually more stringent that the disclosure practices of the host country. With their increased corporate transparency, subsidiaries of MNC improve the information environment of a host country where disclosure rules are weak. Their voluntary disclosure of information facilitates the effective functioning of market intermediaries like equity analysts which is in turn crucial for vibrant financial markets. In the case of DCs with higher levels of internationalization, our finding suggests that increase in internationalization leads to higher corporate transparency. This is because the information asymmetry arising from diversification of global operations increases the incentives for firms to disclose information at a higher level. Moreover, with the additional disclosure, firms with higher internationalization improve the information environment in their home country similar to what subsidiaries of MNCs do. Finally, previous studies on business groups in India have argued that business groups increase efficiency by conducting transactions in the internal capital, labor, and product market among group-affiliated firms. Our findings show the efficiency-enhancing role of business groups may negatively impact the corporate transparency. Due to their reliance on internal markets, group-affiliated firms are less motivated to disclose information to outside constituents, exacerbating the scarcity of information. This restricts the effective functioning of information intermediaries. Information intermediaries such as equity analysts play a transparency-enhancing role in the market. Equity analysts engage in information discovery and their individual efforts collectively improve corporate transparency (Claessens & Fan, 2002). Lack of disclosure will create impediments for these intermediaries to play an efficient role in improving the corporate transparency in the market.

This study, as with most research studies, has some limitations. Firstly, we based our empirical study from 1995 to 2003, when regulations on corporate disclosure were weak. Future studies may focus on a recent time period of improved corporate governance and disclosure practices in India to examine whether corporate governance practices of subsidiaries of MNCs and DCs have converged. In addition, it would be interesting to examine differences in corporate transparency between group-affiliated and unaffiliated firms following the introduction of corporate-disclosure regulations. Secondly, our study examined the internationalization of firms using the ratio of foreign sales to total sales and percentage of foreign ownership. In recent years, the momentum of internationalization of Indian firms has increased substantially. Future studies may need to focus on other firm level internationalization measures to examine their impact on corporate transparency.

In conclusion, on a broader level, this study shows that firms with higher level of internationalization (both subsidiaries of MNCs and DCs with higher internationalization) play a constructive role improving the information environment in an economy, which in turn facilitates the development of market intermediaries like equity analysts. However, domestic firms affiliated with business groups restrict the activities of such market intermediaries in emerging markets like India.

NOTES

1. Before the actual EPS figure is released, analysts usually forecast the EPS of a particular fiscal year several times. The frequency of forecasting differs depending on the analyst. The I/B/E/S collects the forecast data from individual analysts around the world once a month, and with it calculates statistics such as mean, median, standard deviation, etc. Only the final estimates of the analysts are included in the monthly calculation. Thus, the I/B/E/S Summary History Tape provides calculated statistics of analysts' forecasts of EPS once a month. In this study, we use the final, calculated median of analysts' forecasts of EPS before the actual EPS is released.

2. In Table 1, Panel A, the mean and median of Forecast Error is 0.05 and 0.01 respectively. Further, the minimum and maximum values of this variable are 0.00005 and 2.38, respectively. These values show that the distribution of Forecast Error is skewed, and thus log transformation is needed for normality. For example, the mean and median of Log(Forecast Error) are −4.45 and −4.46, respectively, showing that the distribution of Log(Forecast Error) is closer to normality than the Forecast Error.

3. In Table 1, Panel A, the mean of Forecast Dispersion is 0.027, while the median of Forecast Dispersion is 0.01. Further, the minimum and maximum values of this variable are 0.0002 and 1.0181, respectively. These values show that the distribution of Forecast Dispersion is skewed, and thus log transformation is needed for normality. For example, the mean and median of Log(Forecast Dispersion) are −4.46 and −4.57 respectively, showing the distribution of Log(Forecast Dispersion) to be closer to normality than Forecast Dispersion.

4. The economic magnitude of the group dummy is calculated as exp(−0.22.) −1 = −0.197.

5. The economic magnitude of group dummy is calculated as exp(−0.28) −1 = −0.244.

REFERENCES

Alford, A., & Berger, P (1999). A simultaneous equations analysis of forecast accuracy, analyst following, and trading volume. *Journal of Accounting, Auditing and Finance, Summer*, 219–240.

Alpay, G., Bodur, M., Ener, H., & Talug, C (2005). Comparing board-level governance at MNEs and local firms: Lessons from Turkey. *Journal of International Management, 11*(1), 67–86.

Behn, B. K., Nichols, N. B., & Street., D. L (2002). The predictive ability of geographic segment disclosures by U.S. companies: SFAS No. 131 vs. SFAS No. 14. *Journal of International Accounting Research, 1*(3), 1–44.

Bertrand, M., Mehta, P., & Mullainathan, S. (2002). Ferreting out tunneling: An application to Indian business groups. *Quarterly Journal of Economics, 117*(1), 121–148.

Bhat, G., Hope, O-E., & Kang, T. (2006). Does corporate governance transparency affect the accuracy of analyst forecast? *Accounting and Finance, 46*(5), 715–732.

Brown, L., Richardson, G., & Schwager, S. (1987). An informational interpretation of financial analyst superiority in forecasting earnings. *Journal of Accounting Research, 25*(1), 49–67.

Bushman, R., & Smith, A. (2001). Financial accounting information and corporate governance. *Journal of Accounting and Economics, 32*, 237–334.

Bushman, R. M., Piotroski, J. D., & Smith, A. J. (2003). What determines corporate transparency? *Journal of Accounting Research, 42*(2), 207–252.

Cahan, S. F., Rahman, A., & Perera, H. (2005). Global diversification and corporate disclosure. *Journal of International Accounting Research, 4*, 73–93.

Capar, N., & Kotabe, M. (2003). The relationship between international diversification and performance in service firms. *Journal of international Business Studies, 34*(4), 345–357.

Chang, J., Cho, Y. J., & Shin, H-H. (2007). The change in corporate transparency of Korean firms after the Asian financial crisis: An analysis using analysts' forecast data. *Corporate Governance: An International Review, 15*(6), 1144–1167.

Claessens, S., & Fan, J. P. H. (2002). Corporate governance in Asia: A survey. *International Review of Finance, 3*(2), 71–103.

Douthett, JR. W. B., Jung, K., & Kwak, W. (2004). Japanese corporate groupings (Keiretsu) and the characteristics of analysts' forecasts. *Review of Finance and Accounting, 23*(2), 79–98.

Durnev, A., Errunza, V, & Molchanov, A. (2009). Property rights protection, corporate transparency, and growth. *Journal of International Business Studies, 40*, 1533–1562.

Duru, A., & Reeb., D. M. (2002). International diversification and analysts' forecast accuracy and bias. *The Accounting Review, 77*, 415–433.

Eddy, E., & Seifert, B. (1992). An examination of hypotheses concerning earnings forecast errors. *Quarterly Journal of Business and Economics, 31*(2), 22–37.

Geringer, J. M., Tallman, S, & Olsen, D. M. (2000). Product and international diversification among Japanese multinational firms. *Strategic Management. Journal, 21*(1), 51–80.

Ghemawat, P., & Khanna, T. (1998). The nature of diversified business groups: A research design and two case studies. *The Journal of Industrial Economics, 46*(1), 35–61.

Healy, P., & Palepu, K. (2001). Information asymmetry, corporate disclosure, and capital markets: A review of empirical disclosure literature. *Journal of Accounting and Economics, 31*(1–3), 405–440.

Hope, O. (2003). Accounting policy disclosure and analysts forecasts. *Contemporary Accounting Research, 20*(2), 295–321.

Irani, A. J., & Karamanou, I. (2003). Regulation fair disclosure, analyst following, and analyst forecast dispersion. *Accounting Horizons, 17*(1), 15–29.

Khanna, T., & Palepu, K. (1997). Why focused strategies may be wrong for emerging markets. *Harvard Business Review, 75*(4), 41–51.

Khanna, T., & Palepu, K. (1999). Policy shocks, market intermediaries, and corporate strategy: The evolution of business strategy in Chile and India. *Journal of Economics & Management Strategy, 8*(2), 271–310.

Khanna, T., & Palepu, K. (2000). Is group affiliation profitable in emerging markets? An analysis of diversified Indian business groups. *Journal of Finance, 55*(2), 867–891.

Khanna, T., Palepu, K, & Srinivasan, K. (2004). Disclosure practices of foreign companies interacting with U.S. markets. *Journal of Accounting Research, 42*, 475–508.

Khanna, T., & Rivkin, J. (2001). Estimating the performance effects of business groups in emerging markets. *Strategic Management Journal, 22*(1), 45–74.

Khanna, T., & Yafeh, Y. (2007). Business groups in emerging markets: Paragons or parasites? *Journal of Economic Literature, 45*, 331–372.

Kiel, G. C., Hendry, K., & Nicholson, G. V. (2006). Corporate governance options for the local subsidiaries of multinational enterprises, corporate governance. *An International Review, 14*(6), 568–576.

Kostova, T, & Zaheer, S. (1999). Organizational legitimacy under conditions of complexity: The case of the multinational enterprise. *Academy of Management Review, 24*, 64–81.

Kriger, M. P. (1988). The increasing role of subsidiary boards in MNCs: An empirical study. *Strategic Management Journal, 9*, 347–360.

Krishnaswami, S., Spindt, P. A., & Subramaniam, V. (1998). Information asymmetry, monitoring, and the placement structure of corporate debt. Available at SSRN, http://ssrn.com/abstract=120408

Lang, M. H., & Lundholm, R. J. (1996). Corporate disclosure policy and analyst behavior. *The Accounting Review, 71*(4), 467–492.

La Porta, R., Lopez-de-Silanes, F, & Shleifer, A. (1999). Corporate ownership around the World. *Journal of Finance, 54*, 471–518.

Lee, H. Y., & Mande, V. (2008). A Comparison of reporting lags of multinational and domestic firms. *Journal of International Financial Management and Accounting, 19*(1), 28–55.

Leksell, L., & Lindgren, U. (1982). The board of directors in foreign subsidiaries. *Journal of International Business Studies, 13*, 27–39.

Lensink, R., Van der Molen, R., & Gangopadhyay, S. (2003). Business groups, financing constraints and investment: The case of India. *Journal of Development Studies, 40*(20), 93–119.

Luo, Y. (2005). Corporate governance and accountability in multinational enterprises: Concepts and agenda. *Journal of International Management, 11*, 1–18.

McNichols, M., & Trueman, B. (1994). Public disclosure, private information collection, and short-term trading. *Journal of Accounting and Economics*, *17*(3), 41–67.

North, D. C. (1990). *Institutions, institutional change and economic performance*. New York, NY: Cambridge University Press.

Oman, C., Fries, S., & Buiter, W. (2003). *Corporate governance in developing, transition and emerging-market economies*. Policy Brief No. 23. OECD Development Center, Paris, France.

Peng, M. (2006). *Global strategy*. Mason, OH: Thomson South Western.

Rajan, R., & Zingales, L. (1995). What do we know about capital structure? Some evidence from international data. *Journal of Finance*, *55*(1), 35–80.

Rosenzweig, P. M., & Singh, J. V. (1991). Organizational environments and the multinational enterprise. *Academy of Management Review*, *16*(2), 340–361.

Rubach, M. J., & Sebora, T. C. (1998). Comparative corporate governance: Competitive implications of an emerging convergence. *Journal of World Business*, *33*(2), 167–184.

Strange, R, & Jackson, G. (2008). *Corporate governance and international business*. Basingstoke: Palgrave.

Tallman, S., & Li, J. (1996). Effects of international diversity and product diversity on the performance of multinational firms. *Academy of Management Journal*, *39*(1), 179–196.

Williamson, O. (1985). *The economic institutions of capitalism*. New York, NY: Free Press.

PART IV
INVESTORS, ANALYSTS AND INFORMATIONAL TRANSPARENCY

CASH FLOW STABILITY VERSUS TRANSPARENCY: WHAT DO INVESTORS VALUE ABOUT LISTED INFRASTRUCTURE FUNDS?

Florian Bitsch

ABSTRACT

I analyze cash flow and transparency characteristics of listed infrastructure investment companies and funds and compare this unique infrastructure sample with a non-infrastructure reference group. I confirm the common hypothesis that infrastructure investments provide more stable cash flows than non-infrastructure investments. However, I do not find that investors positively value this cash flow stability. Instead, more volatile cash flows are valued with a premium. On the other hand, earnings management is valued with a discount. Together with a punishment for complex financial and governance structures this indicates a punishment for a lack of transparency by investors. My chapter also offers evidence that infrastructure investments in general are valued with a positive "infrastructure premium" that is not driven by more stable cash flows. I find additional evidence that sector specifics and regulatory risk play a significant role for the valuation of infrastructure investment companies and funds.

Transparency and Governance in a Global World
International Finance Review, Volume 13, 199–229

ISSN: 1569-3767/doi:10.1108/S1569-3767(2012)0000013010

Keywords: Infrastructure funds; cash flow stability; earnings management; transparency

JEL classifications: G23; G24

INTRODUCTION

Numerous studies have described and analyzed the so-called infrastructure investment gap. This term describes the fact that globally the need for infrastructure investments significantly exceeds the volume of financing available (e.g., see OECD, 2007). Given financial constraints of the public sector that has served as the major financing source for infrastructure assets so far, alternative financing sources need to be developed.

The solution most often stated is to facilitate investments and thus get the money from the private sector to narrow the investment gap (Chew, 2011). Although the market for infrastructure investments has developed in recent years, it is still not clear what exactly characterizes financing of and investment in infrastructure assets and thus if they would attract private investors sufficiently at all. For example, infrastructure investments are said to offer long-term, stable and predictable, inflation-linked returns with low correlation to other assets as well as stable operating cash flows (see, e.g., Inderst, 2009, 2010; Lawrence & Stapledon, 2008).

Literature on infrastructure investments can be grouped into four categories (Bitsch, Buchner, & Kaserer, 2010). Empirical studies on direct unlisted (i.e., not publicly traded) investments such as public–private partnerships (PPPs) and project finance vehicles include Välilä (2005), Esty (2003), and Esty (2010), respectively. Empirical studies on direct listed investments such as infrastructure stocks and bonds include Rothballer and Kaserer (2012), Roedel and Rothballer (2012), and Sawant (2010a). They find that infrastructure compared to non-infrastructure stocks have significantly lower systematic risk, higher firm-specific risk, but do not provide any significant inflation linkage and thus inflation hedge for investors. However, infrastructure project bonds show more stable cash flows compared to equities and a low correlation with them.

Bitsch et al. (2010) is the first paper that empirically analyzes infrastructure investments by unlisted private equity funds representing unlisted indirect investments. They were also the first to analyze the stability of total cash flows in an infrastructure context. The result was that there is no significant difference between infrastructure and non-infrastructure investments, which could be caused by the peculiarities of private equity investments and therefore not be representative for the overall infrastructure market as the authors suggest.[1] This paper contributes to the existing literature as it analyzes operating cash flow stability and transparency implications of listed infrastructure funds. They represent the fourth category, listed indirect investments. There exist only a few studies that focus on corporate governance issues of listed infrastructure funds. These studies mainly focus on Australia (see Davis, 2009; Lawrence & Stapledon, 2008). However, neither global nor extensive empirical analysis exists so far. Reasons for this include the fact that private investments into infrastructure in general are a rather new phenomenon, infrastructure research is a rather emerging field and data is simply rare or not easily accessible.

I contribute to extant research using a unique global sample of 120 listed infrastructure investment companies and funds. By integrating an international sample of listed private equity (LPE) used in Lahr and Herschke (2009), I am able to compare effects for the infrastructure versus non-infrastructure universe. Studies on capital allocation decisions show on average that investors value smooth cash flows positively (e.g., Badrinath, Gay, & Kale, 1989; Lang, Lins, & Miller, 2003a; Trueman & Titman, 1988). In particular, Rountree, Weston, and Allayannis (2008) show for a sample of US-listed firms that earnings smoothness is associated with superior firm valuation. Also, if decomposing earnings, they show that smoothness of the cash flow as well as the accruals component of earnings positively affects firm value measured based on Tobin's Q. However, investors discriminate between the components and focus on cash flow volatility but ignore accrual volatility. Evidence on valuation and cash flow characteristics as well as earnings smoothness is of particular interest in the context of the valuation of infrastructure funds. Infrastructure is generally assumed to differ not only in operating and risk characteristics, but also to provide a high degree of stable and thus predictable operating cash flows (see, e.g., Davis, 2009; Inderst, 2009, 2010; Lawrence & Stapledon, 2008). However, the relationship between infrastructure funds and cash flow smoothness has not been tested empirically up to date.

This chapter contributes to this research gap as I find no significant difference between infrastructure and non-infrastructure with respect to the volatility of net income. However, decomposing net income into the cash flow and accrual component, I find that infrastructure investments offer significantly lower volatilities of operating cash flows, which is consistent with the general assumption. In a next step, I analyze if and to what extent investors price cash flow volatility at all. Evidence suggests that volatility of net income is not associated with valuation levels. Instead, investors clearly discriminate between the volatility of cash flow and accrual component of earnings which is consistent to Rountree et al. (2008). I find that investors value volatility of the cash flow component with a premium. A positive impact of cash flow volatility on valuation is contrary to Rountree et al. (2008). However, my empirical evidence is by and large in line with theoretical considerations on cash flow volatility. Following Merton (1974) and viewing equity as a call option on firm value, cash flow volatility should indeed add firm value as my results suggest. Chi and Wu (2010) document this positive relation also in an empirical study for a sample of US-listed firms. They find that cash flow volatility is associated with an economically significant increase in firm value and thus support my results.

Contrary to a positive valuation of cash flow volatility I find that investors value volatility of the accrual component with a discount. Following Leuz, Nanda, and Wysocki (2003), I link accrual volatility to earnings management. Based on agency theory, managers have an incentive to engage in opportunistic earnings management (e.g., Healy & Wahlen, 1999; Leuz et al., 2003). By gaining private benefits of control at the expense of investors, this action is valued negatively as my results suggest. Lang, Lins, and Maffett (2012) relate such managerial behavior to a lower level of transparency which implies a negative impact on valuations. I use similar argument to explain the other empirical finding, that infrastructure funds as externally managed vehicles are valued at discount. This is in line with existing literature that argues such structures are often complex and opaque to investors (e.g., Davis, 2009; Lawrence & Stapledon, 2008). Complex financial and governance structures in turn can lead to further misalignment of interests between managers and investors and thus lower valuations. As Orr and Kennedy (2008) point out, transparency is especially important in the infrastructure sector with large and long-term investments, but a little developed capital market. To this extent my chapter is among the first to provide empirical evidence on how a lack of transparency can adversely affect valuation levels of infrastructure funds.

Additionally, I find that investors value infrastructure funds with a general infrastructure premium. Although I cannot find the economics for this premium, I can rule out smoother cash flows as a driver. I also provide evidence on sector specific valuation levels within the infrastructure context.

The chapter is organized as follows: the second section develops the three main hypotheses which will be tested empirically. The third section describes the sample composition and gives details on the construction of variables and descriptive statistics. In the fourth section, I present results from my multivariate analyses of valuation of cash flow volatility and transparency. The fifth section investigates further results on infrastructure specifics and addresses robustness checks, while the sixth section concludes.

HYPOTHESES

Hypothesis 1. Infrastructure investments exhibit low cash flow volatility.

Existing literature mostly assumes that infrastructure investments provide stable operating cash flows (e.g., Davis, 2009; Inderst, 2009, 2010; Lawrence & Stapledon, 2008). The rationale is that infrastructure networks often operate in monopolistic or regulated markets, which directly leads to a stable, low volatile operative business. This is reinforced by the fact that infrastructure provides necessities to the economy such that consumers show relatively inelastic demand for infrastructure services.

However, there exist little empirical findings on cash flow stability of infrastructure investments. For example, Bitsch et al. (2010) do not find that the volatility of total (operating and nonoperating) cash flows differ between infrastructure and non-infrastructure investments. In this chapter, I empirically test the hypothesis that operating cash flows of listed infrastructure funds are less volatile, that is, more stable than non-infrastructure funds.

Hypothesis 2. Smooth cash flows are positively valued by infrastructure investors.

While it is argued that infrastructure investments exhibit low cash flow volatility (see Hypothesis 1 above), this is said to be a favorable investment characteristic for investors. From a theoretical stand point, it can be argued that smooth, that is, nonvolatile, cash flows can reduce cost of financing (e.g., Froot, Scharfstein, & Stein, 1993), or are preferred for capital allocation decisions (e.g., Badrinath et al., 1989; Lang et al., 2003a; Trueman & Titman, 1988). Also Rountree et al. (2008) have empirically shown that smooth cash flows are valued positively by investors. In this chapter, I hypothesize that infrastructure investors also positively value the allegedly infrastructure-specific characteristic of stable cash flows.

In contrast, Chi and Wu (2010) can show for a sample of US-listed firms the opposite direction. This is consistent with Merton (1974). When viewing equity as a call option on firm value, then cash flow volatility should add firm value. Similarly, Pastor and Veronesi (2003) interpret cash flow volatility as uncertainty over future growth opportunities, which imply a positive valuation of cash flow volatility.

Hypothesis 3. Intransparency is negatively valued by infrastructure investors.

It is argued that transparency is crucial in the infrastructure sector with large and long-term investments, but a little developed capital market (Orr & Kennedy, 2008). I proxy (in-) transparency with managerial behavior as well as financial and governance structures.

First, opportunistic managerial behavior such as earnings management leads to a lower level of transparency for investors following Lang et al. (2012). Based on agency theory, managers have an incentive to engage in opportunistic earnings management which implies a negative impact on valuations by gaining private benefits of control at the expense of investors (e.g., Healy & Wahlen, 1999; Leuz et al., 2003). Second, complex structures of externally managed infrastructure funds are often opaque to investors and can lead to less transparency for investors (e.g., Davis, 2009; Lawrence & Stapledon, 2008). Complex financial and governance structures in turn can lead to further misalignment of interests between managers and investors.

In this chapter, I hypothesize that the lack of transparency, proxied by both opportunistic managerial behavior as well as complex structures, is welfare-reducing for infrastructure investors and thus leads to lower valuation levels of listed infrastructure funds.

DATA DESCRIPTION

My sample consists of listed (i.e., publicly traded) *infrastructure investment vehicles* (IIVs). It is based on the universe of global infrastructure equities as described in Rothballer and Kaserer (2012).[2] Out of this sample, I select all vehicles that have as a business model to pool money from investors in order to invest into and manage a portfolio of infrastructure assets. The underlying assets must be primarily nonpublic companies. Thus, an IIV provides the investor with the opportunity to directly participate in a portfolio of nonpublic infrastructure assets.

Sample Composition

Thereby, I derive a sample of 120 IIVs with a majority having their primary listing in the United States (33.3%), Canada (29.2%), Australia or New Zealand (13.3%), and the United Kingdom (11.7%). The remaining sample is listed in the rest of the world including countries such as Brazil, India, or Korea (12.5%). Following Lahr and Herschke (2009), I can split the whole sample of IIVs into internally and externally managed vehicles, which I call *infrastructure investment companies* (IICs) and *infrastructure investment funds* (IIFs), respectively. This gives 45 IICs and 75 IIFs. Table 1 gives a schematic overview of this classification and lists a few examples for each category.

Hereby, I refer to an externally managed vehicle if it contracts out management functions. A well-known example is the so-called "infrastructure fund model" (Davis, 2009, p. 2) or the "[...] asset-manager model for infrastructure, where a sponsoring manager – usually but not always an investment bank – establishes a separate publicly traded entity to own infrastructure assets while contracting out management functions to the sponsor [...]" (Lawrence & Stapledon, 2008, p. 44) to which the entity

Table 1. Overview of Infrastructure Investment Vehicles, Companies, and Funds.

Infrastructure Investment Vehicles (IIVs)	
Internally Managed Infrastructure Investment Companies (IICs)	Externally Managed Infrastructure Investment Funds (IIFs)
• BF Utilities Ltd.	• Brookfield Renewable Power
• Cheung Kong Infrastructure Holdings	• HSBC Infrastructure Company
• Eredene Capital	• Macquarie Infrastructure Group
• GTL Infrastructure Ltd.	• Prime Infrastructure Group
• IPSA Group plc	• Utilico Investment Trust plc

Note: The figure gives an overview of infrastructure investment vehicles (IIVs). They can be categorized in internally and externally managed vehicles, called infrastructure investment companies (IICs) and infrastructure investment funds (IIFs). Examples for each subsample are given.
Source: Own contribution, based on Lahr and Herschke (2009).

pays fees. These fees mostly consist of a base or management and a performance fee. However, the fee can also be a fixed amount written down in a management agreement or include payments to the general partner in case of a limited partnership. Opposite to that, an internally managed vehicle invests into a portfolio of infrastructure assets with no payments to external management. This means they employ their own managers. IICs can be hard to distinguish from operating infrastructure companies and therefore have to make clear statements regarding their business model, for example "[... our] principal objective is to generate substantial capital growth for investors by investing principally in high quality [...] infrastructure assets, providing [...] sustainable cash flows over the long term [...]."[3]

To be able to identify infrastructure-specific characteristics, I include the sample of LPE vehicles used in Lahr and Herschke (2009) and Kaserer, Lahr, Liebhart, and Mettler (2010). Due to the analogous structure of internally managed investment companies versus externally managed investment funds, I can control for fund and management structure and thus compare effects between the infrastructure and non-infrastructure subsamples. Also Davis (2009) as well as Lawrence and Stapledon (2008) point out similarities between LPE and IIVs (see Davis, 2009 or Lawrence & Stapledon, 2008). This adds 240 vehicles to the sample of which 164 are internally and 76 externally managed.

Variables and Descriptive Statistics

Because one focus of this chapter is the valuation of cash flow volatility, I first derive the measures of cash flow and its volatility. I decompose annual net income (NI) into its two components operating cash flow (CF), from now on simply called cash flow, and accruals (ACC). After standardizing net income and cash flow by total assets, accruals are calculated for year t as the difference between net income and operating cash flows following Dechow and Dichev (2002):

$$ACC_t = NI_t - CF_t$$

The standard deviation of the yearly data for $t \in [2000, \dots 2010]$ proxies for volatility for each vehicle in the sample and thus gives the volatility of net income, vola(NI), volatility of cash flow, vola(CF), and volatility of accruals, vola(ACC). Only those year observations are considered for which there exists (i) a matching pair observation for NI and CF as well as (ii) a minimum of three subsequent year observations. Table 2 provides

Table 2. Definition of Variables, Listed Funds

Category	Variable Name	Description
Dependent	tobins*Q*	Average of all available yearly observations for the sum of market capitalization (TOB item: ws. yrendmarketcap) and total debt (TOB item: ws.totaldebt) divided by the sum of total shareholders' equity (TOB item: totalshareholderequity) and total debt (TOB item: ws.totaldebt).
	MVBV	Average of all available yearly observations for market capitalization (TOB item: ws.yrendmarketcap) divided by total shareholders' equity (TOB item: totalshareholderequity).
Earnings component	NI	Average of all available yearly observations of net income (TOB item: ws.netincome) standardized by total assets of the vehicle (TOB item: ws.totalassets).
	CF	Average of all available yearly observations of operating cash flows (TOB item: ws. NetCashFlowOperatingCFStmt) standardized by total assets of the vehicle (TOB item: ws. totalassets).
	ACC	Average of all available yearly observations of accruals, whereby accruals is the difference between standardized yearly net income and operating cash flows (see NI, CF above).
	corr(CF, ACC)	Correlation between standardized yearly cash flow and accrual observations (see CF, ACC above).
	vola(NI)	Standard deviation of yearly, standardized net income observations (see NI above).
	vola(CF)	Standard deviation of yearly, standardized cash flow observations (see CF above).
	vola(ACC)	Standard deviation of yearly, standardized accrual observations (see ACC above).
Accounting	totassets	Average of all available yearly observations for total assets of a vehicle in USD (TOB item: ws. totalassetsUSD).
	debtfin	Average of all available yearly observations of debt (TOB item: ws.totaldebt) divided by total assets of a vehicle (TOB item: ws.totalassets).
	ROA	Average of all available yearly observations for return on assets (TOB item: ws.returnonassets).
Risk	beta_unlev	Beta of a vehicle delivered with its debt-equity ratio using the Hamada equation. Beta is the regression coefficient from the one-factor-model regressing return of the market index on vehicle return. Market index is the MSCI country index for each vehicle. All returns are total monthly returns between 2000 and 2010 and obtained from Thomson Reuters Datastream. Debt-equity ratio is the average of all available yearly observations of debt (TOB item: ws.totaldebt) divided by equity (TOB item: ws.totalshareholderequity). A corporate tax rate of 30% is applied.

Table 2. (*Continued*)

Category	Variable Name	Description
	idio	Annualized idiosyncratic risk, whereby idiosyncratic risk is the square root of the difference between return variance of a vehicle and the product of its squared beta multiplied with its "market index" return variance. All returns are total monthly returns between 2000 and 2010 and obtained from Thomson Reuters Datastream.
Structure/ industry	infra	Dummy variable equal to 1 for infrastructure vehicles.
	external	Dummy variable equal to 1 for externally managed vehicles.
	oil_gas	Dummy variable equal to 1 for vehicles that have invested into oil or gas infrastructure.
	transport	Dummy variable equal to 1 for vehicles that have invested into transportation infrastructure.
	electricity	Dummy variable equal to 1 for vehicles that have invested into electricity infrastructure.

Note: Column "Category" shows if the variable refers to the category earnings management, accounting, risk, or structure/industry. The "Ln"-prefix of a variable name indicates that the natural logarithm of the observations is taken. "TOB item" is the name as indicated in the database ThomsonONEBanker.

detailed information on how each variable is derived and calculated. Table 3 shows the descriptive statistics for the volatility of net income, cash flow, and accruals for the total as well as the two infrastructure/non-infrastructure subsamples.

> **Hypothesis 1**. The volatility of net income vola(NI) does not differ significantly between the infrastructure and non-infrastructure subsamples with standard deviations of 0.29 and 0.28, respectively. Similar holds for the volatility for both subsamples of accruals vola(ACC), which is on a comparable level with standard deviations of 0.27 and 0.25, respectively. The volatility of cash flows vola(CF), however, shows a different relation. I find that with a standard deviation of 0.07, it is significantly lower for IIVs than for the non-infrastructure subsample with a standard deviation of 0.14.[4] This result confirms Hypothesis 1 and is consistent with the common assumption about cash flow stability of infrastructure investments as suggested by prior literature (e.g., Inderst, 2009, 2010; Lawrence & Stapledon, 2008). Being on average less than half of accruals volatility, cash flow volatility forms also the smaller component of total net income volatility.

Due to the fact that I have an unbalanced panel and that I calculate one measure of cash flow volatility per vehicle over the whole period, I reduce the sample to cross-sectional observations. Accordingly, I calculate the mean of the standardized net income, cash flow, and accrual over all available years between 2000 and 2010 for each vehicle to derive NI, CF, and ACC. The descriptive statistics provided in Table 3 indicate on average negative accruals that do not differ significantly between the infrastructure and non-infrastructure subsample. However, IIVs offer significantly higher and positive cash flows than non-infrastructure vehicles over the sample period. Corr(CF, ACC) gives the correlation between cash flows and accruals over all periods per vehicle. The coefficient is −0.36 for the whole sample and does not differ significantly between the two subsamples.

Following the same procedure, I also calculate the mean of all accounting observations such as Tobin's Q, average total assets measures in USD, as well as the average debt–financing ratio. Table 4 also shows the descriptive statistics of the accounting variables for the total sample as well as both subsamples.

To measure valuation levels of the listed vehicles, I apply Tobin's Q. It is a proxy for firm value as it is commonly used in literature (e.g., Fang, Noe, & Tice, 2009; Gompers, Ishii, & Metrick, 2003). I calculate the

Table 3. Cash Flow and Volatility Statistics.

	Infrastructure						Non-Infrastructure							Total Sample					
Variable	Mean	Median	Min.	Max.	SD	*N*	Mean	Median	Min.	Max.	SD	*N*	Sign	Mean	Median	Min.	Max.	SD	*N*
NI	0	0.03	−0.95	0.13	0.14	108	−0.38	0	−16.93	0.11	2.01	139	**	−0.22	0.01	−16.93	0.13	1.52	247
CF	0.06	0.07	−0.57	0.22	0.12	106	−0.06	−0.01	−1.93	0.19	0.21	140	***	−0.01	0.02	−1.93	0.22	0.18	246
ACC	−0.06	−0.06	−0.38	0.25	0.07	109	−0.3	0	−16.05	0.24	1.85	138	–	−0.20	−0.03	−16.05	0.25	1.38	247
Corr(CF,ACC)	−0.42	−0.55	−1.00	0.99	0.5	111	−0.32	−0.46	−1.00	0.99	0.58	142	–	−0.36	−0.53	−1.00	0.99	0.55	253
vola(NI)	0.29	0.04	0.00	23.16	2.21	110	0.28	0.08	0.00	7.00	0.77	139	–	0.28	0.06	0.00	23.16	1.57	249
vola(CF)	0.07	0.04	0.01	1.12	0.12	109	0.14	0.05	0.01	1.64	0.27	141	***	0.11	0.05	0.01	1.64	0.22	250
vola(ACC)	0.27	0.04	0.01	21.00	2.00	110	0.25	0.12	0.00	4.46	0.47	139	–	0.26	0.07	0.00	21.02	1.37	249

Table 4. Risk and Accounting Statistics.

Variable	Infrastructure						Non-Infrastructure							Total Sample					
	Mean	Median	Min.	Max.	SD	*N*	Mean	Median	Min.	Max.	SD	*N*	Sign	Mean	Median	Min.	Max.	SD	*N*
tobins*Q*	1.53	1.43	0.56	3.87	0.58	108	1.11	0.97	0.52	3.38	0.52	139	***	1.29	1.11	0.52	3.87	0.58	247
beta_unlev	0.49	0.48	−0.09	1.48	0.33	98	0.64	0.48	−0.20	2.29	0.52	133	**	0.58	0.48	−0.20	2.29	0.46	231
idio	0.39	0.29	0.15	1.41	0.25	99	0.44	0.39	0.14	1.67	0.26	135	*	0.42	0.34	0.14	1.67	0.26	234
totassets(USDbn)	1.67	0.88	0.00	12.61	2.14	106	0.68	0.09	0.00	11.87	1.74	135	***	1.12	0.26	0.00	12.61	1.99	241
debtfin	0.35	0.33	0.00	0.81	0.19	109	0.20	0.17	0.00	1.00	0.20	154	***	0.27	0.26	0.00	1.00	0.20	224
external	0.61	1.00	0.00	1.00	0.49	111	0.29	0.00	0.00	1.00	0.45	142	***	0.61	0.00	0.00	1.00	0.50	253

Note: Table 3 gives descriptive statistics of cash flow and volatility measures, Table 4 gives descriptive statistics of risk and accounting measures for all vehicles with a minimum number of 3 cash flow observations. Statistics are given for the full sample as well as the infrastructure and non-infrastructure subsamples. Column "Sign" indicates whether the difference between the infra and the non-infra subsample is significant, as measured by the test for difference in mean. The asterisks indicate the level of significance (*, **, ***, significant at the 10%, 5%, and 1% levels, respectively).

variable tobins$Q$ as the ratio of market value of equity plus debt and book value of equity plus debt. While the total sample has an average Tobin's Q of 1.29, the infrastructure subsample shows a higher value of 1.53 than the non-infrastructure subsample of 1.11. This difference is statistically significant and implies that investors value infrastructure vehicles higher than non-infrastructure. I aim to explore in this chapter why this is the case. One possible explanation might be that investors do value smooth cash flows as reported in Rountree et al. (2008). As a consequence, investors might value IIVs higher, because they have significantly lower cash flow volatility, that is, smoother cash flows. Although intuitive, I can see later that this line of argumentation cannot be confirmed by multivariate regressions.

The variable totassets gives the average total assets for each vehicle over time and proxies the size of the vehicles. It is measured in billion USD. The average size of all vehicles in my total sample is USD 1.12 billion, which is close to the average firm size of USD 1.11 billion as reported in Rountree et al. (2008). However, splitting my sample into the infrastructure and non-infrastructure subsamples, I find that IIVs are with average total assets of USD 1.67 billion significantly larger than the non-infrastructure benchmark with USD 0.68 billion. This is consistent with the general assumption that infrastructure assets are specifically large (e.g., see Sawant, 2010b). debtfin gives the average debt-financing-ratio of each vehicle and measures the leverage. Table 4 shows that the leverage of my infrastructure subsample is twice as high as for the non-infrastructure subsample with a statistically significant difference. This is consistent to the general evidence that infrastructure assets have on average a higher leverage than non-infrastructure assets.[5]

For the same time period, I also calculate the unlevered systematic risk beta_unlev and annualized idiosyncratic risk idio based on the monthly total returns provided by Thomson Reuters DataStream. Table 4 also displays the descriptive statistics of the risk measures. The systematic risk is derived from a one-factor model, whereby I regress the total return of a local stock index onto the total return of each vehicle. The resulting levered beta is de-levered by the average debt-financing-ratio as described above and proxies the systematic operative risk of each vehicle. Table 4 shows that IIVs have on average an unlevered beta of 0.49, which is significantly lower than for the non-infrastructure subsample with an average unlevered beta of 0.64. This is close to the results reported by Rothballer and Kaserer (2012) who find an unlevered beta of 0.37 for infrastructure stocks. The idiosyncratic risk is calculated as the residual between total volatility and the product of squared beta of a vehicle with the total volatility of its local market index. The presented variable idio is annualized. Both risk measures are by construction contemporaneous measures to the accounting variables described before.

Table 5 shows the table with correlation coefficients between all variables. It shows that in a univariate analysis none of the risk measure is significantly correlated to firm value. Intuitively, higher levels of net income, cash flows, and accruals are positively correlated to firm value. Consistent with Dechow and Dichev (2002), Table 5 shows significantly positive correlations between net income and cash flow as well as net income and accruals. It also confirms the significant negative correlation between cash flow and accruals as reported in Table 3. However, this correlation is not correlated to firm value. This is also the case for volatility of net income. Interestingly, the volatilities of its two components cash flow and accruals have a significantly different relation with valuation. Volatility of accruals vola(ACC) is significantly negatively related to valuation levels, whereas volatility of cash flows vola(CF) is positively – although not significantly – correlated to valuation levels. This provides first empirical evidence that investors do significantly differentiate between the cash flow and the accrual component, which I aim to further investigate in the following sections. Another significant finding is that large firms as well as firms with higher debt levels are valued with a significant premium and at the same time provide significantly more stable net income, cash flows, and accruals. The relation between size and the three volatility measures is also consistent with Dechow and Dichev (2002).

The fact that the dummy variable for IIVs is highly positively correlated to valuation encourages further exploring the determinants of valuation in the context of infrastructure. However, because IIVs correspond to larger size and higher debt levels at the same time, I need to control for these characteristics in a multivariate analysis.

I therefore apply in the following section multivariate regression analyses to ask if and to what extent investors value cash flow stability of IIVs.

WHAT DO INVESTORS VALUE?

Following Shin and Stulz (2000) as well as Rountree et al. (2008) I run pooled regressions on Tobin's Q, whereby the accounting variables and risk measures described in the previous section serve as independent variables. Because independent and dependent variables refer to the time frame 2000 through 2010, I can verify if there is a contemporaneous effect on the

Table 5. Correlation Matrix

Spearman' s Correlations Coefficients	Tobin's Q	beta_unlev	idio	NI	CF	ACC	Corr(CF, ACC)
Tobin's Q	1.000						
beta_unlev	0.008	1.000					
idio	−0.052	0.362 ***	1.000				
NI	0.302 ***	−0.085	−0.572	1.000			
CF	0.484 ***	−0.096	−0.380 ***	0.672 ***	1.000		
ACC	−0.359 ***	0.004	−0.210 ***	0.301 ***	−0.339 ***	1.000	
Corr(CF,ACC)	0.056	0.136	0.135	−0.170 **	−0.130 *	−0.227 ***	1.000
vola(NI)	−0.085	0.355 ***	0.506 ***	0.423 ***	−0.350 ***	−0.256 ***	0.524 ***
vola(CF)	0.045	0.319 ***	0.459 ***	−0.246 ***	−0.200 ***	−0.199 ***	−0.067
vola(ACC)	−0.212 ***	0.349 ***	0.543 ***	−0.479 ***	−0.446 ***	−0.154 **	0.165 **
totassets	0.323 ***	−0.084	−0.435 ***	0.506 ***	−0.504 ***	0.039	−0.193 ***
debtfin	0.261 ***	−0.263 ***	−0.056	0.174 **	0.348 ***	−0.144 *	−0.244 ***
infra	0.486 ***	−0.202 ***	−0.256 ***	0.329 ***	0.578 ***	−0.340 ***	−0.075
external	−0.006	−0.228 ***	−0.269 ***	0.204 ***	0.219 ***	0.019	−0.215 ***

	vola(NI)	vola(CF)	vola(ACC)	totassets	debtfin	infra	external
vola(NI)	1.000						
vola(CF)	0.608 ***	1.000					
vola(ACC)	0.860 ***	0.694 ***	1.000				
totassets	−0.468 ***	−0.439 ***	−0.482 ***	1.000			
debtfin	−0.333 ***	−0.239 ***	−0.306 ***	0.594 ***	1.000		
infra	−0.370 ***	−0.213 ***	−0.445 ***	0.438 ***	0.375 ***	1.000	
external	−0.413 ***	−0.281 ***	−0.387 ***	0.222 ***	0.160 **	0.325 ***	1.000

Note: Coefficients display Spearman's correlation coefficients for all vehicles with a minimum number of 3 cash flow observations. Exception: the coefficient between dummy variables infra and external displays Cramer's V. The asterisks indicate the level of significance for the test of independence (*, **, ***, significant at the 10%, 5%, and 1% levels, respectively).

level of valuation. In particular, this enables me to analyze if and to what extent investors value cash flow volatility of IIVs. I perform an Ln-transformation with all variables given in a cardinal scale indicated by the Ln-prefix at the beginning of the variable names. This does not only allow for an easier interpretation of log–log regression models, but also further controls for potential outliers (see also Rountree et al., 2008).

In the following regressions, I control for year effects by adding dummies for every year between 2000 and 2010. They take on the value one if for a given vehicle if it was active, that is, listed, in this particular year of observation. Because I use a sample of global vehicles from regions with different regulation or reporting standards and practice, I also control for such institutional characteristics following Leuz (2010). They divide countries into three clusters[6]: (1) outsider economies that are "characterized by large stock markets, low ownership concentration, extensive outsider rights, high disclosure, and strong legal enforcement," (2) insider economies with strong legal enforcement, but "smaller stock markets, higher ownership concentration, weaker investor protection, and lower disclosure levels," and (3) insider economies with similar characteristics as countries in the second cluster but with weak legal enforcement (see Leuz, 2010). The data and clustering is an updated and extended version of Leuz et al. (2003). It is based on reporting practice and regulatory data from Djankov, La Porta, Lopez-de-Silanes, and Shleifer (2008), Licht, Goldschmidt, and Schwartz (2007), and La Porta, Lopez-de-Silanes, and Shleifer (2006) among others. I control for these institutional characteristics by using dummy variables if a vehicle in my sample has its primary exchange listing in one of the clusters described above. Outsider economies in cluster one include countries such as Australia, Canada, the United States, and the United Kingdom – 79.45% of all vehicles in my sample are in this cluster. Cluster two includes most continental European countries such as France, Germany, Netherlands, Switzerland as well as Japan and South Korea – 15.42% of all vehicles in my sample are in this cluster. The remaining 5.14% of my sample is listed in countries such as Brazil, India, or Taiwan, which are contained in cluster three.

I also control if particular infrastructure sectors experienced a significant premium or discount by investors. Hereby I differentiate between the following sectors – transportation, electricity, oil and gas, water, telecommunication, and social infrastructure. I incorporate this by adding dummy variables that take on the value one if the vehicle has invested in this sector in any year between 2000 and 2010.

Regressions (1) and (2) in Table 6 show the regression results with the Ln-transformed Tobin's Q as dependent variable. I apply ordinary least

Table 6. Main Regressions.

Model number	(1)	(2)	(3)
Variables	Ln_tobins*Q*	Ln_tobins*Q*	Ln_tobins*Q*
Ln_beta_unlev	0.0002	0.0043	0.0013
	(0.01)	(0.12)	(0.04)
Ln_idio	0.0244	0.0642	0.0477
	(0.41)	(1.09)	(0.81)
Ln_vola(NI)	0.0343	–	–
	(1.21)	(2.72)	(3.02)
Ln_vola(CF)	–	0.0855***	0.1070***
Ln_vola(ACC)	–	− 0.0758**	− 0.0901***
		(−2.46)	(−2.77)
Corr(CF, ACC)	–	–	0.0920*
			(1.72)
Ln_totassets	0.0194	0.0212	0.0251
	(1.12)	(1.19)	(1.37)
Ln_debtfin	− 0.0093	− 0.0133	− 0.0065
	(−0.60)	(−0.84)	(−0.42)
infra	0.4170***	0.3900***	0.3660***
	(0.88)	(5.27)	(4.92)
external	− 0.1500***	− 0.1650	− 0.1450**
	(−2.65)	(−2.85)	(−2.51)
oil_gas	0.1190**	0.1030*	0.0922*
	(2.16)	(1.89)	(1.72)
transport	− 0.1800***	− 0.1590**	− 0.1640***
	(−2.88)	(−2.58)	(−2.75)
electricity	− 0.1530**	− 0.1450**	− 0.1440**
	(−2.44)	(−2.34)	(−2.34)
constant	0.1500	0.0942	0.1377
	(0.72)	(0.45)	(0.67)
year dummies	Yes	Yes	Yes
Institutional cluster dummies	Yes	Yes	Yes
Number of observations	188	188	188
F-statistic	5.85***	5.55***	5.39***
Max. VIF	5.60	5.40	5.41
Max. VIF without year and institutional cluster dummies	2.24	2.77	2.88
Adjusted R^2	34.10%	36.2%	37.1%

Note: The table gives the results of OLS regressions for the full sample with Ln_tobins*Q* as dependent variable and a minimum of 3 cash flow observations per vehicle. Regression (1) includes volatility of net income vola(NI) as exogenous variable. Regression (2) includes its components volatility of cash flow vola(CF) and accrual vola(ACC) instead. Both regressions use White's heteroskedasticity-consistent estimators. The independent variables are listed in the first column. The second and third columns show the non-standardized coefficients of each exogenous variable and the associated t-statistics. The asterisks indicate the level of significance (*, **, ***, significant at the 10%, 5%, and 1% levels, respectively).

square (OLS) regressions with White's heteroskedasticity-consistent estimators. Although I control for year and institutional effects as described above, I do not display the results for those dummies for a better overview. Both regression specifications are identical except that Regression (1) includes volatility of net income vola(NI) as an independent variable. Regression (2) lacks this variable and splits this into the volatilities of its cash flow and accrual component, vola(CF) and vola(ACC), respectively. Leverage is negatively but not statistically significant associated with valuation level in both regressions. This relationship is similar to the results reported in Rountree et al. (2008). Opposite to this, I find a significant positive relation between the proxy for firm size and valuation. This implies that larger firms trade at a premium compared to smaller ones. The two risk measures for systematic and idiosyncratic risk have both a positive but not significant influence.

Cash Flow Stability

Hypothesis 2. I can confirm the indications of the univariate findings on volatilities reported in Table 5. First, volatility of net income has no significant influence on valuation levels as shown in Regression (1). Instead, I can confirm discriminating effects on valuation when decomposing net income into its components as shown in Regression (2), which is by and large consistent to Rountree et al. (2008). However, I report opposing effects where investors value cash flow volatility positively and accrual volatility negatively. These effects are highly significant and also robust as shown in section "Further Results and Robustness Checks." The decomposition even increases the already high explanatory power of the regression from an adjusted R^2 of 34.1 to 36.2% – compared to 22.9% and 27.3% reported for similar regressions in Rountree et al. (2008). This suggests that investors significantly differentiate between the cash flow and accrual component of net income to a similar magnitude: an increase of cash flow volatility by 1% is associated with an increase in value of approximately 0.09%, whereas an increase of accrual volatility by 1% is associated with a decrease in value of approximately 0.08%. For comparison, Chi and Wu (2010) also find an economically significant increase in value of approximately 0.14% for a 1% increase in cash flow volatility.

The fact that cash flow volatility is positively valued in my sample contradicts my Hypothesis 2 and does not confirm the findings of Rountree et al. (2008) that investors value smooth cash flows. In contrary, following Merton (1974) and viewing equity as a call option on firm value, then cash flow volatility should indeed add firm value which is consistent with what my results suggest. Similarly, Pastor and Veronesi (2003) interpret cash flow volatility as uncertainty over future growth opportunities, which imply a positive valuation of cash flow volatility. Additionally, this positive relation is also documented in the empirical study by Chi and Wu (2010). They even find evidence that the negative impact of cash flow volatility on firm value reported in Rountree et al. (2008) is due to the fact that nonstandardized per-share volatilities were used. If cash flows are standardized for total assets as I did in this chapter, they find that the negative relation turns positive as reported in my chapter. A positive relation can also be supported by the theoretical agency argument that managers cannot diversify sufficiently the stream of income they receive from the firm. As a consequence, they engage in lower levels of firm risk associated with lower cash flow volatilities and thus decrease firm value (Amihud & Lev, 1981; see also Chi & Wu, 2010). Higher firm risk and cash flow volatilities can limit this inefficiency and thus increase firm value. In the context of infrastructure investments, for example, a positive valuation for volatile cash flows can be explained with investors that mainly seek riskier greenfield investments and provide a higher upside potential of returns.

Transparency

Hypothesis 3. In opposite, accrual volatility is clearly valued by investors at a discount. I explain this with opportunistic managers who manipulate accruals and therefore reduce the wealth of shareholders. Based on principal-agent theory, there is an information asymmetry between managers and investors where managers have an informational advantage over the investor about the true state of the company. At the same time, managers have some accounting discretion about accruals and thus reported earnings. Following Leuz et al. (2003) and Healy and Wahlen (1999), the manager has an incentive to use this discretion to misrepresent firm performance in order to gain private control benefits at the expense of the investors.[7] For example, managers could try to avoid the reporting of large losses to mitigate disciplinary action against them (e.g., Degeorge, Patel, & Zeckhauser, 1999). I can therefore interpret accruals and accrual volatility as proxy for earnings management. Because such action by managers reduces the wealth of shareholders, investors value this action with a discount as confirmed in my empirical analysis. Alternatively, Dechow and Dichev (2002) identify both accrual and earnings volatility as a proxy for accrual and earnings quality, where a higher volatility signifies lower quality.

Regression (3) underpins the effect of earnings management by adding corr(CF, ACC) as independent variable. It is commonly used in literature as proxy for earnings smoothing which is a particular form of earnings management (e.g., Barton, 2001; Lang, Raedy, & Yetman, 2003b; Leuz et al., 2003). In times of volatile cash flows, managers can report negative accruals to partially offset high cash flows and vice versa to smoothen net income and earnings. Similar to Rountree et al. (2008), the positive and significant coefficient shows that the more negative the correlation, that is, the more earnings smoothing by the management, the larger the discount for firm value. By adding this variable, not only the significance of the negative impact of accrual volatility on valuation increased, also the R^2 of the regression increased to high 37.1%.

Thus, both proxies for earnings management, correlation between cash flow and accruals as well as volatility of accruals, consistently show that earnings management is valued with a discount by investors. Following Lang et al. (2012), I can also relate earnings management to the level of transparency for investors. The more managers engage in earnings management, the less transparency there is about the true economic performance about the firm, and the more firms are valued with a discount.[8]

Besides the negative impact of earnings management on valuation levels, Table 6 also reveals a highly significant and economically meaningful discount for externally managed vehicles. This indicates another punishment for non-transparency by investors. In the context of infrastructure funds for example, Davis (2009) mentions "complex and opaque financial" structures that "make the true financial position of the fund hard to determine"(p. 47). Such structures also facilitate managers to gain private control benefits or reduce the shareholders' monitoring capabilities, similar to earnings management described above. Furthermore, Lawrence and Stapledon (2008) list concerns about the governance structure that can lead among others to less transparency or misalignment of interests between shareholders and managers and thus reduce valuation of infrastructure funds.

Orr and Kennedy (2008, p. 104) point out that transparency is specifically necessary for financing infrastructure projects through capital markets, which requires "ongoing and high quality disclosure of operating and financial performance" of the assets. Greater transparency further develops this market, increases investment, and ceteris paribus positively affects valuations. Earnings management or intransparent legal and organizational structures, however, is not likely to enhance such qualities.

My findings thus confirm Hypothesis 3 that infrastructure intransparency is negatively by infrastructure investors.

So far, the interpretations of regressions referred to my whole sample of investment vehicles including infrastructure as well as non-infrastructure. One could argue that infrastructure vehicles should then be valued by investors at discounts if they (i) show significantly lower cash flow volatility as reported in Table 3 and (ii) cash flow smoothness is punished by investors as shown above. Nevertheless, I find higher valuation levels for infrastructure vehicles versus non-infrastructure vehicles. Table 4 shows an average Tobin's Q of 1.53 for infrastructure vehicles, which is significantly higher than the one of 1.11 for non-infrastructure vehicles. My regression model suggests that the discount from smooth cash flows for infrastructure vehicles is at least partially offset by a general infrastructure premium shown by the positive and highly significant regression coefficient for the dummy variable infra. For example, Regression (2) in Table 6 implies IIVs on average are ceteris paribus valued 48% higher than non-IIVs. This means despite controlling for risk measures, accounting characteristics, time, or institutional effects, there is an unobserved characteristic of infrastructure vehicles in my model that causes this infrastructure premium. One of the myriad possibilities might be a money chasing deals phenomenon. This describes the empirical fact that private equity can be subject to overinvestment, so that asset prices go up and performance goes down (see, e.g., Gompers & Lerner, 2000 as well as Diller & Kaserer, 2009). Reasons for this include that the market for private equity investments is segmented with a limited number of potential investments that are illiquid. This implies that in times of high capital inflows into this particular market, the supply of potential investments does not adjust sufficiently and valuations increase. Because infrastructure assets are also subject to these conditions, this phenomenon might also occur for IIVs as indicated in previous literature (Orr & Kennedy, 2008; Lawrence & Stapledon, 2008). However, this remains an assumption with no empirical proof.

FURTHER RESULTS AND ROBUSTNESS CHECKS

The regression results in Table 6 also report a significant premium for investment vehicles that invest in the oil and gas sector. On the other hand, vehicles that invest in the transportation and electricity sectors are valued at a significant and economically meaningful discount. These results are also valid after the robustness checks in Table 7. It is likely that those sector-specific valuations depend to a large extent on sector-specific risks and regulations. For example, Bitsch et al. (2010) report significantly higher returns for the transport sector within the infrastructure universe. The authors suggest this might be driven by a high degree of government intervention and less independent regulation. This could lead to higher investment uncertainty and thus higher cost of capital, which could imply lower valuations similar to my results. However, sector-specific risk and return profiles are heterogeneous and require more attention and research to allow for robust conclusions.

To show that the valuation effects described above don't only hold for the total but also for the infrastructure and non-infrastructure subsamples, I perform similar regressions for the two subsamples separately besides other robustness checks.

In Table 7, I perform the same regressions as in Table 6, now separately for the infrastructure (Regressions (1) and (2)) and non-infrastructure sample (Regressions (3) and (4)). Because the number of observations sharply drops, the explanation power of these regressions as well as significance of their independent variables is rather low. Nevertheless, the regressions confirm for both subsamples the positive effect of cash flow volatility and negative effect of accrual volatility on valuation. I find additionally that within the infrastructure sample, leverage has a highly significant and negative impact on valuation. This might be an indicator for the criticism that some IIVs have exceeded optimal levels of leverage (see Davis, 2009; Lawrence & Stapledon, 2008).

Regressions (5) and (6) show that the results on cash flow volatility reported in Table 6 are also robust if I use the Ln-transformation of the market-to-book value Ln_MVBV as an alternative valuation measure.

In Regressions (7) and (8) I have also included return on assets as a proxy of profitability following Rountree et al. (2008). I have not included this variable in the previous analysis in Table 6, because this variable is not available for many observations and thus would further decrease my sample size. The regressions show that including the Ln-transformation of return on assets Ln_ROA, sample size is decreased but explanatory power

Table 7. Robustness Checks.

Model	Min. of 3 Cash Flow Observations, Infra Sample		Min. of 3 Cash Flow Observations, Non-Infra Sample		Min. of 3 Cash Flow Observations, Full Sample		Min. of 3 Cash Flow Observations, Full Sample		Min. of 7 Cash Flow Observations, Full Sample	
NUMBER	(1)	(2)	(3)	(4)	(5)	(6)	(7)	(8)	(9)	(10)
Variables	Ln_tobinsQ	Ln_tobinsQ	Ln_tobinsQ	Ln_tobinsQ	Ln_MVBV	Ln_MVBV	Ln_tobinsQ	Ln_tobinsQ	Ln_tobinsQ	Ln_tobinsQ
Ln_ROA	–	–	–	–	–	–	0.0435	0.0489*	–	–
							(1.30)	(1.70)	–	–
Ln_beta_unlev	0.0255	0.0254	0.0205	0.0199	−0.0793	−0.0736	0.0314	0.047	0.0515	0.0586
	(0.65)	(0.64)	(0.39)	(0.38)	(−1.53)	(−1.43)	(0.74)	(1.26)	(1.18)	(1.58)
Ln_idio	−0.1864	−0.1279	0.1360	0.1490 *	0.0417	0.0952	0.0332	0.0757	−0.0203	0.0246
	(−2.36)	(−1.69)	(1.55)	(1.74)	(0.47)	(1.07)	(0.51)	(1.19)	(−0.33)	(0.42)
Ln_vola(NI)	0.0067	–	0.0346	–	0.0620	–	0.0101	–	0.0184	–
	(0.16)		(1.02)		(1.51)		(0.28)		(0.48)	
Ln_vola(CF)	–	0.0919 *	–	0.0372	–	0.110 **	–	0.0774 ***	–	0.0914 **
		(1.92)		(0.90)		(2.43)		(2.41)		(2.36)
Ln_vola(ACC)	–	−0.1190	–	−0.0210	–	−0.0793 *	–	−0.107 ***	–	−0.1060 **
		(−1.61)		(−0.49)		(−1.76)		(−2.69)		(−2.53)
Ln_totassets	−0.0269	−0.0281	0.0266	0.0247	0.0582 **	0.0607 **	0.0150	0.0139	0.0102	0.0100
	(−0.98)	(−0.99)	(1.37)	(1.15)	(2.49)	(2.35)	(0.70)	(0.64)	(0.44)	(0.41)
Ln_debtfin	−0.0647 ***	−0.0642 **	−0.0148	−0.0191	0.0006 **	−0.0057	−0.0035	−0.0080	−0.0150	−0.0209
	(−2.48)	(−2.32)	(−1.11)	(−1.32)	(0.03)	(−0.30)	(−0.24)	(−0.59)	(−0.53)	(−0.74)
infra	–	–	–	–	0.5860 ***	−0.5600 ***	0.3960 ***	0.3840 ***	0.4970 ***	0.4570 ***
					(5.76)	(4.97)	(4.57)	(4.79)	(5.76)	(5.44)
external	−0.0502	−0.0497	−0.2840 ***	−0.3230 ***	−0.1170	−0.1390 *	−0.1580 **	−0.1890 ***	−0.1940 ***	−0.1990 ***
	(−0.83)	(−0.82)	(−2.83)	(−3.08)	(−1.47)	(−1.71)	(−2.35)	(−2.88)	(−2.92)	(−2.95)
oil_gas	0.1124	0.0936	0.0272	0.0464	0.0681	0.0483	0.0715	0.0515	0.0821	0.0687
	(1.53)	(1.49)	(0.37)	(0.63)	(0.77)	(0.53)	(1.31)	(1.02)	(1.25)	(1.11)
transport	−0.3036 ***	−0.2410 **	−0.0584	−0.0645	−0.2760 ***	−0.2520 ***	−0.2110 ***	−0.1780 ***	−0.1760 ***	−0.1400 ***
	(−3.36)	(−2.50)	(−0.58)	(−0.62)	(−3.24)	(−2.89)	(−3.10)	(−2.83)	(−2.43)	(−1.96)
electricity	−0.2127 **	−0.2083 ***	0.0757	0.0934	−0.2440 ***	−0.2350 **	−0.0720	−0.0574	−0.1440 **	−0.1510 **
	(−2.62)	(−2.77)	(0.81)	(0.96)	(−2.64)	(−2.54)	(−1.05)	(−0.90)	(−2.00)	(−2.14)

constant	−0.3817		0.1597		0.2150		0.1642		0.1540		0.0742		0.1380		0.0789		1.2510	***	1.0560	**
	(−1.40)		(0.66)		(−0.77)		(0.59)		(0.47)		(0.22)		(0.61)		(0.35)		(2.85)		(2.39)	
Year dummies	Yes		Yes		Yes		Yes		Yes		Yes		Yes		Yes		Yes		Yes	
Institutional cluster dummies	Yes		Yes		Yes		Yes		Yes		Yes		Yes		Yes		Yes		Yes	
Number of observations	88		88		100		100		188		188		137		137		128		138	
F-statistic	5.26	***	7.66	***	3.11	***	2.52	***	6.88	***	6.85	***	6.78	***	7.58	***	2.91	***	2.80	***
Max. VIF	4.81		4.62		5.50		5.30		5.60		5.40		5.08		4.87		5.60		5.40	
Max. VIF without year and institutional cluster dummies	2.15		2.58		2.15		2.58		2.24		2.77		2.33		2.73		2.24		2.77	
Adjusted R^2	38.2%		41.8%		23.6%		22.3%		36.0%		36.8%		41.1%		44.4%		36.7%		39.8%	

Note: The table gives the results of OLS regressions with differing specifications. Regressions (1) and (2) reproduce Table 5 for the infrastructure subsample only. Regressions (3) and (4) reproduce Table 5 for the non-infrastructure subsample only. Regressions (5) and (6) reproduce Table 5 with Ln_MVBV instead of Ln_tobins*Q* as dependent variable. Regressions (7) and (8) reproduce Table 5 including Ln_ROA as an additional independent variable. Regressions (9) and (10) reproduce Table 5 for vehicles with a minimum of 7 cash flow observations. All regressions use White's heteroskedasticity-consistent estimators. The independent variables are listed in the first column. The following columns show the non-standardized coefficients of each exogenous variable and the associated t-statistics. The asterisks indicate the level of significance (*, **, ***, significant at the 10%, 5%, and 1% levels, respectively).

significantly increased expressed by an adjusted R^2 of up to 44%. More importantly, the effects of cash flow volatility as described for Table 6 are robust. Also, return on assets has a significantly positive impact on valuation levels. This is consistent with the results reported in Rountree et al. (2008).

The regression results from Table 6 might have also been biased because I constructed the measures of volatilities based on different numbers of cash flow observations due to the unbalanced structure of the panel. With a mean and median number of cash flow observations of 6.52 and 7, respectively, I perform the same regressions as in Table 6 except with a minimum number of cash flow observations of 7 instead of 3. Regressions (9) and (10) in Table 7 show that my results are also robust to this robustness check.

Finally, the elevated variance inflation factors (VIFs) give rise for a concern about multi-collinearity among the independent variables of the regressions in Tables 6 and 7. However, the values of *max VIF without year and institutional cluster dummies* show that for all regressions the maximum VIF is smaller than 3 when the dummy variables controlling for year and institutional effects are not included in the regressions. This shows that some of the control variables are slightly correlated, but multi-collinearity is not an issue among the main explanatory variables.

SUMMARY

It is widely believed that infrastructure investments offer some typical financial characteristics such as long-term, stable and predictable, inflation-linked cash flows with low correlation to other assets. However, research on infrastructure investments is an emerging field and the number of studies is till limited. So far, the existing empirical research on infrastructure mainly focuses on listed infrastructure companies, PPPs, or project finance.

This chapter contributes to a research gap as it provides first empirical evidence for a larger sample of listed IIVs. I categorize them into internally and externally managed vehicles, which I label infrastructure investment companies and infrastructure investment funds, respectively. Comparing this sample to a non-infrastructure reference group of LPE vehicles, I can confirm the common hypothesis that infrastructure investments provide more stable operating cash flows than non-infrastructure investments.

In a next step, I analyze if and to what extent investors price cash flow volatility at all. Evidence suggests that volatility of net income is not associated with valuation levels. Instead, investors clearly discriminate between the volatility of cash flow and accrual component of earnings that is consistent to existing literature. I find that investors value volatility of the cash flow component with a premium. Although existing theoretical as well as empirical literature provides evidence for both a negative and positive relation, I explain this result by viewing equity as a call option on firm value. In this context, cash flow volatility should indeed add firm value as my results suggest.

On the other hand, I find that volatility of the accrual component is valued with a discount on valuation levels. This negative relation between accruals and valuation levels is by and large consistent with existing literature. I relate this finding to discounts for opportunistic earnings management by mangers at the expense of investors. Such managerial behavior can be interpreted as transparency reducing actions. Further results suggest that not only earnings management but also externally managed vehicles are valued at a discount. I relate this to complex financial and governance structures. Possible reasons for this include less transparency that leads to further agency conflicts and lower valuations.

Overall, IIVs are valued at a significant "infrastructure premium" over the non-infrastructure reference group. One rationale for this might be that infrastructure investments considered in this time period have been subject to the so-called money chasing deals phenomenon. Although I have no clear indication for the economics of this result, I can say that it is not the more stable cash flows that lead to the higher valuation levels. I also find that investment vehicles that invest into oil and gas infrastructure are valued at a premium as opposed to vehicles investing into transportation or electricity infrastructure, which are valued at a discount. Likely reasons for this include differing regulatory risks.

Summing up, my chapter supports the perception that IIVs do have specific characteristics that are of interest to institutional investors. Most importantly, they provide more stable operating cash flows. However, investors do not positively value this as it is often perceived. In opposite, investors punish managerial behavior that reduces transparency, as well as opaque and complex governance structures. An overall positive "infrastructure premium" reveals that a more detailed picture regarding the infrastructure market is still needed. For example, the influence of regulatory risk needs to be better understood. In this regard, my chapter offers some limited evidence that can be used as a starting point for future research.

NOTES

1. Another reason could be data-driven, since their data set contained total cash flows only and did not allow disentangling between operating and nonoperating cash flows.

2. Additionally, I also screened the universe of select financials (SIC codes starting with 67, GICS code 4020, Diversified Financials) as well as the oil and gas sector (SIC codes starting with 13, GICS code 101020) backed by an ongoing news search primarily at http://www.infrastructureinvestor.com.

3. http://www.eredene.com/approach/investment-policy. Accessed on April 12, 2012.

4. For comparison, Francis, Lafond, Olsson, and Schipper (2004) report an average cash flow volatility of 0.074 for a large sample of US listed firms between 1975 and 2001, Dechow and Dichev (2002) report a standard deviation of 0.06 between 1987 and 1999.

5. The absolute level of leverage needs to be interpreted with care. Minority investments below 50% are recognized using the equity method according to the International Financial Reporting Standards (IFRS). In this case the leverage in the underlying infrastructure assets is not reflected in the leverage of the investment vehicles and leverage of the investment vehicles in this sample is biased downwards. For example, on an asset level there are reported high average debt-financing ratios of 70% (see Esty, 2003; Weisdorf, 2007).

6. See Leuz (2010), Table 3, Panel C.

7. This action is also referred to as asset expropriation (see Lang & Maffett, 2010). Alternatively, a positive effect of transparency on firm valuation could also be explained by an efficient resource allocation (see Lang & Maffett, 2010).

8. Lang et al. (2012) show empirically for a large sample of international firms that lower transparency lowers liquidity, and thus increases expected return and cost of capital, which leads to lower valuations. The mediator between transparency and valuation is liquidity instead of cash flows. However, the net effect could be positive or negative, considering the possible costs of transparency. For example, earnings management through earnings smoothing could also reduce cost of debt through lower default risk for creditors. See also Lang and Maffett (2010).

ACKNOWLEDGMENTS

The author would like to thank Henry Lahr and Nina Fichtl for support and helpful comments. Financial support by the European Investment Bank through the EIBURS program is also gratefully acknowledged. The findings, interpretations, and conclusions of this article as well as any remaining errors are entirely those of the author.

REFERENCES

Amihud, Y., & Lev, B. (1981). Risk reduction as a managerial motive for conglomerate mergers. *The Bell Journal of Economics*, *12*(2), 605–617.

Badrinath, S. G., Gay, G. D., & Kale, J. R. (1989). Patterns of institutional investment, prudence and the 'managerial safety net' hypothesis. *Journal of Risk and Insurance*, *56*(4), 605–629.

Barton, J. (2001). Does the use of financial derivatives affect earnings management decisions? *The Accounting Review*, *76*(1), 1–26.

Bitsch, F., Buchner, A., & Kaserer, C. (2010). Risk, return and cash flow characteristics of infrastructure fund investments. *EIB Papers*, *15*(1), 106–136.

Chew, D. H. (2011). A message from the editor. *Journal of Applied Corporate Finance*, *23*(3), 2–3.

Chi, J. D. & Wu, J. (2010). Cash-flow volatility and firm valuation, Working Paper, Version September 1, 2010.

Davis, K. (2009). Listed infrastructure funds: Funding and financial management. *The FINSIA Journal of Applied Finance*, *1*, 43–47.

Dechow, P. M., & Dichev, I. D. (2002). The quality of accruals and earnings: The role of accrual estimation errors. *The Accounting Review*, *77*(Suppl.), 35–59.

Degeorge, F., Patel, J., & Zeckhauser, R. (1999). Earnings management to exceed thresholds. *Journal of Business*, *72*(1), 1–33.

Diller, C., & Kaserer, C. (2009). What drives private equity returns? – Fund inflows, skilled GPs, and/or risk? *European Financial Management*, *15*(3), 643–675.

Djankov, S., La Porta, R., Lopez-de-Silanes, F., & Shleifer, A. (2008). The law and economics of self-dealing. *Journal of Financial Economics*, *88*(3), 430–465.

Esty, B. C. (2003). *The economic motivations for using project finance*. Mimeo: Harvard Business School.

Esty, B. C. (2010). An overview of project finance and infrastructure finance – 2009 Update, Harvard Business School Case No. 210-061.

Fang, V. W., Noe, T. H., & Tice, S. (2009). Stock market liquidity and firm value. *Journal of financial Economics*, *94*(1), 150–169.

Froot, K., Scharfstein, D., & Stein, J. (1993). Risk management: Coordinating corporate investment and financing policies. *Journal of Finance*, *48*, 1624–1658.

Francis, J., Lafond, R., Olsson, P. M., & Schipper, K. (2004). Costs of equity and earnings attributes. *The Accounting Review*, *79*(4), 135–176.

Gompers, P. A., & Lerner, J. (2000). Money chasing deals? The impact of fund inflows on private equity valuation. *Journal of Financial Economics*, *55*(2), 281–325.

Gompers, P. A., Ishii, J. L., & Metrick, A. (2003). Corporate governance and equity prices. *Quarterly Journal of Economics*, *118*(1), 107–155.

Healy, P. M., & Wahlen, J. M. (1999). A review of the earnings management literature and its implications for standard setting. *Accounting Horizons*, *13*(4), 365–383.

Inderst, G. (2009). *Pension fund investment in infrastructure*. OECD Working Papers on Insurance and Private Pensions, No. 32. OECD Publishing. Paris, France.

Inderst, G. (2010). Infrastructure as an asset class. *EIB Papers*, *15*(1), 70–104.

Kaserer, C., Lahr, H., Liebhart, V., & Mettler, A. (2010). The time-varying risk of listed private equity. *Journal of Financial Transformation*, *28*, 87–93.

Lahr, H., & Herschke, F. T. (2009). Organizational forms and risk of listed private equity. *The Journal of Private Equity*, *13*(1), 89–99.

Lang, M. H., Lins, K. V. H., & Miller, D. P. (2003a). ADRs, analysts, and accuracy: Does cross listing in the united states improve a firm's information environment and increase market value? *Journal of Accounting Research*, *41*(2), 317–345.

Lang, M. H., & Maffett, M. (2010). Economic effects of transparency in international equity markets: A review and suggestions for future research. *Foundations and Trends in Accounting*, *5*(3), 175–241.

Lang, M. H., Raedy, J. S., & Yetman, M. H. (2003b). How representative are firms that are cross-listed in the United States? An analysis of accounting quality. *Journal of Accounting Research*, *41*(2), 363–386.

Lang, M. H., Lins, K. V., & Maffett, M. (2012). Transparency, liquidity, and valuation: International evidence on when transparency matters most. *Journal of Accounting Research*, *50*(3), 729–774.

La Porta, R., Lopez-de-Silanes, F., & Shleifer, A. (2006). What works in securities laws? *Journal of Finance*, *61*(1), 1–32.

Lawrence, M. & Stapledon, G. P. (2008). Infrastructure funds: Creative use of corporate structure and law – But in whose interests? University of Melbourne Legal Studies Research Paper No. 314. University of Melbourne. Melbourne, Australia.

Leuz, C. (2010). Different approaches to corporate reporting regulation: How jurisdictions differ and why. *Accounting and Business Research, International Accounting Policy Forum*, 229–256.

Leuz, C., Nanda, D., & Wysocki, P. D. (2003). Earnings management and investor protection: An international comparison. *Journal of Financial Economics*, *69*(3), 505–527.

Licht, A. N., Goldschmidt, C., & Schwartz, S. H. (2007). Culture rules: The foundations of the rule of law and other norms of governance. *Journal of Comparative Economics*, *35* (4), 659–688.

Merton, R. C. (1974). The pricing of corporate debt: The risk structures of interest rates. *Journal of Finance*, *29*(2), 449–470.

OECD. (2007). *Infrastructure to 2030, Volume 2, Mapping policy for electricity, water and transport*. Paris: Organisation for Economic Co-operation and Development.

Orr, R. J., & Kennedy, J. R. (2008). Highlights of recent trends in global infrastructure: New players and revised game rules. *Transnational Corporations*, *17*(1), 95–130.

Pastor, L., & Veronesi, P. (2003). Stock valuation and learning about profitability. *Journal of Finance*, *58*(5), 1749–1789.

Roedel, M., & Rothballer, C. (2012). Infrastructure as hedge against inflation – Fact or Fantasy? *The Journal of Alternative Investments*, *15*(1), 110–123.

Rothballer, C., & Kaserer, C. (2012). The risk profile of infrastructure investments: Challenging conventional wisdom. *The Journal of Structured Finance*, *18*(2), 95–109.

Rountree, B., Weston, J., & Allayannis, G. (2008). Do investors value smooth performance? *Journal of Financial Economics*, *90*(3), 237–251.

Sawant, R. J. (2010a). Emerging market infrastructure project bonds: Their risks and returns. *The Journal of Structured Finance*, *15*(4), 75–83.

Sawant, R. J. (2010b). *Infrastructure investing: Managing risks and rewards for pensions, insurance companies and endowments*. Hoboken, NJ: Wiley.

Shin, H.-H., & Stulz, R. M. (2000). *Firm value, risk and growth opportunities*. NBER Working Paper No. 7808. National Bureau of Economic Research. Cambridge, MA.

Trueman, B., & Titman, S. (1988). An explanation for accounting income smoothing. *Journal of Accounting Research*, *26*(Suppl.), 127–139.

Välilä, T. (2005). How expensive are cost savings? On the economics of public-private partnerships. *EIB Papers*, *10*(1), 94–119.

Weisdorf, M. A. (2007). Infrastructure: A growing real return asset class. *CFA Institute Conference Proceedings*, *24*(3), 17–27.

EARNINGS MANAGEMENT BEHAVIOUR UNDER THE RECENT ECONOMIC DOWNTURN IN SPAIN

Josep M. Argilés-Bosch, Josep García-Blandón and Mónica Martínez-Blasco

ABSTRACT

This study analyses the influence of the recent economic downturn on earnings management (EM), as well as the manipulation of real activities through cash flow from operations (CFO), with a sample of Spanish listed firms from 2004 to 2009.

We find evidence that the recent economic downturn has changed the patterns of firms' EM. On the one hand, the crisis influence higher earnings generation as indebtedness increase. On the other hand, results support the hypothesis of an opportunistic behaviour of managers with higher firm market valuation. They have incentives to reduce earnings during the recession and push earnings for the recovery phase of the business cycle.

The study finds also a significant relationship between EM and abnormal CFO generation. The downturn influences positive abnormal CFO generation with indebtedness, as well as negative abnormal CFO generation

Transparency and Governance in a Global World
International Finance Review, Volume 13, 231–255

ISSN: 1569-3767/doi:10.1108/S1569-3767(2012)0000013011

with firm size and market valuation. It has no significant influence through abnormal accruals on abnormal CFO generation.

Keywords: Earnings management; economic downturn; manipulation of cash flow

JEL classifications: D22; E32; M40; M41

INTRODUCTION

Earnings management (EM) has attracted considerable academic attention. EM is usually seen as undesirable from the investor's and stakeholders' point of view. It may thwart their efforts to make a correct assessment of the firm's fundamentals and determine the stock's fair value. Prior studies have shown that under certain circumstances managers try to manage earnings. These include the attainment of earnings thresholds (e.g. Burgstahler & Dichev, 1997; Degeorge, Patel, & Zeckhauser, 1999; Frankel, Johnson, & Nelson, 2002), the realization of initial public offerings or seasoned equity offerings (e.g. Cohen & Zarowin, 2010; Rangan, 1998; Teoh, Wong, & Rao, 1998), the attainment of bonus plans and compensation (e.g. Holthausen, Larcker, & Sloan, 1995; Pourciau, 1993), for smoothing income (DeFond & Park, 1997), in front of debt covenant restraints (e.g. DeFond & Jiambalvo, 1994), etc. The influence of corporate governance on EM has also been studied, finding that independence in board and audit committee (AC) influence significant lower abnormal accruals (e.g. Klein, 2002) and that firms with stronger corporate governance is significantly related with conditional conservatism (García Lara, García Osma, & Penalva, 2009). Roychowdhury (2006) found a significant manipulation of real activities in firms close to the zero earnings benchmark. DeAngelo and DeAngelo (1994) analysed managers' accounting choices in troubled companies. Yoon and Miller (2002) studied EM across different operating performances portfolios. However, previous studies have scarcely studied the influence of economic cycles on EM. Mitton (2002) studied the effect of corporate governance on disclosure quality during the East financial crisis of 1997–1998, but they did not relate it with EM. Davis-Friday, Eng, and Liu's (2006) study on the Asian financial crisis is focused on value relevance. Han and Wang (1998) found evidence of an opportunistic accounting behaviour in oil companies aiming at avoiding political costs during the

1990 Persian Gulf crisis. But this study does not deal with an economic downturn.

There are some empirical studies on the influence of the economic cycle on bank loan provisions. Agarwal, Chomsisengphet, Liu, and Rhee (2007) found evidence of differences in EM behaviour in Japanese banks under different economic environments. They studied Japanese bank practices on four decision variables (lending, securities, loan loss provisions and dividends). Quagliariello (2007) found that banks manage loan provisions in business cycle in order to carry out stress tests. Laeven and Majnoni (2003) found that banks postpone loan provisions during favourable cycles, but he did not analyse loan provision during downturns. Hsieh and Shen (2010) found that banks' loan provisions vary across geographical locations and combinations of growth in both, the economy and bank earnings. Huizinga and Laeven (2009) found evidence of relatively large excess returns in banks with large exposures to mortgage-backed securities. But these studies are focused on provisions and do not analyse total abnormal accruals. Empirical accounting studies on EM usually use samples of non-financial firms.

Additionally, there are the unpublished studies of Qinglu (2005) and Lin and Shih (2002). The former found that EM is significantly larger during recessions, as well as in strong economic growth periods, but they did not consider the complete array of control variables used in accounting studies, and used estimates of cash flow from operations (CFO) in the calculation of accruals. The latter studied the influence of Gross Domestic Product (GDP) growth on discretionary accruals, finding that during recessions managers defer income from periods of weak earnings to future periods. However, they did not accomplish their study using traditional models of EM, and did not analyse factors influencing abnormal accruals. They just performed descriptive analysis of abnormal accruals across periods. The unpublished paper of Navarro and Madrid (2009) investigates the relationship between GDP growth rates and EM with a sample of Spanish real state firms, but it did not perform multivariate analysis. In addition, the period covered in this study does not include a downturn. The authors recognize that the effect of a crisis remains unknown. An additional disadvantage of this study is that they did not find data on CFO, thus relying on estimated cash flows. None of these studies analysed the drivers through which a downturn influences on EM or on the manipulation of real activities.

Our study performs an empirical analysis on the influence of the recent economic crisis on EM through accounting and real activities manipulation with a sample of panel data of Spanish non-financial listed firms from

2004 to 2009. The severe Spanish recent downturn provides an interesting setting to perform such analysis. We find significant influence of the recent financial crisis on accounting manipulation through indebtedness and market valuation of firms. The recent financial crisis accentuates the influence of indebtedness on EM, applying income increasing accruals in order to convey a favourable image of the firm. It also influences income decreasing abnormal accruals with the aim to release profits to reserve earnings for the recovery phase of the business cycle in firms with higher market value. We also find a significant incidence on the effects of indebtedness, size and market valuation of firms on abnormal CFO generation during the financial crisis. Given the increasing difficulties in obtaining loan grants, firms generate abnormal increasing CFO with indebtedness. On the contrary, the recent economic crisis influence abnormal decreasing CFO generation with size and market valuation of firms. Abnormal accruals have a significant negative influence on abnormal CFO generation, but the crisis does not accentuate it.

The remaining of the chapter is organized as follows: the next section discusses the expected influence of economic recessions on EM and formulates hypotheses, we then explain the methodology, describe sample, explain results and then raise concluding remarks.

HYPOTHESES DEVELOPMENT: ECONOMIC RECESSION AND EM

Recessions make the business environment more challenging for firms, while managers try to cope with it managing financial statements according to this adverse economic situation. Investors, auditors, policy makers and stakeholders would be benefited from knowledge of EM under economic downturns.

By smoothing earnings over time, managers convey information to stakeholders about the underlying economic performance of the company, or attempt to influence contractual outcomes that depend on the reported accounting numbers. Healy (1985) argues that managers of firms that perform poorly have incentives to manipulate earnings downwards because they have no chance of receiving a bonus in the current period. Deferring income to the future periods would have no effect on their current total compensation, while would have positive influence in their future bonus. Yoon and Miller (2002) found empirical evidence that when operating performance is extremely poor, firms tend to take a big bath. Future research found empirical evidence of higher levels of EM in firms with higher levels of stock-based incentives for CEOs (e.g. Benesih & Vargus, 2002; Bergstresser & Philippon, 2006).

On the other side, Hayn (1995) demonstrated that the response of stock returns is larger for firms reporting positive earnings than for firms reporting losses. This asymmetric response has also been demonstrated by Basu (1997). Firms would be benefited from EM to the fact that stock prices decrease less with the incidence of negative accruals in periods of negative earnings than they increase when positive accruals impact favourably in periods of positive earnings. According to this, firms that report losses during recessions may be judged less harshly than firms doing so during normal periods, as well as firms that report lower income increasing. Stakeholders are prone to accept losses, or lower income increasing, during recessions. Beatty, Ke, and Petroni (2002) found that publicly held banks report fewer small earnings declines and use loan loss provisions to eliminate small earnings decreases, with respect to privately held. During recessions they may be inclined to loosen this behaviour with respect to normal periods. Assuming that firms perform poorly during recessions, they may have incentives to push earnings even lower (or to avoid to report earning increases) to reserve earnings for the recovery phase of the business cycle. By releasing these earnings reserves after the recession, these firms are likely to report higher earnings in the recovery phase. On the other hand, there is a reaction to the factors that presumably induced the recent economic downturn. Stakeholders and public opinion are cautious with respect to risky business and accounting practices. Therefore, there is more surveillance on firms' management and more awareness on the need of reflecting future risks in firms' accounting. An important restriction for this behaviour is market valuation. Given that abnormal accruals and the subsequent reported earnings convey relevant information (Subramanyam, 1996), firms with lower market valuation will find more restrictions in lowering earnings even more during the crisis, while firms with higher market valuation will be comparatively more prone to apply this opportunistic behaviour.

The present financial crisis entails severe financial restrictions for firms, especially in Spain. Banks and financial institutions restrict loan grants and are more demanding in the assessment of firm financial soundness. Firms face a decrease in revenues and cash flow generation in the present downturn, matched with loan grant restrictions, while they have more urgent need of external funding. According to Watts and Zimmerman (1990) debt covenants influence accounting choices. When firms face a covenant constraint or a danger of a covenant violation, managers try to exercise discretion by choosing income increasing methods that relax debts constraints. Different studies found empirical evidence that firm's indebtedness is positively associated with EM, and more concretely with income increasing accounting practices (e.g. Duke & Hunt, 1990; Holthausen, 1981; Jelinek, 2007). Increasing firm income through EM, managers try to convey a more favourable image of the financial position of the firm that would facilitate access to loan granting. The extraordinary financial constraints in the recent financial crisis will accentuate the influence of firm leverage on EM.

Given that financial constraints and the decrease in market firms' valuation are important consequences of the recent financial crisis, we expect that the interaction between the crisis and both mentioned consequences will significantly impact firms' EM. Accordingly, we formulate the following hypotheses:

Hypothesis 1. The recent economic downturn significantly influences EM.

Hypothesis 2. The recent economic downturn influences income decreasing abnormal accruals in higher market valued firms.

Hypothesis 3. The recent economic downturn increases the influence of indebtedness on income increasing abnormal accruals.

Apart from EM, the recent economic downturn is favouring the manipulation of cash flow generation with the aim of alleviating the financial stress of firms. The recent economic crisis is substantially reducing sales and income, and subsequently affecting firms' cash flow generation and financing. The sharp decrease of stock prices, and specifically in the Spanish Stock Exchange Market, and the shortcut in lending from financial institutions are additional factors that aggravate the availability of sources of financing of firm activities. Managers try to cope with this financial stress managing real activities related to CFO generation, such as selling assets, shortening cash collection terms from customers and clients, delaying any kind of payment, depleting inventories, reducing certain discretionary expenses, etc. Burgstahler and Dichev (1997) and Roychowdhury (2006) found empirical evidence of manipulation of CFO related to reported earnings. More indebted firms are more exposed to such debt grant difficulties, as well as to difficulties to face loan return, and thus will be prone to generate additional cash flow. In the same vein, firms with lower market valuation will have lower opportunities to get external funding, and consequently are in more urgent need of generating abnormal positive cash flows, especially those firms that apply the opportunistic behaviour of reporting more losses during the recession through EM. These firms disclose less favourable financial statements, which consequently aggravate the opportunities for obtaining funding from financial markets or financial institutions, and have more urgent need of manipulating CFO. We, thus formulate the following hypotheses:

Hypothesis 4. The recent economic downturn influences higher generation of abnormal CFO as indebtedness increases, and vice versa.

Hypothesis 5. The recent financial crisis influences lower abnormal CFO generation with higher market firm valuation, and vice versa.

Hypothesis 6. The recent financial crisis stresses the influence of abnormal accruals on abnormal CFO generation: higher abnormal income decreasing accruals urge firms to obtain higher positive abnormal CFO, while higher abnormal income increasing accruals deter firms from generating positive abnormal CFO.

METHODOLOGY

Our empirical study on EM takes the approach used by Klein (2002). We begin by estimating the Dechow, Sloan, and Sweeney (1995) variant of the Jones (1991) expected accruals model:

$$\frac{ACCR_{i,t}}{TA_{i,t-1}} = \alpha_0 + \alpha_1 \cdot \frac{1}{TA_{i,t-1}} + \alpha_2 \cdot \frac{\Delta REV_{i,t} - \Delta REC_{i,t}}{TA_{i,t-1}} + \alpha_3 \cdot \frac{PPE_{i,t}}{TA_{i,t-1}} + \varepsilon_{i,t} \quad (1)$$

where $ACCR$ are total accruals for firm i in period t, TA are total assets, ΔREV and ΔREC are increases in revenues and receivables from previous period respectively, and PPE property, plant and equipment. We use ε as indication of the error term in any equation used in the chapter.

Abnormal accruals (AAC) are then calculated as:

$$AAC_{i,t} = \frac{ACCR_{i,t}}{TA_{i,t-1}} - PREDACC_{i,t} \quad (2)$$

where $PREDACC$ are predicted accruals through the estimation of Eq. (1).

We then explain *AAC* and absolute value of abnormal accruals (*AAAC*) as depending on economic recession, the control variables used in Klein (2002) model and basic corporate governance characteristics.

Predominance of independent directors in board composition influence positive board decisions. Weisbach (1988) shows that the presence of external directors is positively related to CEO removal decisions, while higher executives on the board are associated with higher CEO influence. With majority of external directors in the board, CEOs are expected to be deterred from EM. Similarly, the more the external members participate in the AC, the more the firm will be deterred from EM practices. Specifically, when all members are external, the AC will feel free to detect inadequate accounting statements.

We use a dummy variable (*CRISIS*) for indicating with value 1 that the observation corresponds to the recent economic recession (years 2008 and 2009), and 0 otherwise (years 2004–2007). We use two variables for controlling for basic corporate governance characteristics. The dummy variable *BD51* takes the value of 1 when the firm's board has at least majority of outside directors, and 0 otherwise. The dummy variable *ACOM100* takes the value of 1 when all members of the AC are external and 0 otherwise. Assuming that a board with majority of external members will be less likely influenced by managers, and that the absence of internal members in the AC will provide more ground to monitor firm accounting consistently, we expect significant negative signs for these variables.

The additional control variables used in Klein (2002) are the market value of the total firm over book value of assets, measured at the beginning of the fiscal year (*MVTBV*), the absolute value of the change in net income between years $t-1$ and t ($ABS\Delta NI$), a dummy variable indicating if the firm had two or more consecutive years of negative income (with value 1 and 0 otherwise), ending on the fiscal year prior to the shareholder's meeting (*NEGNI*), long-term debt divided by last year's assets (*LDEBTTA*), and the natural logarithm of book value of total assets (*LNTA*). As suggested in Klein (2002), significant positive signs are expected for $ABS\Delta NI$ and *LDEBTTA*, as well as significant negative signs for *LNTA*, while no specific expectation is formulated for the other two variables.

We also perform additional estimation controlling by the specific circumstance that a given firm, setting aside the existence of a generalized crisis, decrease its activity in the current year. The dummy variable *DECR-REV* indicates, with value 1 that the firm decrease revenues in the current year, and 0 otherwise. The firm may be induced either to adjust its behaviour in EM to the fact that it is facing a decrease in activity, despite there is no general economic recession, or that it is not suffering such a decrease in spite of the fact that it is immersed in a global downturn. Managers may be induced to manage earnings in order to mitigate the effects of the decrease in activity, to defer income to future periods, and/or the benefit from the asymmetric response of stock returns. Thus, a positive sign is expected for this variable.

We then formulate the following model for explaining EM:

$$\begin{aligned} AAAC_{i,t} = {} & \beta_0 + \beta_1 \cdot CRISIS_{i,t} + \beta_2 \cdot MVTBV_{i,t} + \beta_3 \cdot ABS\Delta NI_{i,t} \\ & + \beta_4 \cdot NEGNI_{i,t} + \beta_5 \cdot LDEBTTA_{i,t} + \beta_6 \cdot LNTA_{i,t} + \beta_7 \cdot BD51_{i,t} \\ & + \beta_8 \cdot ACOM100_{i,t} + \beta_9 \cdot DECRREV_{i,t} + \varepsilon_{i,t} \end{aligned} \tag{3}$$

In order to analyse the mechanisms through which economic cycles affects EM we add iterative variables of CRISIS with *MVTBV*, *ABS*Δ*NI*, *NEGNI*, *LDEBTA* and *LNTA*. In addition to *AAAC*, we also use *AAC* as dependent variable, which allows us to analyse the incidence of the independent variables on abnormal firm income.

Following Roychowdhury (2006) we use the following equation for predicting CFO:

$$\frac{CFO_{i,t}}{TA_{1,t-1}} = \gamma_0 + \gamma_1 \cdot \frac{1}{TA_{i,t-1}} + \gamma_2 \cdot \frac{REV_{i,t}}{TA_{i,t-1}} + \gamma_3 \cdot \frac{\Delta REV_{i,t}}{TA_{i,t-1}} + \varepsilon_{i,t} \tag{4}$$

Abnormal CFO (*ACFO*) are then calculated as:

$$ACFO_{i,t} = \frac{CFO_{i,t}}{TA_{i,t-1}} - PREDCFO_{i,t} \tag{5}$$

where *PREDCFO* are predicted CFO through the estimation of Eq. (4).

We then use similar model to that used by Roychowdhury (2006) to explain abnormal CFO as depending on size, market valuation (*MVTBV*) and net income (*NI*). Following this author we use the logarithm of market value at the beginning of the year (*LNMV*) as a proxy for size. We also include the variable AAC to control for the influence of abnormal accruals on the generation of abnormal CFO. We include *CRISIS* to analyse the effect of the economic downturn:

$$\begin{aligned} ACFO_{i,t} = {} & \varphi_0 + \varphi_1 \cdot LNMV_{i,t-1} + \varphi_2 \cdot MVTBV_{i,t-1} + \varphi_3 \cdot NI_{i,t} \\ & + \varphi_4 \cdot CRISIS_{i,t} + \varphi_5 \cdot AAC_{i,t} + \varepsilon_{i,t} \end{aligned} \tag{6}$$

The iterative variables of *CRISIS* with these control variables and with indebtedness allow a more accurate analysis of the mechanisms through which the economic downturn influences abnormal CFO generation.

SAMPLE

We refer our analysis to firms listed in the Spanish Stock Exchange Market. We found our data in different sources. Data on corporate governance were collected in the web site of the *Comisión Nacional del Mercado de Valores*, which is the agency in charge of supervising and inspecting the Spanish Stock Exchange Market and the activities of all the participants in this market. Thomson Reuters and SABI data bases provided data on accounting information between year 2004 and 2009. Finally, the market value of firms were complemented with the web site of *Bolsa de Madrid*. Bank and insurance companies were excluded from our sample, as is usual in empirical studies on EM, because it is difficult to define accruals and abnormal accruals for financial service firms (Klein, 2002).

A final sample of 104 firms and 462 firm-year data was available for all variables needed in our study. Data for 34 firms were available for all considered years, while we got the necessary data for only one year for 12 firms (see Table 1). For descriptive and some variables expressed in non-relative terms, all data are converted into 2009 values, applying the Spanish index of consumer prices. For the purposes of our study, we consider years 2008 and 2009 belonging to the economic downturn, taking into account that mid-September 2007 is considered the start of the financial crisis in the United States, that the crisis burst a little bit later in Spain, and the variation of the Spanish GDP: more than three year percent growth from 2004 to 2007, and 1.4 and 3.0 year percent decrease in 2008 and 2009 respectively.

Table 2 displays descriptive statistics. Firms in our sample performed significantly lower positive and total abnormal accruals with $p < 0.01$ during the crisis with respect to the previous period, which gives a first indication of a change in EM during the economic downturn. However, negative abnormal accruals are not significantly different across both periods. Both abnormal CFO, positive and negative, are significantly higher during the crisis. While there are no significant differences in revenues of firms in our sample between both periods, net income and return on assets decreased significantly with $p < 0.01$ during the downturn, when these firms experienced significantly higher financial stress with $p < 0.1$ (higher median values of long-term debt on total assets). Also, firms in our sample experienced significantly higher absolute change in net income during the downturn with $p < 0.01$. Firms in our sample are homogenous in terms of corporate governance characteristics: outside members of firm's board and AC are majority in most of them. The percentage of firms with 100%

Table 1. Sample Characteristics.

Panel A: Year-Data Observations

Year	Year-Data Observations	% Increase in GDP in Spain[1]
2004	71	3.4
2005	78	3.8
2006	79	4.0
2007	89	3.2
2008	101	− 1.4
2009	44	− 3.0
Total	462	

Panel B: Number of Firms in the Sample

Number of Years in the Sample	Number of Firms
1	12
2	8
3	5
4	10
5	35
6	34
Total	104

[1]*Source*: Spanish *Instituto Nacional de Estadística*. Retrieved from http://www.ine.es/jaxiBD/tabla.do.

of independent members increased significantly (with $p < 0.05$) during the crisis with respect to the previous period.

Panels A and B from Table 3 display Pearson correlations between independent variables of Eqs. (1) and (3) respectively. As correlations are low (the highest coefficient is 0.4403), collinearity is unlikely to affect estimations. Correlations are also not high between independent variables in Eqs. (4) and (6), as can be seen in Panels C and D from Table 3.

RESULTS

As our sample presents the typical autocorrelation pattern of panel data, we perform panel data estimations.

The commonly used Hausman test (Hsiao, 2005) did not reject the null hypothesis of no correlation between individual effects and explanatory

Table 2. Descriptive Statistics: Mean Values.

	Overall Sample	Downturn (2008–2009)	No Downturn (2004–2007)
Positive Abnormal accruals ($AACR > 0$)	0.0792715 (0.0464342)	0.0498633 (0.0389649)	0.0993438 (0.0488762)***
Negative Abnormal accruals ($AACR < 0$)	−0.0656743 (−0.0490164)	− 0.066123 (−0.0379807)	−0.0655357 (−0.0508907)
Absolute value of abnormal accruals (*AAAC*)	0.0719137 (0.0469495)	0.0564793 (0.0388661)	0.0789736 (0.0500382)***
Positive abnormal *CFO*	0.0847053 (0.0590842)	0.1278664 (0.1156099)	0.0659793 (0.0460061)***
Negative abnormal *CFO*	−0.112542 (−0.0666341)	− 0.1664293 (−0.1148104)	−0.0860193 (−0.055508)***
Absolute value of abnormal *CFO*	0.0962135 (0.0617576)	0.1446214 (0.1153739)	0.0740711 (0.0505871)***
Deflated total assets	7157.122 (1118.036)	9167.553 (1482.972)	6237.525 (1077.376)**
Deflated revenues	3678.014 (743.735)	4371.404 (832.73)	3360.848 (724.85)
Deflated net income	324.7234 (33.97)	254.8451 (14.6315)	347.6487 (38.43)***
Return on assets (%)	3.69 (3.95)	1.04 (2.65)	4.91 (4.61)***
Absolute change in net income ($ABS\Delta NI$)	143.821 (18.3025)	241.4928 (29.958)	99.14461 (16.107)***
% of firms with two or more years of negative income	4.76	4.82	4.73
Long-term debt to last year's assets (*LDEBTTA*): median in parenthesis	0.2631867 (0.195159)	0.2521172 (0.2141005)	0.2682501 (0.185818)*
Natural logarithm of assets (*LNTA*):	7.250267 (7.019304)	7.50883 (7.301804)	7.131997 (6.982284)**
% of firms with firm's board with majority of outside members	97.62	99.31	96.84
% of firms with AC with all outside members	79.22	85.51	76.34**

Notes: Median values in parenthesis; Mann–Witney tests for continuous variables and Pearson chi-squared tests of independence for categorical variables.
Significance levels: *$p < 0.1$, **$p < 0.05$ and ***$p < 0.01$.

variables. As individual effects are uncorrelated with the regressors in all estimations, the random effects estimator is consistent and efficient, for the estimation of the explanatory equation of abnormal accruals. The value of the Hausman test (7.43) for the estimation of the reduced model (Eq. (3)) in Table 4 is not significant with $p < 0.05$ for 6 d.f., as well as for

Table 3. Pearson Correlations between Independent Variables (Significance Level).

	$1/TA_{t-1}$	$(\Delta REV_t - \Delta REC_t)/TA_{t-1}$	PPE_t/TA_{t-1}
Panel A: Independent Variables in Eq. (1)			
$1/TA_{t-1}$	1		
$(\Delta REV_t - \Delta REC_{t-1})/TA_{t-1}$	0.012	1	
PPE_t/TA_{t-1}	− 0.0941 **	0.0573	1

	MVTBV	*ABSΔNI*	*NEGNI*	*LDEBTTA*	*LNTA*	*ACOM100*	*BD51*	*CRISIS*	*DECRREV*
Panel B: Independent Variables in Eq. (3)									
MVTBV	1								
ABSΔNI	− 0.0944 **	1							
NEGNI	0.0848 *	− 0.0501	1						
LDEBTTA:	− 0.0678	0.0386	− 0.0145	1					
LNTA	− 0.2027 ***	0.4403 ***	− 0.2007 ***	0.2209 ***	1				
ACOM100	− 0.0439	0.091 *	− 0.136 ***	0.0779 *	0.2704 ***	1			
BD51	0.0248	0.0477	0.0349	0.0112	0.1833 ***	0.2 ***	1		
CRISIS	− 0.0223	0.1448 ***	0.0021	− 0.0143	0.0968 **	0.105 **	0.075	1	
DECRREV	− 0.0808 *	0.0265	− 0.0208	− 0.0705	− 0.0552	− 0.0149	0.0305	0.1903 ***	1

Table 3. (*Continued*)

	$1/TA_{t-1}$	REV_t/TA_{t-1}	$\Delta REV_t/TA_{t-1}$
Panel C: Independent Variables in Eq. (4)			
$1/TA_{t-1}$	1		
REV_t/TA_{t-1}	0.2017 ***		1
$\Delta REV_t/TA_{t-1}$	0.0916	0.501 ***	1

	$LNMV_{t-1}$	$MVTBV_{t-1}$	NI	$CRISIS$	AAC
Panel D: Independent Variables in Eq. (6)					
$LNMV_{t-1}$	1				
$MVTBV_{t-1}$	0.1302 **	1			
NI	0.5548 ***	− 0.0525	1		
$CRISIS$	0.0908 **	0.1535 ***	0.0063	1	
AAC	− 0.0201	0.2005 ***	0.0113	0.0115	1

Note: Significance levels: *$p < 0.1$, **$p < 0.05$ and ***$p < 0.01$.

the enlarged models in Columns B and C in Table 4: 8.98 and 9.61 in the Hausman tests with 8 and 9 d.f. respectively. The subsequent Hausman tests of other estimations in this table, as well as in the following tables, yielded similar results referring to the preference of random over fixed effects. Estimations of accruals with Eq. (1) are also performed with panel data estimations. Table 4 displays estimations for the dependent variable *AAAC*.

All models present significant goodness of fit with $p < 0.01$ for estimations displayed in this table. Most control variables are significant with $p < 0.05$ in the reduced model (Column A). As expected, absolute changes in net income and financial leverage are positively associated with EM, while size significantly influences negative *AAAC*. Moreover, coefficient of market value of firm is positive and significant with $p < 0.05$. All this results are in accordance to expectations and previous empirical research (e.g. Bartov, Givoly, & Hayn, 2002; Frankel et al., 2002; Klein, 2002). However, external predominance on board and AC does not significantly influence EM according to our results (Columns B–E), a fact that contradicts previous empirical research (e.g. Klein, 2002), but is in accordance with Pucheta-Martínez and de Fuentes (2007) findings of no influence of the existence of an AC and its composition on audit quality in Spanish firms. These results cast doubts on the real effectiveness of the board of directors and AC in Spain. However, this finding can be explained in terms of the homogeneity of board and AC characteristics of firms in our sample, as mentioned in section four. Firms listed in the Spanish Stock Exchange Market are usually the biggest firms operating in Spain, and in most of them external members are majority in their boards and AC.

With respect to our variable of interest, results indicate that the existence of an economic downturn significantly influences lower EM (with $p < 0.01$), which provide support for our Hypothesis 1. The significant negative sign of the dummy variable indicates that firms reduce abnormal accruals during the crisis (Columns A–C in Table 4). Estimation replacing the dummy variable *CRISIS* with the continuous variable percent increase in GDP in Spain (Column D) reinforces results on the significant decrease of AAAC during the crisis. Column E displays estimations adding the iterative variables. Pearson correlations of some variables are significant and highly correlated: 0.6781 for *CRISIS* and *CRISIS*LDEBTTA*, 0.7726 for *CRISIS*LNTA* and *CRISIS*LDEBTA*, and 0.8426 for *CRISIS*ABSΔNI* and *ABSΔNI*. Consequently, and considering the variables of interest for testing our hypotheses, we removed the variables *CRISIS*, *ABSΔNI*, *CRISIS*LNTA* and *CRISIS*ABSΔNI*. Estimates for the model with the

Table 4. Random Effects Estimations for Multivariate Models of Absolute Values of Abnormal Accruals (*AAAC*) On *CRISIS*, Basic Board Characteristics and Control Variables (Eq. (3)).

	A		B		C		D		E	
CRISIS	−0.0230882	***	−0.0230502	***	−0.0251674	***				
	(0.006219)		(0.0062758)		(0.0064017)					
Percent increase in GDP							0.0046433	***		
							(0.0011593)			
MVTBV	0.0076899	**	0.0078836	**	0.0084616	**	0.0082948	**	0.0100844	***
	(0.0033161)		(0.0033113)		(0.0033211)		(0.0033221)		(0.0034988)	
ABSΔNI	0.0000218	***	0.0000217	***	0.0000221	***	0.0000217	***	0.000022	***
	(7.99e-06)		(8.01e-06)		(8.00e-06)		(7.98e-06)		(7.90e-06)	
NEGNI	−0.0192573		−0.0171797		−0.0153239		−0.0143392		−0.0101348	
	(0.0195169)		(0.0195449)		(0.0195323)		(0.0195332)		(0.0211942)	
LDEBTTA	0.0694126	***	0.0691118	***	0.0698393	***	0.0696175	***	0.0715821	***
	(0.0061036)		(0.006112)		(0.0061188)		(0.0061149)		(0.0060771)	
LNTA	−0.0072526	**	−0.0070779	**	−0.0067093	**	−0.0065195	**	−0.005717*	
	(0.0031023)		(0.0031745)		(0.0031735)		(0.003176)		(0.003143)	
*BD*51			−0.0347574		−0.035065		−0.035302		−0.0369209	
			(0.028096)		(0.0280297)		(0.0280163)		(0.0276101)	
*ACOM*100			0.007973		0.0079563		0.0078774		0.0076526	
			(0.0106479)		(0.0106229)		(0.0106157)		(0.0104471)	
DECRREV					0.0106229		0.0125875*		0.0097918	
					(0.0071034)		(0.007152)		(0.0069493)	
CRISIS * *LDEBTTA*									−0.0854255	***
									(0.020799)	
CRISIS * *MVTBV*									−0.0042419	
									(0.0039206)	
CRISIS * *NEGNI*									−0.0033706	
									(0.0286679)	
Intercept	0.1054807	***	0.1315576	***	0.0115162	***	0.1080917	***	0.1188678	***
	(0.0232403)		(0.032584)		(0.0326916)		(0.0331929)		(0.0322562)	
R^2	0.2192	***	0.2290	***	0.2330	***	0.2341	***	0.2553	***
Number of observations	462		462		462		462		462	

Note: Parameter estimates and standard deviation in parenthesis.
Significance levels: $*p<0.1$, $**p<0.05$ and $***p<0.01$.

remaining variables are displayed in Column E in Table 4, which reveal that the downturn influences EM through the interaction with indebtedness.

Table 5 displays estimations for the dependent variable *AAC*. The non-significant sign of the dummy variable *CRISIS* (Column A) suggests the existence of opposite effects of the crisis in abnormal accruals. Column B explains these opposite effects. The significant (with $p < 0.05$) negative sign of the iterative variable *CRISIS*MVTBV* supports Hypothesis 2 on the existence of EM during the downturn aiming at releasing earnings for the recovery phase. However, this behaviour is constricted by firm market valuation. The significant positive sign of the iterative variable *CRISIS*LDEBTTA* reveals that the downturn influences higher (lower) income increasing abnormal accruals for higher (lower) indebtedness, which supports Hypothesis 3. This finding suggests that during the downturn indebted firms try to improve their financial statements through EM in order to get better financial access to loan granting.

Table 6 displays more detailed information on the mechanisms through which the downturn influences EM. Overall results in this table reinforce confirmation of Hypotheses 1, 2 and 3. Panel A reveals that the downturn significantly affects EM with $p < 0.05$ only in the subsamples of firms with higher indebtedness (Column A) and market valuation (Column C). Coefficients of the dummy variable are not significant in Columns B and D of this panel, suggesting no different EM behaviour in less indebted and market-valued firms during the downturn. Column A in Panel B displays a significant positive sign for the iterative variable *CRISIS*LDEBTA*, thus revealing that the downturn influences higher income increasing accruals in most indebted firms, which is not the case for less indebted firms (Column B in Panel B). Column C in Panel B displays also a significant positive sign for this variable, as well as a significant negative sign for the iterative variable *CRISIS*MVTBV*, thus suggesting that firms with higher market valuation apply the opportunistic behaviour of pushing earnings down during the downturn to reserve earnings for the recovery phase. There is no significant goodness of fit in the estimation of Eq. (3) with iterative variables for the subsample of firms with lower market valuation (Column D in Panel B).

Panels C and D in Table 6 provide detailed information on positive and negative abnormal accruals. According to these results, the crisis influences a decrease in negative abnormal accruals in firms with higher indebtedness (see the significant positive sign with $p < 0.05$ in Column A of Panel D), but it has no significant influence with respect to positive abnormal accruals in these firms (see Column A in Panel C). According to these

Table 5. Random Effects Estimations for Multivariate Models of Abnormal Accruals (*AAC*) on Iterative Variables of *CRISIS*, Basic Board Characteristics and Control Variables (Eq. (3)).

	A		B	
CRISIS	0.0090275			
	(0.0089482)			
MVTBV	0.019116	***	0.0228112	***
	(0.0046498)		(0.0049252)	
ABSΔNI	− 0.0000114		− 0.0000127	
	(0.0000112)		(0.0000111)	
NEGNI	− 0.0516132	*	− 0.0593328	**
	(0.0273308)		(0.0297636)	
LDEBTTA	0.0687578	***	0.0674454	***
	(0.0085541)		(0.0085011)	
LNTA	− 0.005286		− 0.006779	
	(0.0044447)		(0.0044423)	
*BD*51	− 0.0558251		− 0.056904	
	(0.0392256)		(0.0388473)	
*ACOM*100	0.005083		0.0048807	
	(0.0148654)		(0.0146955)	
DECRREV	0.0073136		0.0088092	
	(0.0099304)		(0.0097202)	
CRISIS * *LDEBTTA*			0.0876219	***
			(0.0290768)	
CRISIS * *MVTBV*			− 0.0116634	**
			(0.0054797)	
CRISIS * *NEGNI*			0.0152792	
			(0.0400502)	
Intercept			0.0587633	
	0.0505856		(0.0455009)	
	(0.0457701)			
R^2	0.1725	***	0.1686	***
Number of observations	462		462	

Note: Parameter estimates and standard deviation in parenthesis.
Significance levels: $*p<0.1$, $**p<0.05$ and $***p<0.01$.

results, more indebted firms convey a more favourable image reducing negative accruals during the downturn. Firms with higher market valuation apply lower positive and negative abnormal accruals during the downturn (see Column C in Panels C and D respectively). Given that the slope for the positive accruals (0.041) is higher that the slope for the negative accruals (0.024), the outcome is a net income decreasing effect. Even the less indebted firms (which have lower financial restrictions) display a

Table 6. Random Effects Estimations for Multivariate Model of Abnormal Accruals for Subsamples with Indebtedness and Market to Book Values above and below Median Values of Total Sample.

	LDEBTTA				*MVTBV*			
	Above Median		Below Median		Above Median		Below Median	
	A		B		C		D	
Panel A: Absolute Value of Abnormal Accruals (AAAC): Eq. (3) (Independent Variables of Column A in Table 5)								
CRISIS	− 0.0303584	***	− 0.0110591		− 0.371373	***	− 0.0113657	
	(0.0074026)		(0.0105446)		(0.0088848)		(0.0098356)	
R^2	0.4682	***	0.1599	***	0.3847	***	0.1188	***
Number of observations	231		231		231		231	
Panel B: Abnormal Acruals (AAC): Eq. (3) with Iterative Variables (Independent Variables of Column B in Table 5)								
*CRISIS * LDEBTTA*	0.0913184	***	0.0943354		0.1531118	***	0.0573991	
	(0.0337164)		(0.1612896)		(0.0511269)		(0.053084)	
*CRISIS * MVTBV*	0.0208217		− 0.0088472		− 0.0141772	**	0.0065805	
	(0.016055)		(0.0073741)		(0.0055985)		(0.0410551)	
*CRISIS * NEGNI*	− 0.0087734		0.0405154		0.0213399		− 0.0278941	
	(0.510339)		(0.0729921)		(0.0512993)		(0.0608664)	
R^2	0.2862	***	0.1487	***	0.2304	***	0.0375	
Number of observations	231		231		231		231	
*Panel C: Positive Abnormal Acruals (*AAC*): Eq. (3) (Independent Variables of Column A in Table 5)*								
CRISIS	0.0034132		− 0.0332173	*	− 0.0416427	***	− 0.0097388	
	(0.0120649)		(0.0178793)		(0.0156927)		(0.0145421)	
R^2	0.6478	***	0.2767	***	0.5042	***	0.2968	***
Number of observations	96		116		116		96	
*Panel D: Negative Abnormal Acruals (*AAC*): Eq. (3) (Independent Variables of Column A in Table 5)*								
CRISIS	0.0292256	**	− 0.0098493		0.0243622	**	− 0.0061452	
	(0.0119882)		(0.0116765)		(0.0116812)		(0.0120605)	
R^2	0.1808	***	0.0926	*	0.2620	***	0.1502	**
Number of observations	135		115		115		135	

Note: Control variables not displayed; parameter estimates and standard deviation in parenthesis. Significance levels: $*p < 0.1$, $**p < 0.05$ and $***p < 0.01$.

significant (only with $p < 0.1$) negative sign in the dummy variable for the subsample of positive abnormal accruals (Column B in Panel C), but no significant (with $p < 0.1$) for the subsample of negative abnormal accruals (Column B in Panel D), suggesting that less indebted firms apply the opportunistic behaviour of releasing earnings for the recovery phase. The non-significant coefficients of the dummy variable in Column D in Panels C and D suggest that firms with *MVTBV* below the median have market constraints to take profit from this EM behaviour.

Table 7 displays random effects estimations of Eq. (6). All models present significant goodness of fit, but unlike Roychowdhury's (2006) study, most control variables are not significant. According to our expectations, the sign of the variable *AAC* is negative and significant in all estimations (Columns A–C), thus providing empirical evidence that firms applying higher income decreasing accruals apply higher abnormal increasing CFO generation (presumably because they have more difficulties in getting financial resources), and vice versa. The negative significant signs of *LDEBTA* (Columns B and C) suggest that firms unable to get financial resources through indebtedness generate them through generation of abnormal increasing CFO. Additionally, more indebted firms have lower possibilities for generating abnormal increasing CFO. The coefficient of the variable *CRISIS* is not significant with $p < 0.1$ (see Columns A and B). Analysing these results together with estimates in Column C suggests the existence of opposite effects across the different mechanism through which the downturn influences abnormal CFO generation. Column C displays estimation of the full model with the iterative variables. Pearson correlations between *MVTBV* and *CRISIS*MVTBV*, as well as between *NI* and *CRISIS*NI* (0.7107 and 0.6731) are high and significant with $p < 0.01$. We consequently removed one variable in any of these pairs of variables. The negative significant sign of *CRISIS*LNMV* provides empirical evidence that the downturn influences higher abnormal increasing CFO in the smallest firms. With respect to our variables of interest, the significant positive sign of variable *CRISIS*LDEBTA* provides support for our Hypothesis 4, while the significant negative sign of *CRISIS*MVTBV* supports our Hypothesis 5. The crisis influences firm abnormal increasing CFO generation with indebtedness, given the difficulties to renew firm loans, as well as the financial stress of more indebted firms to pay back their loans during the crisis. The specific setting of the crisis turns them into influential factors. On the other hand, the downturn influences more abnormal increasing CFO for those firms with lower market valuation, given that the market signal extraordinary difficulties in getting additional funding. It is

Table 7. Random Effects Estimations for Multivariate Model of Abnormal CFO (Eq. (6)).

	A		B		C	
CRISIS	0.0050639		.0043051			
	(0.0108326)		(0.0107243)			
LNMV	0.0064478		0.0047615		0.0037901	
	(0.0076781)		(0.0076709)		(0.0071796)	
MVTBV	− 0.0074029		− 0.0072913			
	(0.0088704)		(0.0088546)			
NI	0.000014		0.0000161		0.0000188	**
	(0.0000101)		(0.00001)		(9.27e-06)	
AAC	− 0.6618375	***	− 0.6007303	***	− 0.6985141	***
	(0.0573491)		(0.0618214)		(0.0649586)	
LDEBTTA			− 0.027255	**	− 0.0260206	***
			(0.0106932)		(0.0098068)	
*CRISIS * LDEBTA*					0.3569233	***
					(0.0493566)	
*CRISIS * LNMV*					− 0.0103418	***
					(0.0026365)	
*CRISIS * AAC*					0.063032	
					(0.1387566)	
*CRISIS * MVTVBV*					− 0.0151771	**
					(0.0061442)	
Intercept	− 0.0414272		− 0.0234534		− 0.0197255	
	(0.0530064)		(0.0532369)		(0.0508819)	
R^2	0.1319	***	0.1333	***	0.1953	***
Number of observations	357		357		357	

Note: Parameter estimates and standard deviation in parenthesis.
Significance levels: $*p<0.1$, $**p<0.05$ and $***p<0.01$.

interesting to point out that while these iterative variables are significant with $p<0.05$, the untransformed variables *LNMV* and *MVTBV* do not significantly influence abnormal CFO generation in our sample. The non-significant sign of variable *CRISIS**ACC* does not provide support for our Hypothesis 6. In spite of the fact that estimations provide empirical evidence on a significant negative relationship between abnormal accruals and CFO generation, the crisis has no significant additional influence on this relationship.

We winsorized values of all variables avoiding 2% extreme values (data below the 1st percentile and data above 99th percentile), and repeated estimations. Results (not displayed) are also essentially the same. The exception is the iterative variable *CRISIS* with the lag value of *MVTVBV* in

Eq. (6) (see the corresponding coefficient in Column C in Table 7), that is no significant with $p < 0.1$, thus providing no conclusive support for Hypothesis 5. However, the estimation with the iterative variable of *CRISIS* with the untransformed *MVTBV* (in period *t*) provide again a significant negative sign with $p < 0.01$.

We have repeated all estimations (not displayed) with fixed effects, as well as adding dummy variables for sector identification. Results are substantially the same with respect to our variables of interest. The iterative variable *CRISIS* with the lag values of *MVTVBV* (corresponding to Column C in Table 7) is now significant with $p < 0.1$ (but not with $p < 0.05$) with fixed effects estimations. Again, the iterative untransformed variable (*CRISIS* with *MVTBV* in period *t*) is significant with $p < 0.01$.

CONCLUSIONS

In spite of the fact that EM has attracted considerable academic attention, previous empirical studies have scarcely studied the effect of economic cycles on EM. To the authors' knowledge, there is no previous empirical research on the incidence of economic downturns on firm real activities manipulation.

In this chapter we assess the association between the present economic recession and EM. We used the classical model used in Klein (2002) to estimate abnormal accruals and analyse the influence of the recent economic downturn in EM, controlling for market to book value, change in net income, indebtedness, firm size, basic corporate governance characteristics and the incurrence in negative income and decrease in activity. We also control for sector variables. Results indicate a significant influence of the downturn in EM behaviour during the crisis. This study provides empirical evidence that the recent economic downturn significantly influences lower EM in Spain. The financial crisis stresses the prevailing tendency to improve firm income with indebtedness. In this vein, more indebted firms reduce income decreasing accruals during the downturn, and more specifically negative abnormal accruals. Additionally, depending on market valuation it influences an opportunistic behaviour of pushing earnings down, to reserve earnings for the recovery phase after the downturn. Firms with market valuation above the median reduce income decreasing accruals, but they also apply a greater reduction in income increasing accruals. The non-significant results for firms with lower market valuation, suggest that there they have no scope for action on this issue.

The recent economic downturn also influences real activities manipulation of CFO. During the crisis firms apply abnormal increasing CFO with indebtedness, as well as abnormal decreasing CFO with size and market valuation. Real activities manipulation of CFO is significantly influenced by EM, but there is no significant change in this behaviour during the downturn.

This study provides new knowledge on EM behaviour and abnormal CFO of firms in the setting of the recent economic recession (in the context of the severe Spanish downturn), which is interesting to academics and stakeholders. However, more in-depth research is needed on this issue, and more specifically on the drivers of EM under this context, as well as on real activities manipulation during the downturn.

ACKNOWLEDGEMENT

The authors are grateful to the University of Barcelona for funding this research.

REFERENCES

Agarwal, S., Chomsisengphet, S., Liu, Ch., & Rhee, S. G. (2007). Earnings management behaviours under different economic environments: Evidence from Japanese banks. *International Review of Economics and Finance*, *16*, 429–443.

Bartov, E., Givoly, D., & Hayn, C. (2002). The rewards to meeting or beating earnings expectations. *Journal of Accounting and Economics*, *32*, 173–204.

Basu, S. (1997). The conservatism principle and the asymmetric timeliness of earnings. *Journal of Accounting and Economics*, *24*, 3–37.

Beatty, A. L., Ke, B., & Petroni, K. R. (2002). Earnings management to avoid earnings declines across publicly and privately held banks. *The Accounting Review*, *77*(3), 547–570.

Beneish, M., & Vargus, M. (2002). Insider trading, earnings quality, and accrual mispricing. *Accounting Review*, *4*, 755–790.

Bergstresser, D., & Philippon, T. (2006). CEO incentives and earnings management. *Journal of Financial Economics*, *80*(3), 511–529.

Burgstahler, D., & Dichev, I. (1997). Earnings management to avoid earnings decreases. *Journal of Accounting and Economics*, *22*, 313–325.

Cohen, D. A., & Zarowin, P. (2010). Accrual-based and real earnings management activities around seasoned equity offerings. *Journal of Accounting and Economics*, *50*(1), 2–19.

Davis-Friday, P. Y., Eng, L. L., & Ch., Liu (2006). The effects of the Asian crisis, corporate governance and accounting systems on the valuation of book value and earnings. *The International Journal of Accounting*, *41*, 22–40.

DeAngelo, H., & DeAngelo, L. (1994). Accounting choice in troubled companies. *Journal of Accounting and Economics*, *17*, 113–143.

Dechow, P. M., Sloan, R. G., & Sweeney, A. P. (1995). Detecting earnings management. *The Accounting Review*, *70*, 195–222.

DeFond, M. L., & Jiambalvo, J. (1994). Debt covenant violation and manipulation of accruals: Accounting choice in troubled companies. *Journal of Accounting and Economics*, *17*, 145–176.

DeFond, M. L., & Park, Ch. W. (1997). Smoothing income in anticipation of future earnings. *Journal of Accounting and Economics*, *23*, 115–139.

Degeorge, F., Patel, J., & Zeckhauser, R. (1999). Earnings management to exceed thresholds. *Journal of Business*, *72*(1), 1–33.

Duke, J., & Hunt, H. (1990). An empirical examination of debt covenant restrictions and accounting-related debt proxies. *Journal of Accounting and Economics*, *12*(1–3), 45–63.

Frankel, R. M., Johnson, M. F., & Nelson, K. K. (2002). The relation between auditors' fees for nonaudit services and earnings management. *The Accounting Review*, *77*(Suppl.), 71–105.

García Lara, J. M., García Osma, B., & Penalva, F. (2009). Accounting conservatism and corporate governance. *Review of Accounting Studies*, *14*, 161–201.

Han, J. C., & Wang, S. (1998). Political costs and earnings management of oil companies during the 1990 Persian Gulf crisis. *The Accounting Review*, *73*(1), 103–117.

Hayn, C. (1995). The information content of losses. *Journal of Accounting and Economics*, *20*, 125–153.

Healy, P. M. (1985). The effect of bonus schemes on accounting decisions. *Journal of Accounting and Economics*, *7*, 85–107.

Holthausen, R. W. (1981). Evidence on the effect of bond covenants and management compensation contracts on the choice of accounting techniques: The case of depreciation switch-back. *Journal of Accounting and Economics*, *3*(1), 73–109.

Holthausen, R. W., Larcker, D. F., & Sloan, R. G. (1995). Annual bonus schemes and the manipulation of earnings. *Journal of Accounting and Economics*, *19*, 29–74.

Hsiao, Ch. (2005). *Analysis of panel data*. Cambridge: Cambridge University Press.

Hsieh, M., & Shean, Ch. (2010). Business cycles and bank regulations – What happens to bank provisioning? A more comprehensive look at 49 countries. *Applied Economics, iFirst*, 1–12.

Huizinga, H. & Laeven, L. (2009). *Accounting discretion of banks during a financial crisis*. Working paper. Retrieved from: http://papers.ssrn.com/sol3/papers.cfm?abstract_id=1462010

Jelinek, K. (2007). The effect of leverage increases on earnings management. *Journal of Busines & Economics Studies*, *13*(2), 24–46.

Jones, J. (1991). Earnings management during import relief investigations. *Journal of Accounting Research*, *29*, 193–228.

Klein, A. (2002). Audit committee, board of director characteristics, and earnings management. *Journal of Accounting and Economics*, *33*, 375–400.

Laeven, L., & Majnoni, G. (2003). Loan loss provisioning and economic slowdowns: Too much, too late? *Journal of Financial Intermediation*, *12*, 178–197.

Lin, Z. X. & Shih, M. S. H. (2002). *Earnings management in economic downturns and adjacent periods: Evidence from the 1990–1991 recession*. Working Paper. Retrieved at: http://papers.ssrn.com/sol3/papers.cfm?abstract_id=331400

Mitton, T. (2002). A cross-firm analysis of the impact of corporate governance on the East Asian financial crisis. *Journal of Financial Economics*, *64*, 215–241.

Navarro, J. C. & Madrid, A. (2009, November 18–20). *La coyuntura económica y la información contable de constructoras e inmobiliarias*. Paper presented at the *VII Workshop de Investigación Empírica en Contabilidad Financiera*. Cartagena, Spain.

Pourciau, S. (1993). Earnings management and nonroutine executive changes. *Journal of Accounting and Economics*, *16*, 317–336.

Pucheta-Martínez, M. C., & de Fuentes, C. (2007). The impact of audit committee characteristics on the enhancement of the quality of financial reporting: An empirical study in the Spanish context. *Corporate Governance*, *15*(6), 1394–1412.

Quagliariello, M. (2007). Bank's riskiness over the business cycle: A panel data analysis on Italian intermediaries. *Applied Financial Economics*, *17*, 119–138.

Qinglu, J. (2005). *Business cycle, accounting behavior and earnings management*. A thesis submitted to the Hong Kong University of Science and Technology in partial fulfillment of the requirement for the Degree of Doctor of Philosophy in Accounting. Retrieved from http://hdl.handle.net/1783.1/2666

Rangan, S. (1998). Earnings management and the performance of seasoned equity offerings. *Journal of Financial Economics*, *50*, 101–122.

Roychowdhury, S. (2006). Earnings management through real activities manipulation. *Journal of Accounting and Economics*, *42*, 335–370.

Subramanyam, K. (1996). The pricing of discretionary accruals. *Journal of Accounting and Economics*, *22*(1–3), 249–281.

Teoh, S. H., Wong, T. J., & Rao, G. R. (1998). Are accruals during initial public offerings opportunistic? *Review of Accounting Studies*, *3*(1–2), 175–208.

Weisbach, M. S. (1988). Outside directors and CEO turnover. *Journal of Financial Economics*, *20*, 431–460.

Watts, R. L., & Zimmerman, J. L. (1990). Positive accounting theory: A ten year perspective. *The Accounting Review*, *65*(1), 131–156.

Yoon, S. S., & Miller, G. A. (2002). Cash from operations and earnings management in Korea. *The International Journal of Accounting*, *37*, 395–412.

THE ROLE OF ANALYSTS' RECOMMENDATION REVISIONS IN HELPING INVESTORS UNDERSTAND THE VALUATION IMPLICATIONS OF ANNOUNCED EARNINGS

Zheng Wang

ABSTRACT

In this study, I investigate analysts' ability to process public information for investors by examining price reactions to a sample of analysts' recommendation revisions issued shortly after quarterly earnings announcements. I find that these recommendation revisions are used by investors to reassess the valuation implications of announced earnings. Confirmatory (contradictory) recommendation revisions that have the same (opposite) sign as prior earnings surprises can cause investors to revise their beliefs about the valuation implications of announced earnings upward (downward) and thus cause price reactions that are positively (negatively) associated with prior earnings surprises. In addition, I find that as the information complexity of earnings announcements

Transparency and Governance in a Global World
International Finance Review, Volume 13, 257–286

ISSN: 1569-3767/doi:10.1108/S1569-3767(2012)0000013012

gets higher, these recommendation revisions play a more important role in helping investors understand the valuation implications of announced earnings. Finally, I find that analysts' ability to interpret the valuation implications of announced earnings for investors has remained at a similar level since the adoption of Regulation Fair Disclosure. Overall, this study provides additional evidence on how analysts help improve corporate information environment.

Keywords: Analyst recommendation; earnings announcement; information environment; valuation implication

JEL classifications: M41; G14; G30

INTRODUCTION

In analyst literature, many researchers assume that analysts are more skillful than ordinary investors in acquiring private information, as well as analyzing and interpreting public information. Although the extant literature has documented analysts' expertise in collecting private information, especially with respect to management's inside information (e.g., Bowen, Davis, & Matsumoto, 2002; Francis, Hanna, & Philbrisk, 1997), analysts' ability to analyze and to interpret information that is public has not been examined fully.

The purpose of this study is to investigate analysts' ability to process public information for investors by examining price reactions to a sample of analysts' recommendation revisions issued subsequent to quarterly earnings announcements within two trading weeks. Following the extant literature, price reactions to announced earnings, are determined by the valuation implications of the currently announced earnings for future earnings such as its persistence and reliability (Easton & Zmijewski, 1989; Kormendi & Lipe, 1987; Schipper & Vincent, 2003).[1] However, the real valuation implications of earnings are uncertain to investors and can only be estimated intuitively based on their knowledge, and therefore can be misassessed by them initially.[2] If analysts are more proficient in analyzing the valuation implications of earnings announcements, then they can identify instances of security mispricing caused by investors' misassessments, and, as a result, will revise their recommendations on the mispriced securities to reveal their opinions. Ivkovic and Jegadeesh (2004) mention that the concentration of recommendation revisions following earnings announcements suggests that analysts identify instances of mispricing during this period. Otherwise, there is no reason to expect that recommendation revisions are triggered by public earnings announcements.

Following this argument, I surmise that when an analyst revises his/her recommendation following an earnings announcement, he/she essentially reveals a disparity between his/her opinion and that of investors about the valuation implications of the released earnings. Thus, investors react to the analyst's recommendation revision by adjusting their initial assessment of the valuation implications of the released earnings, resulting in a corrective price reaction to the released earnings post its announcement. I predict that confirmatory recommendation revisions that have the same sign as prior earnings surprises signal that investors underestimate the valuation implications of announced earnings, and that the earnings announcements should have a stronger impact on security prices. Therefore, after observing confirmatory recommendation revisions, investors will react more to prior earnings surprises and as a result, the corrective price reactions will be positively associated with prior earnings surprises. In contrast, contradictory recommendation revisions with the opposite sign as prior earnings surprises suggest that investors overestimate the valuation implications of announced earnings, and that the earnings announcements should have a smaller impact on security prices. Thus, after observing contradictory recommendation revisions, investors will take actions to offset the impact of announced earnings and as a result, the corrective price reactions will be negatively associated with prior earnings surprises.

The statistical test results reported in this study are consistent with the above predictions. That is, subsequent to earnings announcements, analysts' recommendation revisions can cause corrective price reactions that are positively (negatively) related to prior earnings surprises by making investors reassess the valuation implications of announced earnings upward (downward). The magnitude of the statistical relation between the corrective price reactions and prior earnings surprises represent the extent to which investors' beliefs of the valuation implications of announced earnings are altered by analysts' recommendation revisions. In other words, it measures the distance between analysts' and investors' expertise in processing publicly released earnings information. Specifically, results of this study reveal that the extent of investors' belief revisions can be as much as 13%, suggesting that analysts play a significant role in helping investors understand the valuation implications of announced earnings.

In this study, I also document that analysts' expertise relative to investors', intensifies with the increasing complexity of earnings signals measured by the three-day abnormal trading volumes that surround earnings announcements. Analysts' recommendation revisions can cause larger corrective price reactions when earnings signals are more complex, holding constant the magnitude of prior earnings surprises. It seems that investors become more reliant on analysts' recommendations in the review of the valuation implications of highly complex earnings signals.

Although, analysts are more proficient in processing publicly released earnings news, one can argue that analysts can use inside information from management to analyze the valuation implications of earnings. To yield additional insight to this issue, I examine the impact of Regulation Fair Disclosure (henceforth Reg FD).[3] I find that analysts continue to maintain a similar level of expertise in processing publicly released earnings information in the post Reg FD period. As a matter of fact, confirmatory recommendation revisions have become even more informative about the valuation implications of announced earnings since the adoption of Reg FD. This evidence gives a promising signal that indicates that analysts indeed possess better analytical skills, instead of being better informed than investors in the interpretation and analyses of public information.[4]

This study makes contributions to the extant literature by providing evidence on analysts' ability to process public information for investors, an area that has not been addressed fully in prior literature. Mendenhall (1991) also indicates that investors use analysts' forecast revisions to reassess the persistence of previous earnings forecast errors that are initially underestimated by them. Differing from Mendenhall's study, this paper employs recommendation revisions rather than forecast revisions to examine the role of analysts' information in signaling the valuation implications of previous earnings. While analysts naturally revise their forecasts of future earnings when new information from earnings announcements arrives, they are unlikely to adjust their recommendations if the security prices fully incorporate the information. Therefore, analysts' recommendation revisions are more dependable indicators of investors' misreactions to recent earnings announcements. More importantly, I extend Mendenhall's study in the following two aspects. First, I find that analysts' information becomes more valuable to investors for correctly assessing the valuation implications of announced earnings as the complexity of earnings signals increases, which provides additional evidence on analysts' ability to process public information for investors. Second, by examining the impact of Reg FD, this study confirms that analysts indeed rely on their analytical skills to interpret and analyze the valuation implications of public earnings information.

This study also relates to the literature on analysts' role in improving corporate transparency. Dyck, Morse, and Zingales (2010) find that analysts are the most efficient external whistleblowers for corporate fraud. Yu (2008) shows evidence that equity analysts play a monitoring/governance role in reducing earnings management. Lang, Lins, and Miller (2004) find a positive valuation effect when analysts cover firms that have both potentially poor internal governance and weak country-level external governance, suggesting that analysts play a role in improving corporate governance. These studies provide direct evidence on the role of analysts in corporate governance. Other studies suggest that when analysts engage in private information production, it helps to detect managers' misbehavior and consequently, corporate transparency is improved (e.g., Bushman, Piotroski, & Smith, 2004; Healy & Palepu, 2001). Bushman et al. (2004) also point out that the interpretation and dissemination of corporate financial disclosures by analysts and media is an efficient and important factor that affects corporate governance and they classify it into the financial transparency factor. This study shows evidence that analysts' recommendation revisions help investors interpret public earnings announcements. By analyzing and interpreting public earnings announcements, analysts can help detect managerial misrepresentation and improve corporate information transparency.

The rest of the paper is organized as follows. In the second section, I review the related prior research. In the third section, I develop the research hypotheses. Fourth section describes the research design and the sample selection procedures. In the fifth section, I discuss the empirical results. The sixth section concludes the paper.

PRIOR RESEARCH

Since the 1970s, numerous studies have shown that analysts' information is valuable to investors by examining the market's reaction to revisions of analysts' forecasts or recommendations. Lloyd-Davies and Canes (1978) find, on average, an event-day abnormal return of 0.93% (−2.37%) for new favorable (unfavorable) recommendations that appear in the *Wall Street Journal*. More recent studies (Lys & Sohn, 1990; Mikhail, Walther, & Willis, 2007; Womack, 1996) provide confirming evidence that forecast and recommendation revisions have information content to investors. Bauman, Datta, and Iskandar-Datta (1995) examine both short-run and long-run price reactions to investment recommendations of security analysts and find that such recommendations are even more valuable to long-term investors than to short-term traders. Kim, Lee, and Park (1996) document a positive relationship between the number of transactions around revisions of analysts' earnings forecasts and the magnitude of the revisions. Some other studies have affirmed that the information content of analysts' forecasts or recommendations is related to factors such as analyst reputation, firm size, brokerage profits, and brokerage size, etc. (Frankel, Kothari, & Weber, 2006; Gleason & Lee, 2003; Stickel, 1992).

The value of analysts' forecasts and recommendations stems partially from their ability to collect nonpublic information from management. The SEC is concerned that the issuers' selective disclosure of material nonpublic information to security analysts has hurt uninformed investors. Despite the controversial evidence as to whether private communications between analysts and management make investors better or worse off (Bushman, 1991; Das, Levine, & Sivaramakrishnan, 1998; Francis et al., 1997),[5] Reg FD became effective on October 23, 2000.

Motivated by Reg FD, Ivkovic and Jegadeesh (2004) evaluate the information content of analysts' one-quarter ahead earnings forecasts and recommendation revisions at various points in time relative to earnings announcement dates. They find that price reactions and their sensitivity to revisions are weaker in the week after earnings announcements than in the week before earnings announcements, and conclude that analysts' informational advantage as private information collectors is more important than as public information processors. Asquith, Mikhail, and Au (2005) suggest that analysts may play a role in interpreting information previously released by examining market reactions to analyst reports that occur simultaneously with other information releases. I provide evidence that is consistent with Asquith et al. (2005) by documenting the role of analysts' recommendation revisions in interpreting the valuation implications of announced earnings for investors.

The evidence of investors' misreactions to earnings announcements is mixed. There are several studies trying to explain post-earnings announcement drifts as an initial underreaction to earnings and a subsequent delayed price response in the same direction (Abarbanell & Bernard, 1992; Bernard & Thomas, 1990; Liang, 2003; Mendenhall, 1991; Shane & Brous, 2001). There are also studies documenting prior overreactions to news events (Chopra, Lakonishok, & Ritter, 1992; DeBondt & Thaler, 1985, 1987; Klein, 1990). Abarbanell and Bernard (1992) also find that value line analysts appear to under-react to recent earnings information. However, stock prices appear to under-react to an even greater degree.

The methodology aspect of this paper is in the spirit of Freeman and Tse (1989), Mendenhall (1991), and Koch and Sun (2004). Freeman and Tse (1989) report that investors learn about the valuation implications of previously announced earnings from current earnings announcements. Mendenhall (1991) finds that investors correct their previous under-weights to earnings using analyst forecast revisions. Koch and Sun (2004) show that investors reassess the persistence of recently announced earnings using information released during dividend announcements.

Finally, this study joins a growing literature examining the impact of Reg FD on analysts' information environment. A few studies find that there has been a leveling of the information playing field between analysts and investors and among analysts themselves (Gintschela & Markov, 2004; Mohanram & Sunder, 2006; Zitzewitz, 2002). Some studies show mixed evidence on whether analysts' forecast dispersion and other measures of disagreement increase after the adoption of Reg FD (Agrawal, Chadha, & Chen, 2006; Bailey, Li, Mao, & Zhong, 2003; Heflin, Subramanyam, & Zhang, 2003). This study augments the literature by examining the impact of Reg FD on analysts' role of processing public information for investors.

HYPOTHESIS DEVELOPMENT

Prior studies show that the Earnings Response Coefficient (ERC) is an increasing function of current earnings' valuation implications for future earnings determined by earnings quality such as persistence and reliability, under the assumption of discounted earnings valuation (Collins & Kothari, 1989). However, during an earnings announcement, the real valuation implication of announced earnings is unknown or uncertain to investors. For example, investors may not be able to discern how much of the current earnings surprise will persist in future periods or how reliable the reported earnings number is. Therefore, investors can only react to announced earnings based on their assessment of its valuation implication.

Assuming that, during an earnings announcement, the initial price reaction to the announcement of E_t (period t's reported earnings) is determined as:

$$R = ERC \times (E_t - F_t^{\,t})$$

where ERC is the valuation multiple attached to the announced earnings by investors that is determined by various factors related to earnings quality such as persistence, reliability, and others based on investors' initial assessments of these factors. F_t^t denotes the consensus analyst forecast for E_t before it is announced. Thus, earnings surprise is equal to $(E_t - F_t^t)$. By conducting more proficient analysis on the quality of announced earnings, the analyst who follows the firm, instead believes that the price should react to the announced earnings with an ERC equal to ERC^A.[6] If $ERC^A > ERC$, the analyst would think that investors have underreacted to the recently announced earnings and issue a confirmatory recommendation revision to signal the high valuation implication of the announced earnings: an upward recommendation revision following a positive earnings surprise or a downward recommendation revision following a negative earnings surprise. In contrast, if $ERC^A < ERC$, to the analyst, investors have overreacted to the announced earnings and as a result, the analyst would issue a contradictory recommendation revision to indicate that the earnings news should be less value relevant than expected by investors: a downward recommendation revision following a positive earnings surprise or an upward recommendation revision following a negative earnings surprise.

After receiving the analyst's opinion through his/her recommendation revision, investors will attempt to correct their prior misreaction as follows:

$$R' = (ERC^A - ERC) \times (E_t - F_t^t) \qquad (1)$$

The magnitude of the corrective price reaction is jointly determined by the magnitude of the prior earnings surprise and the extent of the disparity between the analyst's assessment and investors' assessment of the valuation implication of the announced earnings ($|ERC^A - ERC|$). In addition, the corrective price reaction should be positively related to the prior earnings surprise if investors observe confirmatory recommendation revisions from analysts ($ERC^A > ERC$) and negatively related to the prior earnings surprise if they observe contradictory recommendation revisions from analysts ($ERC^A < ERC$). In the former case, investors will try to correct their initial underreaction to announced earnings and continue to react more to the announced earnings post its announcement. In the later case, investors will act to offset the initial impact of the earnings news on security price because they initially overreact to the earnings news.

Based on the discussions above, I hypothesize that a statistical relation between price reactions surrounding analysts' recommendation revisions and prior earnings surprises should exist post earnings announcements if analysts' recommendation revisions issued shortly after earnings announcements can cause investors to reassess the valuation implications of the earnings. The sign of this relation is positive (negative) if the recommendation revisions have the same (opposite) sign as prior earnings surprises. In addition, from Eq. (1), the magnitude of this relation that equals $|ERC^A - ERC|$ represents the distance between analysts' and investors' expertise in assessing the valuation implications of publicly announced earnings and thus can serve as an appropriate measure of the value of analysts' ability to process public information for investors. Specifically, H1 is developed as follows:

> **H1**. When an analyst's recommendation revision issued shortly after an earnings announcement has the same (opposite) sign as the prior earnings surprise, the price reaction surrounding the recommendation revision is positively (negatively) related to the prior earnings surprise.

If I find that analysts' information does help investors resolve their uncertainty about the valuation implications of earnings, then another research question arises: Can analysts' information help resolve more or less uncertainty for investors as the level of information uncertainty (complexity) of earnings announcements increases? When the level of information uncertainty (complexity) gets higher, it is possible that investors' misreactions to earnings announcements can also become more severe because they are likely to make more faulty estimates of the valuation implications of announced earnings. In such situations, analysts' guidance might be more important and valuable to investors for reevaluating previously released earnings, permitting analysts' expertise to be more detectable. As expert information processors, analysts are expected to provide valuable professional guidance to investors in evaluating publicly released information, especially when the information is highly complex.

Therefore, the next hypothesis is developed to examine whether the extent of analysts' information processing expertise becomes more augmented as the level of information complexity of earnings announcements increases. Consistent with prior studies, abnormal trading volumes are used as a proxy for information uncertainty (complexity) of earnings announcements. Prior theoretical studies suggest that trading volume is related to investors' differing opinions on a signal (Holthausen & Verrecchia, 1990; Kim & Verrecchia, 1991, 1994). Higher abnormal trading volume reflects a greater degree of heterogeneity of investors' opinions on the same information signal when they are uncertain about that signal. Based on the above discussions, I hypothesize:

> **H2**. The magnitude of the statistical relation between the price reaction surrounding an analyst's recommendation revision and the prior earnings surprise increases with the level of information uncertainty of the earnings announcement.

Even if analysts are found to be more proficient in processing publicly released earnings news and have a better understanding of its valuation implications, it is still possible that analysts may use inside information from management to help them with this task. Therefore, do analysts truly possess better intellectual skills in processing public information, and can they still play the role of helping investors assess the valuation implications of publicly released earnings without accessibility to any private information from management? The SEC aimed to level the information playing field for market participants by passing Reg FD that requires management to disseminate any material information simultaneously to all market participants. If analysts primarily rely on their accessibility to management's inside information to interpret public information, then after Reg FD became effective, they would no longer exhibit a significant advantage over investors. On the contrary, if they do possess better analytical skills, then they can continue to assist investors in re-evaluating publicly released earnings news and the information content of their recommendation revisions can also remain at a similar level after Reg FD.

Moreover, since private information from management is no longer available to analysts due to Reg FD, all analysts now can only use publicly available information such as earnings announcements to make their recommendations. They can and have to expend all their efforts in analyzing and interpreting public information instead of spending their time developing connections with management to gain private information, thereby further nurturing their skills in processing public information.

As discussed so far, analysts would continue to exhibit significant and similar levels of advantage over investors in interpreting publicly released earnings news after Reg FD only if they are truly more skillful rather than more informed than investors. Hence, the following hypothesis is put forth to investigate the impact of Reg FD:

> **H3**. The magnitude of the statistical relation between the price reaction surrounding an analyst's recommendation revision and the prior earnings surprise remains unchanged after the adoption of Reg FD.

SAMPLE SELECTION AND DESIGN OF EMPIRICAL TESTS

I test these hypotheses using analysts' recommendation revisions recorded in 2007 I/B/E/S database from November 1993 to December 2007. The quarterly earnings announcement dates and reported values of earnings also come from I/B/E/S. The stock return and price data come from the 2007 Center for Research in Security Prices (CRSP) files.

In the sample, I only include the first recommendation revisions issued after quarterly earnings announcements within two trading weeks to make sure that the recommendation revisions are triggered by earnings announcements, not by any other information events such as recommendation revisions issued earlier by other analysts.[7] A sample firm must meet the following data requirements in order to be included in the tests: (1) the first recommendation revision must be issued between the 3rd and 13th trading days from the date of the quarterly earnings announcement; (2) the quarterly earnings information with actual reported value and actual reported date is recorded in I/B/E/S; (3) analysts' forecasts are available to calculate earnings surprises for announced earnings; and (4) the daily stock returns and the beginning of period prices for the three-day window centered on the recommendation revision date are available in the CRSP daily files.

I eliminate recommendation revisions issued within two trading days from the quarterly earnings announcement dates because it is difficult to disentangle the effect of the quarterly earnings announcements on security prices from that of the recommendation revisions when they are too close. I eliminate observations of zero recommendation revisions and zero earnings surprises in order to classify confirmatory and contradictory recommendation revisions. The variables of earnings surprises and the three-day cumulative abnormal returns are winsorized at the 1% and 99% level. The above selection criteria yield 18,010 observations of recommendation revisions and 5,119 firm years in the sample for testing H1.

H1 predicts that confirmatory (contradictory) recommendation revisions signal that prior earnings surprises have greater (smaller) valuation implications than initially estimated by investors. Therefore, as indicated in Eq. (1), confirmatory (contradictory) recommendation revisions cause corrective price reactions that are positively (negatively) related to prior earnings surprises because investors' beliefs about the valuation implications are revised upward (downward). In order to test this hypothesis, I follow Mendenhall (1991) and develop the following regression equation:

$$CAR_{t,i,j} = \alpha + \beta_1 PER_{t,i,j} \times FERROR_{t,i} + \beta_2 NPER_{t,i,j} \times FERROR_{t,i} + \beta_3 REV_{t,i,j} + \varepsilon_{t,i,j} \quad (2)$$

where $PER_{t,i,j}(NPER_{t,i,j})$ is a dummy variable with a value equal to one for confirmatory (contradictory) recommendation revisions that have the same (opposite) sign as prior earnings surprises, and zero otherwise.[8] Although there are two dummy variables for two categories, each dummy variable interacts with $FERROR_{t,i}$. Therefore, the above equation does notsuffer-from perfect collinearity. $CAR_{t,i,j}$ is the cumulative three-day size-adjusted abnormal returns surrounding analyst *j*'s recommendation revision for firm *i*. $FERROR_{t,i}$ is firm *i*'s earnings surprise (forecast error) that is equal to the difference between announced earnings and its consensus forecast (its mean forecast) deflated by the firm's beginning price of the three-day window centered on the recommendation revision date. $REV_{t,i,j}$ is the difference between the numerical values of analyst *j*'s recommendation issued after an earnings announcement and his/her prior recommendation issued before the earnings announcement. I assign a numerical value for each recommendation: 5 for strong buy; 4 for buy; 3 for hold; 2 for underperform; 1 for sell. $REV_{t,i,j}$ is included in the regression to control for the analyst's nonearnings information if any. Since $REV_{t,i,j}$ already contains the information regarding the statistical relation between $CAR_{t,i,j}$ and $FERROR_{t,i}$, a certain degree of multicollinearity occurs after including $REV_{t,i,j}$ in the regression. Therefore, I will mainly use the estimated results of Eq. (2) without $REV_{t,i,j}$ included to test H1. According to H1, β_1 (β_2) is predicted to be positive (negative) because confirmatory (contradictory) recommendation revisions cause corrective price reactions that are positively (negatively) related to prior earnings surprises. The predicted sign for the coefficient on $REV_{t,i,j}$ (β_3) is positive.

H2 is developed to investigate whether analysts' information can provide more guidance to investors to reevaluate the recently announced earnings when they are more uncertain about the valuation implications of these announcements. I use the following equation to test this hypothesis:

$$CAR_{t,i,j} = \alpha + \beta'_1 PER_{t,i,j} \times FERROR_{t,i} + \beta'_2 NPER_{t,i,j} \times FERROR_{t,i} + \beta'_3 AVOL_{t,i} \times PER_{t,i,j} \times FERROR_{t,i} + \beta'_4 AVOL_{t,i} \times NPER_{t,i,j} \times FERROR_{t,i} + \beta'_5 REV_{t,i,j} + \beta'_6 AVOL_{t,i} \times REV_{t,i,j} + \varsigma_{t,i,j} \quad (3)$$

where $AVOL_{t,i}$ measures abnormal trading volume around the three-day announcement window. Like Landsman and Maydew (2002), the variable $AVOL_{t,i}$ is estimated as:

$$AVOL_{t,i} = \sum_{n=-1}^{1} (V_{t,i,n} - \overline{V}_{t,i})/\sigma_{t,i}$$

where $V_{t,i,n}$ is the trading volume of firm i during day n at year t deflated by shares outstanding of the firm on day n during the three-day window (−1,0,1) at year t, with day 0 being the announcement date. For each firm year, I estimate $\overline{V}_{t,i}$ and $\sigma_{t,i}$ – the mean and standard deviation of firm i's daily trading volume divided by daily shares outstanding of the firm during the estimation period (−242, −20). In order to differentiate earnings announcements with high information uncertainty from those with lower information uncertainty, for each year, the value of $AVOL_{t,i}$ is replaced by one if it is higher than the sample average during the year. Otherwise, $AVOL_{t,i}$ takes the value of zero. Therefore, for earnings announcements with high information uncertainty, the coefficients on $FERROR_{t,i}$ are equal to $\beta_1' + \beta_3'$and $\beta_2' + \beta_4'$ for confirmatory and contradictory recommendation revisions, respectively. Since the absolute magnitude of the coefficients on $FERROR_{t,i}$ is predicted to increase with information uncertainty, $\beta_3'(\beta_4')$ has the same sign as $\beta_1'(\beta_2')$, which is positive (negative). β_6' is positive because it is expected that analysts' information is more valuable and crucial to investors when information uncertainty is high. I also estimate Eq. (3) using the continuous variable of $AVOL_{t,i}$, and the inferences of the results remain unchanged. Because additional data are required to estimate $AVOL_{t,i}$, the sample of this test is slightly reduced to 17,050 observations.

The last set of tests is to evaluate the impact of Reg FD on analysts' ability to process public information to unveil the basis of this ability. H3 is tested by estimating the following regression:

$$\begin{aligned} CAR_{t,i,j} = \alpha &+ \beta''_1 PER_{t,i,j} \times FERROR_{t,i} + \beta''_2 NPER_{t,i,j} \times FERROR_{t,i} \\ &+ \beta''_3 POST_{t,i} \times PER_{t,i,j} \times FERROR_{t,i} + \beta''_4 POST_{t,i} \times NPER_{t,i,j} \\ &\times FERROR_{t,i} + \beta''_5 REV_{t,i,j} + \beta''_6 POST_{t,i} \times REV_{t,i,j} + \varsigma_{t,i,j} \end{aligned} \quad (4)$$

where $POST_{t,i}$ is the dummy variable representing the period since the adoption of Reg FD. $POST_{t,i}$ takes the value of one if the earnings announcement date is after the adoption of Reg FD (10/23/2000), and zero otherwise. Therefore, after Reg FD, the magnitude of the statistical relation between the corrective price reactions caused by confirmatory recommendation revisions and prior earnings surprises is measured as $\beta_1'' + \beta_3''$ and for contradictory recommendation revisions, it is $\beta_2'' + \beta_4''$. β_3'' and β_4'' represent any decline or improvement in the informativeness of analysts' recommendation revisions in helping investors reassess the valuation implications of earnings announcements after the adoption of Reg FD.

RESULTS OF EMPIRICAL TESTS

Descriptive Statistics

Panel A of Table 1 shows the breakdown of the sample into confirmatory and contradictory recommendation revisions. There are 9,309 confirmatory recommendation revisions that have the same sign as prior earnings surprises and 8,701 contradictory recommendation revisions that have the opposite sign as prior earnings surprises in the sample.

Table 1 also reports sample descriptive statistics. Panel B shows that the cumulative three-day size-adjusted abnormal returns surrounding recommendation revisions range from -0.197 to 0.228 with a mean equal to -0.003 and a median of 0.001. As indicated in Panel A, more analysts revise recommendations downward than upward in this sample. Thus, the mean and median of recommendation revisions are both negative. The mean of $FERROR_{t,i}$ is negative and the median is close to zero, suggesting that the number of firms that report negative earnings surprises is about the same as the number of firms that report positive earnings surprises, whereas the magnitude of negative earnings surprises is larger than that of positive earnings surprises. As to the abnormal trading volume, it seems that this measure has large variations among the observations of the sample.

The correlation table presented in Panel C shows that the cumulative three-day returns surrounding recommendation revisions are significantly and positively correlated with the revisions, and the extent of the correlation is quite strong ($p = 0.200$). The correlation between returns around recommendation revisions and prior earnings surprises is not statistically significant and the magnitude of the correlation is also very weak ($p = 0.004$). These results indicate that after earnings announcements, returns around recommendation revisions are in general not strongly associated with prior earnings news. Although the magnitude is small, the correlation between recommendation revisions and prior earnings surprises is positive and statistically significant ($p = 0.048$).

Table 1. Sample Descriptive Statistics.

Panel A: Distribution of Revisions and Market Reactions

	Earnings Innovation	
Recommendation Revisions	Positive	Negative
Upward	4,332	4,328
Downward	4,373	4,977

Panel B: Percentiles of Key Variables

	Mean	Max	75%	Median	25%	Min
$CAR_{t,i,j}$	−0.003	0.228	0.027	0.001	−0.024	−0.197
$REV_{t,i}$	−0.061	4	1	−1	−1	−4
$FERROR_{t,i}$	−0.003	0.022	0.001	0.000	−0.002	−0.105
$AVOL_{t,i,j}$	36	1,146	39	15	6	523

Panel C: Pearson Correlations of Key Variables

	$CAR_{t,i}$	$REV_{t,i}$	$FERROR_{t,i}$	$AVOL_{t,i,j}$
$CAR_{t,i}$	1	0.200***	0.004	0.005
$REV_{t,i}$		1	0.048***	−0.003
$FERROR_{t,i}$			1	0.004
$AVOL_{t,i,j}$				1

Notes: This table presents descriptive statistics on a sample of 18,010 (5,119 firm years) recommendation revisions firstly issued within two trading weeks after each quarterly earnings announcement from 1993 to 2007. The variable $CAR_{t,i,j}$ is the cumulative three-day size-adjusted abnormal returns centered on a recommendation revision. The variable $REV_{t,i}$ is the analyst's recommendation revision on firm *i*'s stock following earnings announcements. The variable $FERROR_{t,i}$ is the difference between announced earnings and its consensus analyst forecasts. $FERROR_{t,i}$ is deflated using the beginning price of the three-day window used to calculate $CAR_{t,i,j}$. The variable $AVOL_{t,i}$ is the abnormal trading volumes during the three-day window centered on the earnings announcement.

Regression Results

Main Results

H1 is tested by estimating Eq. (2) and the results are reported in Table 2. Column (1) presents results without $REV_{t,i,j}$ in the regression. The coefficient on $PER_{t,i,j} \times FERROR_{t,i}$ is positive, as hypothesized, and statistically significant at the 0.01 level ($\beta_1 = 0.4821$, $t = 10.48$). The coefficient on $NPER_{t,i,j} \times FERROR_{t,i}$ is negative, as hypothesized, and statistically significant at the

Table 2. Estimated Results of the Relation between Price Reactions around Analysts' Recommendations and Prior Earnings Surprises.

Independent Variable	Predicted Sign	Without $REV_{t,i}$ (1)	With $REV_{t,i}$ (2)
Intercept		0.0029	0.0032
		(7.23)***	(8.04)***
$PER_{t,i} \times FERROR_{t,i}$	+	0.4821	0.1673
		(10.48)***	(3.53)***
$NPER_{t,i} \times FERROR_{t,i}$	–	−0.6770	−0.3071
		(−12.04)***	(−5.32)***
$REV_{t,i}$	+		0.0067
			(22.84)***
Adj.R^2		0.014	0.042
No. of observations	18,010		

Notes: This table reports estimated results of the relationship between the corrective price reactions caused by analysts' recommendation revisions and prior earnings surprises. $CAR_{t,i,j}$ is the cumulative three-day size-adjusted abnormal returns centered on a recommendation revision. The variable $REV_{t,i}$ is the analyst recommendation revision for firm *i*'s stock following earnings announcements within two trading weeks. The variable $FERROR_{t,i}$is the difference between reported earnings and the prior consensus analyst forecasts deflated using the beginning price of the three-day window used to calculate $CAR_{t,i,j}$. The dummy variable $PER_{t,i}$ ($NPER_{t,i}$) takes the value of one if the recommendation revision has the same (opposite) sign as prior earnings surprise and zero otherwise. The *t*-scores are in parentheses. ***,**,* represent statistical significance at 0.01, 0.05, and 0.1 levels, respectively.

$$CAR_{t,i,j} = \alpha + \beta_1 PER_{t,i,j} \times FERROR_{t,i} + \beta_2 NPER_{t,i,j} \times FERROR_{t,i} + \beta_3 REV_{t,i,j} + \varepsilon_{t,i,j} \quad (2)$$

0.01 level ($\beta_2 = -0.6770$, $t = -12.04$). Therefore, as predicted by H1, price reactions caused by confirmatory (contradictory) recommendation revisions are positively (negatively) related to prior earnings surprises, suggesting that investors learn from these recommendation revisions that they initially underestimated (overestimated) the valuation implications of the announced earnings and need to revise their estimates upward (downward).

If solely considering the persistence of earnings and assuming that earnings follow an IMA(1,1) process with a moving average parameter equal to 0.5 and a discount rate equal to 12%, then the ERC of an earnings surprise is equal to 5.17.[9] With an ERC equal to 5.17, results reported in Column (1) indicate that analysts' confirmatory recommendation revisions can alter investors' beliefs about the valuation implications of previous earnings upward by about 9% (0.4821/5.17) and their contradictory recommendation revisions can guide investors to revise down their beliefs by about 13% (0.6770/5.17).

Column (2) reports the estimated results of Eq. (2) with $REV_{t,i,j}$ in the regression to control for nonearnings information. The coefficient on $REV_{t,i,j}$ is positive and statistically significant at the 0.01 level ($\beta_3 = 0.0067$, $t = 22.84$). The adjusted R^2 is increased from 1.4% to 4.2% after including $REV_{t,i,j}$, which indicates that recommendation revisions contain valuable nonearnings information. It is not surprising to find that the magnitude of the coefficients on $PER_{t,i,j} \times FERROR_{t,i}$ and $NPER_{t,i,j} \times FERROR_{t,i}$ decreases after including $REV_{t,i,j}$ in the regression ($\beta_1 = 0.1673$; $\beta_2 = -0.3071$). However, the fact that these two coefficients still have the predicted signs and are statistically significant at the 0.01 level strongly support H1.

In Mendenhall (1991), the adjusted R^2 of his regression equation using analysts' forecast revisions is only 0.9%. A large increase in adjusted R^2 in my model suggests that recommendation revisions are more informative about the valuation implications of earnings than forecast revisions.[10]

Overall, the results reported in Table 2 confirm my prediction that analysts' recommendation revisions issued subsequent to earnings announcements make investors reevaluate the valuation implications of announced earnings. The results directly imply that analysts are regarded by investors as more proficient in processing public information and assessing the valuation implications of public information. Results presented above also reveal that analysts' information can make investors adjust their beliefs about the valuation implications of previous earnings by as large as 15%, which suggests that analysts' expertise in processing public information is quite substantial compared to that of investors.[11]

Information Uncertainty

H2 predicts that analysts' expertise in processing public information becomes more distinctive when the information uncertainty (complexity) of earnings announcements increases. Because of the difficulty involved in processing such complex earnings information, investors might be more uncertain about the valuation implications of announced earnings and demand more of analysts' guidance in this matter. H2 is tested by estimating Eq. (3), the results of which are reported in Table 3. In Column (1), the coefficient on $PER_{t,i,j} \times FERROR_{t,i}$ ($NPER_{t,i,j} \times FERROR_{t,i}$) is positive (negative), as predicted, and statistically significant at the 0.01 level, which confirms that analysts' information can help investors reassess the valuation implications of earnings when information complexity is low. The coefficient on $AVOL_{t,i} \times PER_{t,i,j} \times FERROR_{t,i}$ is positive and statistically

Table 3. Estimated Results of the Effect of Information Complexity.

Independent Variable	Predicted Sign	Without $REV_{t,i}$ (1)	With $REV_{t,i}$ (2)
Intercept		0.0029	0.0032
		(6.96)***	(7.93)***
$PER_{t,i} \times FERROR_{t,i}$	+	0.2810	0.0631
		(3.92)***	(0.75)
$NPER_{t,i} \times FERROR_{t,i}$	−	−0.6187	−0.2352
		(−7.13)***	(−2.37)**
$AVOL_{t,i} \times PER_{t,i} \times FERROR_{t,i}$	+	0.2853	0.1320
		(2.88)***	(1.25)
$AVOL_{t,i} \times NPER_{t,i} \times FERROR_{t,i}$	−	−0.3310	−0.2064
		(−2.73)***	(−1.64)*
$REV_{t,i}$	+		0.0055
			(12.64)***
$AVOL_{t,i} \times REV_{t,i}$	+		0.0028
			(4.63)***
Adj.R^2		0.015	0.047
No. of observations	17,050		

Notes: This table reports the effect of information complexity on the relationship between corrective price reactions caused by analysts' recommendation revisions and prior earnings surprises. $CAR_{t,i,j}$ is the cumulative three-day size-adjusted abnormal returns centered on the recommendation revision. The variable $REV_{t,i}$ is the analyst recommendation revision for firm *i*'s stock following earnings announcements within two trading weeks. The variable $FERROR_{t,i}$ is the difference between reported earnings and the prior consensus analyst forecasts deflated by the beginning price of the three-day window used to calculate $CAR_{t,i,j}$. The dummy variable $PER_{t,i}$ ($NPER_{t,i}$) takes the value of one if the recommendation revision has the same (opposite) sign as prior earnings surprise and zero otherwise. The variable $AVOL_{t,i}$ is the (0, 1) rank of the abnormal trading volumes during the three-day window centered on the announcement. The *t*-scores are in parentheses. ***, **, * represent statistical significance at 0.01, 0.05, and 0.1 levels, respectively.

$$
\begin{aligned}
CAR_{t,i,j} = {} & \alpha + \beta'_1 PER_{t,i,j} \times FERROR_{t,i} + \beta'_2 NPER_{t,i,j} \times FERROR_{t,i} \\
& + \beta'_3 AVOL_{t,i} \times PER_{t,i,j} \times FERROR_{t,i} + \beta'_4 AVOL_{t,i} \times NPER_{t,i,j} \\
& \times FERROR_{t,i} + \beta'_5 REV_{t,i,j} + \beta'_6 AVOL_{t,i} \times REV_{t,i,j} + \varsigma_{t,i,j}
\end{aligned} \tag{3}
$$

significant at the 0.01 level ($\beta'_3 = 0.2853$, $t = 2.88$), which indicates that as the information complexity of earnings announcements increases, confirmatory recommendation revisions can cause even larger corrective price reactions holding constant the magnitude of prior earnings surprises. The coefficient on $AVOL_{t,i} \times NPER_{t,i,j} \times FERROR_{t,i}$ is negative and statistically significant at the 0.05 level ($\beta'_4 = -0.3310$, $t = -2.73$), which indicates that contradictory recommendation revisions also become more informative to investors for reassessing the valuation implications of earnings as the information complexity of earnings announcements gets higher. Overall, the results suggest that investors become more dependent on analysts for guidance in assessing the valuation implications of earnings announcements of higher information complexity.

Column (2) reports similar results as those reported in Column (1). After including $REV_{t,i,j}$ in the regression, the coefficient on $AVOL_{t,i} \times NPER_{t,i,j} \times FERROR_{t,i}$, is still negative and statistically significant at the 0.1 level. Although the coefficient on $AVOL_{t,i} \times PER_{t,i,j} \times FERROR_{t,i}$ is not statistically significant at any conventional level, it still has the predicted positive sign. The coefficient on $REV_{t,i,j}$ is positive, as expected, and statistically significant at the 0.01 level. The coefficient on $AVOL_{t,i} \times REV_{t,i,j}$ is also positive and statistically significant at the 0.01 level, suggesting that analysts' recommendation revisions have larger price impact as the complexity of publicly disclosed earnings information increases.

The Impact of Reg FD

For H3, Eq. (4) is estimated to investigate whether analysts' recommendation revisions, after Reg FD, can still help investors reassess the valuation implications of announced earnings. The results are reported in Table 4. In Column (1), the coefficient on $PER_{t,i,j} \times FERROR_{t,i}$ ($NPER_{t,i,j} \times FERROR_{t,i}$) is positive (negative) as predicted and statistically significant at the 0.01 level, suggesting that before the adoption of Reg FD, analysts' recommendation revisions had caused investors to reassess the valuation implications of earnings announcements and to correct their misreactions to announced earnings. By estimating the coefficients on $POST_{t,i} \times PER_{t,i,j} \times FERROR_{t,i}$ and $POST_{t,i} \times NPER_{t,i,j} \times FERROR_{t,i}$, evidence reveals whether analysts' ability to help investors discern the valuation implications of earnings announcements declines, remains at a similar level, or improves after Reg FD. The results show that the coefficient on $POST_{t,i} \times PER_{t,i,j} \times FERROR_{t,i}$ is positive and statistically significant at the 0.05 level ($\beta''_3 = 0.2238$, $t = 2.48$) and thus suggest that confirmatory recommendation revisions, after Reg FD, can cause even larger corrective price reactions, holding constant the magnitude of prior earnings surprises. As a matter of fact, the magnitude of the coefficient on $PER_{t,i,j} \times FERROR_{t,i}$ increases by as much as 60% (0.2238/0.3717) for confirmatory recommendation revisions. For contradictory recommendation revisions, the coefficient on $POST_{t,i} \times NPER_{t,i,j} \times FERROR_{t,i}$ is negative, but not statistically significant at any conventional level ($\beta''_4 = -0.1409$, $t = -1.26$). This result indicates that

Table 4. Estimated Results of the Impact of Reg FD.

Independent Variable	Predicted Sign	Without $REV_{t,i}$(1)	With $REV_{t,i}$(2)
Intercept		0.0029	0.0032
		(7.20)***	(8.07)***
$PER_{t,i} \times FERROR_{t,i}$	+	0.3717	0.1224
		(5.80)***	(1.85)**
$NPER_{t,i} \times FERROR_{t,i}$	−	−0.5984	−0.2941
		(−7.09)***	(−3.41)***
$POST_{t,i} \times PER_{t,i} \times FERROR_{t,i}$	?	0.2238	0.0867
		(2.48)**	(0.93)
$POST_{t,i} \times NPER_{t,i} \times FERROR_{t,i}$	?	−0.1409	0.0034
		(−1.26)	(0.03)
$REV_{t,i}$	+		0.0051
			(12.78)***
$POST_{t,i} \times REV_{t,i}$	?		0.0036
			(6.09)***
Adj. R^2		0.015	0.044
No. of observations	18,010		

Notes: This table reports the impact of Reg FD on the relation between corrective price reactions caused by analysts' recommendation revisions and prior earnings surprises. $CAR_{t,i,j}$ is the cumulative three-day size-adjusted abnormal returns centered on the recommendation revision. The variable $REV_{t,i}$ is recommendation revisions for firm *i*'s stock following earnings announcements within two trading weeks. The variable $FERROR_{t,i}$is the difference between reported earnings and the prior consensus analyst forecasts deflated by the beginning price of the three-day window used to calculate $CAR_{t,i,j}$. The dummy variable $PER_{t,i}$ ($NPER_{t,i}$) takes the value of one if the recommendation revision has the same (opposite) sign as prior earnings surprise and zero otherwise. The dummy variable $POST_{t,i}$ takes the value of one if the revision date is after the effective date of Reg FD (10/23/2000). The *t*-scores are in parentheses. ***,**,* represent statistical significance at 0.01, 0.05, and 0.1 levels, respectively.

$$\begin{aligned} CAR_{t,i,j} = {} & \alpha + \beta''_1 PER_{t,i,j} \times FERROR_{t,i} + \beta''_2 NPER_{t,i,j} \times FERROR_{t,i} \\ & + \beta''_3 POST_t \times PER_{t,i,j} \times FERROR_{t,i} + \beta''_4 POST_t \times NPER_{t,i,j} \\ & \times FERROR_{t,i} + \beta''_5 REV_{t,i,j} + \beta''_6 POST_t \times REV_{t,i,j} + \zeta_{t,i,j} \end{aligned} \quad (4)$$

the information content of contradictory recommendation revisions, after Reg FD, remains at a similar level in terms of helping investors correct their prior overreactions to announced earnings.

In Column (2), the coefficients on $PER_{t,i,j} \times FERROR_{t,i}$ and $NPER_{t,i,j} \times FERROR_{t,i}$ are not statistically significant at any conventional level. Such results indicate that analysts at least maintain a similar level of expertise in processing public information after Reg FD. The coefficient on

$POST_{t,i} \times REV_{t,i,j}$ is positive and statistically significant at the 0.01 level, which demonstrates that analysts' recommendation revisions driven by earnings announcements have become more informative after Reg FD.

Overall, the results show that analysts continue to help investors assess the valuation implications of earnings announcements after Reg FD terminated their access to management's inside information. In fact, since the adoption of Reg FD, the information content of confirmatory recommendation revisions has improved in clarifying the valuation implications of earnings announcements for investors and there is no evidence to indicate any decline in the information content of contradictory recommendation revisions. The fact that analysts have maintained at least a similar level of expertise in processing public information without the aids of inside information from management suggests that they truly rely on their analytical skills to process public information. Moreover, losing their access to the inside information from firms' management also means that analysts have to exercise greater effort and to work more diligently, which helps to explain why the information content of confirmatory recommendation revisions has improved after Reg FD.

To further prove that analysts are primarily relying on their skills rather than inside information from management to process public information, I examine the effect of Reg FD on upward and downward recommendation revisions separately. Prior studies document that management has incentives to communicate good news to analysts or to give an early peek to analysts when there is more good news than bad news to be shared (Brown, 2001; Chambers & Penman, 1984; Ivkovic & Jegadeesh, 2004). Upward (downward) recommendation revisions usually indicate that analysts have discovered good (bad) news about the security price of a firm. Therefore, examining whether Reg FD has a different impact on the informativeness of upward and downward revisions can shed additional light on this issue. Before Reg FD, since management tended to give analysts early access to good news rather than bad news, there would have been a greater reduction of good news passing from management to analysts after Reg FD. Thus, if analysts' interpretation of public signals had substantially benefitted from the guidance of management, then intuitively, the information content of analysts' upward revisions would definitely decline and decline more than that of downward revisions.

In order to test if upward recommendation revisions have become less informative about the valuation implications of earnings announcements after Reg FD, I split the sample into confirmatory and contradictory recommendation revisions and then test the information content of upward and downward recommendation revisions using each subsample. The following equation is estimated for both confirmatory and contradictory recommendation revisions to check for evidence:

$$\begin{aligned} CAR_{t,i,j} = {} & \lambda_0 + \lambda_1 Upward_{t,i,j} \times FERROR_{t,i} + \lambda_2 Downward_{t,i,j} \times FERROR_{t,i} \\ & + \lambda_3 POST_{t,i} \times Upward_{t,i,j} \times FERROR_{t,i} + \lambda_4 POST_{t,i} \times Downward_{t,i,j} \\ & \times FERROR_{t,i} + \zeta_{t,i,j} \end{aligned} \tag{5}$$

where $Upward_{t,i,j}$ ($Downward_{t,i,j}$) takes the value of one if the analyst recommendation is revised upward (downward) from his/her prior recommendation, and otherwise zero. In 2002, a financial reform was implemented to resolve analysts' conflict of interest when issuing recommendations and it quickly resulted in a large amount of downward recommendation revisions. To eliminate the effect of the 2002 financial reform, all 2002 observations are excluded from this test.[12]

Results reported in Table 5 are contrary to the prediction that the information content of upward recommendation revisions declines after Reg FD. Column (1) reports the results regarding confirmatory recommendation revisions. The coefficient on $POST_{t,i} \times Upward_{t,i,j} \times FERROR_{t,i}$ is positive and significant at the 0.05 level ($\lambda_3 = 1.4949$, $t = 3.14$), which means that the information content of upward recommendation revisions has increased significantly after Reg FD. The coefficient on $POST_{t,i} \times Downward_{t,i,j} \times FERROR_{t,i}$ is also positive and statistically significant at the 0.05 level, but with a much smaller magnitude ($\lambda_4 = 0.2125$, $t = 1.96$). Therefore, for confirmatory recommendation revisions, the information content of upward recommendation revisions has not declined at all after Reg FD. It has in fact increased at an even greater magnitude than that of downward recommendation revisions.

As for contradictory recommendation revisions, the evidence is not consistent with the prediction either. In Column (2), the coefficient on either $POST_{t,i} \times Upward_{t,i,j} \times FERROR_{t,i}$ or $POST_{t,i} \times Downward_{t,i,j} \times FERROR_{t,i}$ is not statistically significant at any conventional level, suggesting that neither upward nor downward recommendation revisions become less informative concerning the valuation implications of earnings.

Overall, I find that analysts' ability to process public information for investors is relatively unaffected since Reg FD came into effect, which provides evidence to support the notion that analysts do depend on their professional analytical expertise to interpret public information.

Table 5. Estimated Results of the Impact of Reg FD on the Information Content of Upward Recommendation Revision Vs. Downward Recommendation Revisions.

Independent Variable	Predicted Sign	Confirmatory (1)	Predicted Sign	Contradictory (2)
Intercept		0.0012		0.0040
		(1.82)*		(5.82)***
$Upward_{t,i,j} \times FERROR_{t,i}$	+	1.9584	–	– 0.5482
		(5.46)***		(– 5.73)***
$Downward_{t,i,j} \times FERROR_{t,i}$	+	0.2673	–	– 2.2580
		(3.68)***		(– 5.99)***
$POST_{t,i} \times Upward_{t,i} \times FERROR_{t,i}$	?	1.4949	?	– 0.1506
		(3.14)***		(– 1.17)
$POST_{t,i} \times Downward_{t,i} \times FERROR_{t,i}$	?	0.2125	?	– 0.2774
		(1.96)**		(– 0.55)
Adj.R^2		0.021		0.023
No. of observations		9,309		8,701

Notes: This table reports the impact of Reg FD on the information content of upward recommendation revisions versus downward recommendation revisions for confirmatory and contradictory recommendation revisions separately. $CAR_{t,i,j}$ is the cumulative three-day size-adjusted abnormal returns centered on the recommendation revision. The variable $FERROR_{t,i}$ is the difference between reported earnings and the prior consensus analyst forecasts deflated by the beginning price of the three-day window used to calculate $CAR_{t,i,j}$. The dummy variable $Upward_{t,i,j}$ takes the value of one if the analyst's recommendation is revised upward from his/her prior recommendation and otherwise zero. The dummy variable $Downward_{t,i,j}$ takes the value of one if the analyst's recommendation is revised downward from her prior recommendation and otherwise zero. The dummy variable $POST_{t,i}$ takes the value of one if the revision date is after the effective date of Reg FD (10/23/2000). The t-scores are in parentheses. ***, **, * represent statistical significance at 0.01, 0.05, and 0.1 levels, respectively.

$$CAR_{t,i,j} = \lambda_0 + \lambda_1 Upward_{t,i,j} \times FERROR_{t,i} + \lambda_2 Downward_{t,i,j} \times FERROR_{t,i} + \lambda_3 POST_{t,i} \times Upward_{t,i,j} \times FERROR_{t,i} + \lambda_4 POST_{t,i} \times Downward_{t,i,j} \times FERROR_{t,i} + \zeta_{t,i,j} \quad (5)$$

Robustness Tests

In this study, I use analysts' recommendation revisions rather than their recommendations (Buy, Hold, or Sell) to derive analysts' opinions about the valuation implications of announced earnings due to two reasons: first, although analysts' recommendations directly reflect their opinions on security misprices, recommendation revisions issued subsequent to earnings announcements reflect the change of analysts' opinions on security prices caused by market's reactions to publicly released earnings news. Second, prior studies show that analysts are reluctant to issue "sell" recommendations (e.g., O'Brien, McNichols, Maureen, & Lin, 2005; Malmendier & Shanthikumar, 2007). In addition, they find that analysts' buy recommendations are discounted by the market and have a weak effect on firm valuation. In fact, in a sample of 18,010 recommendations examined by this study, there are only 1,378 "underperform" or "sell" recommendations.

However, I also estimate Eqs. (2–4) by grouping the observations and defining the variable $PER_{t,i,j}$ based on confirmatory recommendations and contradictory recommendations. Confirmatory recommendations are buy (sell) recommendations following positive (negative) earnings surprises. Contradictory recommendations are buy (sell) recommendations following negative (positive) earnings surprises. The implications of the results, which are not reported here for brevity, remain unchanged, but the adjusted R^2 of the equations becomes very small because there is only a very small fraction of "underperform" or "sell" recommendations in the sample.

In the main tests, recommendation revisions are classified as confirmatory if $REV_{t,i,j}$ and $FERROR_{t,i}$ have the same sign and contradictory if $REV_{t,i,j}$ and $FERROR_{t,i}$ have the opposite sign. Since $REV_{t,i,j}$ and $CAR_{t,i,j}$ are highly correlated, to make sure that the estimated results of Eq. (2) are not caused by how the observations are grouped, I also test H1 by regressing the following equation:

$$\begin{aligned} CAR_{t,i,j} = a &+ b_1 PER1_{t,i,j} \times FERROR_{t,i} + b_2 PER2_{t,i,j} \times FERROR_{t,i} \\ &+ b_3 NPER1_{t,i,j} \times FERROR_{t,i} + b_4 NPER2_{t,i,j} \times FERROR_{t,i} \\ &+ b_5 REV_{t,i,j} + \varepsilon_{t,i,j} \end{aligned}$$

where $PER1_{t,i,j}(PER2_{t,i,j})$ is equal to one if the recommendation revision and the earnings surprise both have the positive (negative) sign, and zero otherwise. $NPER1_{t,i,j}(NPER2_{t,i,j})$ is equal to one if the recommendation revision is negative (positive), but the earnings surprise is positive (negative), and zero otherwise. Therefore, the expected signs of b_1 and b_2 should be positive and the expected signs of b_3 and b_4 should be negative.

The estimated results are not reported here for brevity, but they show that all the coefficients have the predicted signs and are at least statistically significant at the 0.05 level. Moreover, the adjusted R^2 improves compared to that of Eq. (2). Therefore, the estimated results of the above equation provide consistent evidence that supports H1.

I also use the above specification to test H2 and H3 by interacting $PER1_{t,i,j}$, $PER2_{t,i,j}$, $NPER1_{t,i,j}$ and $NPER2_{t,i,j}$ with $AVOL_{t,i}$ and $POST_{t,i}$, respectively. The implications of the estimated results remain unchanged.

CONCLUSION

In this study, I investigate analysts' expertise in processing public information by focusing on how investors re-examine the valuation implications of announced earnings using analysts' recommendation revisions issued shortly after earnings announcements. Confirmatory (contradictory) recommendation revisions that have the same (opposite) sign as prior earnings surprises can cause investors to revise their initial assessment of the valuation implications of recently announced earnings upward (downward) and thus cause corrective price reactions that are positively (negatively) associated with prior earnings surprises. The fact that investors react to analysts' recommendation revisions by revising their initial assessments of the valuation implications of announced earnings indicates that analysts are regarded by them as more proficient in processing public information.

Furthermore, analysts' expertise in processing public information relative to that of investors widens even further as the information complexity of earnings announcements intensifies. When investors are more uncertain about the valuation implications of announced earnings, the extent of their misreactions to the earnings news can also be greater. I find that analysts' recommendation revisions can cause larger corrective price reactions as the earnings news becomes more complex, holding constant the magnitude of the earnings surprises.

In the investigation to determine the effect of Reg FD, evidence indicates that analysts' ability to process public information has remained at a similar level despite the adoption of Reg FD. Moreover, I find that the information content of confirmatory recommendation revisions in fact has increased post Reg FD. Seemingly, this ability of analysts' is attributable to their analytical and interpretation proficiency rather than accessibility to insider information from management.

The findings of this study have implications on the role of analysts in corporate governance. By interpreting public information for investors, analysts not only help disseminate corporate financial disclosures, in this process, they can also help detect managerial misrepresentation and improves information transparency. Furthermore, it shows in this study that analysts' information is more useful when earnings announcements are more complex to process. This provides further support that analysts play an important role in enhancing corporate transparency.

Overall, this paper provides evidence on the value of analysts' ability to process public information for investors by examining how analysts' recommendation revisions alter investors' opinions toward the valuation implications of publicly announced earnings. The limitation of such an approach is that it measures analysts' expertise perceived by investors instead of their actual expertise in processing public information. However, this approach is consistent with the methodology adopted in those value-relevance studies that gauge the value of announced information by the amount of reactions from investors. In addition, one of the merits of this approach is that it provides direct evidence on analysts' role as public information processors by showing the impact of their information on changing investors' opinions of the valuation implications of publicly released earnings information.

ACKNOWLEDGMENT

The author would like to thank workshop participants at University of Hong Kong and participants of 2008 American Accounting Association annual meeting in Annaheim for their many helpful comments and suggestions.

NOTES

1. It is documented in those studies that persistent and reliable earnings have larger valuation implications and price impact.

2. There are many studies investigating investors' learning process under parameter uncertainty (e.g., Chen, Francis & Jiang, 2005; Lewellen & Shanken, 2002).

3. Reg FD prohibits selective disclosure of material information to financial professionals, including analysts, and requires broad, nonexclusionary disclosure of such information. Recent studies have shown evidence that Reg FD is taking effect in reducing management's inside information to analysts (e.g., Gintschela & Markov, 2004; Sunder, 2003; Zitzewitz, 2002).

4. This study does not completely rule out the possibility of analysts using management's private information to interpret public information. Rather, it aims to prove analysts' intellectual skills in processing public information.

5. Bushman (1991) argues that selective disclosures of private information before public release may make traders better off. Francis et al. (1997) find that both firms and analysts benefit from corporate presentations to security analysts. Das et al. (1998) find that analysts issued optimistic forecasts to gain their access to management's nonpublic information.

6. Barker and Imam (2008) conclude that the importance of accounting-based information relating to earnings quality exerts a significant influence on the analysis and recommendations in analysts' reports.

7. I also shorten the window between earnings announcements and the first analyst recommendation revisions to be one trading week and the inferences of the results remain unchanged.

8. Following Freeman and Tse (1989) and Mendenhall (1991), I do not include an interaction variable of the intercept and dummy variables in Eq. (2). To check the robustness of the results, I estimated the following equation using the same sample: $CAR_{t,i,j} = \alpha_1 PER_{t,i,j} + \alpha_2 NPER_{t,i,j} + \beta_1 PER_{t,i,j} \times FERROR_{t,i} + \beta_2 NPER_{t,i,j} \times FERROR_{t,i} + \beta_3 REV_{t,i,j} + \varepsilon_{t,i,j}$, Both α_1 and α_2 are similar to α and the other coefficients are also similar to those estimated using Eq. (2).

9. In Collins and Kothari (1989), the sum of the present value of expectation changes on earnings of all the future periods is equal to $(1 - \theta\ )/r$ if earnings are assumed to follow an IMA(1,1) process with the moving average parameter equal to θ where r is the discount rate. Therefore, ERC should be equal to $1 + (1 - \theta)/r$.

10. Mendenhall's sample covers a different period (from 1982 to 1986) and he uses analysts' forecasts from the Value Line Investment Survey.

11. In order to exclude the possibility that analysts simply pick up in their recommendation revisions information that is already known to investors, I examine the stock price changes in the period between earnings announcements and analysts' recommendation revisions. I do not find that stock prices reflect any information contained in analysts' recommendation revisions before they are issued.

12. The implications of test results with 2002 data included in the sample remain similar.

REFERENCES

Abarbanell, J. S., & Bernard, V. L. (1992). Tests of analysts' overreaction/underreaction to earnings information as an explanation for anomalous stock price behavior. *Journal of Finance*, *47*(3), 1181–1207.

Agrawal, A., Chadha, S., & Chen, M. A. (2006). Who is afraid of Reg FD? the behavior and performance of sell-side analysts following the SEC's fair disclosure rules. *Journal of Business*, *79*(6), 2811–2837.

Asquith, P., Mikhail, M. B., & Au, A. S. (2005). Information content of equity analyst reports. *Journal of Financial Economics*, *75*(2), 245–282.

Bailey, W., Li, H., Mao, C. X., & Zhong, R. (2003). Regulation fair disclosure and earnings information: Market, analyst, and corporate responses. *Journal of Finance*, *58*(6), 2487–2514.

Barker, R., & Imam, S. (2008). Analysts' perceptions of earnings quality. *Accounting & Business Research*, *38*(4), 313–329.

Bauman, W. S., Datta, S., & Iskandar-Datta, M. E. (1995). Investment analyst recommendations: a test of "the announcement effect" and "the valuable information effect". *Journal of Business Finance & Accounting*, *22*(5), 659–670.

Bernard, V., & Thomas, J. (1990). Evidence that stock prices do not fully reflect the implications of current earnings for future earnings. *Journal of Accounting and Economics*, *13*(4), 305–340.

Bowen, R. M., Davis, A. K., & Matsumoto, D. A. (2002). 'Do conference calls affect analysts' forecasts? *The Accounting Review*, *77*(2), 285–316.

Brown, L. D. (2001). A temporal analysis of earnings surprises: profits versus losses. *Journal of Accounting Research*, *39*(2), 221–241.

Bushman, R. M. (1991). Public disclosure and the structure of private information market. *Journal of Accounting Research*, *29*(2), 261–276.

Bushman, R. M., Piotroski, J. D., & Smith, A. J. (2004). What determines corporate transparency? *Journal of Accounting Research*, *42*(2), 207–252.

Chambers, A. E., & Penman, S. H. (1984). Timeliness of reporting and the stock price reaction to earnings announcements. *Journal of Accounting Research*, *22*(1), 21–47.

Chen, Q., Francis, J., & Jiang, W. (2005). Investor learning about analyst predictive ability. *Journal of Accounting and Economics*, *39*(1), 3–24.

Chopra, N., Lakonishok, J., & Ritter, J. (1992). Measuring abnormal performance: Do stocks overreact? *Journal of Financial Economics*, *31*(2), 235–268.

Collins, D. W., & Kothari, S. P. (1989). An analysis of intertemporal and cross-sectional determinants of earnings response coefficients. *Journal of Accounting and Economics*, *11*(4), 143–181.

Das, S., Levine, C. B., & Sivaramakrishnan, K. (1998). Earnings predictability and bias in analysts' earnings forecasts. *The Accounting Review*, *73*(2), 277–294.

DeBondt, W. F. M., & Thaler, R. H. (1985). Does the stock market overreact? *Journal of Finance*, *40*(3), 793–805.

DeBondt, W. F. M., & Thaler, R. H. (1987). Further evidence of investor overreaction and stock market seasonality. *Journal of Finance*, *42*(3), 557–582.

Dyck, A., Morse, A., & Zingales, L. (2010). Who blows the whistle on corporate fraud? *Journal of Finance*, *65*(6), 2213–2253.

Easton, P. D., & Zmijewski, M. E. (1989). Cross-sectional variation in the stock market response to accounting earnings announcement. *Journal of Accounting and Economics*, *11*(2–3), 117–141.

Francis, J., Hanna, J. D., & Philbrisk, D. R. (1997). Management communications with securities analysts. *Journal of Accounting and Economics*, *24*(3), 363–394.

Frankel, R., Kothari, S. P., & Weber, J. (2006). Determinants of the informativeness of analyst research. *Journal of Accounting and Economics*, *41*(1–2), 3–50.

Freeman, R. N., & Tse, S. (1989). The multiperiod information content of accounting earnings: Confirmations and contradictions of previous earnings reports. *Journal of Accounting Research*, *27*(Suppl.), 49–79.

Gintschela, A., & Markov, S. (2004). The effectiveness of regulation FD. *Journal of Accounting & Economics*, *37*(3), 293–314.

Gleason, C. A., & Lee, C. M. C. (2003). Analyst forecast revisions and market price discovery. *The Accounting Review*, *78*(1), 193–225.

Healy, P., & Palepu, K. (2001). Information asymmetry, corporate disclosure, and the capital markets: a review of the empirical disclosure literature. *Journal of Accounting and Economics*, *31*(1–3), 405–440.

Heflin, F., Subramanyam, K. R., & Zhang, Y. (2003). Regulation FD and the financial information environment. *The Accounting Review*, *78*(1), 1–37.

Holthausen, R. W., & Verrecchia, R. E. (1990). The effect of informedness and consensus on price and volume behavior. *The Accounting Review*, *65*(1), 191–208.

Ivkovic, Z., & Jegadeesh, N. (2004). The timing and value of forecast and recommendation revisions. *Journal of Financial Economics*, *73*(3), 433–463.

Kim, J., Lee, J., & Park, T. H. (1996). Transaction responses to analysts' earnings forecasts, news type and trade type. *Journal of Business Finance and Accounting*, *23*(7), 1043–1058.

Kim, O., & Verrecchia, R. (1991). Trading volumes and price reactions to public announcements. *Journal of Accounting Research*, *29*(2), 302–321.

Kim, O., & Verrecchia, R. (1994). Market liquidity and volume around earnings announcements. *Journal of Accounting and Economics*, *17*(1), 41–67.

Klein, A. (1990). A direct test of the cognitive bias theory of share price reversals. *Journal of Accounting and Economics*, *13*(2), 155–166.

Koch, A. S., & Sun, A. X. (2004). Dividend changes and the persistence of past earnings changes. *The Journal of Finance*, *59*(5), 2093–2116.

Kormendi, R., & Lipe, R. (1987). Earnings innovations, earnings persistence, and stock returns. *Journal of Business*, *60*(3), 323–344.

Landsman, W., & Maydew, E. (2002). Has the information content of quarterly earnings announcements declined in the past three decades? *Journal of Accounting Research*, *40*(3), 797–808.

Lang, M. H., Lins, K. V., & Miller, D. P. (2004). Concentrated control, analyst following, and valuation: do analysts matter most when investors are protected least? *Journal of Accounting Research*, *42*(3), 589–623.

Lewellen, J., & Shanken, J. (2002). Learning, asset-pricing tests, and market efficiency. *Journal of Finance*, *57*(3), 1113–1145.

Liang, L. (2003). Post-earnings announcement drift and market participants' information processing biases. *Review of Accounting Studies*, *8*(2–3), 321–345.

Lloyd-Davies, P., & Canes, M. (1978). Stock prices and the publication of second-hand information. *Journal of Business*, *51*(1), 43–56.

Lys, T., & Sohn, S. (1990). The association between revisions of financial analysts' earnings forecasts and security-price changes. *Journal of Accounting and Economics*, *13*(1), 341–363.

Malmendier, U., & Shanthikumar, D. (2007). Are small investors naive about incentives? *Journal of Financial Economics*, *85*(2), 457–489.

Mendenhall, R. R. (1991). Evidence on the possible underweighting of earnings-related information. *Journal of Accounting Research*, *29*(1), 170–179.

Mikhail, M. B., Walther, B. R., & Willis, R. H. (2007). When security analysts talk who listens?. *Accounting Review*, *82*(5), 1227–1253.

Mohanram, P. S., & Sunder, S. V. (2006). How has regulation fair disclosure affected the functioning of financial analysts? *Contemporary Accounting Research*, *23*(2), 491–525.

O'Brien, P. C., McNichols, M. F., Maureen, F., & Lin, H. (2005). Analyst impartiality and investment banking relationships. *Journal of Accounting Research*, *43*(4), 623–650.

Schipper, K., & Vincent, L. (2003). Earnings quality. *Accounting Horizons*, *17*(Suppl.), 97–110.

Shane, P., & Brous, P. (2001). Investor and (value line) analyst underreaction to information about future earnings: the corrective role of non-earnings-surprise information. *Journal of Accounting Research*, *39*(2), 387–404.

Stickel, S. E. (1992). Reputations and performance among security analysts. *Journal of Finance*, *47*(5), 1811–1836.

Sunder, S. V. (2003). *Investor access to conference call disclosures: Impact of regulation fair disclosure on information asymmetry*, Working Paper, The University of Arizona.

Womack, K. (1996). Do brokerage analysts' recommendations have investment value? *The Journal of Finance*, *51*(1), 137–168.

Yu, F. (2008). Analyst coverage and earnings management. *Journal of Financial Economics*, *88*(2), 245–271.

Zitzewitz, E. (2002). *Regulation fair disclosure and the private information of analysts*. Stanford University: Working Paper.

DOES BROKER ANONYMITY HIDE INFORMED TRADERS?

Andrew Lepone, Reuben Segara and Brad Wong

ABSTRACT

This study investigates whether broker anonymity impairs the ability of the market to detect informed trading in the lead up to takeover announcements. Our research represents the first study in this area to analyse the effects of broker anonymity in the context of significant information asymmetry. Results indicate that informed traders are less detected, and therefore better off when broker identifiers are concealed. This finding has important policy implications for exchange officials deciding whether or not to reveal broker identifiers surrounding trades, especially considering that almost all prior research suggests that broker anonymity is correlated with improved liquidity.

Keywords: Broker anonymity; informed trading; stock exchange; takeovers

JEL classifications: G10; G14; G34

Transparency and Governance in a Global World
International Finance Review, Volume 13, 287–317

ISSN: 1569-3767/doi:10.1108/S1569-3767(2012)0000013013

INTRODUCTION

One of the most prominent market design issues considered by exchange officials of electronic order-driven markets in recent years is the decision regarding whether to reveal broker identifiers surrounding trades. Between 1999 and 2005 no fewer than seven exchanges made changes to their respective broker identification regimes, and the high incidence of such changes has led to an equally high incidence of academic studies investigating the effect of the transparency change on market quality. Foucault, Moinas, and Thiessen (2007) investigate the switch to pre-trade broker anonymity on the Paris Bourse in April 2001 and find that quoted bid-ask spreads decrease after the change and that spreads become less informative about future volatility. Comerton-Forde, Frino, and Mollica (2005) examine the affects of broker identification changes on the Paris Bourse, the Tokyo Stock Exchange and the Korean Stock Exchange and find that improved market quality, in the form of reduced relative and effective bid-ask spreads, is correlated with pre-trade broker anonymity. Finally, Comerton-Forde and Tang (2009) document decreased bid-ask spreads, increased depth and greater order flow after the Australian Stock Exchange (ASX) removed pre-trade broker identifiers and delayed the reporting of post-trade broker identifiers on 28 November 2005. Table A summarizes the recent broker identification changes implemented by electronic exchanges and related academic studies.[1] The focus of such studies is broad in nature, with an emphasis on the effects of the transparency change on general market quality indicators.

Despite the extensive literature on broker identification in electronic markets, no study in this area examines how a change in broker anonymity affects market participants during periods of large information asymmetry. This is an important distinction since one would naturally expect that anonymity is more relevant during periods of high information asymmetry vis-à-vis periods when no information event is pending. Intuitively, broker anonymity impairs the ability of uninformed traders, followers and dealers to discern the advent of some significant price-sensitive announcement from the pool of liquidity-motivated trades.[2] The hidden nature of broker identifiers is not as problematic (beneficial) for uninformed (informed) traders when no information event is about to occur. Furthermore, the interpretation of market quality statistics can be fundamentally altered depending on the level of informed trading across the period analysed. For example, during periods when no information event is pending, tight bid-ask spreads represent lower transaction costs for uninformed traders, whereas tight bid-ask spreads before unanticipated material announcements with active informed traders imply that liquidity providers are not adequately engaging in price protection. It is not possible to disentangle the two scenarios by examining, as previous studies have, market quality statistics averaged across all market conditions.

The purpose of this study is to investigate whether the removal of broker identifiers camouflages the presence of informed traders prior to a significant information event. To perform this analysis, we investigate pre-announcement trading in a sample of 258 takeovers, announced between 28 November 2003 and 28 November 2007, corresponding to a time period two years either side of the aforementioned transparency change that occurred on the ASX on 28 November 2005. As recognized by Cao, Chen, and Griffin (2005), takeover announcements provide an ideal setting to test hypotheses related to information transmission in markets. The magnitude of potential returns provides a strong incentive for informed traders to trade and indeed it is well established that informed traders are active prior to takeover announcements (Jarrell & Poulson, 1989; Keown & Pinkerton, 1981; Meulbroek, 1992). Furthermore, unlike earnings announcements, the timing and occurrence of takeover announcements is completely unknown to uninformed traders. As such, if abnormal volume or price activity occurs before these announcements, it most likely coincides with trading by informed participants.

This study, therefore, explicitly addresses the issue of broker anonymity effects in the context of large information asymmetry. This is important given the frequency of changes to broker transparency that have occurred in electronic order-driven markets in recent years and the fact that almost all studies to date suggest that improved liquidity (in the form of tighter bid-ask spreads) is correlated with an anonymous regime. Our results indicate that informed traders are better off after a switch to anonymity, a finding which needs to be considered together with previous studies when assessing the implications of broker anonymity changes on market quality.

This chapter is also related to studies which investigate the relationship between broker anonymity and information transmission in securities markets other than electronic order-driven markets. Benveniste, Marcus, and Wilhelm (1992) develop a model that describes the interactions between a specialist and broker intermediaries on a floor traded market. Their model supposes that specialists are better able to detect informed trading because the nature of repeat (non-anonymous) face-to-face interactions between floor brokers and the specialist provides incentives for brokers to be candid about whether their client is informed or otherwise. In contrast, market makers in electronic markets, who do not benefit from repeated face-to-face interactions with brokers, are less able to detect informed trading. The predictions of the model are confirmed by Garfinkel and Nimalendran (2003) who find that informed trading[3] is correlated with larger effective bid-ask spreads for New York Stock Exchange (NYSE)-listed stocks relative to NASDAQ-listed stocks. Umlauf (1991) examines the effects of broker anonymity in the over-the-counter market for U.S. government bond securities. In his paper, certain traders – primary dealers – have access to all brokers, while other traders – secondary dealers – have access to only a subset of brokers. Secondary dealers effectively exist in a market with partial broker transparency. The chapter shows that primary dealers' price expectations lead those of secondary dealers, because brokers provide valuable information to clients via video screen, such as the limit orders of other traders and recent transaction prices.

Our chapter extends these studies in two important ways. The first extension relates to the mechanism of information transmission. In Benveniste, Marcus, and Wilhelm (1992) and Umlauf (1991), information transmission occurs because brokers actively divulge price-sensitive information to the specialist or other traders respectively. In this chapter, we show that it is possible for the mere identity of the broker to provide valuable information to other market participants. Furthermore, while the results of Garfinkel and Nimalendran (2003) support the predictions of Benveniste, Marcus, and Wilhelm, (1992), it is possible that their results are driven by some other difference between the NYSE and NASDAQ, unrelated to information sharing by brokers.[4] This study takes advantage of a natural experiment in which the market structure remains essentially the same, except for the change in broker identification rules, allowing for a clearer inference on the relationship between broker anonymity and information transmission.

This study benefits significantly from access to a proprietary data set provided by the ASX which contains the broker counterparties to every trade executed on the exchange. Prior studies, including all those listed in Table A in the appendix, which investigate changes in the transparency of broker identifiers have yet to utilize data of this nature, resorting instead to broad trade and quote level data. While this can be suitable, and indeed two of the hypotheses in this chapter require only trade and quote level data, one could argue that the most natural observational unit for a study of broker identifier transparency is the individual broker. To the best of our knowledge, this is the first study of broker transparency to incorporate within its analysis, research directed at the level of the individual broker.

We use the data set provided by the ASX to calculate the average permanent price impact of each broker's trades and the dispersion of this variable *across brokers*. The rationale for examining this metric is that, all other things being equal, the dispersion of permanent price impact across brokers provides an indication of the extent to which the market utilizes the identifier to distinguish informed from uninformed trades. For example, all other things being equal, if the dispersion of average permanent price impact across brokers is zero, then the market places no informational weight on the identifier. Clearly in the anonymous broker regime it is impossible for the market to extract any information from the broker identifier. We compare the dispersion of broker price impact before and after the change to determine if the identifier has incremental signalling value in the transparent period in the lead up to takeover announcements. If it contains value, then by definition, its absence suggests that informed traders are less detectable after the change to anonymity.

To enhance this analysis, we also investigate the extent to which liquidity suppliers adequately price protect themselves as well as the ability of the market to correctly interpret the information content of order imbalances in 40 days prior to takeover announcements. We choose to examine bid-ask spreads since it provides a natural indication of whether informed traders are being detected by liquidity providers (Bagehot, 1971; Copeland & Galai, 1983; Easley & O'Hara, 1987; Glosten & Milgrom, 1985). Furthermore, we measure the strength of the order imbalance to price relationship in the days leading up to the announcement as another indicator of how well-informed traders can disguise their status.[5] Studies show that informed trading is likely to manifest itself as an imbalance between buyer- and seller-initiated trades (Easley, Kiefer, O'Hara, & Paperman, 1996; Easley, Kiefer, & O'Hara, 1997). Since we analyse periods where informed trading is likely to occur, the extent to which the market reacts to order imbalances during this time is another measure to assess the ability of informed traders to remain hidden from the market.

The results of this study indicate that the dispersion in the average permanent price impact across brokers is lower after the change to broker anonymity with the standard deviation of average price impact across brokers dropping from 32.34 basis points to 27.72 basis points. The reduction in dispersion is most pronounced for trades executed by brokers that are between one to five times the median trade size for the security. We also find that bid-ask spreads are significantly lower in the anonymous market setting. The magnitude of this reduction, 24 basis points, is material even after controlling for firm size, volume and volatility. Additional tests indicate that the decrease is attributable to a reduction in the adverse selection component of the spread. With respect to the order imbalance-price relationship, results indicate that both before and after the switch to anonymity excessive buyer-initiated days correspond to days of greater returns. However, this relationship is significantly weaker in the post period. Overall the results of this study suggest that informed traders remain less detected by the market and are therefore better off after a switch to broker anonymity.

The rest of this chapter is organized as follows. The third section outlines the theory underpinning the hypotheses of the chapter. The third section describes the institutional detail and data used for this study. The fourth section provides the results of the analysis. In fifth section, we perform additional robustness tests, and the sixth section concludes.

HYPOTHESIS DEVELOPMENT

In this section, we outline three hypotheses which allow us to test whether informed traders are more hidden after the removal of broker identifiers. The first hypothesis relates to permanent price impact, and how an investigation of this metric at the broker level reveals the extent to which the identifier is used to distinguish informed and uninformed traders. Secondly, we explain how bid-ask spreads reflect informed trading in an electronic market where all traders can provide liquidity. Thirdly, we discuss the price-order imbalance relationship and its connection with informed trading.

Dispersion in Broker-Level Permanent Price Impact

The price impact of a trade can be divided into two components: transitory and permanent (Kraus & Stoll, 1972). The transitory component measures the price impact associated with temporary liquidity constraints at the time of the trade. In contrast, the permanent component measures the longer lasting price impact of the trade. In this study, we are interested in the permanent component because it can be used to ascertain the market's assessment of the information content of that order. Since broker identifiers are attached to all orders in the transparent regime, but not in the anonymous regime, a comparison of permanent price impact across regimes provides some insight into the information content of the identifiers, if any.

Consider two brokers, one which is perceived by the market to execute trades from informed traders, broker *I* and another broker *U*, which executes trades from uninformed investors. In terms of real-world examples, broker *I* could fit the description of an institutional broker and broker *U* could be a discount Internet broker catering mainly for retail investors. All other things being equal, the trades executed by broker *I* will have greater permanent price impact than those of broker *U*. Now consider the case where the market cannot identify the broker behind each trade and thus cannot use the incremental signalling value it provides. In this case, all other things being equal, the trades of broker *I* and broker *U* should have the same perceived information content and thus the same permanent price impact. Therefore, in the transparent regime, *assuming the broker identifiers have some informational value*, the dispersion in the average permanent price impact across brokers should be higher than in the anonymous regime. However, if the broker identifiers have no value, then the dispersion should be similar across the regimes. By definition, if broker identifiers have informational value, then the absence of these identifiers means that informed traders are more hidden after the change to anonymity. Therefore, an investigation of the dispersion in permanent price impact furthers the overall aim of this study – namely, whether the removal of broker identifiers hides informed traders.

> **H1**. In the lead up to takeover announcements, the dispersion in permanent price impact across brokers is narrower after the switch to anonymity.[6]

Bid-Ask Spread

It is well established that the bid-ask spread incorporates the risk associated with trading with an informed trader (Bagehot, 1971). Therefore, the magnitude of the bid-ask spread should be an increasing function of the probability of informed trading in the market (Copeland & Galai, 1983; Easley & O'Hara, 1987; Glosten & Milgrom, 1985). However, this relationship breaks down when liquidity providers and dealers incorrectly assess the probability of informed trading or at the extreme fail to discern the presence of informed traders whatsoever. For example, Fishe and Robe

(2004) show that NASDAQ dealers did not widen bid-ask spreads in the presence of trading by those who had foreknowledge of the influential *Business Week* stock analysis column, 'Inside Wall Street'. Therefore, assuming informed traders are active in a market, one can examine bid-ask spreads to determine the extent to which other market participants have detected informed traders. Indeed, Garfinkel, and Nimalendram (2003) use bid-ask spreads as a means to determine the extent to which traders are recognized as informed on the NYSE compared to the NASDAQ.

The above reasoning applies when informed traders act as liquidity demanders in a market. However, in an electronic limit order book with no designated dealers such as the ASX, informed traders are also free to act as liquidity suppliers. In this situation, we contend that the bid-ask spread is still a useful indicator of the extent to which participants are recognized as informed. Foucault et al. (2007) provide a model of an electronic limit order book where informed traders possess information about a stock's future volatility and act as liquidity suppliers. They compete for order flow with uninformed liquidity suppliers, who behave according to the participation rate of informed dealers in the market. Nature decides whether an information event occurs, and if so, informed dealers enter the market and act first by posting limit orders which maximize their expected profit. If there is no information event, a pre-committed dealer acts first. Uninformed liquidity suppliers post orders after the initial round. By definition, uninformed liquidity suppliers cannot tell whether an information event has occurred, but they can infer the presence of an informed dealer by the state of the order book when it is their turn to post orders.[7] The authors consider two scenarios: one in which informed dealers are known to others as signalled by their broker identity (transparent market) and one in which informed dealers are unknown (anonymous market). The anonymous market is the only scenario relevant to the discussion of informed trader detection since in a transparent market, uninformed dealers behave as if they have perfect information as to whether an order book is set by an informed dealer or otherwise. For an anonymous market, when the participation rate of informed dealers is low, uninformed liquidity suppliers never assign a large enough probability of an information event (even when the order book looks like it has been set by an informed dealer), such that the profit maximizing response is to provide price improvement (i.e. reduce the spread). Similar reasoning leads the authors to conclude that, when the participation rate of informed dealers is large, spreads widen such that there is a positive correlation between bid-ask spreads and the participation rate of informed dealers.

Foucault et al. (2007) assume that uninformed traders are able to accurately assess the participation rate of informed dealers and act accordingly. In reality, however, the behaviour of uninformed dealers is not determined by the participation rate of informed dealers, but rather the uninformed dealers' *beliefs* about the participation rate of informed dealers. The bid-ask spread is therefore an indicator of such beliefs and prior to significant information events the bid-ask spread is an appropriate measure of the extent to which uninformed liquidity suppliers can discern the presence of informed liquidity suppliers.

Whether informed traders demand or supply liquidity, we hypothesize that if informed traders are able to conceal their informed status as a result of broker anonymity, then other liquidity suppliers should factor in a lower adverse selection cost component into the spread.

H2. The bid-ask spread of target firms in the lead up to the takeover announcement is lower in the anonymous broker regime.

Order Imbalance and Returns

The third metric we use to determine the extent to which informed traders are detected is the relationship between order imbalances and returns. Order imbalance is a measure of excess buyer over seller-initiated trading in a given period. Easley et al. (1996) formalize the intuition that this measure can be used to ascertain the extent of informed trading in markets. Cao et al. (2005) show that contemporaneous and lagged order imbalances are positively related to stock returns prior to takeover announcements, providing empirical evidence that order imbalances are a manifestation of information transmission in markets.

Before outlining our hypothesis, it is important to note the inferential differences between order balances in a specialist or dealer market compared to a completely order-driven market. At the most basic level, order imbalances are equivalent in either market structure – order imbalances measure the difference between liquidity demanded by buyers over liquidity demanded by sellers of securities. The primary difference between the markets is that in order-driven markets public traders, rather than dealers, provide the liquidity. As such, there is an argument to suggest that the term order imbalance, in the context of order-driven markets, is a misnomer and therefore uninformative, since 'for every buyer there is also a seller'. We do not take this view, but note the difference in interpretation of order imbalances in an order-driven market vis-à-vis specialist or dealer markets.

In an order-driven market, order imbalance represents the magnitude of excess buy *market* orders over sell *market* orders. This metric is not completely uncorrelated with the extent of informed trading in the market, since it can be argued that informed traders are more likely to use market orders, rather than limit orders, to rapidly utilize their information before others trade on the same information (Conroy & Winkler, 1981; Glosten, 1994; Harris, 2003). This might be particularly the case in the period leading up to takeover announcements where it is likely that a larger group of individuals (employees of the target, the bidder and the corporate and legal advisors for both parties) possess the price-sensitive information, compared to company-specific announcements such as earnings reports. If market orders are in general correlated with informed trading during the periods analysed in this study, and broker anonymity impairs the discovery of informed traders, then this can manifest itself in two ways within the order imbalance–return relationship. Firstly, for a given return, if uninformed traders cannot discern which trades are informed, then they are less likely to trade in the same direction as informed traders, reducing the level of order imbalance. Alternatively, for a given order imbalance, trades by informed individuals should incur a smaller permanent price impact if anonymity means that the market does not correctly interpret the information content of their trades. In either case, the correlation between order imbalance and returns should be weaker when informed traders are hidden due to broker anonymity.

H3. In the lead up to a takeover announcement, the relationship between order imbalances and returns for target firms is weaker in the anonymous broker regime.

INSTITUTIONAL DETAIL AND DATA

The ASX operates a centralized electronic limit order book similar to other prominent exchanges in Europe (e.g. Euronext) and Asia (e.g. Tokyo Stock Exchange, Hong Kong Stock Exchange and Korea Stock Exchange). The market opens with a call auction and thereafter all trading is conducted via a continuous order-driven auction, until the close of the day when another call auction is used to set the closing price. During normal trading, brokers submit orders with size and price conditions which are matched with an order(s) on the opposite side of the book, if possible, otherwise they remain in the limit order book. Orders with the most competitive price are executed first and where prices are the same, orders that were submitted first have precedence. Prior to 28 November 2005, brokers were able to see broker identifiers of other limit orders as well as the broker counter parties to a trade after a transaction occurred.[8] Since the change to an anonymous regime, all pre-trade identifiers have been removed. In terms of post-trade information, participants can obtain, for a fee, an aggregated summary of each broker's transactions after the close of trading. The summary provides the total volume per broker per security traded on that day. Complete trade by trade broker counterparty information, formerly reported immediately after trade, is now only available three trading days after the initial transaction. In this study, we investigate how this change in the disclosure of pre- and post-trade broker identifiers allows informed traders to conceal themselves from other market participants. This research investigates the ability of the market to detect informed trading in 40 days prior to takeover announcements announced two years either side of the transparency shift on 28 November 2005.

A list of merger and takeover announcements is obtained from Thomson DataStream and supplemented by another list obtained from Bloomberg. To ensure the cleanliness of the pre-announcement period, where a firm has been the subject of multiple takeover offers, we only consider the first announcement in the list.

The intraday trade and quote data used in this study is obtained from two sources: the Securities Institute Research Centre of Asia-Pacific (SIRCA) and the internal database of the ASX. Both data sets include the price, size and time of every trade for each firm in the sample. Trades that occur during the opening and closing call auctions are excluded from the sample. The SIRCA data set provides best quotes that prevailed immediately before each trade (required for the calculation of trade direction), while the ASX data provides the broker counterparties to each trade. The SIRCA data set covers a period that allows analysis of all takeover announcements made two years either side of the transparency change – 28 November 2003 to 28 November 2007.[9] This dataset is used to test *H2* and *H3*. The data set sourced internally from the ASX covers only one year either side of the change, 28 November 2004 to 28 November 2006. This data set is merged with the SIRCA data set and is used to test *H1*.

If a trade is executed at the prevailing ask price (or greater if the order walks up the book), then the trade is classified as buyer initiated. Seller-initiated trades are classified in a similar way. Unlike studies conducted in U.S. markets, trade classification via an algorithm, such as Lee and Ready (1991), is unnecessary since the structure of the ASX requires that trades are executed against existing standing limit orders. Therefore, there is less ambiguity with respect to whether a trade is buyer or seller initiated, with all trades classified accurately.

We are primarily interested in 40 days prior to the takeover announcement not including the day of the takeover announcement (hereafter, the 'pre-announcement period'). However, we also require intraday trading data up to 150 days prior to the announcement to ascertain benchmark metrics for the calculation of abnormal volume and returns. The benchmark period in our sample is from days $t=-50$ to $t=-150$, where $t=0$ is the day of the announcement. A target firm is purged from the sample if it does not have at least 20 days of trading during the pre-announcement period or at least 50 days of trading during the benchmark period. For the main analysis, we also exclude 10 firms whose pre-announcement period spans both the transparent and anonymous regimes. These firms are kept aside for an additional robustness test to ascertain whether the observed results are caused not by the switch to anonymity but by broader market trends. After all filters are applied, this leaves a total of 258 takeover targets over the period 28 November 2003 to 28 November 2007. Of our final sample, 95 were announced in the transparent broker regime and 163 announcements occurred in the anonymous broker regime. For the restricted ASX sample used to test *H1*, there are 178 takeover targets, 68 in the transparent regime and 110 in the anonymous regime.

Summary statistics of the target firms for the entire sample are presented in Table 1. The statistics indicate that the nature of the takeover firms is not materially different between the two sample periods. The mean value for market capitalization of the firms (calculated by taking the average daily market capitalization in the benchmark period) is reasonably similar between the regimes taking the value of $686.44 million in the transparent environment compared to $765.92 million in the anonymous environment. This is important since firm size is correlated with a number of important metrics such as the level of informed trading (Hasbrouck, 1991), the bid-ask spread (Roll, 1984) and the magnitude of the stock price to volume relationship (Breen, Hodrick, & Korajczyk, 2002). This makes it less likely that our results are driven by differences in the characteristics of the firms across the two regimes. The daily pre-announcement traded

Table 1. Summary Statistics.[a]

	Mean	Median	Max	Min	SD
Panel A: All Takeovers (n = 258)					
Market capitalization (pre run-up, $millions)	736.6	112.8	15,893	2.12	1,780
Daily trading volume ('000s shares)	2,610	968.0	34,799	2.79	47,840
Trade size ('000s shares)	13.31	6.96	180.9	0.14	21.11
Daily volatility (%)	3.31	3.00	12.68	0.61	1.73
Pre-announcement return (%)	6.61	4.68	121.3	− 80.52	20.63
Post-announcement return (%)	9.10	4.77	79.37	− 14.99	14.00
Panel B: Transparent Regime (n = 95)					
Market capitalization (pre run-up, $millions)	686.4	140.8	7,408	6.52	1,373
Daily trading volume ('000s shares)	2,465	1,157	29,926	2.79	4,279
Trade size	13.90	8.42	117.3	0.63	19.41
Daily volatility	2.98	2.70	12.68	0.80	1.71
Pre-announcement return (%)	7.26	3.12	121.3	− 80.52	21.44
Post-announcement return (%)	8.11	2.56	79.37	− 14.68	14.22
Panel C: Anonymous Regime (n = 163)					
Market capitalization (pre run-up, $millions)	765.9	106.8	15,893	2.12	1,982
Daily trading volume ('000s shares)	2,694	806.5	34,799	4.32	5,067
Trade size	12.96	6.10	180.94	0.14	22.09
Daily volatility	3.51	3.26	9.14	0.61	1.72
Pre-announcement return (%)	6.23	5.54	89.33	− 50.49	20.20
Post-announcement return (%)	9.96	6.34	54.19	− 14.99	13.56

[a]This table reports summary statistics of the takeover targets in the sample. *Market capitalization* is the average daily market capitalization of the firm during the 'benchmark period' (days $t = -150$ to $t = -50$ where the announcement date is $t = 0$). *Daily trading volume* is the average daily number of shares traded in the firm's stock during the 'pre-announcement' period (days $t = -40$ to $t = -1$). *Trade size* is the average size of each trade during the pre-announcement period. Daily volatility is the average daily value of (High − Low)/(High + Low)÷2 for each firm. *Pre-announcement return* is the simple return over the pre-announcement period. *Post-announcement return* is the return from days $t = 0$ to $t = 2$.

volume during both periods is similar, with a mean value of 2,465,070 shares in the transparent regime compared to 2,694,620 shares in the anonymous regime. Again, this is a reassuring statistic since overall trading activity is a known determinant of bid-ask spreads (Demsetz, 1968; McInish & Wood, 1992) and price impact (Breen et al., 2002). Other potential indicators of informed trading such as trade size and volatility are also reasonably similar between the two trading environments. In the transparent (anonymous) period, the mean trade size is 13,900 (12,960) shares and the average daily volatility is 2.98% (3.51%).

There is a difference in the ratio of pre-announcement and post-announcement stock abnormal return before and after the structural change. The ratio between mean pre- to post-announcement abnormal returns is higher when broker identifiers are visible (0.89) compared to when they are anonymous (0.63). This result provides the first indication that informed traders are generally more hidden after the switch to an anonymous regime since less of the overall abnormal stock return occurs before the announcement is made. We investigate this issue with greater rigour in the following section by examining bid-ask spreads, the order imbalance to return relationship and the dispersion in permanent price impact using univariate and multivariate analyses.

METHODOLOGY AND RESULTS

Dispersion in Permanent Price Impact Across Brokers

In this section, we calculate the dispersion in broker-level permanent price impact and compare this metric between the two regimes. For each buyer-initiated market order in the sample, indicated by the subscript i, the permanent price impact is calculated as:

$$\text{Permanent Price Impact (or PPI}_i) = \frac{P_{i,t=+5} - P_{i,t=-5}}{P_{i,t=-5}} \tag{1}$$

where $P_{i,t}$ represents the midpoint of the bid-ask spread at time t, which denotes the trade relative to the trade of interest $P_{i,t=0}$.[10,11] Since an important determinant of price impact is the size of the trade, trades are divided into four relative trade size groups. This is accomplished by first calculating each stock's median trade size during the pre-announcement period and then comparing each trade to the median value:

$$\text{Relative Trade Size} = \frac{\text{Trade Size}}{\text{Median Trade Size}} \tag{2}$$

Trade size groups are defined as follows: *Group 1* contains all trades where Relative Trade Size (RTS) $<$ 1; *Group 2* contains all trades where $1 \le RTS < 2$; *Group 3* contains all trades where $2 \le RTS < 5$ and Group 4 contains all trades where $RTS \ge 5$.[12] Our variable of interest is the average permanent price impact per broker, b, per trade size group, g subdivided by the two market structure regimes, denoted by the Bernoulli variable d ($d=0$ for the transparent broker regime):

$$\frac{\sum_{i=1}^{N(i_{b,g,d})} \text{PPI}_{i,b,g,d}}{N(i_{b,g,d})} = \overline{\text{PPI}}_{b,g,d} \tag{3}$$

where $N(i_{b,g,d})$ equals the number of market-order buys initiated by broker b, falling into trade size group g, in market structure regime d. The dispersion characteristics of this value are compared between different transparency regimes. Two measures of dispersion are used. The first measure is the standard deviation (or its square, the variance) of average permanent price impact across brokers. Differences between the regimes are tested using the traditional F-test for equal variances.

The second measure of dispersion, developed by Fligner and Killeen (1976), is a non-parametric measure which utilizes the ranks of the absolute deviates from the median, $|\overline{\mathrm{PPI}}_{b,g} - \mathrm{Median}(\overline{\mathrm{PPI}}_{b,g})|$. Once ranked, the variables are transformed into scores according to $s_{b,g} = \left[\Phi^{-1}\left(\frac{N(b_g)+1+r_{b,g}}{2(N(b_g)+1)}\right)\right]^2$, where Φ is the function for the standard normal distribution, $N(b_g)\frac{1}{2}$ is the number of brokers which executed trades of size g and $r_{b,g}$ is the rank of broker b's absolute deviate from the median for size group g. The Fligner–Killeen (FK) (1976) test statistic is calculated by summing these scores across the transparent regime, $FK_g = \sum_{b=1}^{N(b_{g,d=0})} s_{b,g}$. Following Donnelly and Kramer (1999), we take the z-approximation of the *FK* statistic.[13] The FK test is preferred to the traditional F-test for equal variances, since the F-test is very sensitive to non-normality (McGrath & Yeh, 2005). Furthermore, the FK test accounts for differences in scale of the underlying comparison variables. Finally, Donnelly & Kramer (1999) show that the Fligner–Killeen (1976) is superior to a number of other tests for equal dispersion in terms of maintaining an appropriate balance between Type I and Type II error rates. Nevertheless, the traditional F-test is included for completeness.

Table 2 reports the results of both tests for equal dispersion. The results indicate that the standard deviation of permanent price impact across brokers experiences a reduction from 32.34 basis points to 27.72 basis points. This reduction is not significant at the 5% level based on the traditional F-test (*p-value* is 0.09) but exhibits significance at that level based on the Fligner–Killeen (1976) test. When stratified by trade size group, the dispersion of permanent price impact between brokers is lower after the switch to broker anonymity. The results are significant at the 1% level for all groups except *Group 1* and *Group 4* under the Fligner–Killeen (1976) test, where the test statistics are significant at the 5% level. The greater dispersion in permanent price impact across brokers in the transparent regime suggests that broker identifiers have incremental signalling value when they are visible to the market in the lead up to takeover announcements.

Table 2. Dispersion in Permanent Price Impact Across Brokers.[a]

	Transparent Regime		Anonymous Regime		Test of Differences	
	SD (bp)	No. of brokers	SD (bp)	No. of brokers	F-statistic	Fligner–Killeen statistic
All	32.34	73	27.72	77	1.36	1.67*
Group 1	39.95	68	29.34	76	1.86**	1.81*
Group 2	47.37	70	23.58	75	4.02**	3.09**
Group 3	46.88	68	25.46	74	3.39**	2.75**
Group 4	40.77	51	25.01	75	2.66**	1.65*

*Indicates significance at the 5% level.

**Indicates significance at the 1% level.

[a]This table reports the standard deviation of permanent price impact across brokers according to the size of the trade. The trade size groups are defined as: *Group 1* contains all trades where *relative trade size (RTS)* < 1; *Group 2* contains all trades where 1 ≤ *RTS* < 2; *Group 3* contains all trades where 2 ≤ *RTS* < 5 and Group 4 contains all trades where *RTS* ≥ 5 where *RTS* is defined as the size of the trade divided by the median trade size in the pre-announcement period. The table reports the F-statistic for the test of equal variances and the z-approximation to the FK statistic for equal dispersion. Both tests are unidirectional tests against a null hypothesis of equal dispersion between the regimes.

The incremental signalling value appears to be greatest for the intermediate trade size groups (*Groups 2 and 3*) which possess the largest test statistics under both dispersion tests. This might be expected given the information asymmetry potential of medium-sized trades. Barclay and Warner (1993) show that 'medium-sized' trades rather than large trades are perceived by the market to contain the greatest information value, though of course, not all medium-sized trades are motivated by information. Indeed Chakravaty (2001) shows that it is not medium-sized trades per se that generate permanent price movements, but rather, medium-sized trades initiated by institutional investors that alert other participants to the presence of informed trading. Given this uncertainty for medium-sized trades, it might be possible that the broker identifiers are used to distinguish medium-sized trades which originate from institutional investors (and are therefore more likely to represent informed trading), against those which are less likely information motivated. The data do not allow for an exploration of this hypothesis, since the broker identifiers are simply alphanumerical codes and cannot be linked (by the researcher) to institutional investors. Nevertheless, the results of this section suggest that broker identifiers possess some informational value. As such, informed traders are more concealed after the change to an anonymous broker market.

Bid-Ask Spread

Table 3 compares the magnitude of bid-ask spreads between the two broker identification regimes. Using univariate analysis, there is mixed evidence that spreads have declined, and therefore informed traders are less detected, after the switch to anonymity. We sample bid-ask spreads immediately before each trade for a given security in a given day and use the trade-weighted average as a measure of the stock's percentage bid-ask spread for that day. After pooling all daily observations across all stocks and all days, we calculate the mean and median of daily percentage bid-ask spreads. These results are presented in Table 3 as well as parametric and non-parametric tests for differences between the regimes. Univariate analysis provides mixed evidence for *H1*. Both mean and median daily percentage spreads are lower in the post period. The mean (median) percentage bid-ask spread decreases from 1.70% (1.24%) in the transparent regime to 1.67% (1.11%) in the anonymous regime. A one way t-test indicates that daily percentage bid-ask spreads are not significantly lower at the 5% level after the switch to anonymity. However, a non-parametric Wilcoxon two-sample rank sum test, indicates that daily percentage bid-ask spreads are significantly lower in the anonymous period. The z-statistic approximation to the Wilcoxon statistic is 3.87 which is significant at the 1% level.

To further investigate the robustness of our univariate results we also examine the change in the adverse selection component of the spread.

Table 3. Bid-Ask Spreads: Univariate Analysis.[a]

	Mean		Median		Tests for Differences	
	Transparent	Anonymous	Transparent	Anonymous	T-test	Wilcoxon
Percentage bid-ask spreads (%)	1.71	1.67	1.24	1.11	1.09	3.87**
Adverse selection component (%)	32.09	27.26	32.21	26.82	2.65**	2.94**

**Indicates significance at the 1% level.

[a]This table reports the mean and median of the average daily percentage bid-ask spread as well as the mean and median adverse selection cost component of the spread. This table also reports tests of the hypothesis that the value in the transparent broker identifier regime is larger than the value in the anonymous broker identifier regime (one-tailed test). The difference is tested using a parametric t-test and a non-parametric Wilcoxon test.

We perform this analysis because the theory underpinning our hypothesis is that liquidity suppliers are less able to detect informed trading in an anonymous regime and therefore factor in a lower adverse selection component into the bid-ask spread. Statistics examining total bid-ask spreads might therefore be capturing changes in some other aspect of the spread (inventory holding or order processing) that is unrelated to adverse selection and as such uninformative about our hypothesis. We calculate the adverse selection cost component of the bid-ask spread using the method developed in Lin, Sanger, and Booth (1995) and subsequently applied to an electronic limit order market in Brockman and Chung (1999). The adverse selection component is calculated by estimating the following regression for each firm over the entire 40-day pre-announcement period:

$$\Delta Q_{t+1} = \lambda z_t + e_{t+1} \tag{4}$$

where Q is the natural log of the bid-ask spread midpoint, z is the natural log of the difference between the transaction price and the bid-ask spread midpoint and e is a normally distributed error term. The coefficient on z, λ, measures the adverse selection component of the bid-ask spread. Table 3 presents the calculated values of the adverse selection cost component, averaged across the number of firms in the respective regime, before and after the switch to broker anonymity. The results indicate that the mean (median) adverse selection component decreases from 32.09% (32.21%) to 27.26% (26.82%) in the anonymous period. The adverse selection cost component is significantly lower at conventional levels when assessed using a t-test or a Wilcoxon two sample rank sum test. The results suggest that informed traders are not as easily detected after the removal of broker identifiers since liquidity suppliers do not incorporate as large an adverse selection cost component into the bid-ask spread.

Finally, to ascertain the extent to which informed traders go undetected by liquidity suppliers in the market in a multivariate setting the following pooled cross-sectional regression is estimated:

$$\text{PBAS}_{jt} = \beta_0 + \beta_1{}^{*} D_{jt} + \beta_2{}^{*}\ \text{Volume}_{jt} + \beta_3 \text{Volatility}_{jt} + \sum_{i=1}^{3} \gamma_i{}^{*}\ \text{Size}_{jti} \tag{5}$$

PBAS is the (trade-weighted average) daily proportional bid-ask spread for firm j on day t, where as previously, the bid-ask spread is sampled immediately before each trade. The dummy variable, D, takes the value 0 during the transparent regime and 1 during the anonymous regime. Volume, volatility and market capitalization variables are also include in the regression specification as control variables (McInish & Wood, 1992). *Volume* is the firm's turnover for the day. *Volatility* is defined as the natural log of the day's price range divided by the closing price. To avoid contamination from the stock run up that occurs during the pre-announcement period, firm size is calculated by averaging the daily market capitalization of the firm over the benchmark period. The firms are then ranked and placed into four groups based on quartile ranking. The quartile cut-off values are \$41.92 million (25th percentile), \$112.85 million (50th percentile), \$507.38 million (75th percentile) and \$15,894 million (100th percentile). In the regression, γ_i is equal to 1 if the firm is in size quartile i and 0 otherwise. The results of the regression are presented in Table 4. We report the results based on the entire pre-announcement period and for robustness, sub-groups of observations according to proximity to the announcement date.

The results indicate that after controlling for volatility, volume and firm market capitalization, during the pre-announcement period, bid-ask spreads are smaller in the anonymous broker regime. The coefficient on the anonymity dummy variable is negative and significant and indicates that spreads are 24 basis points per trade lower when broker identifiers are hidden (Table 4, column 1). This suggests that liquidity suppliers are not price protecting as aggressively and that informed traders are therefore, more concealed after a switch to broker anonymity.

An analysis of the results based on the time to the announcement date indicates that this result is robust across the pre-announcement period. The magnitude of the coefficient on the dummy variable is greatest in the period furthest away, that is 40 to 31 days, prior to the announcement (Table 4, column 5). The value of the coefficient is −39 basis points. In the final 30 days the results are reasonably consistent across the sub-periods, ranging between 18 and 20 basis point reductions in bid-ask spreads (Table 4, columns 2–4). This result indicates that in the anonymous market, despite the fact that there is less detection of informed trading as indicated by the negative coefficient on the dummy variable, the ability of informed traders to remain hidden is lower in the final 30 days leading up the announcement compared to days −40 to −31. This might be because other indicators, unrelated to broker identifiers, such as rumours, volume or price run-ups reveal the presence of informed traders to the market and these indicators are more prevalent closer to the

Table 4. Bid-Ask Spreads: Multivariate Analysis.[a]

	Days −40 to −1	Days −10 to −1	Days −20 to −11	Days −30 to −21	Days −40 to −31
Intercept	4.99	4.84	5.04	4.95	5.24
	(64.44)	(32.95)	(31.98)	(31.95)	(32.28)
D	− 0.24	− 0.18	− 0.20	− 0.19	− 0.39
	(− 7.86)	(− 3.11)	(− 3.24)	(− 3.15)	(− 6.00)
Volume	− 21.53	− 16.55	− 33.65	− 25.43	− 20.32
	(− 13.89)	(− 5.43)	(− 7.04)	(− 7.19)	(− 8.35)
Volatility	0.43	0.43	0.40	0.44	0.46
	(21.23)	(11.24)	(10.06)	(10.70)	(10.97)
Size 2nd Q	− 1.53	− 1.40	− 1.68	− 1.55	− 1.50
	(− 33.60)	(− 16.17)	(− 18.16)	(− 17.46)	(− 15.66)
Size 3rd Q	− 2.21	− 2.12	− 2.38	− 2.12	− 2.22
	(− 48.87)	(− 24.63)	(− 26.05)	(− 23.87)	(− 23.39)
Size 4th Q	− 2.75	− 2.65	− 2.86	− 2.67	− 2.81
	(− 59.74)	(− 30.20)	(− 30.61)	(− 29.59)	(− 29.11)
N	8755	2146	2224	2168	2210
Adjusted R^2	41.11%	42.25%	41.35%	41.96%	39.52%

$$PBAS_{jt} = \beta_0 + \beta_1{}^*D_{jt} + \beta_2{}^*Volume_{jt} + \beta_3 Volatility_{jt} + \sum_{i=1}^{3} \gamma_i{}^*Size_{jti}$$

D is a dummy variable which takes a value of 1 during the anonymous broker regime and 0 otherwise; *Volume* is the firm's turnover for the day; and *Volatility* is defined as the natural log of the day's price range divided by the closing price. *Size 2nd Q* is a dummy variable which takes the value of 1 if the firm falls within the second quartile of firms by market capitalization and 0 otherwise. *Size 3rd Q* and *Size 4th Q* are similarly defined. The regression is estimated using daily trading data from 40 days prior to 252 takeover announcements. The regression is also estimated using various sample subsets partitioned according to proximity to the announcement date. The relevant hypothesis is whether the coefficient on the anonymity switch dummy variable is significantly less than zero, that is, H_a: $\beta < 0$.

[a]This table reports the coefficient values and t-statistics (in brackets) of a regression of daily median percentage bid-ask spread (PBAS) on the following independent variables.

announcement date. Alternatively, it is possible to argue that there is negligible informed trading in the period −40 to −31 during the anonymous regime and the result in this period is driven not by a lack of detection, but a lack of informed trading whatsoever. To ensure the robustness of our results, we rerun the analysis with only a 30-day pre-announcement window. The coefficient on the broker anonymity dummy variable is negative (−0.19) and significant at the 1% level. Therefore, our conclusions remain unchanged.

Order Imbalance and Returns

In this section, we test the sensitivity of daily returns to contemporaneous order imbalances. The following pooled cross-sectional regression is estimated:

$$R_{jt} = \beta_0 + \beta_1{}^*D_t + \beta_2{}^*OI_{jt} + \beta_3{}^*OI_{jt}{}^*D_t + \sum_{i=1}^{3} \gamma_i{}^*\text{Size}_{jti} + \sum_{m=1}^{4} \phi_m{}^*\text{Day}_m + \sum_{k=1}^{5} \lambda_k R_{it-k} + \varepsilon \qquad (6)$$

where R_{jt} and OI_{jt} represent the standardized beta-adjusted excess return[14] and standardized order imbalance respectively of firm j on day t, and D_t is a dummy variable which takes the value of 1 if the day falls on or after 28 November 2005 and zero otherwise. Included within the regression are dummy variables to control for the effect that firm size and day of the week might have on excess returns. Finally, we also include five lags of the dependent variable to control for possible autocorrelation in excess returns. Following Cao et al. (2005) both excess returns and order imbalances are standardized by the mean and standard deviation of the variables over the benchmark period. Specifically, the dependent variable is the excess return standardized by the standard deviation of excess returns during the benchmark period. Order imbalance is calculated by first taking the difference between the number of buyer-initiated market orders and the number of seller-initiated market orders for a given day then dividing by the average volume over the benchmark period. The variable is then standardized using its mean and standard deviation during the benchmark period. The standardization allows observations from different firms, with potentially divergent return and volume characteristics, to be more suitably combined in a pooled cross-sectional regression.

The results of the regression are presented in Table 5. The results indicate that in both regimes greater order imbalance leads to larger returns. The coefficient on OI_{jt} is positive and significant at 0.351 which indicates that when order imbalance is one standard deviation greater than its benchmark mean excess returns are 0.351 standard deviations greater than zero. This result is consistent with the notion that excess buying conveys positive information about the firm. However, as indicated by the coefficient on the interaction variable $OI_{jt}{}^*D$, −0.032, this relationship is significantly weaker when broker identifiers are anonymous. During the anonymous broker regime vis-à-vis the transparent market, similar levels

Table 5. Order Imbalance and Returns.[a]

Variable	Order Imbalance	Volume Imbalance
Intercept	0.018	− 0.009
	(0.06)	(− 0.03)
D	0.351	0.437
	(1.40)	(1.71)
OI_{jt}	0.244	0.327
	(28.90)	(26.98)
$OI_{jt}{}^{*}\ D$	− 0.032	− 0.193
	(− 2.59)	(− 13.52)
N	8116	8116
Adj. R^2	14.73%	11.43%

$$R_{jt} = \beta_0 + \beta_1{}^{*}D_t + \beta_2{}^{*}OI_{jt} + \beta_3{}^{*}OI_{jt}{}^{*}D_t + \sum_{i=1}^{3}\gamma_i{}^{*}\text{Size}_{jti} + \sum_{m=1}^{4}\varphi_m{}^{*}\text{Day}_m + \sum_{k=1}^{5}\lambda_k R_{it-k} + \varepsilon$$

The dependent variable is the beta-adjusted daily excess return standardized by the variable's standard deviation over the benchmark period. D is a dummy variable which takes a value of 1 during the anonymous broker regime and 0 otherwise. OI_{jt} is the standardized daily order imbalance or the total volume imbalance. The relevant hypothesis is whether the coefficient on the interaction variable $OI_{jt}{}^{*}\ D$ is significantly less than zero, that is, $H_a{:}\beta < 0$.

[a]This table reports the coefficients and t-statistics (in brackets) of the variables of interest based on the following regression model.

of order imbalance do not lead to as large a price movement in target firms prior to the takeover announcement. This might be because, for a given return, other traders do not trade as much in the same direction as informed traders or, for a given imbalance, there is a lower permanent price impact after buying (or both). In any case, it appears that the market does not respond as strongly to trading which suggests that a takeover announcement is imminent, after the removal of broker identifiers. To test the robustness of our results the same regression is estimated using total volume imbalance, rather than order imbalance (which disregards the magnitude of the trades). The results based on volume imbalance provide corroborating evidence that the switch to an anonymous broker market impairs the ability of the market to detect informed trading.

ADDITIONAL TESTS

One argument that can be made against any research that investigates the effects of a one-off change to market structure is that the results could be driven by broader market trends over the sample period rather than being directly related to the structural change.[15] Applied specifically to this study, this argument questions whether the results of the preceding analysis are driven by the change in broker anonymity or, alternatively, gradual changes to the various metrics being analysed. For example, it is well accepted that bid-ask spreads decrease over time, casting doubt over the results presented in section 'Bid-Ask Spreads'.

A second criticism that can be laid against the findings in the fourth section is that the results indicate a reduction in informed trading, rather than impaired detection. For example, the adverse selection component of bid-ask spreads might be lower in the anonymous regime because there are less informed traders, not because the market has become less efficient at detecting informed traders. This might occur because the markets information asymmetry is decreasing over time, or there is something particular about the takeovers in the anonymous regime, relative to the transparent regime, that lends itself to having less information asymmetry. As a counter to this argument we note that the *ex ante* expectation of increased broker anonymity is that there would be *greater* information asymmetry rather than less. Indeed Rindi's (2008) model of information acquisition and transparency predicts that broker anonymity is correlated with more informed traders, since the benefits of becoming informed are larger in an anonymous market. Therefore, if any bias exists it is likely to be directed against our findings.

To address both criticisms empirically, we investigate 10 firms whose 40 day pre-announcement period straddles the change to an anonymous regime on 28 November 2005. These firms were excluded from the original analysis. The sample period of this subset of firms is 71 trading days from 11 October 2005 to 20 January 2006. The rationale for analysing this sample is that these firms span the shortest possible time frame for which there is still variation in the transparency of broker identifiers, thereby minimizing the effect of any gradual improvement in liquidity while still making it possible to perform the analyses conducted in the fourth section.

In terms of the second criticism, it is our expectation that the level of information asymmetry within a particular event is relatively constant throughout the pre-announcement period. At the very least, the intra-event variation in information asymmetry is likely to be less than inter-event variations in information asymmetry. As such, analysing these 10 firms minimizes the possibility that the results are driven by changes in the level of information asymmetry.

As per the analysis in the fourth section, the dispersion in permanent price impact across brokers is calculated for this robustness sample. Since the number of firms is much smaller than the main analysis, there are many brokers which only execute a handful of trades in these 10 securities. To ensure that we have an appropriate representation of the average information content of a given broker's trades, brokers who execute less than 15 trades in these 10 securities are not considered for analysis. This leaves a total of 20 active brokers in the transparent regime and 18 in the anonymous regime. When not stratified by trade size, the standard deviation of permanent price impact across brokers falls from 43.40 basis points to 19.81 basis points. This implies an F-statistic of 4.79 which is significant at the 1% level. In the Fligner–Killeen (1976) test for equal dispersion, the z-approximation to FK-statistic is 1.77 which is significant at the 5% level.[16] These results validate the findings of the initial analysis and provide evidence that the results are not driven by broader market trends or differences in the takeover targets before and after the anonymity switch.

To ensure the robustness of the bid-ask spread analysis we re-estimate Eq. (4), the results of which are presented in Table 6. While estimated on a small independent sample of firms, the results are reasonably similar to the main analysis. The coefficient on the anonymity change dummy variable indicates that this sample experiences an 18 basis point reduction in bid-ask spreads after a switch to broker anonymity compared to a 24 basis point reduction for the main sample. This result is significant at the 10% level, when tested against the hypothesis that the coefficient is less than zero. Given the proximity of the sub-sample sample to the anonymity switch, this indicates that the concealment effect of informed trades appears to have occurred immediately or very soon after the change.[17] The results of this robustness test suggest that broader improvements to market quality are not driving the results of the main analysis.

The regression of order imbalance and returns is re-estimated using the observations of those firms whose pre-announcement period straddles the change on 28 November 2005. The results are presented in Table 7. The coefficients on the variables of interest are similar to those in the main analysis. Excess returns are significantly positively related to order imbalance with a coefficient of 0.688 and also total volume imbalance which has a coefficient of 0.549. The coefficient on the interaction variable is negative at −0.135 and −0.110 for order imbalance and total volume imbalance respectively. This indicates that after the switch to anonymity the relationship between returns and imbalances is weaker, a finding which reconfirms *H3*. The results of this robustness test indicate that informed traders

Table 6. Additional Test for Bid-Ask Spreads.[a]

	Coefficient		t-Statistic
Intercept	4.79		15.61
D	− 0.18		− 1.42
Volatility	0.62		7.59
Volume	− 55.06		− 4.97
Size 2nd Q	− 0.38		− 1.69
Size 3rd Q	− 0.95		− 6.72
Size 4th Q	− 1.55		− 7.44
N		324	
Adjusted R^2		37.82%	

D is a dummy variable which takes a value of 1 during the anonymous broker regime and 0 otherwise; *Volume* is the firm's turnover for the day; and *Volatility* is defined as the natural log of the day's price range divided by the closing price. *Size 2nd Q* is a dummy variable which takes the value of 1 if the firm falls within the second quartile of firms by market capitalization and 0 otherwise. *Size 3rd Q* and *Size 4th Q* are similarly defined. The relevant alternative hypothesis is whether the coefficient on the anonymity switch dummy variable is significantly less than zero, that is, H_a: $\beta < 0$. The coefficient on the anonymity switch dummy variable is −0.18 which has a *p-value* of 0.078 with respect to the alternative hypothesis.

[a]This table reports the results of the same regression model documented in Table 4, using a smaller sample of 10 firms whose pre-announcement period includes the date of the transparency change.

$$\text{PBAS}_{jt} = \beta_0 + \beta_1{}^*D_{jt} + \beta_2{}^*\text{Volume}_{jt} + \beta_3\text{Volatility}_{jt} + \sum_{i=1}^{3}\gamma_i{}^*\text{Size}_{jti}$$

appear to be better hidden after the switch to anonymity and this finding is not driven by a secular change in the relationship between returns and imbalances over time.

CONCLUSION

In this study, we present three pieces of evidence that show that, in the lead up to takeover announcements, informed traders are more concealed, and therefore, better off after broker identifiers were removed from the electronic trading screen at the ASX on 28 November 2005. Firstly, we show that the dispersion in permanent price impact of trades across brokers is significantly lower after the change. This suggests that the market used the identifiers to help distinguish informed from uninformed trades during the transparent regime. Put differently, our results suggest that broker identifiers have informational value. The fact that they have been

Table 7. Additional Test for Order Imbalance and Returns.[a]

Variable	Order Imbalance	Volume Imbalance
Intercept	− 1.497	0.389
	(− 1.47)	(0.40)
D	2.483	0.648
	(2.04)	(0.55)
OI_{jt}	0.688	0.549
	(13.44)	(15.50)
OI_{jt}* *D*	− 0.135	− 0.123
	(− 1.93)	(− 2.38)
N	303	303
Adjusted R^2	52.17%	55.48%

The dependent variable is the beta-adjusted daily excess return standardized by the variable's standard deviation over the benchmark period. *D* is a dummy variable which takes a value of 1 during the anonymous broker regime and 0 otherwise. *OIjt* is the standardized daily order imbalance or the total volume imbalance. The relevant hypothesis is whether the coefficient on the interaction variable OI_{jt}* *D* is significantly less than zero, that is, $H_a{:}\beta<0$. With respect to this alternative hypothesis, the coefficient on OI_{jt}* *D* where OI_{jt} is measured by the order (volume) imbalance, is significant at the 5% (1%) level.

[a]This table reports the coefficients and t-statistics (in brackets) of the variables of interest based on the below regression model for a smaller sample of 10 firms whose pre-announcement period includes the date of the transparency change.

$$R_{jt} = \beta_0 + \beta_1{}^*D_t + \beta_2{}^*OI_{jt} + \beta_3{}^*OI_{jt}{}^*D_t + \sum_{i=1}^{3}\gamma_i{}^*\text{Size}_{jti} + \sum_{m=1}^{4}\varphi_m{}^*\text{Day}_m + \sum_{k=1}^{5}\lambda_k R_{it-k} + \varepsilon$$

removed indicates that informed traders are more concealed after the transparency change.

Secondly, we show that after the removal of broker identifiers bid-ask spreads are significantly lower in the days leading up to a takeover announcement. This suggests that liquidity suppliers are not engaging in as much price protection compared to when identifiers were revealed. Indeed, the adverse selection component of the spread falls significantly in the anonymous regime suggestive of the fact that informed traders remain less detected by the market. Finally, an analysis of the relationship between returns and order imbalances shows that while there is a positive relationship between the two variables, the relationship is weaker in the anonymous broker regime. Again, this suggests that the market is not able to detect informed traders as readily when broker identifiers are concealed.

The results have important policy implications for exchange officials of electronic markets considering whether to reveal or hide the identities of brokers surrounding trades. Evidence from prior literature indicates that the concealment of identifiers is correlated with lower bid-ask spreads (Comerton-Forde & Tang, 2009; Comerton-Forde et al., 2005; Foucault et al., 2007). However, the results of this study indicate that bid-ask spreads remain lower, even when a significant information announcement is pending. Taken together the research suggests that the removal of broker identifiers has a mixed effect for uninformed traders. When no information event is pending, uninformed traders enjoy improved liquidity. However, when information asymmetry is large, the ability of uninformed traders to detect and protect themselves from the informed is impaired. To resolve the issue as to whether broker identifiers should be revealed or not, research is required which analyses and quantifies the trade-off between these two competing factors. We leave this as a possible avenue for future investigation.

NOTES

1. Theoretical work by Foucault et al. (2007) and Rindi (2008), and a study conducted in an experimental market by Perotti and Rindi (2006) support these empirical results. The overwhelming consensus amongst published literature is that pre-trade or post-trade broker anonymity reduces bid-ask spreads.

2. This reasoning is in the same spirit as Pagano and Röell (1996). However, their paper concerns the effects of order book price and depth transparency rather than broker identifiers.

3. The authors use medium-sized trades (500–9900 shares) of corporate insiders as a proxy for informed trading. They justify this proxy with reference to Barclay and Warner (1993) who show that informed traders are more likely to use medium-sized trades and Seyhun (1986) who shows that insider trades earn abnormal profits, and are therefore, likely to be information-motivated.

4. For example, Gleason (2007) documents that market maker competition dampens market-wide ability to detect informed trading. It is possible then that the results of Garfinkel and Nimalendran (2003) are driven by this difference between the exchanges.

5. Another data-related advantage arises from the fact that the market being analysed is a centralized electronic limit order market. Therefore, trade classification algorithms, such as the Lee and Ready (1991) algorithm commonly adopted in studies of U.S. markets, are not required to discern trade direction. Since all trades (excluding upstairs trading) must be executed at either the best prevailing bid or ask, it is possible to classify with certainty whether a trade is buyer or seller initiated. This facet of the data allows us to accurately calculate order imbalances for the firms in our sample.

6. Note this hypothesis does not require us to identify which broker identifiers are associated with informed trading and which ones are not.

7. A wide bid-ask spread indicates a greater probability that an information event has occurred.

8. The identifiers are alphanumeric codes and therefore do not explicitly identify the broker. However, the identifiers, once allocated, are fixed over time and discussions with officials at the ASX indicate that market participants can link alphanumeric codes to the relevant broker.

9. The actual data set sourced from SIRCA spans a period slightly longer than four years, since we also require 150 days of trading data prior to the announcement in order to calculate various benchmarks for volume and returns.

10. We focus only on buyer initiated orders in order to restrict the sample to trades which can be motivated by information. We make the assumption that seller initiated trades prior to a takeover announcements are not informed trades.

11. For robustness we also consider alternative specifications, where the permanent price impact is calculated from $t = -10$ to $t = +10$, from $t = -1$ to $t = +5$ and from $t = open$ to $t = close$. The conclusions drawn from the results of these alternate specifications are not different. Thus, only the results from $t = -5$ to $t = +5$ are presented.

12. These values are chosen to approximately represent the following percentile groups: Group 1 – 0 to 50th percentile; Group 2 – 50th to 75th percentile; Group 3 – 75th to 90th percentile; Group 4 – 90th to 100th percentile. Other cut-off values are considered with similar results.

13. $z = \frac{FK_g - E(FK_g)}{\sqrt{Var(FK_g)}}$

where $E(FK_g) = N(b_{g,d=0})^* \overline{s_g}, \overline{s_g}$ is the average score for trade size group g and

$$Var(FK_g) = \frac{N(b_{g,d=0})^* N(b_{g,d=1})}{(N(b_g) - 1)^* N(b_g)} * \sum_{b=1}^{N(b_g)} \left[s_{b,g} - \bar{s}_g \right].$$

14. Each firms' beta is calculated by estimating the market model of returns over the benchmark period.

15. See Majois (2007) for a critique of natural experiments methodology.

16. We also perform the analysis with stratification on trade size, though the statistical tests lack power due to the very small number of observations. When we stratify into two trade size groups divided at $RTS = 1$, the sample size pairs for (transparent, anonymous) are (11,11) and (12,13) for the small and large trade size group respectively. Nevertheless, the standard deviation for the small group falls from 47.21 basis points to 32.91 basis points, while for the large trade size group the standard deviation falls from 32.98 to 17.89. The F-statistics implied by these values are 2.06 and 3.40 respectively, the latter of which is significant at the 5% level. The corresponding (raw) Fligner-Killeen test statistics are 11.68 and 13.78 respectively. While still in the expected direction these values are not significant at conventional levels.

17. In an additional test, we estimate firm-specific time series regressions rather than a pooled cross-sectional regression. While the small sample size of each regression (maximum number of observations is 40) reduces the precision of the parameter estimates, they are nevertheless unbiased. The results indicate that eight out of the ten firms have a negative value on the anonymity switch dummy variable.

REFERENCES

Bagehot, W. (1971). The only game in town. *Financial Analysts Journal, 27*(2), 12–14.

Barclay, M. J., & Warner, J. B. (1993). Stealth trading and volatility: Which trades move prices? *Journal of Financial Economics, 34*(3), 281–305.

Benveniste, LM, Marcus, AJ, & Wilhelm, WJ (1992). What's special about the specialist? *Journal of Financial Economics, 32*(1), 61–86.

Breen, W. J., Hodrick, L. S., & Korajczyk, R. A. (2002). Predicting equity liquidity. *Management Science, 48*(4), 470–483.

Brockman, P., & Chung, D. Y. (1999). Bid-ask spread components in an order-driven environment. *Journal of Financial Research, 22*(2), 227–246.

Cao, C., Chen, Z., & Griffin, J. M. (2005). Informational content of option volume prior to takeovers. *Journal of Business, 78*(3), 1073–1109.

Chakravarty, S. (2001). Stealth trading: Which traders' trades move stock prices? *Journal of Financial Economics, 61*, 289–307.

Comerton-Forde, C., Frino, A., & Mollica, V. (2005). The impact of limit order anonymity on liquidity: Evidence from Paris, Tokyo and Korea. *Journal of Economics and Business, 57*(6), 528–540.

Comerton-Forde, C., & Tang, K. M. (2009). Anonymity, liquidity and fragmentation. *Journal of Financial Markets, 12*(3), 337–367.

Conroy, R. M., & Winkler, R. L. (1981). Informational differences between a limit and a market order for a market maker. *Journal of Financial and Quantitative Analysis, 16*(5), 703–724.

Copeland, T. E., & Galai, D. (1983). Information effects on the bid-ask spread. *Journal of Finance, 38*(5), 1457–1469.

Demsetz, H. (1968). The cost of transacting. *Quarterly Journal of Economics, 82*(1), 33–53.

Donnelly, S. M., & Kramer, A. (1999). Testing for multiple species in fossil samples: An evaluation and comparison of tests for equal relative variation. *American Journal of Physical Anthropology, 108*(4), 507–529.

Easley, D., Kiefer, N. M., & O'Hara, M. (1997). One day in the life of a very common stock. *Review of Financial Studies, 10*(3), 805–835.

Easley, D., Kiefer, N. M., O'Hara, M., & Paperman, J. B. (1996). Liquidity, information and infrequently traded stocks. *Journal of Finance, 51*(4), 1405–1436.

Easley, D., & O'Hara, M. (1987). Price, trade size and information in securities markets. *Journal of Financial Economics, 19*(1), 69–90.

Fishe, R. P. H., & Robe, M. A. (2004). The impact of illegal insider trading in dealer and specialist markets: Evidence from a natural experiment. *Journal of Financial Economics, 71* (3), 461–488.

Fligner, M. A., & Killeen, T. J. (1976). Distribution-free two sample tests for scale. *Journal of the American Statistical Association, 71*(353), 210–213.

Foucault, T., Moinas, S., & Thiessen, E. (2007). Does anonymity matter in electronic limit order markets? *Review of Financial Studies, 20*(5), 1707–1747.

Garfinkel, J. A., & Nimalendran, M. (2003). Market structure and trader anonymity: An analysis of insider trading. *The Journal of Financial and Quantitative Analysis, 38*(3), 591–610.

Gleason, K. (2007). Does market maker competition affect the response to insider trading? *Applied Financial Economics, 17*(9), 691–700.

Glosten, L. R. (1994). Is the electronic limit order book inevitable? *Journal of Finance*, *49*(4), 1127–1161.

Glosten, LR, & Milgrom, PR (1985). Bid, ask and transaction prices in a specialist market with heterogeneously informed traders. *Journal of Financial Economics*, *14*(1), 71–100.

Hachmeister, A., & Schiereck, D. (2010). Dancing in the dark: Post-trade anonymity, liquidity and informed trading. *Review of Quantitative Finance and Accounting*, *34*(2), 145–177.

Harris, L. (2003). *Trading and exchanges*. New York, NY: Oxford University Press.

Hasbrouck, J. (1991). Measuring the information content of stock trades. *Journal of Finance*, *46*(1), 179–207.

Jarrell, G. A., & Poulsen, A. B. (1989). Stock trading before the announcement of tender offers: Insider trading or market anticipation? *Journal of Law, Economics and Organization*, *5*(2), 225–248.

Keown, A., & Pinkerton, J. (1981). Merger announcements and insider trading activity: An empirical investigation. *Journal of Finance*, *36*(4), 855–869.

Kraus, A., & Stoll, H. (1972). Price impacts of block trading on the New York stock exchange. *Journal of Finance*, *27*(3), 569–588.

Lee, C., & Ready, M. (1991). Inferring trade direction from intraday data. *Journal of Finance*, *46*(2), 733–746.

Lin, J., Sanger, G. C., & Booth, G. G. (1995). Trade size and components of the bid-ask spread. *Review of Financial Studies*, *8*(4), 1153–1183.

Maher, O., Swan, P., & Westerholm, J. (2008). Twilight falls on the limit order book: Endogeneity and the demise of broker identity. Available at SSRN, http://ssrn.com/abstract=1090001 or http://dx.doi.org/10.2139/ssrn.1090001

Majois, C. (2007). Natural experiments methodology and global liquidity in financial markets. Working paper. Retrieved from http://ssrn.com/abstract = 1008753.

McGrath, R. N.,, & Yeh, A. B. (2005). A quick, compact, two sample dispersion test: Count five. *The American Statistician*, *59*(1), 47–53.

McInish, T. H., & Wood, R. A. (1992). An analysis of intraday patterns in bid/ask spreads for NYSE stocks. *Journal of Finance*, *47*(2), 753–764.

Meulbroek, L. K. (1992). An empirical analysis of illegal insider trading. *Journal of Finance*, *47*(5), 1661–1699.

Pagano, M., & Röell, A. (1996). Transparency and liquidity: A comparison of auction and dealer markets with informed trading. *Journal of Finance*, *51*(2), 579–611.

Perotti, P., & Rindi, B. (2006). Market for information and identity disclosure in an experimental open limit order book. *Economic Notes*, *35*(1), 97–119.

Rindi, B. (2008). Informed traders as liquidity providers: Anonymity, liquidity and price formation. *Review of Finance*, *12*(3), 497–532.

Roll, R. (1984). A simple implicit measure of the effective bid-ask spread in an efficient market. *Journal of Finance*, *39*(4), 1127–1139.

Seyhun, H. (1986). Insiders' profits, costs of trading, and market efficiency. *Journal of Financial Economics*, *16*(2), 189–212.

Umlauf, S. R. (1991). Information asymmetries and security market design: An empirical study of the secondary market for U.S. Government Securities. *Journal of Finance*, *46*(3), 929–953.

APPENDIX – TABLE A

Exchange	Date of Change	Academic Literature
Australian Stock Exchange	28 November 2005	Comerton-Forde and Tang (2009)
Paris Bourse	23 April 2001	Foucault et al. (2007); Comerton-Forde et al. (2005)
Korea Stock Exchange	25 October 1999	Comerton-Forde et al. (2005)
Tokyo Stock Exchange	30 June 2003	Comerton-Forde et al. (2005)
Deutsche Börse	27 March 2003 to 10 April 2003	Hachmeister and Schiereck (2010)
Brussels Stock Exchange	21 May 2001	Maher et al. (2008)
Borsa Italiana	21 January 2004	No academic literature to the best of our knowledge

PART V
TRANSPARENCY IN THE PUBLIC SECTOR

CENTRAL BANK AND PRIVATE SECTOR'S WELFARE UNDER PARTIAL TRANSPARENCY VERSUS PUBLICITY: A TWO-PLAYER MONETARY POLICY GAME

Emna Trabelsi

ABSTRACT

This chapter contributes to the continuous debate on the effects of public information. The debate initiated with Morris and Shin (2002) who showed that heightening the precision of public information can be detrimental to welfare in a beauty contest framework, because when agents have both private and public information, they may overreact to the public information since it acts as a focal point. If the private agents overreact to public information, then a policy of limited transparency may be warranted. Some researchers suggest partial announcement (limited publicity), others propose to disseminate the public information privately to each agent (limited precision) with some idiosyncratic noise in order to reduce overreaction. Those chapter, however, miss the following fact;

Transparency and Governance in a Global World
International Finance Review, Volume 13, 321–335

ISSN: 1569-3767/doi:10.1108/S1569-3767(2012)0000013014

they don't take into account the interaction between private sector and the central bank. We extend those studies by setting the framework as a two-player monetary policy game between the central bank and the private sector by allowing explicitly for a central bank to be one of the many contributors of the public signal. We show (1) how introducing a certain degree of opacity affects both players and determines the conditions under which an intermediate transparent strategy improves the outcome of the private sector, as well as of the central bank. We find that reducing transparency doesn't affect the two players in the same way. (2) It turns out that respective players' losses are strictly identical when the central bank implements the optimal degree of transparency or the optimal degree of publicity. We establish then an equivalence relationship in terms of effects between publicity and transparency for both actors.

Keywords: Transparency; public information; monetary policy game; central bank

JEL classifications: D82; E58

INTRODUCTION

Shall central banks talk too much? Most economists are instinctually of the view that more information is better than less and hence agree that openness and communication with the public are crucial for the effectiveness of monetary policy, in allowing the private sector to improve expectations.

Not everyone agrees with that theory. Morris and Shin (2002) argue that noisy public information may be detrimental to welfare because agents may put too much weight on public information relative to private signals since it serves as a focal point. Morris and Shin (2002) suggest reducing the precision of public information or even withholding it. In order to reduce overreaction to public information, Cornand and Heinemann (2008) claimed that private sector's welfare increases in the precision of public information if the degree of publicity is sufficiently small. While Heinemann and Illing (2002) argue that the central bank should release information to each agent privately with some idiosyncratic noise to avoid commonality. In this note, we would like to discuss further those ideas by introducing two main points: We allow explicitly for a central bank to be one of the many contributors of the public signal in the spirit of Demertzis and Hoeberichts (2007). Monetary policy is now a game of two players: the central bank and the private sector. The second innovation concerns the equivalence in terms of effects between both partial transparency regimes mentioned above.

The reminder of this chapter is follows; we describe the loss function to be minimized by the central bank in the second section, we give in the third section the informational structure relative to both partial transparency regimes (limited precision versus limited publicity). The fourth section concerns the welfare effects and the section five illustrates the equivalence effect. Finally, some concluding remarks are offered in the sixth section.

DESIGNING THE CENTRAL BANK'S LOSS

We assume a quadratic loss function for the central bank, constrained by the standard Lucas supply function that takes the following form:

$$\begin{cases} \text{Min}_{\pi} E(L^{CB}) = E[(\pi - \pi^T)^2 + bx^2] \\ s.tx = \pi - \pi^e + s \end{cases} \tag{1}$$

where π denotes a measure of inflation, π^T is the inflation target, x represents the output gap, b is the weight on output gap stabilization relative to the inflation stabilization, such that $b > 0$ and s is a shock with mean 0 and variance σ_s^2. Such a function means that the central bank conducts the monetary policy so as to stabilize inflation around the target, but it also attaches some weight to stabilizing the real economy as represented by the output gap, the employment gap, or the unemployment gap. This describes a flexible inflation targeting central bank. However, in what follows, even if the central bank is conservative (i.e., less flexible), this will not change the qualitative nature of our results[1]. The optimization of Eq. (1) implies

$$\pi|_s = \frac{1}{1+b}\pi^T + \frac{b}{1+b}(\pi^e - s) \tag{2}$$

where π is the ex post inflation outcome given the shock s and π^e is the collective private sector expectation about the rate of inflation. We assume for simplification that $s = 0$, and we rewrite Eq. (2) in a general form:

$$\pi = (1 - r)\pi^T + r\pi^e \tag{3}$$

where r represents the coordination motive whose values lie between 0 and 1 (as it will be shown in subsequent subsections).

The timing of the game is as follows; the central bank provides its public signal (whether partially or with idiosyncratic noise) to the private sector, the latter forms its expectations. Following that the central bank needs to implement the policy rule.

THE FORMATION OF EXPECTATIONS

We depart from a commitment setup and allow agents to form expectations based on all available information. Let π_j^e be the individual expectation of inflation by an individual j. The average expectation across all agents is given by

$$\pi^e = \int \pi_j^e dj$$

The model is a two-stage game in which the private sector interacts with the central bank. The private sector's objective would be minimizing the following disutility function:

$$\underset{\pi_j^e}{\text{Min}}\, u_j(\pi^e, \pi^T) = E_j(\pi_j^e - \pi)^2 \tag{4}$$

Agent j decides his action π_j^e based on the first-order condition of Eq. (4):

$$\pi_j^e = E_j(\pi)$$

And from Eq. (3)

$$\pi_j^e = E_j((1-r)\pi^T + r\pi^e) = (1-r)E_j(\pi^T) + rE_j(\pi^e) \tag{5}$$

The optimal expected inflation by an agent j is thus a function of two things: the view about the true state of the inflation target and the view concerning the collective expected inflation.

Limited Precision: Idiosyncratic Public Noise

In practice, even signals that are released as common signals may evoke private information. In their speculative-attack game, Heinemann and

Illing (2002) discuss an alternative way of reducing the degree of common knowledge: instead of releasing a common signal, the central bank might want to release information to agents in private. We will take this alternative and remodel it in a context a beauty contest model.

We suppose that the central bank targets π^T, but the public receives, instead, two types of signals:

A private signal:

$$p_j = \pi^T + \varepsilon_j \tag{6}$$

And a biased (with more or less ambiguity) *public signal*:

$$u_j = \pi^T + \eta + \varphi_j \tag{7}$$

where ε_j, η, and φ are normal with 0 mean and variances $V(\varepsilon_j) = \sigma_\varepsilon^2, V(\eta) = \sigma_\eta^2$ and $V(\varphi_j) = \sigma_\varphi^2$ respectively.

Based on these two signals, and applying Eqs. (6) and (7) on Eq. (5), we obtain

$$\pi_j^e = \frac{(1-r)\sigma_\eta^2 + \sigma_\varphi^2}{\sigma_\varepsilon^2 + (1-r)\sigma_\eta^2 + \sigma_\varphi^2} p_j + \frac{\sigma_\varepsilon^2}{\sigma_\varepsilon^2 + (1-r)\sigma_\eta^2 + \sigma_\varphi^2} u_j \tag{8}$$

Proof. See appendix.

Note that when $\sigma_\varphi^2 = 0$, the decision rule in Eq. (8) is reduced to that of Morris and Shin (2002).

Limited Publicity: P-Common Beliefs

Walsh (2006) and Cornand and Heinemann (2008) propose an original definition of transparency based on the degree of information dissemination: in this new framework, the central bank may decide to reveal its information, not only to all agents but also to a part of the population. Walsh (2006) used this definition in terms of information dissemination, while Cornand and Heinemann (2008) also retain the definition of transparency in terms of information more or less noisy. The authors show, based on the results of Morris and Shin, in situations such as public information is not desirable because of its effect of coordinating the expectations on an equilibrium that moves away from the optimum, a more precise public signal, but revealed only to a portion of the population is higher from a welfare perspective than a signal of low precision revealed to all agents. The fact that information is not revealed to the general population reduces the incentives of individuals to overreact to the public signal, and therefore reduces the deleterious effect associated with higher-order beliefs. Reducing the number of agents who receive the public signal is, according to these authors, an effective way to avoid the negative effects resulting from the coordination of expectations. Ultimately, if the public signal is very accurate, then the central bank has the interest to reveal it to all agents. In contrast, information with low precision should make the object of a partial publication, that is, a limited number of individuals. Accordingly, the informational structure would be

A private signal: $p_j = \pi^T + \varepsilon_j$

And a *public signal*: $u = \pi^T + \eta$ observed by a proportion P of the population.

P measures the degree of publicity such as $0 < P < 1$.

Based on these two types of signals, the optimal individual action is given by

$$\pi_j^e = \frac{(1-rP)\sigma_\eta^2}{\sigma_\varepsilon^2 + (1-rP)\sigma_\eta^2} p_j + \frac{\sigma_\varepsilon^2}{\sigma_\varepsilon^2 + (1-rP)\sigma_\eta^2} u \tag{9}$$

Proof. See appendix for details

Clearly, $P = 1$ corresponds to the particular case of Morris and Shin (2002). The weight attached to the public signal is smaller than the weight attached to fully public information (see Table 1 for comparison).

Table 1. Comparison Between Weights Attached to Public Information

Cases		Weight in the Case of Full Publicity $\frac{\sigma_\varepsilon^2}{\sigma_\varepsilon^2+(1-r)\sigma_\eta^2}$
Idiosyncratic public noise	$\delta_2 = \frac{\sigma_\varepsilon^2}{\sigma_\varepsilon^2+(1-r)\sigma_\eta^2+\sigma_\phi^2}$	$<$
Limited publicity	$\lambda_2 = \frac{\sigma_\varepsilon^2}{\sigma_\varepsilon^2+(1-rP)\sigma_\eta^2}$	$<$

Note: The table shows how implementing limited transparency generates a smaller weight to the public information than when it is fully disseminated.

WELFARE EFFECTS

Limited Precision: Idiosyncratic Public Noise

The central bank is faced with this optimization problem:

$$\begin{cases} \text{Min}_\pi\, E(L^{CB}) = E[(\pi - \pi^T)^2 + b(\pi - \pi^e)^2] \\ s.t\ \pi^e = \delta_1 \pi^T + \delta_2 u \end{cases} \tag{10}$$

Optimization of Eq. (10) implies

$$\pi^* = \pi^T + \frac{b}{1+b}\delta_2 \eta = \pi^T + \frac{b}{1+b}\frac{\sigma_\varepsilon^2}{\sigma_\varepsilon^2 + (1-r)\sigma_\eta^2 + \sigma_\varphi^2}\eta \tag{11}$$

The unconditional expected loss function is written as

$$E(L^{CB}) = E(\pi^* - \pi^T)^2 + bE(\pi^* - \pi^e)^2$$

We replace π^* by its expression in Eq. (3), we obtain finally

$$E(L^{CB}) = \frac{b}{1+b}\frac{\sigma_\varepsilon^4 \sigma_\eta^2}{[\sigma_\varepsilon^2 + (1-r)\sigma_\eta^2 + \sigma_\varphi^2]^2} \tag{12}$$

Differentiating with respect to σ_φ^2 yields

$$\frac{\partial E(L^{CB})}{\partial \sigma_\varphi^2} = \frac{b}{1+b}\frac{-2\sigma_\varepsilon^4 \sigma_\eta^2}{[\sigma_\varepsilon^2 + (1-r)\sigma_\eta^2 + \sigma_\varphi^2]^3} \leq 0$$

This means that increasing σ_φ^2 (i.e., reducing transparency) decreases the central bank's expected loss.

Turning to the private sector, we have

$$E(L^{PS}) = E(E_j(\pi) - \pi^T)^2 = \frac{\sigma_\varepsilon^2[\sigma_\varphi^2 + (1-r)\sigma_\eta^2]^2 + \sigma_\varepsilon^4(\sigma_\eta^2 + \sigma_\varphi^2)}{(\sigma_\varepsilon^2 + (1-r)\sigma_\eta^2 + \sigma_\varphi^2)^2} \tag{13}$$

$$\frac{\partial E(L^{PS})}{\partial \sigma_\varphi^2} = \frac{\sigma_\varepsilon^4[\sigma_\varepsilon^2 + (1-3r)\sigma_\eta^2 + \sigma_\varphi^2]}{(\sigma_\varepsilon^2 + (1-r)\sigma_\eta^2 + \sigma_\varphi^2)^3} \leq 0 \Rightarrow \sigma_\varphi^2 \leq \sigma_\varepsilon^2 + (3r-1)\sigma_\eta^2$$

Furthermore, it is also true that reducing transparency doesn't affect the two players in the same way. It follows that

Proposition 1. *For any decreases in the precision of the public signal (i.e.,* $\partial\sigma_{\varphi}^2 > 0$*), the central bank benefits more than the private sector.*

Proof. As the differentiation of the central bank expected loss to σ_{φ}^2 is not sensitive to parameter b, we can write $\frac{\partial E(L^{CB})}{\partial\sigma_{\varphi}^2} = \frac{-2\sigma_{\varepsilon}^4\sigma_{\eta}^2}{[\sigma_{\varepsilon}^2+(1-r)\sigma_{\eta}^2+\sigma_{\varphi}^2]^3}$ and then, we have

$$\frac{\partial E(L^{CB})}{\partial\sigma_{\varphi}^2} - \frac{\partial E(L^{PS})}{\partial\sigma_{\varphi}^2} = -\frac{\sigma_{\varepsilon}^4(\sigma_{\varepsilon}^2 + 3(1-r)\sigma_{\eta}^2 + \sigma_{\varphi}^2)}{[(\sigma_{\varepsilon}^2 + (1-r)\sigma_{\eta}^2 + \sigma_{\varphi}^2]^3} \leq 0$$

Fig. 1 demonstrates this for a given parameterization of $r=0.6$. We observe a decrease in the difference between both marginal losses as σ_{φ}^2 increases.

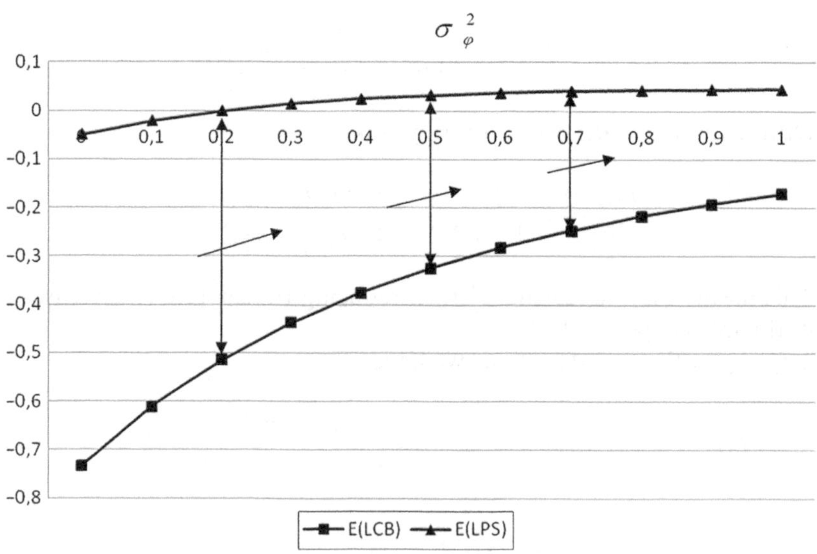

Fig. 1. Marginal Losses of Both Players Against σ_{ϕ}^2. Parameters Used for Calibration ($\sigma_{\varepsilon}^2 = 1, \sigma_{\eta}^2 = 1,5$, $r=0,6$).

Limited Publicity: P-Common Beliefs

The central bank is faced now with this optimization problem:

$$\begin{cases} \text{Min}_\pi E(L^{CB}) = E[(\pi - \pi^T)^2 + b(\pi - \pi^e)^2] \\ s.t \quad \pi^e = P(\lambda_1 \pi^T + \lambda_2 u) + (1-P)\pi^T \end{cases} \tag{14}$$

Optimization of Eq. (14) implies

$$\pi^* = \pi^T + \frac{b}{1+b} P \lambda_2 \eta = \pi^T + \frac{b}{1+b} P \frac{\sigma_\varepsilon^2}{\sigma_\varepsilon^2 + (1-rP)\sigma_\eta^2} \eta \tag{15}$$

The unconditional expected loss function is written as

$$E(L^{CB}) = E(\pi^* - \pi^T)^2 + bE(\pi^* - \pi^e)^2$$

We replace π* by its expression in Eq. (7), we obtain finally

$$E(L^{CB}) = \frac{b}{1+b} \frac{\sigma_\varepsilon^4 \sigma_\eta^2 P^2}{[\sigma_\varepsilon^2 + (1-rP)\sigma_\eta^2]^2} \tag{16}$$

Differentiating with respect to

$$P: \frac{\partial E(L^{CB})}{\partial P} = \frac{b}{1+b} \sigma_\varepsilon^4 \sigma_\eta^2 P \frac{2[\sigma_\varepsilon^2 + (1-rP)\sigma_\eta^2] + 2r\sigma_\eta^2 P}{\left[\sigma_\varepsilon^2 + (1-rP)\sigma_\eta^2\right]^3} \geq 0$$

When the publicity degree P increases, the expected loss of the central bank increases.

On the other hand,

$$\frac{\partial E(L^{PS})}{\partial P} = \frac{\sigma_\varepsilon^2 \sigma_\eta^4 (1-rP)^2 + \sigma_\varepsilon^4 \sigma_\eta^2}{[\sigma_\varepsilon^2 + (1-rP)\sigma_\eta^2]^2} + \frac{2r^2 P^2 \sigma_\varepsilon^4 \sigma_\eta^4}{\left[\sigma_\varepsilon^2 + (1-rP)\sigma_\eta^2\right]^3} - \sigma_\varepsilon^2$$

As both expressions are not unequivocally signed, we will determine the condition required for the derivatives to sign one way. Starting with the central bank, it is clear that increasing the publicity degree P is always harmful to its welfare.

For the private sector, the necessary condition for which increasing the publicity degree is detrimental to the welfare is

$$\frac{\partial E(L^{PS})}{\partial P} \geq 0 \Rightarrow \frac{\sigma_\varepsilon^2 + \sigma_\eta^2}{3r\sigma_\eta^2} \leq P \leq 1$$

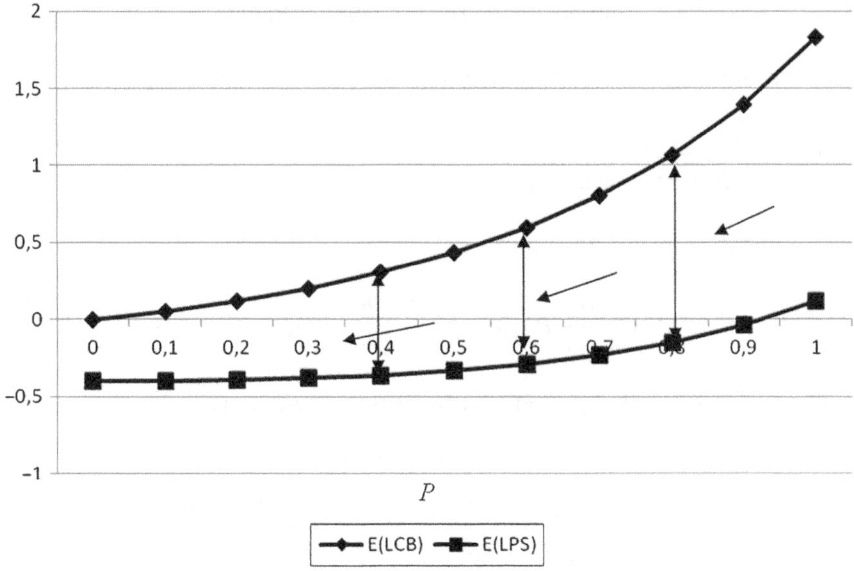

Fig. 2. Marginal Losses of Both Players Against *P*. Parameters Used for Calibration ($\sigma_{\varepsilon}^{2} = 1, \sigma_{\eta}^{2} = 1,5, r = 0, 6$).

If *P* is low, the difference between players' marginal losses tends to decrease (see Fig. 2). This means that the difference is not unequivocally signed and then there are instances for which One of the players benefits the most. In fact, we observe an inverted pattern of the Fig. 1, which means, if we replace the x-axis with $1/P$ values, we will have the same shape as in Fig. 1.

We can now draw the following proposition:

Proposition 2. *When the public information is less precise* ($\partial\sigma_{\varphi}^{2} > 0$) *or partially disclosed (P low), the central bank benefits more than the private sector.*

WELFARE UNDER OPTIMAL PUBLICITY VERSUS OPTIMAL TRANSPARENCY

Now, we propose to establish an equivalence relationship between both intermediate transparency regimes.

Optimal transparency: For the private sector, the first-order and second-order condition yield

$$\begin{cases} \dfrac{\partial E(L^{PS})}{\partial \sigma_{\varphi}^2} = 0 \Leftrightarrow \sigma_{\varphi}^2 = (3r-1)\sigma_{\eta}^2 - \sigma_{\varepsilon}^2 \\ \dfrac{\partial^2 E(L^{PS})}{\partial (\sigma_{\varphi}^2)^2} \geq 0 \Leftrightarrow \sigma_{\varphi}^2 \leq (4r-1)\sigma_{\eta}^2 - \sigma_{\varepsilon}^2 \end{cases} \tag{17}$$

The second-order condition is satisfied for $\sigma^{*2}_{\varphi} = (3r-1)\sigma_{\eta}^2 - \sigma_{\varepsilon}^2$. Finally, the optimal degree of transparency would be $\sigma^{*2}_{\varphi} = \text{Max}\,(0, (3r-1)\sigma_{\eta}^2 - \sigma_{\varepsilon}^2)$

Proposition 3. *If $\sigma_{\varepsilon}^2 < (3r-1)\sigma_{\eta}^2$ and $r > \frac{1}{3}$, then the best strategy for the central bank is to disseminate privately its information to the private sector. If $\sigma_{\varepsilon}^2 > (3r-1)\sigma_{\eta}^2$ or the coordination motive is small ($r < \frac{1}{3}$), then disseminating fully the public information turns to be the best strategy.*

The respective players' expected loss functions that result from this optimum are given by

$$E(L^{CB}) = \text{Min}\left(\frac{b}{1+b}\frac{\sigma_{\varepsilon}^4\sigma_{\eta}^2}{[\sigma_{\varepsilon}^2 + (1-r)\sigma_{\eta}^2]^2}, \frac{b}{1+b}\frac{\sigma_{\varepsilon}^4}{4r^2\sigma_{\eta}^2}\right)$$

$$E(L^{PS}) = \text{Min}\left(\frac{\sigma_{\varepsilon}^2[(1-r)\sigma_{\eta}^2]^2 + \sigma_{\varepsilon}^4\sigma_{\eta}^2}{(\sigma_{\varepsilon}^2 + (1-r)\sigma_{\eta}^2)^2}, \frac{\sigma_{\varepsilon}^2(4r\sigma_{\eta}^2 - \sigma_{\varepsilon}^2)}{4r\sigma_{\eta}^2}\right)$$

Optimal publicity degree: We derive the optimal degree of P^*. The first and second derivations of the unconditional private sector's expected loss are

$$\begin{cases} \dfrac{\partial E(L^{PS})}{\partial P} = 0 \Rightarrow P = \dfrac{\sigma_{\varepsilon}^2 + \sigma_{\eta}^2}{3r\sigma_{\eta}^2} \\ \dfrac{\partial^2 E(L^{PS})}{\partial P^2} \geq 0 \Leftrightarrow P(3 - 6(1-r) + 3(1-r)^2)\sigma_{\eta}^2 \geq 0 \end{cases} \tag{18}$$

For the sake of generality, the optimal degree of publicity is given by $P^* = \min\left\{1, \frac{\sigma_{\varepsilon}^2+\sigma_{\eta}^2}{3r\sigma_{\eta}^2}\right\}$

Reducing the degree of publicity is optimal when the precision of central bank's information is low, and when the degree of strategic complementarities (r) is strong.

Proposition 4. *If* $P^* < 1 \Leftrightarrow \sigma_\varepsilon^2 < (3r-1)\sigma_\eta^2$ and $r > \frac{1}{3}$, *then the best strategy for the central bank is to disseminate its information only to a portion of the private sector. If* $\sigma_\varepsilon^2 > (3r-1)\sigma_\eta^2$ or the coordination motive is small ($r < \frac{1}{3}$), *then disseminating fully the public information turns to be the best strategy.*

In the same vein, the expected loss functions of the central bank and the private sector at the optimum are written as

$$E(L^{CB}) = \mathrm{Min}\left(\frac{b}{1+b}\frac{\sigma_\varepsilon^4\sigma_\eta^2}{[\sigma_\varepsilon^2+(1-r)\sigma_\eta^2]^2}, \frac{b}{1+b}\frac{\sigma_\varepsilon^4}{4r^2\sigma_\eta^2}\right)$$

$$E(L^{PS}) = \mathrm{Min}\left(\frac{\sigma_\varepsilon^2[(1-r)\sigma_\eta^2]^2+\sigma_\varepsilon^4\sigma_\eta^2}{(\sigma_\varepsilon^2+(1-r)\sigma_\eta^2)^2}, \frac{\sigma_\varepsilon^2(4r\sigma_\eta^2-\sigma_\varepsilon^2)}{4r\sigma_\eta^2}\right)$$

It turns out that both losses are identical to the case of optimal transparency.

CONCLUDING REMARKS

To sum up, the central bank can indifferently implement one of both disclosure strategies to reduce the degree of common knowledge since implementing a limited degree of transparency or a limited degree of publicity yields the same welfare effects and the same welfare value at the optimum. From practical point of view, limiting the publicity as recommended by Cornand and Heinemann (2008) would be hard to implement in real world, given the widespread development of media compared to limiting the precision of public information. In fact, a recent comparison between both regimes has been made available through experimental economics by Cornand and Baeriswyl (2011)[2] and their results state that partial publicity would be difficult to implement due to discrimination and fairness issues.

This note sheds light on key issues that face central bankers, such as communication and transparency and helps to think strategically about solutions that focus on best practices and adding value. Furthermore, with respect to the loss function of the central bank designed in the second section, we have considered the transparency problem that arises from misunderstanding about the value π^T that the central bank is expected to implement. This is what we call *economic transparency*. However, transparency problems may also arise from misunderstanding about the true value of the preference b or the shock s. Such issues have to be further examined.

Admittedly, the model of Morris and Shin and its related framework are controversial (see, e.g., Svensson, 2006) but the possibility that more transparency may not always lead to better outcome should be borne in mind. An example of a recent paper, though complex by Goesslin, Lotz, and Wyploz (2009) have extended the arguments of Morris and Shin (2002) to the context of interest rate publication by the central banks and who favor an intermediate transparent strategy, but under circumstances.

ACKNOWLEDGMENT

We are indebted to Walid Hichri for precious comments on an earlier draft.

NOTES

1. The results are totally independent from the exact loss function assumed for the central bank. We can even write $L^{CB} = a(\pi - \pi^T)^2 + bx^2$or suppose that the sum of weights equals one.
2. The experiment takes into account only the effect of such strategies on private sector's welfare.

REFERENCES

Cornand, C., & Heinemann, F. (2008). Optimal degree of public information dissemination. *Economic Journal, 118*(518), 718–734.

Cornand, C., & Baeriswyl, R. (2011). Reducing overreaction to central bank's disclosure: Theory and experiment. GATE Working Paper No. 1141. Retrieved from http://halshs.archives-ouvertes.fr/docs/00/65/79/43/PDF/1141.pdf. Accessed on August 9, 2012.

Demertzis, M., & Hoeberichts, M. (2007). The costs of increasing transparency. *Open Economies Review, 18*(3), 263–280.

Goesslin, P., Lotz, A., & Wyploz, C. (2009). Interest rate signals and central bank transparency (NBER Chapters). In R. Clarida & F. Giavazzi (Eds.), *NBER international seminar on macroeconomics 2007* (pp. 9–51). National Bureau of Economic Research. Retrieved from http://www.nber.org/chapters/c2997

Heinemann, F., & Illing, G. (2002). Speculative attacks: Unique sunspot equilibrium and transparency. *Journal of International Economics*, *58*, 429–450.

Morris, S., & Shin, H. S. (2002). The social value of public information. *American Economic Review*, *92*, 1521–1534.

Svensson, L. E. O. (2006). Social value of public information: Morris and Shin (2002) is actually pro transparency, not con. *American Economic Review*, *96*, 448–451.

Walsh, C. E. (2006). Transparency, flexibility, and inflation targeting. In F. Mishkin & K. Schmidt-Hebbel (Eds.), *Monetary policy under inflation targeting* (pp. 227–263). Santiago, Chile: Central Bank of Chile.

APPENDIX

How to derive mathematically δ_1, δ_2, λ_1, and λ_2?

1. Recall: $\pi_j^e = E_j(\pi)$ be the expected inflation by the individual/agent j conditional on both types of signals. The average expected inflation by the private sector collectively is $\pi^e = \int E_j(\pi)dj$
2. In each case of partial transparency regimes, $E_j(\pi)$ (and therefore π^e) is made a linear function of signals and we know that $E_j(\pi) = E_j((1-r)\pi^T + r\pi^e) = (1-r)E_j(\pi^T) + rE_j(\pi^e)$

Case 1. *Idiosyncratic public signal*

We have $E_j(\pi) = \delta_1 p_j + \delta_2 u_j$
Given

$$E_j(\pi^T) = \frac{\sigma_\eta^2 + \sigma_\varphi^2}{\sigma_\varepsilon^2 + \sigma_\eta^2 + \sigma_\varphi^2} p_j + \frac{\sigma_\varepsilon^2}{\sigma_\varepsilon^2 + \sigma_\eta^2 + \sigma_\varphi^2} u_j$$

$$E_j(u) = \frac{\sigma_\varphi^2}{\sigma_\varepsilon^2 + \sigma_\eta^2 + \sigma_\varphi^2} p_j + \frac{\sigma_\varepsilon^2 + \sigma_\eta^2}{\sigma_\varepsilon^2 + \sigma_\eta^2 + \sigma_\varphi^2} u_j$$

Where the weights attached to signals can be obtained by minimizing $E(E_j(\pi^T) - \pi^T)^2$and $E(E_j(u) - u)^2$, respectively.

We replace $E_j(\pi^T)$ and $E_j(\pi^e) = \delta_1 E_j(\pi^T) + \delta_2 E_j(u)$ by their expressions in Eq. (5) and rearranging terms, we obtain δ_1 *and* $\delta_2 / \delta_1 + \delta_2 = 1$.

Case 2. *P-common beliefs*

We have $E_j(\pi) = \begin{cases} p_j \ \ if \ \ j \in [P, 1] \\ \lambda_1 p_j + \lambda_2 u \ \ if \ \ j \in [0, P] \end{cases}$
Given

$$E_j(\pi^T) = \frac{\sigma_\eta^2}{\sigma_\varepsilon^2 + \sigma_\eta^2} p_j + \frac{\sigma_\varepsilon^2}{\sigma_\varepsilon^2 + \sigma_\eta^2} u$$

$$E_j(\pi^e) = (P\lambda_1 + 1 - P)E_j(\pi^T) + P\lambda_2 E_j(u)$$

$$E_j(u) = u$$

Inserting $E_j(\pi^T)$ and $E_j(\pi^e)$ in Eq. (5) and rearranging terms, we obtain the final weightsλ_1 *and* $\lambda_2 / \lambda_1 + \lambda_2 = 1$.

APPENDIX

OPACITY IN LATIN AMERICA: ARGENTINA AND CHILE: A CASE STUDY COMPARISON

Harvey Arbeláez and Rie Tanaka

ABSTRACT

Governance and opacity issues have increased since the early 1990s and several governance indicators are introduced by international organizations and NGOs. The governance indicators have been used in various sectors, directly affecting a nation's political reputation. This study analyzes the context of governance and opacity in Argentina and Chile and assesses the relationship between the cultural pattern and the functioning of institutions. A first approximation to the analysis of Argentina and Chile seems to lead to the conclusion of the existence of homogeneity between them as a result of a similar background. However, differences in geography and history generate different societal norms, and functioning of institutions within them. Chile's geographical isolation and limited natural resources leads the country toward economic growth and political stability. By contrast, in Argentina, populist regimes undermine the foundations of its economy while its middle class struggles and loses public trust. The various factors interactively affect quality of public policies and governance and, consequently, are conducive to differences in the perceived and real levels of opacity between both countries. Is

Transparency and Governance in a Global World
International Finance Review, Volume 13, 337–377

ISSN: 1569-3767/doi:10.1108/S1569-3767(2012)0000013015

corruption a culture-specific issue? If yes, then, is governance a consequence of culture too? Therefore, it is important to interpret a context behind governance in order to establish appropriate anticorruption reform in practice. This chapter seeks to address some of these issues by means of a case study comparison between Argentina and Chile and contribute to the understanding of the context in which negotiations may occur when FDI and M&A deals take place.

Keywords: Corruption; emerging markets; governance; Latin America; opacity; transparency

JEL classifications: D72; D73; D78; O54

INTRODUCTION

Emerging Awareness of Opacity Issues and Purpose of the Study

A report that emerged over the third weekend of April 2012 revealed a significant case of corruption that involved Wal-Mart in Mexico. The revelations that Wal-Mart greased the wheels of international business with briberies exceeding $24 million were dismissed neither by the media nor by the U.S. government. As a result the market immediately penalized Wal-Mart's wrongdoing with a decline in its stock price by 7% and which in a two-day session meant a value destruction of $10 billion.[1] In addition, by the end of the same week and to incinerate the significance of corruption issues nowadays, Argentina, in a confusing case of clashing interests decided to expropriate the investment of Repsol of Spain in YPF (Yacimientos Petrolíferos Fiscales) by assuming a 51% control of the partnership and with auspices to a return to the days of predominant nationalistic postures such as the Calvo Doctrine policy.

Since early 1990s, there has been growing awareness around the world that corruption is one of the biggest obstacles restraining nation's development, and the corruption issue should be addressed to improve governance effectiveness. Is corruption specific to a country or to a culture? Kersnar (2007) do not think so as a result of an analysis after 37 countries signed the Organization for Economic Cooperation and Development's (OECD) Anti-Bribery Convention. The annual cost of corruption is estimated at $80 billion worldwide, although the cost is believed only as "the tip of the iceberg." According to the IMF, corruption can reduce a country's economic growth rate by more than 0.5 % of GDP (Richardson, 2001). Governance and corruption issues have become widespread in international community, not only for international development sector but also for private business sector. Numerous investigations have been done only in a last decade and various organizations have started to undertake this issue as a prioritized strategy. These organizations include the IMF, the World Bank, the OECD, the United Nations, regional organizations (such as the Inter-American Development Bank and the Asian Development Bank), as well as international nongovernmental organizations (NGOs), especially Transparency International (TI), a leading NGO of anticorruption programs.

Purpose and Organization of the Study

This study aims to interpret the context of opacity in two similar countries, Argentina and Chile, yet so different in many ways. Understanding the real context of opacity is necessary to initiate a further reform. To analyze in depth the context of opacity, this case study compares two countries: Argentina and Chile. These two neighboring countries seem to have relatively similar historical and political background including independence from Spain in the 19th century, experience of authoritarian military dictatorship after WW II, and transition to democracy in 1980s (for an evidence see Adams, 2000; Becker, 2011; Campbell, 2000; Morrison & Conaway, 2007; Toll & Garone, 1997). However, Argentina and Chile have very different reputations in terms of governance indicators. For example, "Chileans value honesty and place much emphasis on reputation" (Toll & Garone, 1997, pp. 25, 29).

A narrative approach from an examination of culture patterns is necessary to interpret each country's governance performance in depth. Following this cultural sequential model, the ensuing sections of the chapter analyze cultural patterns and governance in Argentina and Chile, from exogenous factors to national origins, societal norms, and consequences. The case study examines similarities and differences of each phase between the two countries, and how these different factors consequently affect quality of governance in Argentina and Chile. This analysis could enable to come up with suitable policy reforms to improve the conditions of both countries' governance and contribute to the reduction in opacity, especially for Argentina, whose ranks of governance indicators are lower than in Chile. Following this introduction, the chapter is organized as follows: the second section discusses the meaning of opacity (corruption) and governance as well as the measurement aspects of the governance indicators. The third section describes salient background considerations of both Argentina and Chile, and focuses on societal norms by discussing also specifics of the two countries in the context of their similarities and differences. The fourth section discusses the constitutional and institutional framework of both countries. The fifth section proposes a model of governance as a consequence of culture. The sixth section concludes with a summary of the findings and implications from a comparative analysis of Argentina and Chile, and discusses how to interpret a context of opacity in different countries, particularly in the Latin American region.

OPACITY, GOVERNANCE, AND MEASUREMENT

What Is Opacity and Governance?

Opacity, from the Latin words opacitas or opacus, or corruption, from the Latin word *rumpere*, is any intentional act that breaks integrity, virtue, moral principle, social code of conduct, or an administrative rule that impairs the fulfillment of official policy requirements. A most used definition of corruption is probably "the abuse of public office for private gain," including bribery and extortion, which involve at least two parties, and fraud and embezzlement, which a public official can carry out alone (Gray & Kaufmann, 1998). Corruption includes any immoral or dishonest behavior of people in authority. According to the Organization of American Studies, the formulation of corruption is as follows (Organization of American States, 2007):

$$\text{Monopoly} - \text{Transparency} + \text{Discretion} = \text{Corruption}$$

Applying this formulation, those in absolute power in a nation (e.g., President, or Prime Minister) are more likely to be engaged in corrupt acts, depending on governmental power balance, transparency, and discretion. In the case of an international setting, corruption may mean any intentional attempt to break the organizational requirements of a viable relationship between the political process and the economic changes of the new international political economy, and obstruct reciprocal gains in wealth, well-being, security, and power. Therefore, corruption is generally discussed as a consequence of weak governance and institutions.

The World Bank defines governance as "the traditions and institutions by which authority in a country is exercised. This includes the process by which those in authority are selected, monitored and replaced; the capacity of the government to effectively manage its resources and implement sound policies; and the respect of citizens and the state for the institutions that govern economic and social interactions among them" (Kaufman & Kraay, 2007, p. 6).

Although public attention to governance and corruption issues have rapidly increased in the last decade, corruption itself is not a newborn subject, but a permanent phenomena based on the human nature and condition (Malraux, 1933). In ancient Greece, Plato said that humans naturally seek individual gain or pleasure, and according to Hobbes, a modern philosopher, "cooperative or altruistic behaviors are necessary evils for calculating selfish individuals" (Masters, 1989, p. 3). As discussed among historical philosophers, human beings have both "good" and "evil" sides by nature and opacity is based on the part of "evil," seeking selfish individual gain. Importantly also, it is highlighted that "Ethics and economics were once tightly interwoven. The patriarch of economics, Adam Smith, was actually a scholar of moral philosophy" (Bruner, 2010). This brief reference to the philosophical underpinning of opacity prompts to consider if opacity as a phenomenon is culture specific. This consideration is timely relevant because of the rapid transformation that many economies experience around the world to the point that it makes sense to reflect also on the role of culture as a driver of economic development or, on the contrary, that economic activity influences culture (Finel-Honigman, 2010). Therefore, it may be legitimate to argue the existence of an inclination to opacity in some countries at all costs, if certainly it is needed to avoid missing an opportunity window leading to accelerate plans sought to attain a higher level of economic development, status, and well-being.

Despite the nature of opacity, until the early 1990s, there were few efforts to confront the problem and measure its magnitude. Corruption had been accepted as unavoidable phenomena in many countries with weak institutions and a tradition of bribery (Richardson, 2001). There was also common consensus that opacity or corruption was an untouchable subject in international relations in terms of interference of domestic politics, and most multinational assistance agencies considered it as a political issue and beyond their purview.

There are several reasons why governance and opacity issues started to gain more public attention in the world. The main reasons include (1) the end of Cold War, (2) globalization, and (3) the emergence of an active civil society. According to Tanzi, "the end of Cold War has stopped the political hypocrisy and that had made the decision makers in some industrial countries ignore the political corruption that existed in particular countries" (Tanzi, 1998, p. 561). After the disappearance of the primary ideological conflict between democracy and socialism, governance and anticorruption have emerged as a new strategic ideology for "western" countries and international organizations. Second, globalization has enabled more capital and human mobility among countries, raising more public attention to the countries where corruption is epidemic (Tanzi, 1998). Especially since foreign direct investment (FDI) and capital markets have been growing rapidly, more private companies have seriously considered country and political risk for their trade businesses. Third, since early 1990s, in part because of the pervasive role of information technology, civil societies have started to undertake governance and anticorruption as a development matter. Especially, TI, a NGO located in Germany, has played a significant role in generating broad public recognition that governance and corruption undermine country's development and effectiveness of aid programs. In the case of Latin America, it is worth to note that prior to the 1990s, executives in Latin America spent an inordinate amount of time, energy, and (frequently off-the-books) cash maneuvering within the political system. "The combination of stifling bureaucracy, corrupt officials, and state-owned enterprises that monopolized key areas of the economy made it essential to focus daily management attention on complying with, circumventing, undermining, or swaying an unworkable structure of regulations, laws, and enforcement procedures" (Becker, 2011). Clearly, a "confirmatory bias" toward the prevalence of corruption, bribery and nonethical actions, more than an anxiety it was a reality inviting to frequent situations in which these practices were most likely welcome as ways of doing business as usual.

Nowadays, Latin America means business although not necessarily as usual. Indeed, the backbone of democracy provides healthy rewards to most enterprises in the region after realizing the need to increase their competitiveness and comply with the rule of the law and be less tolerant to corruption by eliminating the necessity to pay bribes to succeed in business. This new posture is well supported by researchers' findings that indicate that as countries become more exposed to globalization and openness of their economies, and become more democratic-oriented, they also experience lower levels of corruption (Sandholtz & Koetzle, 2000; Wei, 2000) even if it is not possible yet to state that corruption is on the defeat. Sadly, it is still rampant in many countries. For example, despite the U.S. Foreign

Corrupt Practices Act (FCPA) of 1977 that brought an added importance to internal auditing procedures of U.S. multinationals and made for the first time "the internal control a question of law and not simply one of technical proficiency" (Ricchiute, 1980), the U.S. Justice Department has recently brought FCPA charges against prominent companies such as Siemens, Alcatel, Willbros, Tyco, and IBM (Tillen & Ellis, 2009). In short, corruption is a delicate issue and, regardless of the analogy, is both a coin with two sides and a knife with a sharp cutting edge.

Governance Indicators

Along with growing international awareness of governance and corruption issues, governance-related indicators have been established to measure each country's governance performance and magnitude of corruption. The well-recognized indexes include Corruption Perception Indexes (CPI) of TI, and Worldwide Governance Indicators (WGI) of the World Bank. The CPI ranks 180 countries by their perceived levels of corruption, as determined by expert assessments and opinion surveys, and ranges between 10 (highly clean) and 0 (highly corrupt) (http://www.transparency.org/policy_research/surveys_indices/cpi/2011). Table 1 shows the CPI score for several countries of the word, Argentina and Chile included, and their respective country and regional country ranks. The World Bank reports 212 countries and territories for six dimensions of governance: voice and accountability, political stability and absence of violence, government effectiveness, regulatory quality, rule of law, and control of corruption.

Their basic processes of determining indicators are as follows: (1) collect data from different organizations and (2) standardize the value of each country based on their own statistical methodology. The original data sources are from various survey institutes, think tanks, NGOs, international organizations, and commercial risk rating agencies.[2] For example, the World Bank uses 311 variables drawn from 33 sources and 30 different organizations for the 2007 WGI. Some of the data sources are surveys of individuals or domestic firms with first-hand knowledge of the governance situation in the country. The data sources include the perceptions of country analysts at the major multilateral development agencies, reflecting their in-depth experience working on the countries. Other data sources from NGOs and commercial risk rating agencies base their assessments on a global network of correspondents typically living in the country they are

Table 1. 2011 Corruption Perception Index Regional Highlights: The Americas.

Country Rank	Regional Country Rank	Country/Territory	CPI Score 2011
10	1	Canada	8.7
16	2	Barbados	7.8
21	3	Bahamas	7.3
22	4	**Chile**	7.2
24	5	United States	7.1
25	6	Saint Lucia	7.0
25	6	Uruguay	7.0
36	8	Saint Vincent and the Grenadines	5.8
39	9	Puerto Rico	5.6
44	10	Dominica	5.2
50	11	Costa Rica	4.8
61	12	Cuba	4.2
73	13	Brazil	3.8
80	14	Colombia	3.4
80	14	El Salvador	3.4
80	14	Peru	3.4
86	17	Jamaica	3.3
86	17	Panama	3.3
91	19	Trinidad & Tobago	3.2
100	20	**Argentina**	3.0
100	20	Mexico	3.0
100	20	Suriname	3.0
118	23	Bolivia	2.8
120	24	Ecuador	2.7
120	24	Guatemala	2.7
129	26	Dominican Republic	2.6
129	26	Honduras	2.6
134	28	Guyana	2.5
134	28	Nicaragua	2.5

Source: Transparency International (2011).

rating as indicated in the following web site: http://info.worldbank.org/governance/wgi/pdf/table1.pdf.

Both CPI and WGI receive extensive international publicity and discussion, and have created political embarrassment in countries ranked near the bottom. International investors have used these indicators to help estimate country-related risks (Richardson, 2001). Governance-related indicators have become widespread and powerful enough to affect country's international reputation, foreign investment environment, and capital market.

Despite widespread recognition and powerful influence of governance-related indicators, however, the real context that determines these indicators remains unclear. Unlike other economic and environmental indicators based on specific facts (e.g., GDP growth and COs emission), governance-related indicators reflect surveys and experts' country assessments, which are not unique "facts" with specific evidence. Governance-related indicators tell just rankings reflecting current governance performance and magnitude of corruption; however, it is not clear how these ranks are determined, and what makes differences among countries despite that, based on 13 independent surveys, it makes more transparent the prevalence of bribery. For example, according to the CPI 2011, New Zealand, Denmark, and Finland are least corrupt countries in the world (while Afghanistan, Myanmar, North Koran, and Somalia are the worst); however, it is unclear why these countries are ranked higher than other countries, and what environment allows corruption. What we need to know is not only indicators (statistical aggregation) but also factors that make difference in each country's governance and corruption level. Otherwise, the indicators could not effectively be applied into practical reform.

Governance-related indicators are of the most importance because, in particular, they help answer the question of what works differently in emerging markets? For some aspects, it is well known that *information is scarce and unevenly distributed* in most countries of the world; in other respects, these markets are at the mercy of *institutions that lack strength and credibility*. As per the latter, it is meant that, "frequently, the legal and regulatory frameworks in emerging markets are poorly defined, inadequate, and full of contradictions. Further, judicial authorities tend to act in an erratic fashion and are occasionally corrupt. Therefore, contracts entered into these markets can be unreliable" (Sabal, 2002).

Fig. 1 shows WGI results of Argentina and Chile. There are remarkable differences between the two countries. Chile is ranked significantly higher than Argentina in all six scores of WGI. Also, Chile's 2011 CPI worldwide country rank is 22 and regional country rank is 4, respectively, while Argentina's rank in 2011 is 100 and 20, respectively. Chile's ranks are outstandingly higher than other Latin America and the Caribbean countries, and Argentina is ranked lower than the average of the region, even lower than some countries whose income levels (GDP per capita) are lower than Argentina, including Colombia, Dominica, El Salvador, Jamaica, and Peru. Clearly some questions arise: Why is Chile ranked much higher than

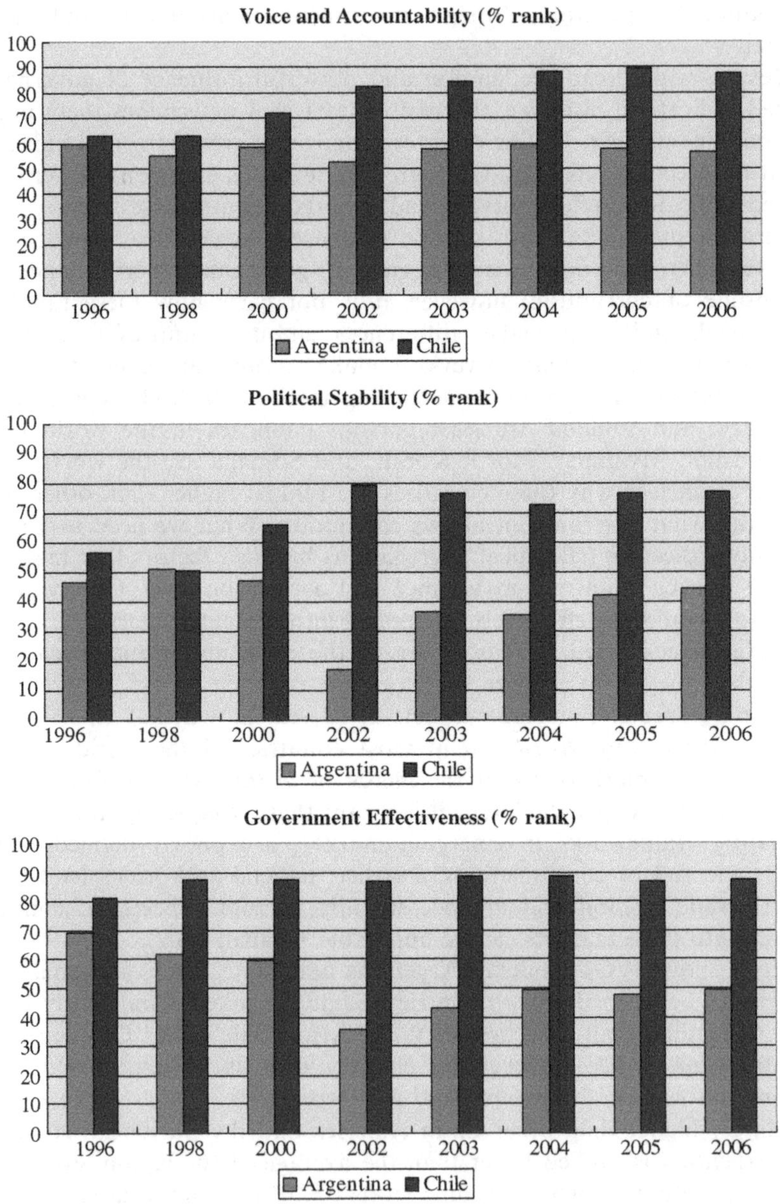

Fig. 1. Worldwide Governance Indicators, 1996–2007. *Source*: World Bank, 2007

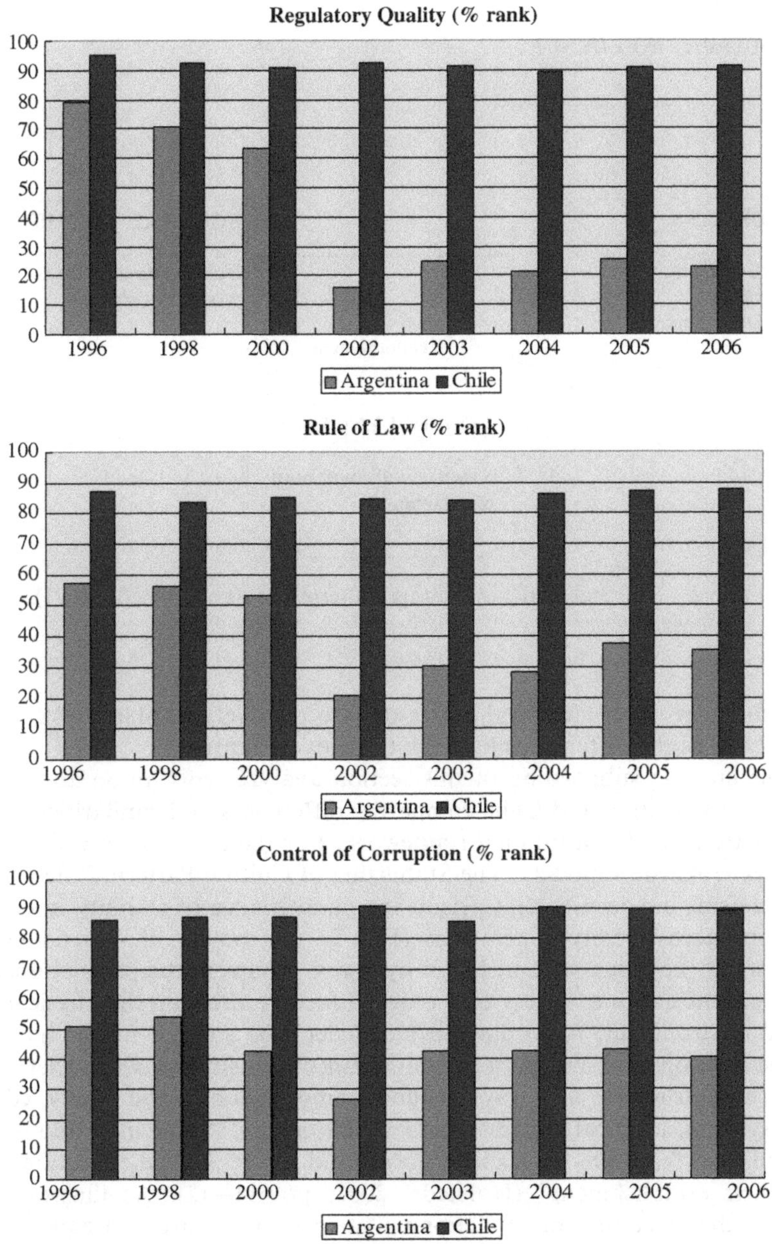

Fig. 1. (Continued).

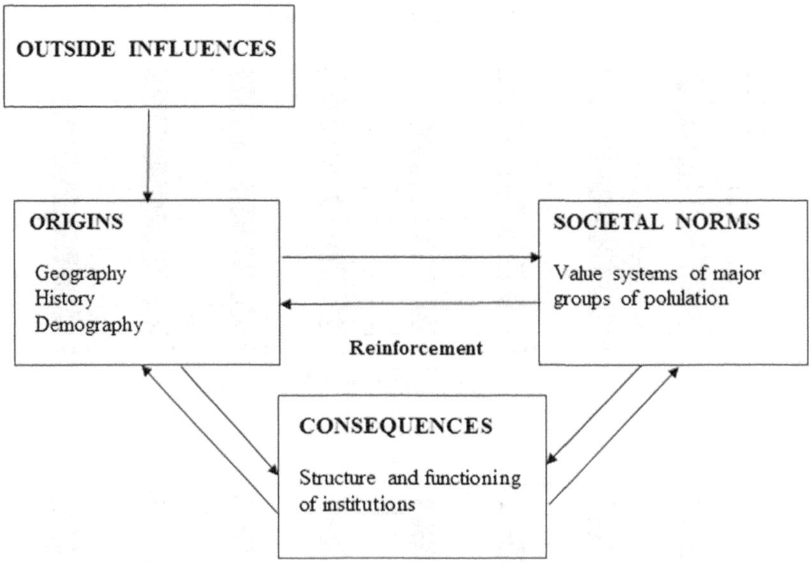

Fig. 2. The Stabilizing of Culture Patterns. *Source*: Hofstede (2001).

Argentina in governance indicators despite relatively similar background? What makes the differences between these two countries?

The ensuing subheading of this section analyzes corruption and governance in Argentina and Chile comparing differences and similarities in culture patterns and institutional framework. For the analysis, this case study follows Hofstede's model, "The Stabilizing of Culture Patterns," describing mechanisms in societies that permit the maintenance of stability in culture patterns across many generations (Fig. 2).[3] A system of societal norms consists of the value system shared by major groups in the population, and their origins are in a variety of ecological factors affecting the physical and social environment. According to Hofstede, "the societal norms have led to the development and pattern maintenance of institutions in society with particular structures and ways of functioning, including the family, education systems, political systems, and legislation" and "these institutions, one established, reinforce the societal norms and the ecological conditions that led their establishment" (Hofstede, 2001, pp. 11–12). As illustrated in Fig. 2, the structure and functioning of institutions are consequences of culture patterns across many generations.

EXOGENOUS FACTORS AND NATIONAL ORIGINS

Outside influences and national origins in Argentina and Chile are a sine a qua noncondition for analyzing similarities/differences between the two countries and the consequences as a result of the interplay of a background rooted in history, politics, policies, and societal interfaces. Outside influences as exogenous factors include forces of nature and forces of human creation (e.g., trade, domination, and scientific discovery), which countries inevitably face. Origins include ecological factors (geography, history, demography, and economy) as distinctive dimensions of a nation-state.

Argentina

In terms of geography and natural resources, it is appropriate to point out that a local saying states that "Argentina was blessed by resources, but cursed by politics." The latter will make perfect sense once the history, economics, and politics are discussed in ensuing sections of this chapter. Argentina is the second largest country in South America, occupying 2,766,890 sq. km. It borders the South Atlantic Ocean, between Bolivia, Brazil, Chile, Paraguay, and Uruguay. Argentina also claims the Falkland Islands (the Islas Malvinas), South Georgia, the South Sandwich Islands as part of Argentina. The climate varies from Patagonia, generally with moderate summer rainfall (The Europa World, 2006). Because of the fertile plains of the pampas, the main industry is agriculture: soybeans, corn, peanuts, and sunflower seeds. Additional natural resources include lead, zinc, tin, copper, iron ore, manganese, petroleum, and uranium (CIA, 2007a).

With respect to demography, the population of Argentina exceeds the 41 million inhabitants and the annual population growth rate is 1.05%. The major ethnic group is European (97%), mostly of Spanish and Italian descent, and 3% are Mestizo, Amerindian, or other nonwhite groups. The great majority of the population practice Christianity: about 92% are Roman Catholics and about 2% Protestants. Over one-third of population lives in the greater Buenos Aires area. Argentine educational level is relatively high due to the 10 years' compulsory and free education system (elementary and secondary school level). Adult literacy rate is 97.2%. Infant mortality rate is 16.16/1,000 and life expectancy is 75.48 years. Workforce proportion divided up as follows: industry and commerce 36%, agriculture 19%, and transport and communication 6% (U.S. Department of State, 2006).

History in a nutshell means that the name of Argentina is derived from the Latin term *argentum* (silver). The first Spanish conquistadors named the country for the rich amount of silver they found there. Following its independence from Spain in 1816, foreign investment and immigration from Europe (mostly Spain and Italy) speeded the economic revolution in the late 19th century. From 1880 to 1930, Argentina became one of the world's 10 wealthiest nations based on rapid expansion of agriculture and foreign investment in infrastructure (U.S. Department of State, 2006).

The military forced out the constitutional government in 1943. Juan Domingo Perón was elected to the presidency in 1946. His emphasis was to empower the working class and nationalize industries. He aimed to change Argentina's traditional socioeconomic mechanism based on agricultural industries, which were controlled by the conservative forces including the propertied class. His populist policies attracted widespread support and generated a number of empowered and unionized workers. However, the biased industrialization consequently undermined Argentina's traditional industry structure and Argentina entered an era of chronic political instability and repeated military intervention.

After Perón died in 1974, the military government formally exercised power until 1983. During this period, it is said that 10,000–30,000 persons disappeared under state control, known as the "Dirty War." The power of the military government decreased through several economic crises, domestic and international criticism toward governmental invasion of human rights, and defeat in the Falklands War. In 1983, the democratization occurred and Raúl Alfonsín took office with strong public support. However, weakened industry and government debt from the populist era caused severe economic stagnation and several hyperinflations occurred in the 1980s. The Alfonsín government could not maintain public confidence through the economic crises.

When Carlos Menem (Justicialist Party – JP) was elected as president in 1989, he undertook neoliberalism economic reform, and pursued the so-called "Washington Consensus" prescriptive approach of opening the economy to FDIs and privatizing state-owned enterprises. In addition, Menem introduced the fixed exchange rate between Argentinean peso and the U.S. dollar in order to resolve hyperinflation. Menem's liberal economic reform promoted international and domestic investment in the early 1990s; however, after the late 1990s, economic conditions went downward due to fiscal deficit and increased external debt. Criticism toward weak public institutions and widespread corruption was increased as well.

In 1999, presidential candidate De La Rúa took office after Menem's two-term presidency. However, after continuing economic pressure as a result of an unbearable recession, De la Rúa announced a foreign debt default of more than $81 billion in 2001, the largest sovereign debt default in history. After an interim administration, Néstor Kirchner (JP) took office in 2003. President Kirchner focused on consolidating his political strength and alleviating social problems (U.S. Department of State, 2006). Strong economic growth after the 2001 crisis assisted a high public support toward the Kirchner government. He was succeeded by his wife Cristina Fernández de Kirchner who, incidentally, has recently begun her second term in office.

Argentina's economy has drastically improved from its deep recession in 1999–2002, stimulated by the devaluation of the peso and high commodity prices. According to INDEC, the national statistics agency, the economy expanded 7.9% year-to-year in February 2007. However, its export-led growth is vulnerable to any reversal of these factors. Argentina traditionally has inflation risks due to the past regimes' loose economic management. Argentina's Central Bank has managed monetary policy in support of a competitive peso, but an inflation rate of 12.3% in 2005 remains a concern (U.S. Department of State, 2006).

Argentina's foreign exchange reserves has accumulated due to the foreign debt default; however, the sovereign debt default strongly damaged Argentina's market credibility and made Argentina less attractive to international investors. Argentina has been restricted in the international capital market.

Since the socioeconomic crisis in 2001, the unemployment rate has been improved through a high GDP growth going down from 21.5% during the 2002 economic crisis to 10.2% during the third quarter of 2006 (U.S. Department of State, 2007). However, there is still a significant amount of population living in poverty. About 33.5% out of the total population in the largest urban areas lives in poverty and almost 12% live in extreme poverty (Sullivan, 2006). The income gap between urban and rural areas has also been increased in Argentina. In sum, it can be stated that Argentina is a country that, after the founding of its stock market in 1872, has emerged (late 1800s, 1930s, 1975, 1990s,) submerged (1965, 2001), and has sought to remerge again.

Chile

Chile is the longest country in the world, narrowly bordering about 2,700 miles of South America's west coast, and sharing border with Argentina, Bolivia, and Perú. The territory includes Easter Island, the Juan Fernández Islands, and other smaller Pacific territories. The climate varies from a desert in the North to cool damp weather in the South. Chilean natural resources include copper, timber, iron ore, nitrates, and precious metals. Chile is a geographically isolated country with limited natural resources.

The population is above 16 million and the annual population growth rate is 0.916%. The main ethnic group is Spanish-Native-American (mestizo), European, and Native American. About 85% out of the total population are Roman Catholic. Over 40% of the population lives in the greater Santiago area. Adult literacy rate is 95.7% and infant mortality rate is 8.36/1,000.

From a history standpoint, it is imperative to state that after gaining independence from Spain in 1810, Chile defeated Peru and Bolivia in the War of the Pacific (1879–1883) and obtained the control of the Atacama Desert, the present northern regions, and its rich mineral resources. Although a parliamentary regime took office in 1891 after the Chilean Civil War, the upper class (mainly owners of large states and wealthy business people) dominated the society.

After the failures of several democratic regimes to accomplish social reforms following WW II, Salvador Allende took office in 1970. Chile became the first American republic to choose a Marxist president by constitutional election. Allende's revolutionary "Popular Unity" program included the nationalization of state-owned enterprises, redistribution of social benefits, and a more independent foreign policy. However, Allende gradually lost support of the middle class, the legislature, the judiciary, and the military (Banks, Muller, & Overstreet, 2007). In 1973, Augusto Pinochet seized power in a military coup.

Pinochet exercised power on the basis of the military support. During his term, especially in early 1970s, many people were arrested, tortured, and murdered as opponents of the Pinochet regime. There have been arguments calling for justice about human right abuses of the Pinochet regime in Chile. However, the Pinochet regime undertook liberal economic policies and increased domestic and foreign private investment. In 1980, a new constitution was approved by the election and Pinochet became president of the Republic for an eight-year term.

In 1990, after a plebiscite rejected Pinochet's second eight-year term, Patricio Aylwin, from a Coalition of Parties for Democracy (CPD), became president with 53.8% vote and served four years. In 1994, Eduardo Frei (CPD) took office with 58% support. Although CPD could obtain majorities of elected Senate and Chamber members, it could not control nonelective lifelong senators appointed for eight-year term during Pinochet regime. In November 2004, the constitutional amendment eliminated such positions, granting the president authority to remove the commanders (Banks et al., 2007).

In 2005, Michelle Bachelet won a majority and became the first female president in Chile. The current president of Chile is Sebastián Piñera, a successful entrepreneur himself before becoming interested in politics. Chile has maintained constant economic growth since the 1980s and is regarded as a regional and international model of sound economic policies and democratic government.

As an economic miracle and model, there is much more to indicate, of course, than Chile's GDP of $118 billion, and per capita GDP is $12,737. The main industry is manufacturing (17% of GDP) and 13% of GDP is mining industry. Chilean economy is market oriented, especially characterized by a high level of foreign trade. The exports include mining, forestry, and fishing. Chile is the world's leading producer of copper, bringing 60% of total exports from the copper industry. At the same time, Chile heavily depends on imports of other commodities, especially oil and natural gas.

During 1990s, Chile was regarded as a model of economic reform with constant economic growth. The average real GDP growth rate became 8% from 1991 to 1997. The global financial crisis in late 1990s led to negative economic growth for the first time in more than 15 years, reducing crop yields and causing hydroelectric shortfalls. However, Chile could maintain its reputation for strong financial institutions and sound policies that have given it the strongest sovereign bond rating in South America. Chile has maintained a 2–6% GDP growth rate between 2000 and 2006 from high copper prices, solid export earnings, and growing domestic consumption. Because of its geographical isolation and limited natural resources, Chile has one of the most liberal trade policies in the world, with the signing of a free trade agreement with various countries, including the United States, Japan, EU, South Korea, New Zealand, Singapore, China, and India. Chile has attracted FDI; however, 80% of FDI continues to go to only four sectors: electricity, gas, water, and mining. The unemployment rate dropped to 7.8% by the end of 2006. Although Chile has a high international reputation due to its stable economic growth, poverty and unequal income distribution has remained problematic in Chile for decades: the highest 10% household share 47% of the income, and the lowest 10% share 1.2%.

Similarities and Differences Between Argentina and Chile

The comparison of exogenous factors and national origins of Argentina and Chile facilitates a description of the similarities and the differences between both countries as nation-states.

Similarities

- Independence from Spain: Like many Latin American countries, Argentina and Chile were Spanish colonies from the Age of Geographical Discovery (independence was in 1816 and 1810, respectively).
- Religion: The majority of people are Roman Catholic (92% in Argentina, 89% in Chile)
- Population concentration in the country's capital: Over 30% living in the greater Buenos Aires, and 40% living in the greater Santiago.
- Authoritarian military regime experience after WW II: Human rights violation and "desaparecidos" as a result of "dirty wars" and internal armed conflicts.
- High income gap: Household income or consumption by percentage share in Argentina: highest 10% households share 35% and lowest 10% share 1%, Chile: highest 10% households share 47% income, lowest 10% share 1.2%.

Differences

- Natural resources and self-sufficiency: Argentina benefits from rich natural resources including fertile plains (pampas), oil, minerals, and uranium. Chile is geographically isolated with relatively scarce natural resources. Chile' main natural resource is copper. Argentina has a high sufficiency of natural resources compared to Chile.
- Industrial structure and trade policy: Since Chile is an export-oriented country (mainly copper) and highly depends on imports of other commodities, it signed free trade agreements with various countries.
- Political regime and stability: There are fewer military coups and populist regimes, and more political stability in Chile than in Argentina.

- Economic performance under military regime: The Chilean military government maintained constant economic growth during 1970–1980s, while the Argentine military regime failed in economic management.
- Economic growth: Argentina's economic growth volatility is higher than Chile.
- Price instability: Argentina has experienced several economic crises, hyperinflation, and social disorder.

There are some similarities about basic social structures (e.g., religion and language) between Argentina and Chile due to some common historical dimensions in the national origin of both nation-states as a result of their independence from Spain. There are income gaps in both countries; however, historically the middle class in Argentina was larger before the 2001 crisis, while Chile has traditionally relied on an income hierarchy based on social stratification.

It is clear that an endowment of natural resources enables and directly influences the countries' industrial structure and capacity, trade policies, and diplomatic strategies. Because of geographic isolation and scarcity of natural resources, Chile is highly dependent on exports, especially the copper industry, and imports of other commodities. Since trade is a key factor for Chilean economy, Chile's government has needed to keep stable international relationship with as many countries as possible in order to maintain its trade. This characteristic forces Chile to restrain itself from political and economic instability, which could damage international reputation and trade environment. Indeed, Chile has never experienced inflation and economic crisis as severe as in Argentina. Consequently, Chile's economic growth has been more stable over the years, while Argentine economic volatility has been significant (Fig. 3).

At the detailed level, the political changes experienced by Argentina and Chile have been different, especially when the attention turns toward their economic policies and likely consequences. Perhaps one of the most important differences in political history between Argentina and Chile is the influence of populism. Drake states that, "Chile has never been ruled by a mesmerizing leader of a multi-class urban movement committed to rapid elevation of the workers and hothouse industrialization" (Drake, 1999, p. 63). Populism has been common in Latin America where competitive party systems have been weak and military interventions were frequent, as in Argentina. However, it has been uncommon in nations with strong party systems and a relatively noninterventionist military, as in Chile, with

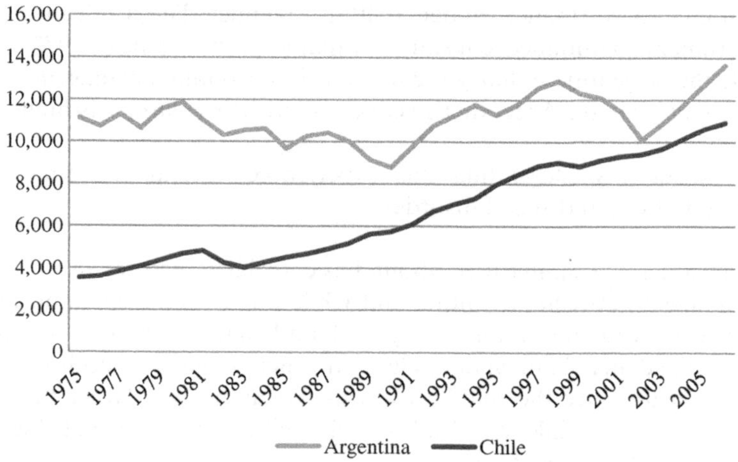

Fig. 3. GDP Per Capita, PPP (Constant 2000 International $). *Source*: WDI 1975–2006. GDP per capita based on purchasing power parity (PPP). Data are in constant 2000 international dollars.

the exception of the years in the recent history of the country when it was under the regime of Augusto Pinochet.

Drake suggests that Latin American populism has exhibited the following three interconnected features: (1) domination by paternalistic, personal, often characteristic leadership and mobilization from the top down; (2) involvement by multiclass incorporation of the masses, especially urban workers but also middle sectors; and (3) emphasis on integrationist, reformist, and nationalist development programs for the state to promote simultaneously redistributive measures of populist supporters and import-substitution industrialization (Drake, 1999).

Populist regimes undertook nationalistic policies and empowered Argentine middle-class labors. These policies extensively increased public expenditure, increasing inflation and foreign debt, generating economic crisis and national instability. The populist regimes' nationalistic industrialization also ignored its natural comparative advantage, plentiful natural resources, and undermined Argentine industrial structure. Populism has left a significant influence on Argentine society: empowered middle-class labors and created a fragile foundation of Argentine development.

Societal Norms

This section of the chapter analyzes societal norms of Argentina and Chile. In this study, societal norms refer to citizens' values and behaviors in a nation. The section seeks to demonstrate how outside influence and national origin have effects on shaping different societal norm in Argentina and Chile.

Experience of Perón-Style Politics and Its Consequences

As discussed in the previous section, one of the most remarkable historical differences between the two countries is an experience of populist regimes. Populist regimes left significant influences on Argentine economic/political structure and citizens' societal norms.

Juan Domingo Perón was one of the most typical populist leaders, who embodied as a legacy the so-called "Peronism." As discussed in a variety of literatures, the legacies of populism still remain in Argentina, and there is a reluctance to accept other parties as legitimate political candidates (Horowitz, 1999, p. 42). For instance, those interviewed who supported Menem did so because they identified him with Peronism and, in spite of Menem's rather un-populist behavior, which included neoliberal policies that were perceived as favoring business and political elites, a reputation for cozy relationships with the business establishment, and repeated public denials that poverty was a problem (Powers, 2001, p. 31).

Empowered Middle Class and Public Trust

The populist regimes emphasized on empowering working labors and involving multiclass incorporation of the masses. Argentina has traditionally had strong labor unions, actively organizing strikes against companies and government policies. In Chile, however, there has been traditional income inequality among people, and middle class has not been empowered by populist regimes as in Argentina. Consequently, level of political turmoil in Chile has been lower than in Argentina.

Experience of political/economic instability has influenced the level of public trust in Argentina and Chile. According to the Global Competitiveness Report, the level of public trust of politicians in Argentina and Chile are considerably different. As showed in Table 2, Argentina is ranked 107 out of 117 countries, while Chile's rank is 23. In response to middle-class workers' demand, populist regimes had undertaken loose fiscal and monetary policies and caused socioeconomic instability in Argentina. By

Table 2. Notable Competitive Differences.

	Rank/117 countries	
	Argentina	Chile
Public trust of politicians	107	23
Judicial independence	105	47
Favoritism in decisions of government officials	97	20
Wastefulness of government spending	91	19
Burden of government regulation	101	18
Efficiency of legal framework	98	35
Extent and effect of taxation	101	26
Effectiveness of antitrust policy	79	22

Source: The World Economic Forum (2006).

repeatedly experiencing economic crisis and governments' inability of policy implementation, Argentine citizens' have become disappointed with government and lost public trust in politicians. In Chile, since there have been much less economic crisis and political chaos, people have more public trust in politicians than in Argentina.

Individualism and Short-Term Perspective

Another different characteristic between Argentina and Chile is individualism. Personal independence is regarded one of the most important qualities in Argentina (Whittle, 1998). Hofstede's value score model illustrate interesting differences on individualism between Argentina and Chile.[4]

Fig. 4 shows the differences on four dimensions between Argentina and Chile. The most notable difference between the two countries is individualism, the degree to which individuals are integrated into groups. According to Hofstede's model, Argentina is a more individualist society than Chile. Hofstede also explains key differences between collectivist and individualist societies (Table 3), and interestingly, these differences are seen in the case of Argentina and Chile, especially stronger development of middle class, and survival more dependent on individual initiative.

In Argentina, people had to survive on individual initiative in order to protect themselves from several economic crises. During hyperinflation, the currency decreased in value every single day. For example, value of salary became less than half within a week. Under that situation, people could not prospect tomorrow's currency value, and their priority became to minimize devaluation of their money in order to protect their own family lives. These survival experiences have made Argentine citizens become more

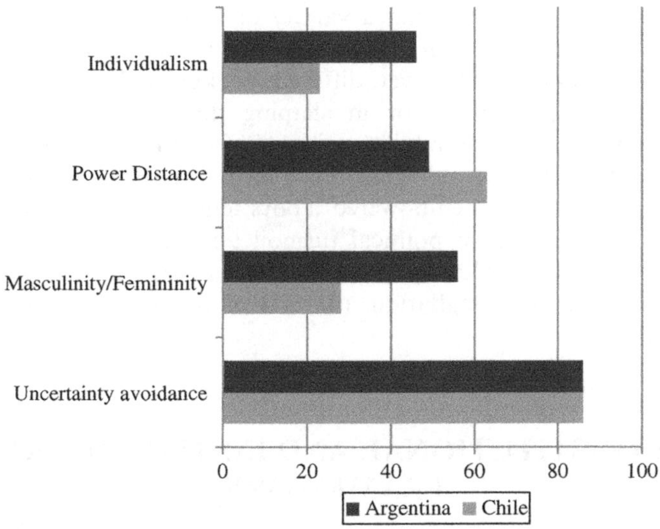

Fig. 4. Hofstede's Value Score Model of Argentina and Chile. *Source*: Hofstede, Hofstede, and Minkov (2010).

Table 3. Key Differences Between Collectivist and Individualist Societies.

Collectivist societies	Individualist societies
Less social mobility	Greater social mobility
Weak development of middle class	Stronger development of middle class
Survival less dependent on individual initiative	Survival more dependent on individual initiative
Collective interests prevail over individual interests	Individual interests prevail over collective interests
Economy based on collective interests	Economy based on individual interests

Source: Hofstede (2001).

individualist and seek short-term economic benefit based on individual interests.

Indeed, despite President Alfonsín's large support for his democratic discipline at the time of transition, the support rate started to decline along with economic downfall and increased level of discontent. According to Catterberg, "these attitudes are rooted in Argentine political culture that people have not undergone significant changes, and a strong attachment to them crosses the different social sectors" (Catterberg, 1991, p. 45).

It is tantamount to state that a variety of factors is related to societal norms and political culture in a country and it is difficult to determine the influence of each factor. However, different background of political history should be an important factor in shaping different societal norms in Argentina and Chile. Especially, experiences of populist regimes and severe economic crises have affected Argentina's level of public trust and individualism. Also, Argentina's empowered labors tend to organize strikes more frequently, causing risk of political turmoil and damaging business environment in Argentina. However, since Chile has experienced less populist regimes and economic stagflation, its level of public trust is higher than Argentina.

CONSTITUTIONAL AND INSTITUTIONAL FRAMEWORK

The last phase of the stabilizing of culture pattern as a construct in the case of an institutional approach is consequences in terms of the structure and functioning of institutions. Argentina and Chile basically have similar political systems: republic and presidential government with bicameral National Congress. The president is both the chief of state and head of government and elected by popular vote.

Despite similar basic constitutional structure, institutions function differently in Argentina and Chile. This section discusses the functioning of key institutions, including the president, the congress and the political parties, the judiciary (Supreme Court), and the bureaucracy, and then analyzes similarities/differences between the two countries under consideration.

President

In Argentina, under the constitution of 1994, the president and vice president are elected for four-year terms by popular election, and eligible for a second term. In addition, they are allowed to stand for a third term or more after interval of at least one term. The first-round election requires a 45% majority – a 40% in the event of a gap greater than 10% between the two leading contenders (Banks et al., 2007). The constitution provides the president with considerable power, including authority to enact laws under conditions of "urgency and necessity" and the line-item veto.

In September 1980, Chile's Constitution was approved under the Pinochet regime. After the transition to democracy, the constitution was amended in 1994, providing a new presidential term of six years. In November 2004, the constitution was amended and the presidential term was reduced to four years, with simultaneous presidential and congressional elections. The 2004 constitutional amendments also include eliminating the positions of appointed senators and senators for life, granting the president authority to remove the commanders (Banks et al., 2007).

The president of both Argentina and Chile is provided with an extensive constitutional power to declare legislation urgent. The Argentine president can exercise decrees of necessity and urgency (DNUs) and the item veto, and the Chilean president has three levels of urgency (simple urgency, extreme urgency, and immediate discussion as interpreted from their sense of urgency in Spanish: *simple urgencia, suma urgencia* y *discusión inmediata*), requiring different speed with which presidential initiatives must be considered (Siavelis, 2002, p. 92).

Despite this similarity in the constitutional structure of both countries, there are significant differences in practical exercise of presidential power between them. In Chile, urgencies are generally used to give priority to the president's own initiatives; however, the veto power is not necessary absolute power to control Chilean Congress. Fig. 5 shows approval rate for executive initiatives with and without urgency in Chile. The 637 total initiatives were presented by the president, including 375 with urgency. However, there were not significant differences between the approval ratings for initiatives with and without urgency: 64% with urgency and 62.6% without urgency.

According to this data, use of emergency did not have a large effect on approval rating. Because of power balance among multipolitical parties, the Chilean president cannot automatically obtain majority support in Congress (the ensuing section discusses the functioning of the Chilean Congress). Therefore, Chilean legislators have been an influential actor in legislative process, and the president needs to negotiate with them to obtain congressional approval. In practice, the Chilean president has not exercised presidential urgency powers in a strict and inflexible manner as expected in the constitution. The president has more incentives to cooperate with other parties to precede legislative process.

However, in Argentina, the president's veto and the DNUs have been exercised as a strong tool to influence policy outcomes and avoid negotiation with other parties, when the president lacks a majority in the legislature (Mustapic, 2002). The use of veto tends to be linked to structural

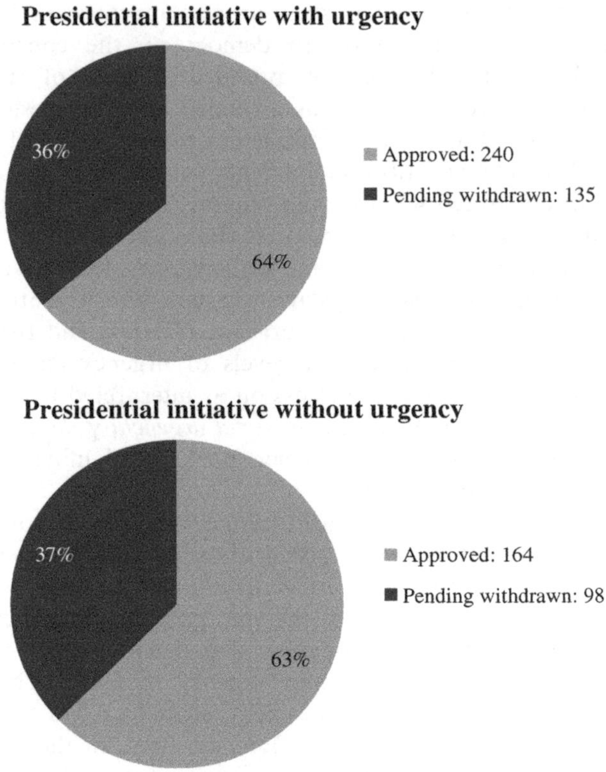

Fig. 5. Summary of Approval Rate for Executive Initiatives with and without Urgency in Chile (1990–1993). *Source*: Siavelis (2002).

reform policies initiated by the executive in Argentina. Especially during the Menem government, the president exercised his urgency power to control legislative process of the privatization of state-owned enterprises (gas, electricity, and oil). Fig. 6 provides a comparison of the presidential vetoes for presidents Alfonsín and Menem during their administrations while Fig. 7 shows a list of necessity and urgency decrees in Argentina for the period 1983–1998.

Reelection eligibility is another important difference of the presidential power in Argentina and Chile. Since President Menem amended the

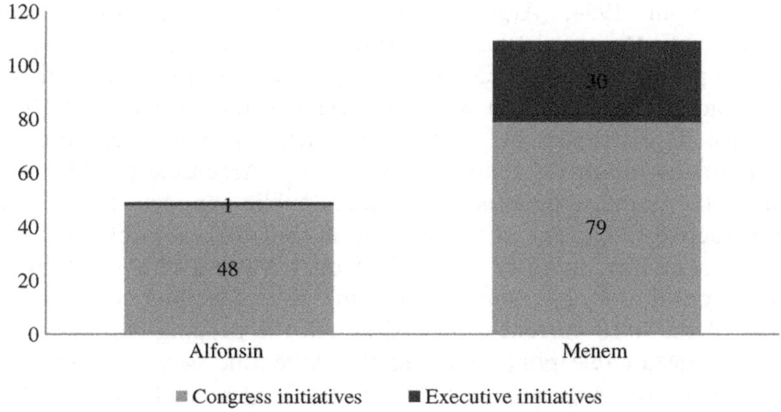

Fig. 6. Presidential Vetos in Argentina: During Alfonsin and Menem Regime. *Source*: Mustapic (2002).

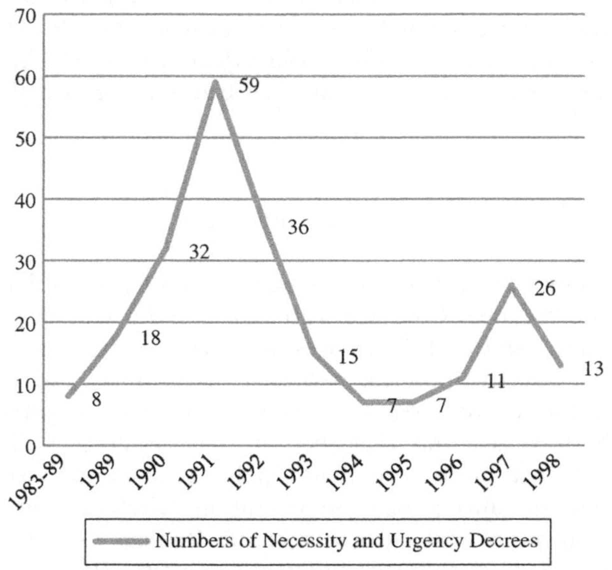

Fig. 7. Decrees of Necessity and Urgency(DNUs) in Argentina. *Source*: Spiller and Tommasi (2000).

constitution in 1994, Argentine constitution provides the president with consecutive renewal (this constitutional reform itself shows how the Argentine president can exercise absolute presidential power to further his/her own goals. This situation was made clear in the reelection of Cristina Fernández de Kirchner, the current president of Argentina, last year). Because of the incentives for next election, the Argentine presidents tend to undertake populist policies to maintain public support. These policies seem attractive to citizens in the short-term, but, irresponsible in the long term. For example, in early 1990s, President Menem could obtain large public support for his accomplishment of controlling hyperinflation because of the fixed currency rate. Although the pegging currency system was not a sustainable policy making the Argentine peso was overvalued and damaging the Argentine economy in the long term, President Menem continued enjoying short-term benefit and obtained the majority of the public support for his second term. Argentine weak macroeconomic policies were results of a strong and selfish president with less control of the Congress.

By contrast, the Chilean constitution does not allow a presidential reelection, and the presidential term was shortened by the 2004 constitution. This constitutional reform is a clear evidence that the Chilean politics has more balance of power so that they can even reduce the executive power.

Congress and Political Parties

In regard to political parties and balance of power, Argentina and Chile have bicameral National Congress with Senate and Chamber of Deputies.[5] One of the most significant differences in Argentine and Chilean politics is the number of effective political parties. In Argentina, only one political party, Front for Victory, the late president Kirchner's party, currently dominates both Senate and Chamber of Deputies. Fig. 8 illustrates the absolute dominance of the president's political party in Argentine Congress. In addition, during his administration Kirchner had support of members of other political parties including Radical Civic Union, which has been traditionally a political opponent against the Peronist parties.

By comparison, in Chilean Congress, there are more than five effective political parties in both Senate and Chamber of Deputies. Because of balance of the power based on the Chilean multiparty system, unlike legislatures in Argentina, Chile's National Congress has been historically an

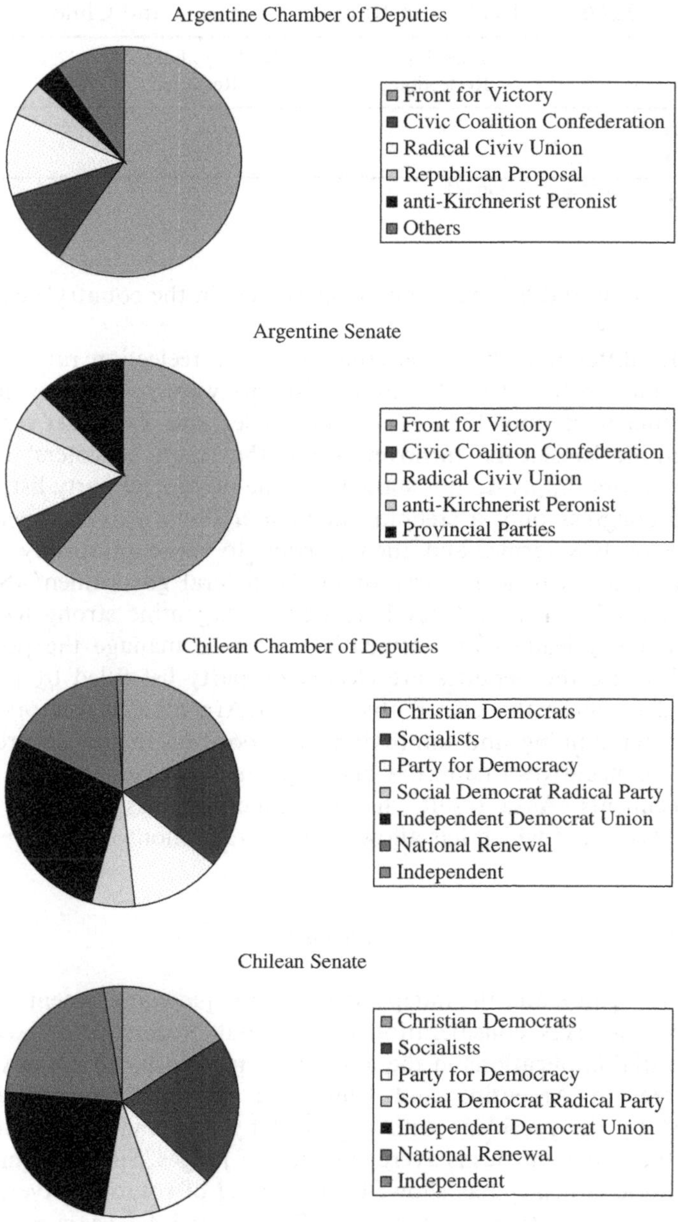

Fig. 8. National Congress in Argentina and Chile: Number of Seats by Parties (November 2007). *Source*: CIA 2007a, 2007b

Table 4. Reelection Rates in Argentina and Chile.

Country	% Seeking Reelection	% of Candidates Reelected	Total % Reelected
Argentina (1997)	26	67	17
Chile (1993)	76	78	59

Source: Spiller and Tommasi (2007).

influential actor and has had significant powers in the country's experience with democracy.

Another difference about the congress is the reelection rate of legislators. In Chile, 59% out of the total legislators were reelected, while those of Argentina were only 17% (Table 4). Spiller and Tommasi report that the Argentine legislators' turnover is not the result of voters' rejection. Most legislators simply do not show up in the provincial party list, because they find congress only a stepping in their political careers, spending at most one or two terms, and then moving to more politically lucrative activities in the provinces, party or at the federal government (Spiller & Tommasi, 2007). This tendency is related to Argentine strong federalism. Provincial party leaders are influential actors to manage the politicians' careers, because the deputies are elected by party list filled by provincial party leaders. Since the career objectives of Argentine legislators are not based on maintaining and improving their position in the congress, they do not have incentives to approve and implement policies for their political accomplishments. As a result, the Argentine congress has been a weak political player and which has allowed unilateral actions by the president.

Judiciary

The average tenure and the independence of the judiciary system is another aspect that deserves consideration as potential precursors of governance with potential implications in the analysis of propensity to opacity in kind and degree. In Argentina and Chile, the Supreme Court judges are appointed by the president with approval by the senate. One difference between the two countries is average tenure of judges. Since the mid 1940s, the Argentine judiciary has showed a high level of rotation. Average judicial tenure in Argentina and Chile is 5.7 years and 4.4 years, respectively (Table 5). According to the report introduced by Inter-American

Table 5. Supreme Court Justices' Average Tenure in Selected Countries 1960–1990.

Country	Judicial Tenure (Number of Years)
USA	18.8
Canada	14.2
Brazil	7.2
Nicaragua	7.1
Chile	**5.7**
Argentina	**4.4**
Peru	4.0
Dominican Rep.	3.6
Mexico	3.3
Honduras	2.8
Colombia	1.9
Ecuador	1.9
Guatemala	1.8
Paraguay	1.1

Source: Spiller and Tommasi (2007).

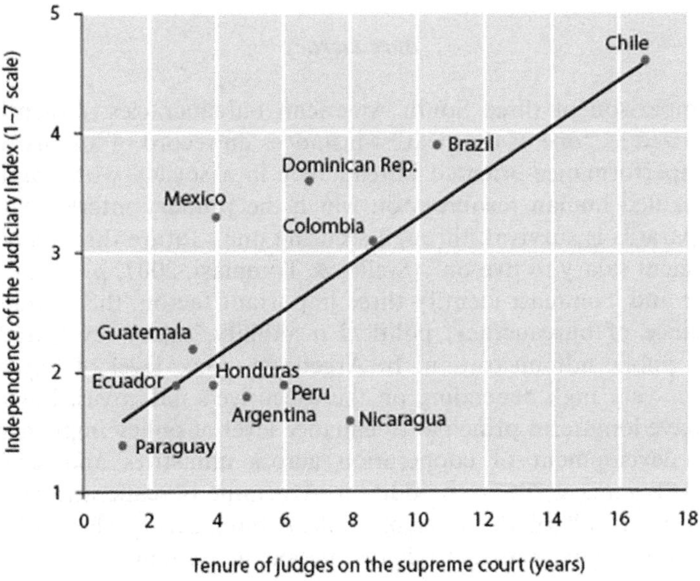

Fig. 9. Supreme Court Tenure and Judicial Independence. *Source*: IADB, 2005.

Development Bank, there is a statistical relationship between tenure of judges and judicial independence (Fig. 9, IADB, 2005). As discussed elsewhere in the literature, the Argentine court was not independent and frequently intervened by the government. For example, President Menem expanded the court from five to nine members in order to control the opposition and obtain judicial majority on behalf of his interest.

Short-tenure provides judges with only short-term incentives, making them more vulnerable to political power game. Indeed, Argentine judges tend to support governments when governments were strong and to desert them when governments grew weak (Helmke, 2002). This lack of independence allowed the executive to exceed its constitutional powers.

The Chilean Supreme Court is regarded as the most independent judicial institution in the region. The following brief and nonexhaustive list of examples show evidences of the Chilean judicial independence: prosecution against former President Pinochet for corruption and human rights violation as well as former Peruvian President Alberto Fujimori, and the 2004 constitutional reform reducing executive power and eliminating heritages from Pinochet's era. Argentine Supreme Court has not achieved faire and drastic judgments as Chile.

Bureaucracy

In a comparison of three South American bureaucracies, Argentina was characterized as "one of the clearest instances on record of an institutionalized, nonperformance-oriented bureaucracy in a society with ample numbers of skilled human resources on which the primary interest within the state apparatus is survival, through securing one's future through a limited but sufficient salary to live on" (Spiller & Tommasi, 2007, p. 157).

Spiller and Tommasi identify three important factors that influence the performance of bureaucracy: political instability, salary level, and confidence in public administration. In Argentina, since level of bureaucratic rotation is very high depending on the executive's initiatives, bureaucracy cannot have long-term principal to enhance level of policy implementation, and the development of cooperation across ministries and secretariats (Spiller & Tommasi, 2007). In addition, Argentine bureaucratic salary level is low, almost half of the level of Chilean bureaucracy (Fig. 10). Salary level is a key factor to attract talented people in a country. Because of low salary level, Argentine bureaucracy is less attractive job market for the talented Argentine citizen.

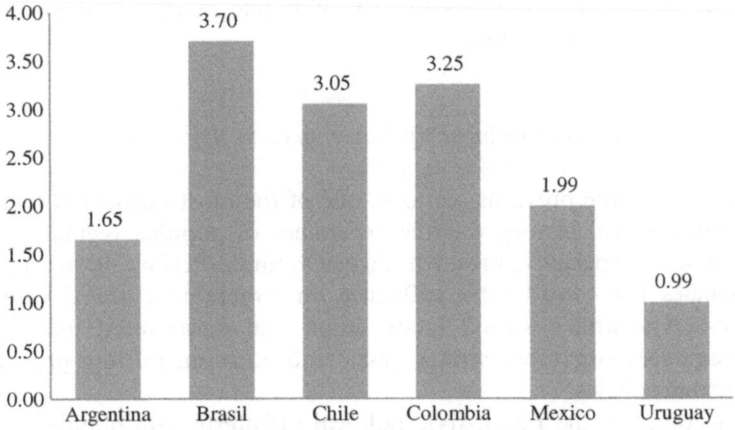

Fig. 10. Central Government Wages Divided by GDP per Capita, 1999. *Source*: Spiller and Tommasi (2007).

The third factor is public confidence in civil services. Since the country lacks a well-structured civil service, Argentine citizens have a low confidence in the quality of public administration (Spiller & Tommasi, 2007). That makes bureaucracy an even less attractive job market in Argentina. These three factors negatively influence each other and create low level of Argentina's bureaucracy. In Chile, these three factors are opposite to Argentina: more political stability, more public trust, and higher bureaucratic salary level make bureaucracy more attractive to Chilean citizens and improve bureaucratic performance.

DOES GOVERNANCE FOLLOW CULTURE?

This study discusses the relationship between the cultural pattern and the functioning of institutions, and compares the cases of Argentina and Chile. These two neighboring countries seem to have similar background; however, a variety of factors is different, generating a dissimilar societal norm, and a contrasting functioning of the institutions in Argentina and Chile. This final section of the chapter establishes a framework of cultural pattern and its consequences in both countries, by integrating the analysis from the previous sections. The study focuses next on how the role of identified factors differentiates quality of public policies and governance between Argentina and Chile.

Factors Influencing Governance in Argentina

As discussed in the previous sections, one of the most influential factors in Argentine political history was the experience of populist regime and economic crises.[6] Especially, President Juan Domingo Perón and his nationalistic policies left considerable influence on Argentine citizens' value and attitudes. Argentina's strong labor union and empowered middle class have frequently organized strikes and demonstration, putting pressure on government policies.

To accomplish the Perón-style political manifesto, the populist regimes undertook loose fiscal and monetary policies. These irresponsible and unsustainable policies led political instability and economic crisis composed of hyperinflation and international debt. Repeated hyperinflation and political chaos generated public distrust in the government, the public services, and the economy as a whole. The traumas of socioeconomic crisis also created citizens' individualism, based on short-term economic interest.

The president, by nature, cares about public opinion and attitudes in order to gain broad public support. Since Argentine citizens mainly expect the government to improve the economic management and performance to enhance their living environment in the short term, Argentine presidents tend to undertake populist and materialistic public policies (including raising wages, fixing currency rate, and freezing prices). These policies look attractive to the public, and then it is easy for the president to gain large support.

In a pure functional institutional framework, the executive, the legislative, and the judicial branches should be independent. However, in the Argentine congress, the president's political party absolutely dominates both the senate and the chamber of deputies, so the president can obtain major support of congress automatically. Legislatures also lack incentives in policy making and implementation, because they see congress as a transitional position in their political career. Lack of judicial independence allows the executive to exercise unilateral power for further his/her own goal. In addition, less attractive bureaucracy undermine level of civil services, causing more citizens' distrust in public administration. As a result, weak institutional framework allows the president to exercise his/her

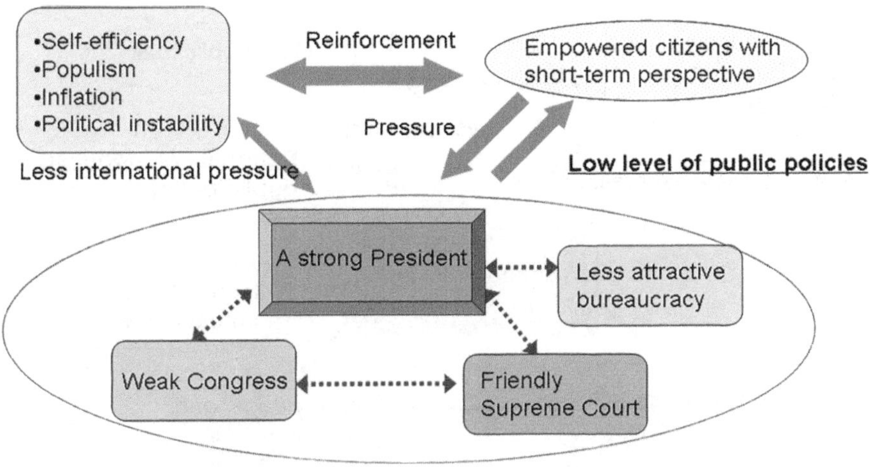

Fig. 11. Framework in Argentina. *Source*: Authors' elaboration.

absolute power to make irresponsible public policies, causing socio-economic instability, public distrust and citizens' individualism in Argentine society.

As illustrated in the framework (see Fig. 11), this negative circulation reinforces each other in each phase. The consequences of current political policies will become a history in the future, influencing again citizens' values and attitudes against government.

Factors Influencing Governance in Chile

In the case of Chile, geographical isolation and low self-sufficiency are key factors. Because of Chile's dependence on trade, the Chilean government needs to keep its international reputation and trade relationship with as many countries as possible. This characteristic leads Chile toward a low political instability and constant economic growth. Also, Chile has never had populist regime and economic crises as have been common and recurrent in Argentina. The economic growth and political stability generated more public confidence among Chilean citizens. Indeed, Chilean political attitudes have been historically more moderate than Argentine citizens.

In Chile's institutional framework (Fig. 12), the congress plays a more influential role in the legislative process than in Argentina. Since there is a

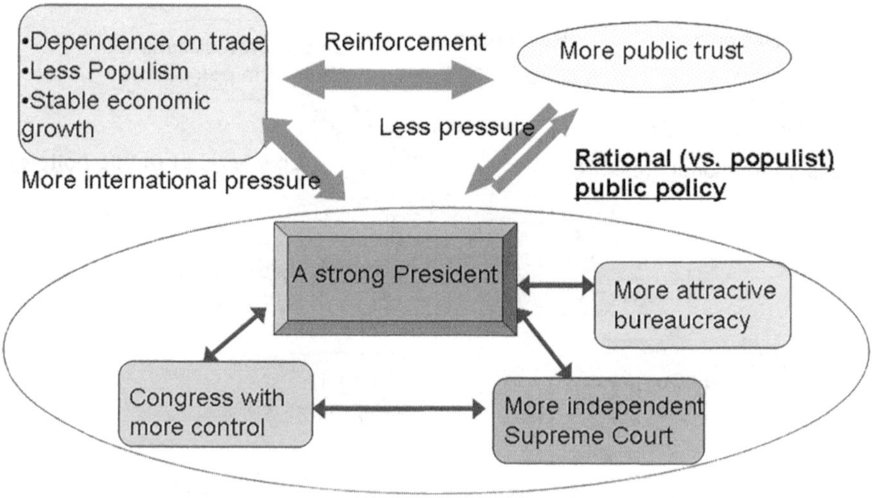

Fig. 12. Framework in Chile. *Source*: Authors' elaboration.

more balanced power among various effective political parties, the Chilean president has more incentive to negotiate with other parties to obtain congressional approval. The Supreme Court's independence permits also to control the excessive use of presidential power. Finally, the Chilean bureaucracy is more stable and attractive, improving bureaucratic performance and level of civil services.

What Argentina Needs to Do to Improve Governance?

Comparing the frameworks of both countries, what does Argentina need to do to improve its governance? One approach is constitutional reform. Current constitution provides the Argentine president extensive power without functional control within an institutional framework. Especially the presidential reelection system creates more presidents' incentives to undertake irresponsible policies from the short-term prospective in order to gain broad public support for next election. Eliminating the reelection system will be significant to change presidential behavior and to promote more rational public policy making.

In addition, the Argentine citizens also need to change their behavior. Rather than calling for immediate economic benefit from the government, they need to accept more rational public policies. Although such policies might be painful in the short term, the outcome will be more sustainable and beneficial for the Argentine society in the long term. For obtaining public support for these public policies, the Argentine government should open as much information to the public as possible, and explain the policies' context and the prospective consequences in the long term.

At a specific level, it has been observed the cognitive styles of Argentines and how they organize and process information and how the value systems are their basis for behavior and which, to some extent could explain why, "corrupt officials, especially rural policemen, have been known to extort fines from travelers. This seems to be on the increase since the economic dislocations of 2001." By contrast, in Chile "corruption (aside from tax evasion) is uncommon. Even the Chilean traffic police (the Carabineros) tend to be honest; they make take an attempt to bribe them as an insult" (Morrison & Conaway, 2007) because they "are not notably prone to bribery" (Becker, 2011).

CONCLUSION

Throughout this chapter, the case study comparison between Argentina and Chile discusses the cultural pattern and functioning of institutions in both countries. A variety of factors shape a unique cultural pattern in each country, and the cultural pattern influences the functioning of institutions. As a result, the functioning of institutions directly contributes to a level of opacity and corruption. As shown in the second section, the fundamental equation of corruption proposed from the perspective of the Organization of American States is: Monopoly − Transparency + Discretion = Corruption. Since Argentine institutional framework provides presidents with higher level of autonomy, monopoly, discretion, and less transparency, the Argentine president tends to exercise the executive power for his/her own gain. However, in Chile, because there are more balance of power and judiciary independence, the Chilean president has less incentive and opportunity to be engaged in acts of corruption. In addition, Chile's geographical isolation and dependence on trade force Chile's government to keep more stability and transparency than Argentina to ensure its reputation intact. These different factors interactively affect quality of public policies and governance, and consequently, the level of corruption.

Governance is a consequence of culture. As each country has an unique culture, each country should have a different governance context. Therefore, each country needs different approaches to improve governance and combat corruption. Two countries with same ranks of governance indicators might need totally different reforms to improve their governance, depending on their cultural pattern and functioning of institutions. Interpreting a context behind governance is necessary to establish appropriate anticorruption reform in practice that results in a lower characterization of a rampant existence of opacity and lack of transparency in a country's daily affairs.

ACKNOWLEDGMENTS

The authors acknowledge and are grateful for comments to earlier drafts by Professor J. Jay Choi, *IFR* Editor in Chief, and Professor Heibatollah Sami, co-editor of this volume of the *International Finance Review* published by Emerald in helping us revise this chapter. One of the authors is also appreciative of the discussions held with Guillermo Vidal, a prestigious Argentinean jurist and author, because his timely observations and comments on the issues of opacity, corruption, transparency, presidential powers, and the interpretation and application of the law in Argentina became a timely critical test to the chapter before its publication. The authors alone are responsible for all limitations and errors that may relate to this study. Send correspondence to Harvey Arbeláez, Monterey Institute of International Studies, Graduate School of International Policy and Management, Fisher International MBA Program, 460 Pierce Street, Monterey, CA 93940; telephone: +1-831-647-4176; email: harvey.arbelaez@miis.edu.

NOTES

1. According to David Barstow of *The New York Times* who reported the story, the bribes were directed by the man who went to become the vice-chairman and head of Wal-Mart's U.S. division. In effect, further reports such as the ones provided in *The Daily Ticker* by Henry Blodget (April 23, 2012) in a story titled "Busted: Wal-Mart Caught In Massive Bribery Scandal That Goes All the Way to the Top," indicate how Wal-Mart through its actions overlooked some key points such as, first, believing that "this is the way things are done in Mexico;" second,

dismiss "The Foreign Corrupt Practices Act of 1977" (FCPA) that makes illegal to bribe officials in countries in which American companies do business; and third, "the bribes involved internal accounting fraud."

2. These organizations include Business Environment Risk Intelligence, Global Insight, Economist Intelligence Unit, Political Risk Services, and World Economic Forum.

3. Hofstede treats culture as the collective programming of mind that distinguishes the members of one group or category of people from another. This implies everything in Kluckhohn's more extensive definition as follows: Culture consists in patterned ways of thinking, feeling, and reacting, acquired and transmitted mainly by symbols, constituting the distinctive achievements of human groups, including their embodiments of traditional (i.e., historically derived and selected) ideas and especially their attached values (as cited in Hofstede, 2001, p. 9).

4. The Hofstede's value score examines national and regional culture values that affect the behavior of societies and organizations from four cultural dimensions including Power Distance Index (PDI), Individualism (IDV), Masculinity (MAS), and Uncertainty Avoidance Index (UAI). PDI is the extent to which the less powerful members of organizations and institutions (like the family) accept and expect that power is distributed unequally. This represents inequality (more versus less), but defined from below, not from above. IDV is the degree to which individuals are integrated into groups. On the individualist side, we find societies in which the ties between individuals are loose: everyone is expected to look after him/herself and his/her immediate family. MAS refers to the distribution of roles between the genders that is another fundamental issue for any society to which a range of solutions are found, in short, the opposite to femininity. UAI indicates to what extent a culture programs its members to feel either uncomfortable or comfortable in unstructured situations (http://www.geert-hofstede.com/index.shtml).

5. Argentine Senate has 72 seats, and senators are elected by popular vote; one-third of members elected every two years to serve six-year terms. The Chamber of Deputies has 257 seats, and members are elected by popular vote; one-half of the members elected every two years to serve four-year terms. Chilean Senate has 38 seats, and senators are elected by popular vote to serve eight years; one-half elected every four years. Chamber of Deputies has 120 seats, and members are elected by popular vote to serve four-year terms (CIA, 2007a, 2007b).

6. This framework is applied to Hofdtede's "The Stabilizing of Cultural Pattern" discussed in the first section of the chapter.

REFERENCES

Adams, F. (2000). *Culture shock! A guide to customs and etiquette: Argentina*. Portland, OR: Graphic Arts Center Publishing Company.

Banks, A. S., Muller, T. C., & Overstreet, W. R. (Eds.). (2007). *Political handbook of the world 2007*. Washington, DC: CQ Press.

Becker, T. H. (2011). *Doing business in the new Latin America: Keys to profit in America's next-door markets*. Santa Barbara, CA: Praeger.

Bruner, R. F. (2010). Ethics in finance. In R. F. Bruner, K. M. Eades & M. J. Schill (Eds.), *Case studies in finance: Managing for corporate value creation* (6th ed.). New York, NY: McGraw-Hill Irwin.

Campbell, A. (2000). *Passport Argentina: Your pocket guide to Argentinean business, customs & etiquette*. Novato, CA: World Trade Press.

Catterberg, E. (1991). *Argentina confronts politics: Political culture and public opinion in the argentine transition to democracy*. Boulder, CO: Lynne Rienner Publishers.

Central Intelligence Agency. (2007a). The world factbook-Argentina. Retrieved from https://www.cia.gov/library/publications/the-world-factbook/geos/ar.html. Accessed on April 30, 2007.

Central Intelligence Agency. (2007b). The world factbook-Chile. Retrieved from https://www.cia.gov/library/publications/the-world-factbook/print/ci.html. Accessed on November 30, 2007.

Drake, P. W. (1999). Chile's populism reconsidered, 1920s–1990s. In M. L. Conniff (Ed.), *Populism in Latin America* (pp. 63–74). Tuscaloosa, AL: The University of Alabama Press.

Finel-Honigman, I. (2010). *A cultural history of finance*. New York, NY: Routledge.

Gray, C. W., & Kaufman, D. (1998). Corruption and development. *Finance & Development*, *35*(March), 7–11.

Helmke, G. (2002). The logic of strategic defection: Court-executive relations in Argentina under dictatorship and democracy. *The American Political Science Review*, *96*(2), 291–304.

Hofstede, G. H. (2001). *Culture's consequences: Comparing values, behaviors, institutions, and organizations across nations* (2nd ed.). Thousand Oaks, CA: Sage.

Hofstede, G. H., Hofstede, G. J., & Minkov, M. (2010). *Cultures and organizations: Software of the mind* (3rd ed.). New York, NY: McGraw-Hill.

Horowitz, J. (1999). Populism and its legacies in Argentina. In M. L. Conniff (Ed.), *Populism in Latin America* (pp. 22–42). Tuscaloosa, AL: The University of Alabama Press.

Inter-American Development Bank. (2005). *The politics of policies*. Washington, D.C.: Harvard University Press.

Kaufman, D., & Kraay, A. (2007). Governance indicators: Where are we? Where should we be going? Policy research working paper, 4370. Retrieved from http://siteresources.worldbank.org/INTWBIGOVANTCOR/Resources/wps4370.pdf. Accessed on December 6, 2007.

Kersnar, J. (2007). View from Europe: Global Bribery. CFO Magazine. Retrieved from http://www3.cfo.com/article.cfm/9211033. Accessed on November 3, 2012.

Malreaux, A. (1933). *La Condition Humaine*. Paris, France: Gallimard.

Masters, R. D. (1989). *The nature of politics*. New Haven, CT: Yale University Press.

Morrison, T., & Conaway, W. A. (2007). *Kiss, bow, or shake hands: Latin America*. Avon, MA: F + A Publications Company.

Mustapic, A. M. (2002). Oscillating relations: President and congress in Argentina. In S. Morgenstern & B. Nacif (Eds.), *Legislative politics in Latin America* (pp. 23–47). Cambridge: Cambridge University Press.

Powers, N. R. (2001). *Grassroots expectations of democracy and economy: Argentina in comparative perspective*. Pittsburgh, PA: University of Pittsburgh Press.

Ricchiute, D. N. (1980). Illegal payments, deception of auditors, and reports on internal control. *MSU Business Topics*, *28*(2), 57–62.

Richardson, P. (2001). Corruption. In P. J. Simmons & C. Oudraat (Eds.), *Managing global issues: Lessons learned* (pp. 75–105). Washington, D.C.: Carnegie Endowment for International Peace.

Sabal, J. (2002). *Financial decisions in emerging markets*. New York, NY: Oxford University Press.

Sandholtz, W., & Koetzle, W. (2000). Accounting for corruption: economic structure, democracy and trade. *International Studies Quarterly*, *44*, 31–50.

Siavelis, P. M. (2002). Exaggerated presidentialism and moderate presidents: executive – legislative relations in Chile. In S. Morgenstern & B. Nacif (Eds.), *Legislative politics in Latin America* (pp. 79–113). Cambridge, MA: Cambridge University Press.

Spiller, P., & Tommasi, M. (2000). The institutional foundations of public policy: A transactions approach with application to Argentina. Retrieved from http://www.lacea.org/meeting2000/MarianoTommasi.PDF. Accessed on August 24, 2012.

Spiller, P., & Tommasi, M. (2007). *The institutional foundations of public policy in Argentina*. Cambridge, MA: Cambridge University Press.

Sullivan, M. (2006). Argentina: Political and economic conditions and U.S. relations. CRS Reportfor Congress, RS21113. Retrieved from http://fpc.state.gov/documents/organization/75250.pdf. Accessed on November 30, 2007.

Tanzi, V. (1998). Corruption around the world. *International Monetary Fund Staff Papers*, *45*(4), 559–595.

The Europa World Year Book (2006). London, UK: Routledge.

The Organization of American States. (2007). Chile: Estudio preliminar. Retrieved from http://www.oas.org/juridico/spanish/agendas/Chileprelim.htm. Accessed on December 7, 2007.

The World Bank. (2007). Governance matters 2007: Worldwide governance indicators, 1996–2006. Retrieved from http://info.worldbank.org/governance/wgi2007/. Accessed on October 10, 2007.

Tillen, J. G., & Ellis, J. M. (2009). Confronting corruption in Latin America. World Trade, 8 (February).

Toll, E. E., & Garone, C. F. (1997). *Doing business in Latin America video series.Videos 3 and 4: Argentina & Chile*. Boulder, CO: Big World Inc.

Transparency International. (2011). Corruption perception index 2011 regional. Retrieved from http://cpi.transparency.org/cpi2011/results/. Accessed on August 24, 2012.

U.S. Department of State. (2006). Country background notes: Argentina. Retrieved from SAT-USA/Internet. Accessed on May 1, 2007.

U.S. Department of State. (2007). Country background notes: Chile. Retrieved Novemver 1, 2007, from SAT-USA/Internet.

Wei, S. J. (2000). Natural openness and good government. National Bureau of Economic Research Working Paper, June. Washington, DC.

Whittle, J. (Ed.). (1998). *Argentina business: The portable encyclopaedia for doing business with Argentina*. San Rafael: World Trade Press.

World Economic Forum., (Ed.). (2006). *The Latin America competitiveness review 2006*. Geneva: The World Economic Forum.